Jim Crow Moves North

This book, which is a history of various efforts to desegregate northern schools during the nineteenth century and the first half of the twentieth century, explores two dominant themes.

The first theme considers the role of law in accomplishing racial change. Most northern state legislatures enacted legislation after the Civil War that prohibited school segregation, and most northern courts, when called upon, enforced that legislation. Despite the legal prohibition of school segregation, government-sponsored school segregation – such as the assignment of black children to separate "colored" schools or classrooms – persisted in open defiance of state law in many northern communities until the late 1940s and early 1950s. This book tries to make sense of this sharp dissonance between legal rule and educational reality.

The second theme this book considers is the ambivalence in the northern black community over the importance of school integration. Since the antebellum era, northern blacks have sharply divided over the question of whether black children would fare better in separate black schools or in racially integrated ones. This book attempts to understand the competing visions of black empowerment in the northern black community over time as reflected in the debate over school integration.

Davison M. Douglas is the Arthur B. Hanson Professor of Law at the William and Mary School of Law, where he teaches courses in American constitutional law and history. From 1997 to 2004, he served as Director of the Institute of Bill of Rights Law at William and Mary. Douglas received a Ph.D. in American history (1992), a law degree (1983), and a master's degree in religion (1983) from Yale University. He has written or edited several books dealing with American constitutional history, including *Reading, Writing, and Race: The Desegregation of the Charlotte Schools* (1995) and *Redefining Equality* (edited with Neal Devins, 1998). He has lectured on American constitutional law and history at universities throughout the United States, Africa, Asia, Australia, and Europe.

CAMBRIDGE HISTORICAL STUDIES IN AMERICAN LAW AND SOCIETY

Series Editor

Christopher Tomlins, *American Bar Foundation*

Previously published in the series:

Michael Grossberg, *A Judgment for Solomon: The d'Hauteville Case and Legal Experience in the Antebellum South*

David M. Rabban, *Free Speech in Its Forgotten Years*

Robert J. Steinfeld, *Coercion, Contract, and Free Labor in Nineteenth-Century America*

Michael Vorenberg, *Final Freedom: The Civil War, the Abolition of Slavery, and the Thirteenth Amendment*

Jenny Wahl, *The Bondsman's Burden: An Economic Analysis of the Common Law of Southern Slavery*

Barbara Young Welke, *Recasting American Liberty: Gender, Race, Law, and the Railroad Revolution, 1865–1920*

Michael Willrich, *City of Courts: Socializing Justice in Progressive Era Chicago*

To the Memory of Arthur S. Link

Jim Crow Moves North

The Battle over Northern School Segregation,
1865–1954

Davison M. Douglas

William and Mary School of Law

CAMBRIDGE
UNIVERSITY PRESS

CAMBRIDGE UNIVERSITY PRESS
Cambridge, New York, Melbourne, Madrid, Cape Town, Singapore, São Paulo

Cambridge University Press
40 West 20th Street, New York, NY 10011-4211, USA

www.cambridge.org
Information on this title: www.cambridge.org/9780521845649

First published 2005

Printed in the United States of America

A catalog record for this publication is available from the British Library.

Library of Congress Cataloging in Publication Data

Douglas, Davison M.
Jim Crow moves North : the battle over northern school segregation, 1865–1954 /
Davison M. Douglas.
p.   cm. – (Cambridge historical studies in American law and society)
Includes bibliographical references and index.
ISBN 0-521-84564-5 (hardback) – ISBN 0-521-60783-3 (pbk.)
1. African Americans – Education – History.   2. Segregation in education –
United States – History.   3. Segregation in education – Law and legislation –
United States.   I. Title.   II. Series.
LC2741.D68   2005
379.2′63′0973 – dc22   2005001649

ISBN-13   978-0-521-84564-9 hardback
ISBN-10   0-521-84564-5 hardback

ISBN-13   978-0-521-60783-4 paperback
ISBN-10   0-521-60783-3 paperback

Contents

Acknowledgments		*page* ix
1	Introduction	1
2	The Struggle for Black Education in the Antebellum North	12
3	Legislative Reform: Banning School Segregation, 1865–1890	61
4	The Spread of Northern School Segregation, 1890–1940	123
5	Responding to the Spread of Northern School Segregation: Conflict within the Black Community, 1900–1940	167
6	The Democratic Imperative: The Campaign against Northern School Segregation, 1940–1954	219
7	Conclusion	274
References		281
Index		307

Acknowledgments

Though the life of the scholar has its solitary aspects, the academic life also affords the opportunity to engage with and enjoy the support of many others in the course of doing one's research and writing. One of the pleasures of seeing this book in print is the opportunity to express my appreciation to those persons and institutions who assisted me along the way.

First of all, I would like to thank the Spencer Foundation and the National Academy of Education for their splendid financial support that permitted me to do much of the extensive research that this book required. I also thank the College of William and Mary School of Law for a variety of forms of support – leave time, research assistance, and superb library support. The nature of this book required me to make extensive use of interlibrary loan services, and I thank Joan Pearlstein of the William and Mary law library for her tireless efforts in tracking down numerous elusive sources.

No historian's work is possible without the support of those historians and archivists who tend to the manuscript collections at the great libraries of the world. I have been wonderfully assisted by archivists at many collections, with particularly lengthy stays at the Library of Congress, the Schlesinger Library at the Radcliffe Institute, the Chicago Historical Society, the Schomberg Center at the New York Public Library, and the Western Reserve Historical Society.

I presented various portions of this book at the annual meetings of the American Society for Legal History, the Association of American Law Schools, the Australia and New Zealand Legal History Society, the History of Education Society, the Law and Society Association, the National Academy of Education, and the Southern Historical Association. I also presented portions of this book at the law schools of the University of Cincinnati, Emory University, Florida State University, University of Georgia, Hokkaido University (in Sapporo, Japan), the University of Iowa, the University of Notre Dame, St. Louis University, and the College of William and Mary, as well as to a conference at the University of Kent in Canterbury, England. I wish to express my appreciation to the participants in these various conferences and presentations for their helpful comments and stimulating questions.

Many friends and colleagues also read and commented on a chapter or more of the book, including Robert Cottrol, Neal Devins, Paul Finkelman, Michael Klarman, Patricia Sullivan, Carl Tobias, and Mark Tushnet. On several occasions, their insights helped me move in a new and useful direction. And I give special thanks to Lewis Bateman of Cambridge University Press, truly one of the great editors and a very patient man.

For the past several years, I have enjoyed research support from numerous William and Mary law students who helped me track down difficult-to-find source materials and cases; these students include David Blessing, Noelle Coates, Rebecca Ebinger, Jonathan Garlough, David Hitchens, Amber Jannusch, and Chris Secord. I am deeply appreciative of their diligence.

My wife, Kathy Urbonya, has lived with me throughout the research and writing of this book. I thank her for her love, support, and reminders that all books must come to an end.

Finally, I dedicate this book to the memory of my uncle, Arthur S. Link, who introduced me to the joys of history at a young age and encouraged me as I pursued an academic career. His life was an inspiration to me in so many ways, and I miss him.

1

Introduction

Power concedes nothing without a demand. It never did and it never will.

— Frederick Douglass, 1857[1]

For most of our history, African Americans have viewed education as essential to their quest for equality. Although many blacks have expressed frustration at the inability of education to move them into the political and economic mainstream, faith in the potential of education has remained strong. As historian Kevin Gaines has noted, "African Americans have, with an almost religious fervor, regarded education as the key to liberation."[2]

Indeed, education has been linked to notions of equality and uplift by both blacks and whites for almost two centuries. Horace Eaton, the first state superintendent of education in Vermont, commented during the antebellum era: "Let every child in the land enjoy the advantages of a competent education at his outset in life – and it will do more to secure a general equality of condition than any guarantee of equal rights and privileges which constitution or laws can give." Ohio Governor Thomas Corwin claimed in 1843 that "by educating the poor children . . . we place them, to some extent, at least, upon a footing of equality with the fortunate inheritors of rich estates. It is of all agencies yet discovered the most efficient in producing that perfect and just equality among men which brings harmony into the social system and gives permanency to free government." A Massachusetts legislative committee stated in 1855: "One of the great merits of our system of public instruction is the fusion of all classes which it produces. From a childhood which shares the same bench and sports there can hardly arise a manhood of aristocratic prejudice or separate castes and classes.

---

[1] Douglass, "The Significance of Emancipation in the West Indies: An Address Delivered in Canandaigua, New York, on 3 August 1857," in Blassingame, 3 *The Frederick Douglass Papers*, p. 204.
[2] Gaines, *Uplifting the Race*, p. 1.

Our common-school system ... promotes ... the habits of republican equality."[3]

Almost a century later, writing in 1944, Gunnar Myrdal identified education as central to the American ethos: "Education has always been the great hope for both individual and society. In the American Creed it has been the main ground upon which 'equality of opportunity for the individual' and 'free outlet for ability' could be based." When the National Association for the Advancement of Colored People (NAACP) began its assault on segregation in earnest during the 1930s, it focused in significant measure on schools, in part because of the perceived importance of education to the quest for racial equality. President Lyndon Johnson declared during the 1960s that proper education could prevent poverty and backed up that claim with a dramatic increase in federal funding for public schools. In recent years, many scholars of education have disputed this optimistic assessment of education, arguing that schools have done less than promised for America's poor and racial minorities, but the embrace of education as fundamental to equality and uplift remains deep within the American psyche.[4]

Yet education has not come easily for African Americans in much of our nation's history. During the antebellum era, many southern states prohibited the education of free blacks and made it a crime to teach a slave to read and write. Although southern states established public schools for blacks during Reconstruction, those schools would remain separate and grossly unequal until the second half of the twentieth century.

The story of black education in the North is far more complicated. During the antebellum era, northern school authorities frequently excluded black children from the newly established common schools. Those black children who did attend school before the Civil War tended to do so on a separate and unequal basis. After the war, blacks gained access to public schools in those parts of the North where they had been excluded, but were frequently assigned to racially separate and inferior schools.

Confronted with both exclusion from public schools and then relegation to racially separate schools, northern blacks fought back,

---

[3] For the Eaton quote, see Perkinson, *The Imperfect Panacea*, p. 12; for the Corwin quote, see B. W. Arnett, "The Black Laws!" p. 13 (1886), in Daniel A. P. Murray Collection, Ohio Historical Society; for the Massachusetts committee quote, see "Equal School Rights," *Frederick Douglass' Paper*, Apr. 13, 1855.

[4] For Myrdal quote, see Myrdal, *An American Dilemma*, p. 882; for discussion of Johnson, see Tyack and Cuban, *Tinkering Toward Utopia*, p. 27; for recent critiques of education, see, e.g., Bowles and Gintis, *Schooling in Capitalist America*; Katznelson and Weir, *Schooling for All*; Feinberg, *Reason and Rhetoric*.

insisting on their right to attend school on a nondiscriminatory basis. By 1870, those northern states that had excluded blacks from public schools had reversed course. Moreover, during the quarter century following the end of the Civil War, most northern states enacted legislation that prohibited racial segregation in public education. Most northern courts, when called upon to enforce this newly enacted antisegregation legislation, did so, ordering the admission of black children into white schools.

Notwithstanding a legal regime clearly aligned against the continuation of racial segregation in public education, school segregation persisted in some northern communities in open defiance of law during the late nineteenth century. Moreover, with the migration of hundreds of thousands of southern blacks into northern communities during the first half of the twentieth century, northern school segregation dramatically increased. Indeed, by 1940, northern school segregation was more extensive than it had been at any time since Reconstruction.

Northern school districts segregated black and white schoolchildren through a variety of devices. Some northern school segregation, later denominated "de facto" segregation, was due to residential segregation. Indeed, as northern ghettos grew in size over the course of the twentieth century, most urban school segregation could be attributed to residential segregation.

But much northern school segregation during the late nineteenth and early twentieth centuries was far more deliberate, in clear violation of state law prohibiting racial separation. School administrators in dozens of northern school districts assigned black children to separate "colored schools" irrespective of geographic location in a manner typical of southern states. Other school administrators assigned black and white children to separate classrooms within the same school building or placed black children in an annex adjacent to the main school building reserved for white children. Some fenced off racially separate playgrounds and flew separate American flags. In many communities, racially gerrymandered school district lines or racially conscious transfer policies ensured the racial homogeneity of northern schools.

The extent of this deliberate, or "de jure," school segregation in northern states has been misunderstood by many government officials, courts, and scholars who have assumed that explicit school segregation in this country was essentially a southern phenomenon and that racial isolation in northern schools has largely been a function of residential segregation. In 1953, attorneys representing the defendant school boards in the *Brown v. Board of Education* litigation before the United States Supreme Court conducted an extensive survey of education officials throughout the United States, seeking to establish which states had operated racially segregated schools at *any* point in their history.

Most northern states that had in fact engaged in school segregation at some point so acknowledged. But officials in several northern states inexplicably denied that there had ever been any school segregation in their state.

Connecticut denied any history of school segregation despite racially explicit school assignments in Hartford until the late 1860s. Iowa ignored an 1858 statute that permitted school segregation throughout the state and the entrenchment of school segregation in several communities such as Keokuk and Dubuque until the mid-1870s. Massachusetts denied a history of school segregation despite explicit segregation in the Boston schools until the state legislature ended the practice in 1855. New Jersey falsely reported that "[a]t no time has segregation by race been established by law in the public schools of New Jersey," ignoring state legislation in 1844 and 1850 that expressly granted local communities the right to establish segregated schools, a right that many local communities exercised and would continue to exercise until the early 1950s in violation of an 1881 statute that forbade such segregation.[5]

Since 1954, other northern school officials have continued to maintain the fiction that they never operated segregated schools. In 1959, the Dayton, Ohio, school superintendent wrote that "to the best of my knowledge Dayton has never maintained legally segregated schools," even though his city maintained explicitly and notoriously segregated schools from the 1920s until the early 1950s in open disregard of a 1926 decision of the Ohio Supreme Court ordering an end to school segregation in that city. During the 1970s and early 1980s, the Ohio State Board of Education denied knowledge of school segregation in Ohio schools at any point during the twentieth century, even though its predecessor State Department of Education had, until 1955, required local school districts to submit regular reports setting forth the number of children attending "separate schools for colored children."[6] Explicit, government-directed school segregation persisted in many Ohio communities until after the 1954 *Brown* decision.

Some courts have also misconstrued the history of northern school segregation. In 1965, the New Jersey Supreme Court made the extraordinary claim that New Jersey's "policy against racial discrimination and segregation in the public schools has been long standing and vigorous" since the enactment of the 1881 statute that prohibited school segregation, notwithstanding the fact that New Jersey had a long history of explicit racial separation in many of its public schools,

---

[5] Reams and Wilson, *Segregation and the Fourteenth Amendment*, pp. 60, 177, 277, 398–9.

[6] For the quote from the Dayton school superintendent, see Watras, *Politics, Race, and Schools*, p. 89; for the State Department of Education requirement, see *Penick v. Columbus Board of Education*, 663 F.2d 24, 27–8 (6th Cir. 1981).

particularly in the state's southern counties, until the middle of the twentieth century.[7]

Distinguished scholars have also misperceived the extent of northern school segregation. In his magisterial 1944 study of race in America, *An American Dilemma*, Gunnar Myrdal, whose consideration of black education focused primarily on the South, erroneously concluded that in northern states, "Negroes have practically the entire educational system flung open to them without much discrimination.... It is unnecessary to take up the Negro school in the North since it hardly exists as a separate entity." A leading historian of the Civil War and Reconstruction eras wrote in 1965 that "[p]ublic schools in many parts of New York, New Jersey, Pennsylvania, Ohio, Illinois, and Indiana – where the large majority of northern Negroes lived – remained segregated until the last two decades of the nineteenth century...." In fact, many schools in each of those states remained rigidly segregated until the middle of the twentieth century; indeed, school segregation was particularly widespread in Indiana, which expressly permitted school segregation by state law until 1949. In 1995, a distinguished scholar of contemporary school desegregation efforts explained the dearth of northern school desegregation litigation during the 1950s and 1960s as due to the fact that litigation during those years was limited to states that "had at some time operated a dual school system,"[8] ignoring the fact that many local school districts in the North operated a dual school system until the 1950s in defiance of state law.

Not surprisingly, the struggle to end school segregation in the North has received far less scholarly attention than has the more dramatic campaign to desegregate southern schools. Moreover, while many scholars have skillfully chronicled the NAACP's campaign against southern school segregation that culminated in the United States Supreme Court's decision in *Brown v. Board of Education*, few have paid attention to the NAACP's simultaneous campaign against northern school segregation.[9]

---

[7] *Booker v. Board of Education*, 45 N.J. 161, 173–4 (1965).

[8] For the Myrdal quote, see Myrdal, *An American Dilemma*, pp. 879, 945; for the Civil War historian quote, see McPherson, "Abolitionists and the Civil Rights Act," p. 495; for the quote from the desegregation scholar, see Rossell, "The Convergence of Black and White Attitudes on School Desegregation Issues," p. 617.

[9] Both Mark Tushnet's and Richard Kluger's excellent accounts of the NAACP's campaign against segregated education focus exclusively on the organization's activities in southern states. Neither addresses the NAACP's simultaneous campaign against segregated schools in northern states. Tushnet, *The NAACP's Legal Strategy against Segregated Education*; Kluger, *Simple Justice*. Similarly, neither Greenberg, *Crusaders in the Courts*, nor Tushnet, *Making Civil Rights Law*, discusses the northern campaign against segregated education.

The relative lack of scholarly attention to northern school segregation during the pre-*Brown* era is unfortunate, because the struggle against northern school segregation took place in a very different legal context than its southern counterpart. Whereas in the South, school desegregation efforts – particularly those of the NAACP – focused on securing incremental judicial precedents as part of a gradual attack on the constitutionality of state segregation statutes that culminated in the *Brown* decision, in the North, the greatest barrier to integrated schools was not legal – in a constitutional or statutory sense – but rather political and cultural. Most northern states prohibited school segregation by statute during the nineteenth century, and most northern courts enforced those statutes when asked to do so. Nevertheless, many local school boards continued to separate schoolchildren by race in defiance of state law and many northern blacks acquiesced in this separation, believing that their children would fare better in black schools with black teachers.

This book's focus on African Americans is not meant to suggest that they were the only racial or ethnic group subjected to school segregation. Various states, particularly in the West, also segregated other groups of schoolchildren during the nineteenth and twentieth centuries, including children of Chinese, Mongolian, Japanese, and Korean ethnicity, as well as Native Americans and, later, children of Hispanic ethnicity. Each of these groups also engaged in efforts to challenge school segregation, but those efforts are beyond the scope of this book. Moreover, although this book focuses on school desegregation battles in northern states – with primary emphasis on New England, the mid-Atlantic, and the Midwest – occasional reference will also be made to western states, as they confronted similar desegregation issues.

The history of northern school desegregation inevitably draws us into two important political and intellectual debates: the importance of racial mixing for African-American uplift and the role of law in accomplishing racial change.

The issue of school integration has been enormously controversial in the black community since the antebellum era. African-American challenges to northern school segregation during both the nineteenth and twentieth centuries have consistently raised one critical issue: How important is it for a black child to attend a racially mixed school?

Since the antebellum era, many northern blacks have displayed ambivalence concerning the importance of racially mixed schools. Though African Americans have consistently embraced the importance of education, the issue of racially mixed schools has been far more complex. Many African Americans have opposed school

integration, fearing, with good reason, the loss of jobs for black teachers, mistreatment of black students, and the end of black-controlled educational institutions. Others have viewed the elimination of school segregation as essential to black efforts to achieve social and political equality, construing state-mandated racial separation as contributing to a racial caste system with devastating consequences for assimilation.

In literally dozens of northern school districts, the African-American community bitterly divided over the issue of school segregation, especially during the first half of the twentieth century. In many instances, some blacks opposed efforts by other blacks to challenge school segregation. NAACP leaders expressed frustration over the lack of commitment to integrated schools among many northern blacks. Such division made desegregation campaigns far more difficult to conduct. This division within the black community over the importance of racial mixing continues today. Although the integrationist vision of the Supreme Court's *Brown* decision has dominated this country's intellectual discourse about race for the past half century, a substantial dissenting tradition, represented by individuals such as Malcolm X and organizations such as the Congress of Racial Equality, has persisted until the present.[10] Much of the contemporary debate concerning the importance of racially mixed schools has intellectual antecedents in the northern black community of the nineteenth and early twentieth centuries.

A second central issue that emerges from the history of northern school desegregation is the role of law in accomplishing racial change. Educational conflicts in this country have generally been defined and debated in the context of legal rights, either through litigation or legislation. As legal scholar Patricia Williams has noted, blacks in particular have "believed in [rights] so much and so hard that we gave them life where there was none before; we held onto them, put the hope them into our wombs, mothered them. . . ."[11] Not surprisingly, northern blacks desirous of challenging school segregation used both lawsuits and legislative lobbying to pursue their goals. But many northern blacks also used extralegal means, such as school boycotts, to pursue similar ends. This book examines each of these strategies, seeking understand both their efficacy and their interplay.

Central to the examination of black efforts to desegregate northern schools is this question: why did the legislation enacted by 1

---

[10] See, e.g., Malcolm X, *The Autobiography of Malcolm X*, pp. 300–7; Congress of Equality, "A True Alternative to Segregation: A Proposal for Community School tricts," February 1970, in "Brief for CORE as Amicus Curiae," *Swann v. Ch Mecklenburg Board of Education*, in Douglas, *The Development of School Busing*, p.

[11] Williams, *The Alchemy of Race and Rights*, p. 163.

northern states during the post–Civil War era banning school segregation and the numerous court decisions enforcing that legislation
fail to eliminate school segregation? As noted, the overwhelming majority of northern state legislatures prohibited school segregation by
statute during the quarter century following the conclusion of the
Civil War, and the vast majority of state courts, when called upon,
enforced those statutes. With this type of legal support for racial
mixing, one might expect to find thoroughly desegregated northern
school systems. Yet despite this legal prohibition on school segregation,
government-sponsored school segregation – such as the assignment of
black children to separate colored schools or classrooms – persisted
in open defiance of state law in many northern communities until
the late 1940s and early 1950s. This book explores the reasons for
this dissonance between legal rule and educational reality and seeks
to provide insight into the broader question of how legal rules affect
racial change. Scholars have urged consideration of these questions
for some time. As historian Robert Cottrol has noted: "Legal historians
need to probe beyond the egalitarianism of northern law. Race-neutral
legal doctrines must be measured against the way law was actually
applied."[12]

During the past forty years, courts have been widely celebrated as
important agents of racial change, with *Brown v. Board of Education*
as the paradigmatic example of the ability of the judiciary to foster
racial progress in the face of significant cultural and political opposition. Yet in recent years, numerous scholars have questioned the
ability of courts to function as a significant force for racial progress
without broad political and cultural support. Some of these scholars have concluded that the traditional emphasis on the role of the
courts – especially the *Brown* Court – in securing racial gains is over-
stated and that certain aspects of racial reform, such as southern school
desegregation, did not take place in this country until the elective
branches of government embraced the desegregation agenda in the
mid-1960s. These scholars suggest that courts, even the United States
Supreme Court, are considerably more limited in their ability to effect
social reform in the absence of significant legislative and executive
support than was previously imagined. Other scholars, associated with
the critical race theory movement, go even further and conclude that
the inherent conservatism of courts inhibits their willingness to produce meaningful change on behalf of racial minorities. Both groups
of scholars suggest that courts alone are unable to bring about significant racial change absent broader political and cultural support.

---

[12] Cottrol, "Law, Politics and Race," p. 534.

The history of northern school desegregation litigation supports the notion that courts are constrained by larger cultural and political dynamics.[13]

While the issue of the ability of courts to effectuate racial change has received considerable scholarly attention in recent years, less attention has been paid to the ability of law more broadly defined – as manifest in legislative and executive actions as well as court decisions – to secure social reform. This book seeks to broaden the conversation about law and racial change by examining the interplay between legal rules – manifest in both court decisions *and* legislation – and racial progress in the context of the campaign against school segregation in northern states prior to the Supreme Court's 1954 decision in *Brown v. Board of Education.*[14]

The capacity of statutory law to promote social change appears obvious, because statutes presumably reflect the majoritarian support that makes legislative change possible. But on occasion, legislative enactments do not reflect majoritarian values. Some statutes are enacted to satisfy a narrow constituency, but without the strong support of the majority necessary for meaningful enforcement. Statutes that seek to reverse longstanding and embedded cultural understandings – particularly those associated with race and ethnicity – may prove especially difficult to enforce. Moreover, cultural attitudes may shift over time; temporary imperatives that helped fuel support

---

[13] For scholars emphasizing the crucial importance of the *Brown* decision, see, e.g., Neier, *Only Judgment,* p. 9 ("Since the early 1950s, the courts have been the most accessible and, often, the most effective instrument of government for bringing about the changes in public policy sought by social protest movements."); Wilkinson, *From Brown to Bakke,* pp. 3, 6 (describing *Brown* as "the most important political, social, and legal event" of the twentieth century and emphasizing the necessity of the Supreme Court for effectuating social change); Cover, "The Origins of Judicial Activism," p. 1316 (describing *Brown* as a "paradigmatic event"). For recent scholarship questioning the impact of Brown, see, e.g., Rosenberg, *The Hollow Hope;* Klarman, *From Jim Crow to Civil Rights;* Klarman, "*Brown,* Racial Change, and the Civil Rights Movement." For a sampling of critical race theory scholars, see Bell, *And We Are Not Saved;* Delgado and Stefancic, *Failed Revolutions: Social Reform and the Limits of Legal Imagination;* Spann, *Race Against the Court.* See generally Scheingold, "Constitutional Rights and Social Change: Civil Rights in Perspective," pp. 74–5 (describing the "democratic" perspective on law and racial change, which celebrates the role of the courts in black liberation, and the "hegemonic" perspective, which concludes that courts have not only failed to liberate blacks, they have contributed to black oppression).

[14] A few scholars – on both the left and the right – have argued that the Civil Rights Act of 1964 failed to achieve workplace equality, thereby implicitly critiquing the ability of at least this one important statute to accomplish racial change. See, e.g., Bell, *Race, Racism and American Law,* pp. 831–906; Epstein, *Forbidden Grounds: The Case against Employment Discrimination Laws.*

for new legislation may fade in the face of changed realities. In short, although statutes may reflect the values of dominant political coalitions at a particular moment in time, they do not necessarily evidence broad and sustained cultural support for the regulated matter.

Each of these factors operated to undermine vigorous enforcement of the nineteenth-century antisegregation legislation. The nineteenth-century antisegregation statutes did not necessarily reflect a broad commitment to school integration. Rather, they reflected a combination of Reconstruction-era racial idealism among some white northerners, a desire to capture black votes in closely contested elections, and the high cost of dual schools. Moreover, all of these statutes were enacted at a time when the northern black population was a tiny fraction of the total population. This commitment to pupil mixing eroded in the wake of the migration of hundreds of thousands of southern blacks into northern communities during the first half of the twentieth century and as a result, noncompliance with the antisegregation legislation sharply increased.

Eventually, the political and cultural environment in the North changed, creating support for integration. By the 1940s, northern black political power had dramatically increased as a result of several decades of black migration. Moreover, encouraged by the NAACP, increasing numbers of African Americans demanded integrated schools. Anxious to capture black electoral support, to serve certain wartime and Cold War objectives, and to defuse racial tensions in several northern cities, white politicians took various actions during the late 1940s favorable to desegregation efforts, including the threat of withholding educational monies from recalcitrant school districts. As a result, by the time of the *Brown* decision, only a handful of northern school districts maintained explicit, officially sanctioned school segregation in defiance of state law. Yet at the same time, these desegregation initiatives left untouched the increasingly prevalent urban school segregation caused not by explicit racial separation but rather by residential segregation. Thus, northern white politicians of the late 1940s and early 1950s could capture black political support by championing school desegregation initiatives that eliminated the most blatant instances of school segregation, primarily in low-population rural school districts, but that left untouched the burgeoning racial separation of schoolchildren in large cities. Since the early 1950s, the requisite political and cultural support for racial mixing has not developed in most northern cities to overcome patterns of residential segregation; as a result, most urban school districts are still beset with significant racial isolation.

The campaign to desegregate northern schools thus exposes the difficulties of using law to force racial change. Just as the *Brown* decision failed to desegregate southern schools during the 1950s and early 1960s until both the president and the Congress committed themselves to racial desegregation with the enactment of the Civil Rights Act of 1964, so, too, court decisions and statutes could not eliminate officially sanctioned northern school segregation during the pre-*Brown* era until a political and cultural environment developed in which majoritarian interests were served by desegregation. The enactment of the nineteenth-century antisegregation legislation had been an important first step in the campaign against state-mandated segregation in northern schools, but the campaign would need seventy years of cultural and political change to achieve success. And even then, that success, as has been true of so many racial gains in this country's history, proved somewhat hollow, as it left untouched the explosive growth of northern residential segregation. Law – both litigation and legislation – has been crucial to racial progress throughout American history, but as desegregation proponents have repeatedly learned, law does not operate in isolation from its cultural context.[15]

---

[15] As to the failure of *Brown* to secure widespread desegregation, only a few southern black schoolchildren – 1.2% – had won entry into an integrated school by the tenth anniversary of the decision. In 1964, Congress, pressured by the demands of the civil rights movement and the violent reaction to that movement, enacted the Civil Rights Act of 1964, which provided in part for the withholding of federal funds from southern schools that refused to desegregate. As a result, southern school desegregation dramatically increased. Southern Education Reporting Service, *Statistical Summary State by State of School Segregation-Desegregation*, pp. 27–30; Orfield, *The Reconstruction of Southern Education*, pp. 46–8, 355. As for the convergence of interests, this has been noted by Derrick Bell in his landmark 1980 article in the *Harvard Law Review*, "*Brown v. Board of Education* and the Interest-Convergence Dilemma."

2

The Struggle for Black Education in the Antebellum North

We also wish to secure, for our children *especially*, the benefits of education, which in several States are entirely denied us, and in others are enjoyed only in name. These, and many other things, of which we justly complain, bear most heavily upon us as a people; and it our right and our duty to seek for redress. . . .

– Samuel H. Davis, addressing the National Convention of Colored Citizens, Buffalo, New York, 1843[1]

Enos Van Camp decided that it was time for his young son and his young apprentice to receive an education. In his small village of Logan, in southern Ohio, the town leaders had established five schools. Early on February 24, 1855, Van Camp took the two boys to a nearby school to enroll them. But the school officials turned them away. Why? Because they looked like they might be "colored" children.

Until 1848, Ohio had excluded all colored children from public schools. Finally, the state legislature decided that separate schools could be established for children of color, but only if sufficient taxes could be raised from black and mulatto families to pay the necessary expenses. In 1855, relatively few blacks lived in Logan, Ohio, and hence there were no schools for their children.

But were Van Camp's son and his apprentice really colored? Many people in Ohio had mixed-race ancestry. As a result, more than twenty years earlier, the Ohio Supreme Court had had to decide who was "white" for purposes of Ohio law. The determination was enormously important. Whether one could vote, attend school, testify in court, serve on a jury, or even settle in the state depended on whether one was deemed white or colored. In 1834, the Ohio Supreme Court had resolved the issue this way: if you had more than one-half white "blood," then you were white, regardless of how you looked. Otherwise, you were colored. Enos Van Camp, his wife, his son, and his apprentice

---

[1] Minutes of the National Convention of Colored Citizens (Buffalo, 1843), reprinted in Bell (ed.), *Minutes of the Proceedings of the National Negro Conventions*, p. 5.

were all five-eighths white, so the two boys were entitled under Ohio law to attend the white school in Logan.[2]

But the local school officials did not see it that way. The two boys *looked* colored. The Ohio Supreme Court might think the Van Camps were white, but the people of Logan did not. Van Camp sued, but a local court ruled against him. In 1859, the Ohio Supreme Court heard Van Camp's appeal. Though the court's relevant precedents favored the Van Camps, three of the five justices determined that the Van Camps, because they had a "*visible taint* of African blood," were indeed colored and hence had no place in Ohio's white schools. The court acknowledged that under its earlier precedents the Van Camps were white, but pointed out that those earlier cases "did not receive the hearty approval of the state at large." In fact, in much of Ohio, the court claimed, whites held "an almost invincible repugnance to ... communion and fellowship with ... blacks and mulattoes," and such "prejudice of ages could not be dissipated" by a judicial decision. The court elaborated: "If those a shade more white than black were to be forced upon the white youth against their consent, the ... prejudice and antagonism of the whites would be aroused; bickerings and contentions become the order of the day, and the moral and mental improvement of both classes retarded." And so, the Van Camp children would receive no education.[3]

Enos Van Camp was hardly alone. Across the North, children of color were routinely excluded from white schools whether or not another school was available for them. It would take years for children like the Van Camps to receive their full education rights.

The common school movement of the 1830s and 1840s brought schoolhouses to cities and towns across the North. Although common schools were developed in part to promote civic and moral virtue and to assimilate America's expanding immigrant population, this assimilationist goal did not include all Americans. Many northern school authorities were overtly hostile to the educational aspirations of black and mulatto children, and either excluded them from the common schools altogether or relegated them to racially separate and inferior schools. By the onset of the Civil War, black education in the North was sporadic, largely separate, and inferior to white education.

But during the antebellum era, the beginnings of a black protest movement emerged that challenged the exclusion of African Americans from the common schools. These efforts at inclusion eventually

---

[2] For the 1834 decision on who was white under Ohio law, see *Williams v. School District,* 1 Wright 578 (1834).

[3] *Van Camp v. Logan,* 9 Ohio St. 406, 408, 410, 412 (1859) (emphasis added).

succeeded in much of the North. Ending racial segregation, however, proved far more difficult. By the end of the antebellum era, some northern schools allowed black and white children to learn together, but most did not.

The Common School Movement

During the first half of the nineteenth century, proponents of public schools enjoyed success throughout the North. The "common school" movement, which built on the urban charity schools developed at the end of the eighteenth century, expanded significantly during the 1830s and 1840s. Prior to 1830, few northern communities offered publicly supported education, as most schools were financed by private charitable interests. Between 1830 and 1860, however, the number of public schools in the North dramatically increased, greatly enhancing the availability of education. The decade of the 1840s witnessed a particularly dramatic rise in the number of children in public schools, with increases from 27,000 to 675,000 in New York, 52,000 to 484,000 in Ohio, and 74,000 to 414,000 in Pennsylvania. By 1860, approximately two-thirds of all white children in the free states between the ages of six and twenty (compared to 44 percent in the slave states) attended school in the United States, a sharp increase from 1840. On the eve of the Civil War, the United States enjoyed one of the highest literacy rates in the world.[4]

Those educators at the center of the common school movement emphasized the importance of inculcating civic and moral virtue in order to preserve America's republican form of government. Indeed, the link between education and the stability of the republic became an article of faith during the early nineteenth century. The majority of newly promulgated state constitutions during the eighteenth and early nineteenth centuries cited education as important to the preservation of civil society and republican self-government. At least seventeen states included language in their constitutions that specifically addressed the political and moral purposes of education. The Minnesota constitution of 1857, for example, provided: "The stability of a republican form of government depending mainly upon the intelligence of the people, it shall be the duty of the legislature to establish a general and uniform system of public schools." Ohio's first constitution described education as "essentially necessary to good government." Ohio Governor

---

4 Reynolds, "Politics and Indiana's Public Schools," p. 3; Reid, "Race, Class, Gender and the Teaching Profession," p. 14; U.S. Bureau of the Census, 1840, 1850, 1860; Finkelman, "Prelude to the Fourteenth Amendment," p. 475; Tyack and Hansot, *Managers of Virtue*, pp. 28–9.

Jeremiah Morrow explained in 1823: "No sentiment is more generally held to be incontrovertible among enlightened free men than that morality and knowledge are necessary to good government. The necessary dependence which civil liberty and free institutions in government have on the moral qualities and intelligence of the people, give importance to the provisions for the encouragement and regulation of common schools." In a similar fashion, an 1826 United States House of Representatives committee on public lands, which unsuccessfully urged that half the proceeds of the sale of public lands go to public schools, argued that education "contemplates giving additional stability to the government, and drawing round the republic new and stronger bonds of union."[5]

Promoters of the common school movement also believed that public schools would help assimilate children into the common culture. America experienced significant immigration during the antebellum era, and many reformers promoted the common schools as a means of assimilating and controlling the immigrant poor and reducing religious and ethnic divisiveness. As Benjamin Rush had claimed during the late eighteenth century, education would "render the mass of people more homogeneous" by inculcating schoolchildren with common values.[6]

In connection with this goal of assimilation, many saw education as a means of reducing the social conflict, crime, and violence that accompanied the trend toward urbanization in antebellum America. As one nineteenth-century educator announced: "If we were to define the public school as an instrument for disintegrating mobs, we would indicate one of its most important purposes." The *New York Commercial Advertiser* in 1824 noted "the vast difference in appearance of those children [who attend school], and those idle ones who are suffered to grow up uncultivated, unpolished, and heathenish in our streets; and who, for the want of care and instruction, are daily plunging in scenes of sloth, idleness, dissipation and crime, until they pass from step to step over the tread mill, into the state prison, and at last up to the gallows." A legislative committee in Ohio commented in 1825: "A wise legislature will endeavor to prevent the commission of crimes – not only by the number and rigor of her penal statutes – but by affording

---

[5] For the link between education and republican government, see Tyack, James, and Benavot, *Law and the Shaping of Public Education*, pp. 14, 20, 30. For Minnesota constitutional language, see the Minnesota Constitution of 1857, Article VIII, Section 1. For the Ohio constitutional language, see Mayo, "Education in the Northwest," pp. 1531, 1538. For the quote from Morrow, see B. W. Arnett, "The Black Laws!" p. 12 (1886), Daniel A. P. Murray Collection, Ohio Historical Society. For the House committee quote, see Tyack, James, and Benavot, *Law and the Shaping of Public Education*, p. 28.

[6] Quoted in Kirp, *Just Schools*, p. 33.

the whole rising generation, the means of moral and virtuous education." Horace Mann, writing in 1841, expressed his enthusiasm for the common school's ability to control crime: "Let the Common School be expanded to its capabilities, let it be worked with the efficiency of which it is susceptible, and nine tenths of the crimes in the penal code would become obsolete." A popular slogan in antebellum educational journals urged citizens to "[p]ay your school tax without grumbling. It is the cheapest premium of insurance on your property."[7]

Not all parts of the new nation embraced the common school movement with equal enthusiasm. New England states established common schools earlier than did states in the Midwest or the South. By 1840, approximately 54 percent of the children attending a public school in the United States lived in New England. Moreover, those parts of the North settled primarily by New Englanders, such as the Western Reserve of Ohio, developed common schools earlier than did those parts settled primarily by southerners. The southernmost counties of Ohio, Indiana, and Illinois, for example, settled in significant measure by white southerners, were slow to embrace the notion of taxation for "schooling other people's children." In 1849, the Indiana state legislature decided to allow each county to determine for itself whether to operate publicly supported schools. About a third of the state's counties declined to do so; even the state capital, Indianapolis, provided no public schools until 1853. According to the 1850 census, the five northern states with the highest percentage of children attending school were in New England; by contrast, four of the five northern states with the lowest percentage of children attending school were in the Midwest.[8]

---

[7] For early purposes of education, see Tyack, *The One Best System*, p. 29; for the nineteenth-century educator quote, see Lazerson, *Origins of the Urban School*, p. 30; for the *New York Commercial Advertiser* quote, see Andrews, *The History of the New-York African Free-Schools*, p. 45; for the Ohio legislative committee quote, see Hurt, *The Ohio Frontier*, p. 383; for the Mann quote, see Glenn, *The Myth of the Common School*, p. 80; for the school tax quote, see Jorgenson, *The Founding of Public Education*, p. 114.

[8] For 1840 education levels, see U.S. Bureau of the Census, 1840; for education in Ohio, see Mayo, "Education in the Northwest," pp. 1542–4; for Indiana school information, see Reynolds, "Politics and Indiana's Public Schools," pp. 7–8 and Mayo, "Education in the Northwest," p. 1537. The five states with the highest education levels in 1850 were Maine (87%), New Hampshire (85%), Vermont (85%), Massachusetts (72%), and Connecticut (72%). The states with the lowest education levels in 1850 were Iowa (46%), New Jersey (54%), Wisconsin (54%), Illinois (54%), and Indiana (55%). This excludes California, which did not become a state until 1850, at which time only 10% of its children attended school. All education figures include both white and black children. For education information, see U.S. Bureau of Census, 1850; Finkelman, "Prelude to the Fourteenth Amendment," pp. 472–3.

Black Support for Education

African-American leaders embraced education as a central feature of racial uplift during the first half of the nineteenth century and vigorously sought to secure education for black children in either privately supported schools or the newly developed common schools. The notion of racial uplift, and the necessity of education to achieve that goal, was a constant theme at Negro conventions and in black newspapers during the antebellum era.[9]

The Negro convention movement, which constituted one of the first organized efforts to attack the climate of racial oppression in America, flourished on the national and state levels from 1830 until 1860. Although many of the conventions emphasized moral reform issues such as temperance and frugality, many also emphasized the importance of education and the link between education and full citizenship rights. One of the first Negro national conventions, held in Philadelphia in 1832, resolved: "If we ever expect to see the influence of prejudice decrease, and ourselves respected, it must be by the blessings of an enlightened education." An 1847 state Negro convention in Indianapolis similarly resolved: "That the white people of this state ought not to reproach us with being ignorant, degraded and poor . . . while denying to ours the benefits and blessings" of education.[10]

Many black newspapers of the antebellum era also urged the importance of education to black uplift. The *North Star*, a black newspaper in Albany, New York, exhorted its readers on the importance of education: "There is no one subject that should claim so much of the attention of our people as the education of our youth, for on that alone, in a great measure, depends our future prosperity and happiness." The *Freedom's Journal* in 1827 blamed the poor condition of many blacks on their lack of education: "Writers, old and young are fond of exclaiming 'there is a wide difference in point of intellect between the African and the European. . . .' [W]e call upon the advocates of the system to point to us one *individual* who has enjoyed to the full extent all the privileges of his fairer brethren."[11]

---

9 Rael, "The Lion's Painting," Introduction, pp. 18–19, 102–3, 124–8.

10 On the Negro convention movement, see Goodman, *Of One Blood,* p. 33; Reid, "Race, Class, Gender, and the Teaching Profession," pp. 54–5; Bethel, *The Roots of African-American Identity,* pp. 137–8. For the Philadelphia convention quote, see *Minutes and Proceedings of the Second Annual Convention, for the Improvement of the Free People of Color in these United States* (Philadelphia, 1832), reprinted in Bell, *Minutes of the Proceedings,* p. 34. For the Indianapolis convention quote, see Heller, "Negro Education in Indiana," p. 63.

11 For the *North Star* quote, see Sacks, "'We Rise or Fall Together,'" pp. 12–13; for the second quote, see *Freedom's Journal* (New York), June 1, 1827, in Dann, *The Black Press,* p. 295.

Abolitionists – both black and white – urged black education, recognizing the link between learning and emancipation. Antislavery societies formed education committees to promote the development of black schools to prepare for "that state in society upon which depends our political happiness." Black abolitionist Alexander Crummel explained to a group of London abolitionists in 1851: "As the *free* coloured population go up in the scale of intelligence, increase in mental capacity, and demonstrate their intellectual power, the whole fabric of slavery proportionably crumbles and totters." A national Negro convention in Rochester, New York, in 1848 made a similar claim: "In the Northern states, we are . . . largely responsible for [the slaves'] continued enslavement, or their speedy deliverance from chains. For in the proportion in which we shall rise in the scale of human improvement, in that proportion do we augment the probabilities of a speedy emancipation of our enslaved fellow-countrymen. It is more than a mere figure of speech to say that we are as a people, chained together. . . . As one rises, all must rise, and as one falls, all must fall." Even schoolchildren understood the connection between education and abolition. One black student in Cincinnati in the 1840s wrote an essay on Alfred the Great: "at one time [Alfred] did not know his a, b, c, but before his death he commanded . . . nations. . . . I think if the colored people study like King Alfred they will soon do away with the evil of slavery."[12]

Before and after the development of publicly supported common schools, both blacks and whites, frequently those associated with abolitionist efforts, established private schools to educate black children. For example, the New York Manumission Society helped establish African Free Schools for black children in New York City beginning in 1787 for the purpose of helping blacks transition from slavery to freedom. These schools offered instruction in both academic subjects and the manual arts. In 1828, the New York Manumission Society reported that "such has been the happy influence of the system pursued in our African schools, that the trustees have never known any scholar regularly educated in them, to have been convicted of crime, in any of our courts of justice." The *New York Commercial Advertiser* also gave high marks to the African Free Schools in 1824: "It is education – it is the cultivation of the mind and the heart, which teaches them to be honest, makes them quiet and orderly citizens. . . . [T]he African

---

[12] For abolitionists and black education, see Tyack, *The One Best System*, p. 111; for antislavery society education committees, see Woodson, *The Education of the Negro*, pp. 71–2; for the Crummel quote, see Crummell, "Speech" in C. Peter Ripley, ed., *The Black Abolitionist Papers*, Vol. I, p. 277; for the quote from the Rochester convention, see Rael, "The Lion's Painting," p. 154; for the quote from the Cincinnati student, see Cheek and Cheek, "John Mercer Langston," p. 70.

Free School is...snatching [the children] from a state of ignorance, superstition, credulity, and crime." By 1837, one-quarter of New York City's black children attended an African Free School.[13]

Blacks and sympathetic whites established private schools for black children in other parts of the antebellum North as well. In Philadelphia, Quakers provided schools for blacks during the late eighteenth century and helped fund several private schools established by blacks during the early nineteenth century. Quakers also supported the establishment of private black schools in several antebellum Indiana communities; as a result of these efforts, about 20 percent of Indiana black children attended some kind of school in 1850, even though they were legally barred from Indiana's public schools. In fact, the vast majority of northern black children who received schooling prior to 1850 did so in private schools. For example, black children would be excluded from Cincinnati's common schools until the early 1850s, but by 1834, Cincinnati was home to six privately supported schools for black children,one of which, Gilmore High School, attracted students from as far away as New Orleans. Many of these schools required tuition, which made attendance difficult for poorer children, but they provided essential training at a time when public schools were frequently closed to blacks. Schools were not the only venue for black education in the antebellum North. Benevolent societies and colored literary societies throughout the North provided educational opportunities for adults eager to learn, as did church Sunday schools.[14]

Beneath this pursuit of educational opportunities lay a conflict in the northern black community over the importance of assimilation into the dominant white culture. Black leaders articulated a variety of perspectives on this issue. Some favored emigration in the face of racial oppression, while others insisted on inclusion in a variety of

---

[13] For New York's African Free Schools, see Mabee, *Black Education in New York State*, p. 21; Bethel, *The Roots of African-American Identity*, pp. 67, 133; Andrews, *The History of the New-York African Free-Schools*, p. 31; Woodson, *The Education of the Negro*, pp. 97–9; Thurston, "Ethiopia Unshackled," p. 216. For the quote from the New York Manumission Society, see Andrews, *The History of the New-York African Free-Schools*, p. 56. For the quote from the *New York Commercial Advertiser*, see ibid., p. 47. For African School attendance, see *The Colored American*, New York, July 1, 1837, in Dann, *The Black Press*, p. 311.

[14] Horton and Horton, *In Hope of Liberty*, pp. 150–1; Thornbrough, *The Negro in Indiana*, p. 317; U.S. Bureau of Census, 1850; Finkelman, "Prelude to the Fourteenth Amendment," p. 472; Woodson, "The Negroes of Cincinnati," pp. 18–20; Pease and Pease, *They Who Would Be Free*, p. 147; Woodson, *The Education of the Negro*, pp. 245, 327; Gerber, *Black Ohio and the Color Line*, p. 4; Woodson, *The Education of the Negro*, p. 149; Bethel, *The Roots of African-American Identity*, p. 67; Ment, "Racial Segregation in the Public Schools," p. 16; Smith, "Native Blacks and Foreign Whites," p. 314.

white institutions including schools. These differences would eventually manifest themselves in the debate over integrated schools.

Antiblack Sentiment in the Antebellum North

Despite black enthusiasm for education, many white northerners who promoted public education did not include African Americans in their common school vision. Throughout much of the antebellum era, strong antiblack sentiment loomed large in much of the North, particularly in the Midwest. To be sure, the racial climate in the antebellum North was not static, varying significantly over time and among states (and even within certain states). In most of New England, blacks experienced relatively few legal disabilities, although local school authorities engaged in racial segregation in a few New England towns and cities during much of the antebellum era. The Midwest, on the other hand, was far less hospitable to African Americans, imposing a variety of legal disabilities, although racial attitudes in the Midwest tended to vary both geographically and over time. For example, in Ohio, racial attitudes dramatically differed between the state's racially conservative southern counties and the abolitionist Western Reserve in the state's northeast corner. Moreover, Ohio enacted harsh "Black Laws" during the early nineteenth century that imposed a variety of legal restraints on blacks but repealed many of those laws during the late 1840s. Those counties in Indiana with a large Quaker population held racial views sharply at odds with those of the rest of the state throughout the antebellum era. The racial attitudes of southern Illinois bore greater similarity to those of the nearby slave states of Kentucky and Missouri than to those of the state's northern counties. Upstate New York was far more sympathetic to black concerns than was Long Island.

Moreover, the sectional crisis over fugitive slaves that erupted during the late 1840s and early 1850s had the collateral effect of improving the status of blacks in a few northern states, such as Massachusetts, where the negative reaction to the Fugitive Slave Act of 1850 contributed to enactment of a statutory ban on segregation in 1855.[15] The rise of the Republican Party during the 1850s also boded well for African Americans and their right to an education. Although a majority of Republicans in the 1850s, including Abraham Lincoln, were not prepared to enfranchise African Americans, they did favor the elimination of various legal disabilities imposed on free blacks such as their exclusion from public schools. Nevertheless, the political and civil status of northern blacks, particularly outside of New England,

---

[15] Finkelman, "Prelude to the Fourteenth Amendment," p. 424.

remained generally poor throughout most of the antebellum era. Although some northern whites favored removing all legal disabilities imposed on blacks, their voices, particularly in the Midwest, remained in the minority until after the Civil War.

During the first half of the nineteenth century, many whites embraced the view that race was "a matter of biological reality, permanent and inescapable, and that character and behavior are inextricably tied to this reality," rejecting eighteenth-century notions of racial differences grounded in environmental and cultural differences. Phrenologists and ethnologists classified African Americans as intrinsically different from whites and "lacking in certain moral and mental capacities." As historian Carl Kaestle has noted, "[n]atural philosophers of the antebellum period forged theories about the separate creation of the races, speculated that blacks and whites were of different species, and fretted than an increase in the black population would cause the downfall of the republic." Some antebellum school textbooks expressed these sentiments.An 1839 text published in Connecticut claimed of blacks: "As a race, phrenologists have pronounced them incapable of any high attainments as well from the shape and configuration of their heads as from their general appearance. Every feature of the negro, except his clear, white teeth, are abhorrent from [sic] all European ideas of personal beauty or enlargement of the intellect. One great cause of their degraded condition in their own country is the total want of ambition and of all incentives to mental improvement." By the middle of the nineteenth century, white conceptions of African Americans as inherently inferior to whites were widespread. Such views contributed to the notion among many whites that blacks could never be incorporated into the body politic.[16]

These racist views were widely expressed. Eliphalet Nott, president of Union College, claimed that African Americans "have remained already to the third and fourth, as they will to the thousandth

---

[16] For the quote concerning race as biological reality, see Dain, "A Hideous Monster of the Mind," p. 14; for the quote concerning moral and mental capacities, see Glaude, *Exodus!* p. 61; for the Kaestle quote, see Kaestle, *Pillars of the Republic*, p. 88; for the textbook quote, see Parillo, "Images of Blacks," p. 83 (quoting Samuel Perkins, *The World as It Is*, p. 444 [1839]). In reality, northern textbooks varied. As one scholar of antebellum textbooks has concluded, "antebellum school children were being exposed to materials written by white advocates of black emancipation, proponents of removing blacks through colonization, as well as apologists for continued slavery." Parillo, "Images of Blacks," p. 111. On the widespread nature of notions of black inferiority, see Glaude, *Exodus!* pp. 65–7. As Rogers Smith has noted of the early nineteenth century: "Assertions of the irrevocable inferiority of blacks . . . by political leaders as well as intellectuals, North and South, became more and more common." Smith, *Civic Ideals*, p. 175.

generation – a distinct, a degraded, and a wretched race." At the Pennsylvania state constitutional convention of 1837 that stripped blacks of the right to vote, one delegate referred to African Americans as "a race of criminals." An Ohio politician in 1833 described free blacks as "the only evil" imperiling "the perfection of our social and political system." De Tocqueville offered this observation of northern attitudes toward blacks in the 1830s: "Race prejudice seems stronger in those states that have abolished slavery than in those where it still exists, and nowhere is it more intolerant than in those states [of the Midwest] where slavery was never known."[17]

Not all white northerners, of course, shared this pessimistic assessment of African Americans as inherently inferior. Abolitionist Lydia Maria Child, for example, published *An Appeal in Favor of Americans Called Africans* in 1833 that argued that "the present degraded condition" of blacks was "produced by artificial causes, not by the laws of nature." But Child's views of African Americans did not predominate in the white antebellum North.[18]

Many northern whites viewed African Americans as unwanted competition for jobs. White workers often refused to work with blacks and sometimes would strike to force them from a job site. Some white skilled laborers refused to hire black apprentices, forcing black workers to scramble for unskilled jobs. White workers in Boston sought legislation during the early 1820s that would have excluded blacks from their state; white artisans in Pennsylvania sought similar legislation in 1834. The president of a mechanical association in Cincinnati was "tried" by members of his organization during the 1830s for the offense of helping a black person learn a trade. One young black man, speaking in 1819, expressed the despair of racial barriers to work opportunities: "Why should I strive hard, and acquire all the constituents of a man, if the prevailing genius of the land admit me not as such, or but in an inferior degree! . . . Shall I be a mechanic? No one will employ me; white boys won't work with me. Shall I be a merchant? No one will have me in his office; white clerks won't associate with me. Drudgery and servitude, then, are my prospective portion. Can you be surprised at my discouragement?" Even in New Bedford, Massachusetts, one of the most racially liberal communities in the antebellum North, Frederick Douglass was denied work in 1838 as a caulker because white caulkers refused to work with him. Douglass commented in a letter in 1853: "In times past we have been the hewers

---

[17] For the Nott quote, see Ratner, *Powder Keg*, p. 18; for the Pennsylvania quote, see ibid., p. 21; for the Ohio quote, see Goodman, *Of One Blood*, p. 20; for the De Tocqueville quote, see De Tocqueville, *Democracy in America*, p. 343.

[18] Quoted in Earhart, "Boston's 'Un-Common' Common," pp. 44–6.

of wood and the drawers of water for American society, and we once enjoyed a monopoly in menial employments, but this is so no longer – even these employments are rapidly passing away out of our hands."[19]

The white popular press played to fears of free blacks – and newly emancipated slaves – taking white jobs. The *Cincinnati Enquirer* editorialized in 1861: "The hundreds of thousands, if not millions of slaves [the Civil War] will emancipate will come North and West, and will either be competitors with our white mechanics and laborers, degrading them by the competition, or they will have to be supported as paupers and criminals at the public expense."[20]

The northern Democratic Party, which gained increasing power during the first half of the nineteenth century, catered to and helped foment working-class antagonisms toward blacks. Many Democratic politicians, virulently antiblack, portrayed African Americans "as an enemy and one to be severely dealt with." Indeed, antiblack rhetoric emerged as a major weapon of the northern Democratic Party during the antebellum era. In 1846, the *New York Tribune* castigated that state's Democratic Party for using race hatred to win votes: "Hostility to 'Niggers' is their great card, by which they hope to [capture support]." Ohio Republican Governor Salmon Chase complained in the 1850s of the Ohio Democratic Party that all they wanted was "simply to talk about the universal nigger question, as they call it. All that they seem to say is 'nigger, nigger, nigger.'" Many historians have noted that the egalitarianism of Jacksonian democracy, manifest in part in the extension of the franchise to all white men, was grounded in part on the oppression of African Americans.[21]

In some northern cities, racial conflicts erupted into violence. On several of these occasions, black homes were burned and black citizens assaulted. In some communities, blacks were forcefully driven out. The

[19] For white workers' attitudes toward blacks, see Woodson, *The Education of the Negro*, p. 286; Fishel, "The North and the Negro," p. 41; Sacks, "'We Rise or Fall Together,'" p. 9; Woodson, *Century of Negro Migration*, pp. 24–5; Turner, *The Negro in Pennsylvania*, p. 159; Woodson, "The Negroes of Cincinnati," p. 5; for the quote from a black worker, see Tyack, *The One Best System*, p. 123; for the Douglass quote, see Letter from Frederick Douglass to Mrs. H. B. Stowe, Mar. 8, 1853, in Proceedings of the Colored National Convention (Rochester, 1853), in Bell (ed.), *Minutes of the Proceedings of the National Negro Conventions*, p. 37. For Douglass, see also Douglass, *Life and Times of Frederick Douglass*, pp. 210–11.

[20] Quoted in Voegeli, *Free But Not Equal*, p. 6.

[21] For antiblack Democratic rhetoric, see Franklin, *Education of Black Philadelphia*, p. 10 and Cottrol, "Law, Politics and Race," pp. 507–8 (including the quote); for the *New York Tribune* quote, see Benson, *The Concept of Jacksonian Democracy*, p. 320; for the Chase quote, see Foner, *Free Soil, Free Labor, Free Men*, p. 264; for Jacksonian democracy, see Cottrol, "Law, Politics and Race," p. 511, n. 192; Fredrickson, *The Black Image in the White Mind*, pp. 61–8, 91–6; Benson, *The Concept of Jacksonian Democracy*, pp. 318–20.

racial conflict in Cincinnati, the nation's sixth largest city during the mid-nineteenth century, was particularly dramatic. Enforcement of Ohio's Black Laws, which required in part that each black person post a $500 surety bond guaranteeing good behavior in order to remain in the state, had been quite lax during the early nineteenth century. But a sharp increase in Cincinnati's black population during the late 1820s – from 600 to over 2,000 – along with a growing tide of German and Irish immigrants, provoked conflict, as these groups competed for work in the Cincinnati economy. Many whites insisted on enforcement of the bond requirement. In response, the city's trustees announced in 1829 that they would give the entire black population sixty days to meet the bond requirement or else leave the city. In the meantime, an impatient mob of whites attacked the city's black population. In response to this eruption of white hostility, about half of the city's black population of more than 2,000 migrated to Canada. Black leaders called a national Negro convention in Philadelphia in 1830 to assist the beleaguered black community in Cincinnati, decrying the "vulgar race prejudice which reigns in the breasts" of working-class whites.[22]

Racial conflict and calls for black expulsion in Cincinnati would continue. Rioters in 1836 destroyed the printing press of the city's abolitionist newspaper, *The Philanthropist*, and dumped it into the Ohio River. In 1841, renewed calls for the expulsion of Cincinnati's entire black population, motivated in part by job competition, helped trigger "the most destructive and violent riot in the city's history," which prompted additional black migration to Canada and more than 100 blacks to post the hated surety bond. Once again, the printing press of *The Philanthropist* wound up at the bottom of the Ohio River.[23]

These racial antagonisms were present throughout much of the North, but were particularly harsh in those counties just north of the Ohio River in southern Ohio, Indiana, and Illinois that were populated primarily by whites of southern origin who feared an influx of free

---

[22] From 1829 until 1841, antiblack (and anti-abolitionist) riots plagued cities such as Cincinnati (1829, 1831, 1836, 1841), New York City (1834), Philadelphia (1834, 1835, 1842), Pittsburgh (1835, 1839), and Providence (1831) and smaller communities such as Burlington, Pennsylvania (1835), Utica and Palmyra, New York (1834, 1839), and Portsmouth, Ohio (1830). Grimsted, *American Mobbing*, pp. 9, 30, 36, 59, 62, 299 n. 89; Woodson, *The Education of the Negro*, p. 284; Turner, *The Negro in Pennsylvania*, pp. 159–61; Bethel, *The Roots of African-American Identity*, p. 123; Cheek and Cheek, "John Mercer Langston," p. 48; Franklin, *From Slavery to Freedom*, pp. 184–5; Glaude, *Exodus!* pp. 234–5. For Cincinnati violence, see Cheek and Cheek, "John Mercer Langston," pp. 30–2; Bertaux, "Structural Economic Change and Occupational Decline," pp. 129–30; Woodson, "The Negroes of Cincinnati," pp. 6–7; Wade, "The Negro in Cincinnati," pp. 51–6; Woodson, *The Education of the Negro*, p. 286 (quote).

[23] Cheek and Cheek, "John Mercer Langston," p. 66 (quote); Grimsted, *American Mobbing*, p. 62; Montgomery, "Racial History of the Cincinnati and Suburban Public Schools," p. 21 (1983), Cincinnati Historical Society.

blacks. Many white midwesterners during the antebellum era would concede blacks the right to be free of slavery but little more. As an Indiana abolitionist, George Julian, commented in 1858: "Our people [of Indiana] hate the Negro with a perfect if not supreme hatred."[24]

Historian Eric Foner has suggested that the more fluid social structure of the Midwest that allowed some blacks to rise economically and socially may have contributed to the region's particularly strong racial animosities. Those blacks arriving in the Midwest were better able to challenge the status and prerogatives of whites than were blacks living back East, provoking white fears and resentments. As an English visitor to Cincinnati noted in 1834, many whites spoke of blacks "with a degree of bitterness that dictated a disposition to be more angry with their virtues than with their vices." The *Cincinnati Daily Gazette* wrote in 1841 of white workers reacting to black prosperity with "jealousy and heart burning."[25]

This deep-seated antiblack feeling resulted in a variety of legal restrictions on African Americans during the first half of the nineteenth century. For example, many northern and western states either considered banning or did ban the entry of black immigrants during the antebellum era. Ohio, Indiana, Illinois, and the Michigan Territory enacted Black Laws, requiring in part that blacks certify their free status, register with county officials, and post a security bond guaranteeing their good behavior in order to settle in the state. These laws also made it illegal to hire a black person who had not met these statutory requirements.[26]

These measures were not widely enforced, and efforts at repeal were frequent; the Michigan Territory and Ohio, for example, repealed most of their Black Laws in 1837 and 1849, respectively. But these laws nevertheless reflected the intense antiblack feeling of many white midwesterners. On some occasions, the Black Laws were enforced, either through legal channels or by vigilante violence. As noted, white insistence on enforcement of the bond requirement in Cincinnati in 1829 forced the removal of half of the city's black population. Similarly, in 1833, the mayor of Detroit issued a proclamation that ordered all blacks who could not post the required bond to leave the city.[27]

---

[24] For the Julian quote, see Voegeli, *Free But Not Equal*, p. 1.

[25] For Foner, see Foner, *Free Soil, Free Labor, Free Men*, p. 262; for the English visitor quote, see Cheek and Cheek, "John Mercer Langston," p. 61; for the *Cincinnati Daily Gazette* quote, see Woodson, "The Negroes of Cincinnati," p. 13.

[26] Banks, *Black Intellectuals*, p. 12; Middleton, *The Black Laws in the Old Northwest*, pp. 15–17, 202–3, 293–8, 346; Finkelman, "Prelude to the Fourteenth Amendment," pp. 434–5.

[27] Middleton, *The Black Laws in the Old Northwest*, pp. 15–17, 202–3, 293–8, 346; Finkelman, "Prelude to the Fourteenth Amendment," pp. 434–5; Thornbrough, *The Negro in Indiana*, p. 63; Katzman, *Before the Ghetto*, pp. 7, 11.

Many midwestern newspapers urged enforcement of the Black Laws. "By enforcing this law," a Richmond, Indiana, newspaper wrote, "we should rid ourselves of a worse than useless population, drive away a gang of pilferers, make an opening for white laborers to fill the places of the blacks, and relieve our town of the odium now resting on it." A New Albany, Indiana, newspaper argued that without enforcement, "we shall soon be overrun with all the worthless, idle, and dissolute Negroes in the surrounding counties." A newspaper editor in the Western Reserve of Ohio opposed the legislation as immoral but made clear his lack of enthusiasm for black settlement: "We have no special affection for negroes. We neither desire their companionship or their society. . . . We would be glad if there was not one in the State or one in the United States."[28]

Proponents of the Black Laws were motivated in part by the desire to discourage settlement of free blacks and emancipated slaves. Indeed, as southern states imposed additional restrictions on free blacks during the 1830s and 1840s, scores of southern blacks crossed the Ohio River into the lower Midwest. Moreover, an English visitor to Indiana in the 1830s reported that it was a common practice for Kentucky slaveholders to bring their slaves who were too old or feeble to work to Indiana and emancipate them, despite their inability to provide for themselves. The Kentucky constitutional convention of 1850 provided for the imprisonment of any emancipated slave who did not leave the state. Other southern states enacted similar legislation. White antagonism toward free blacks was exacerbated by the efforts of Quakers during the 1830s and 1840s to buy southern slaves and resettle them in the Midwest.[29]

Many white northerners – even those who opposed slavery – feared that emancipation would trigger an exodus of blacks into northern states. As a result, during the 1820s and 1830s, many northern whites, even abolitionists, supported the colonization of blacks in Africa. Founded in 1817, the American Colonization Society gave voice to those who sought to rid the new nation of African Americans. Many of those supporting colonization argued that free blacks were hopelessly degraded and could never be assimilated into white society. For many supporters of colonization, black education was pointless. Some midwestern states, such as Indiana, expressly supported, either by resolution or legislative appropriation, the colonization of northern blacks

---

[28] For the Richmond quote, see Thornbrough, *The Negro in Indiana*, p. 62; for the New Albany quote, see ibid., p. 63; for the Western Reserve quote, see Voegeli, *Free But Not Equal*, p. 29.

[29] Heller, "Negro Education in Indiana," p. 146; Woodson, "The Negroes of Cincinnati," p. 3.

in Liberia while at the same time denying black children access to public schools.[30]

Some northern blacks, though not a majority, also favored emigration. Black conventions at Dayton in 1848 and Cincinnati in 1850, for example, expressed support for colonization efforts. Martin Delany, one of the proponents of emigration, expressed frustration about the possibility of blacks ever obtaining equal rights in America. Delany explained his views to William Lloyd Garrison in 1852: "I am not in favor of caste, nor a separation of the brotherhood of mankind, and would as willingly live among white men as black, if I had an *equal possession and enjoyment* of privileges.... If there were any probability of this, I should be willing to remain in the country, fighting and struggling on, the good fight of faith. But I must admit, that I have no hopes in this country – no confidence in the American people – with a *few* excellent exceptions – therefore I have written as I have done. Heathenism and Liberty, before Christianity and Slavery." These sentiments increased in response to enactment of the Fugitive Slave Act of 1850 that left many free blacks, though not fugitives from bondage, vulnerable to southern slave catchers. As a result, many northern blacks, fearing capture, moved further north; Pittsburgh, for example, lost 42 percent of its black population during the 1850s. Between 1820 and 1860, almost 75,000 African Americans, about 20 percent of the free black population, left America for Canada or Haiti.[31]

During the 1850s, antiblack sentiment and fears of black immigration intensified, particularly in the Midwest. During that decade, Illinois, Indiana, and Iowa enacted legislation prohibiting *all* black immigration, while Ohio narrowly defeated such a proposal. Indiana's experience is illustrative. Indiana's constitutional convention of 1850 voted by a margin of more than two to one for a provision providing that "No negro or mulatto shall come into, or settle in the State, after the adoption of this Constitution." One proponent of black exclusion at the Indiana constitutional convention of 1850 outrageously suggested "that it would be better to kill them off at once, if there is no other way to get rid of them." Another proponent of exclusion commented: "The negro race and the white race cannot live together; and it behooves us, under these circumstances, not only to furnish no

[30] Middleton, *The Black Laws in the Old Northwest*, pp. 219–20; Thornbrough, *The Negro in Indiana*, pp. 74–5.

[31] For black conventions, see Meier, "The Emergence of Negro Nationalism, Part I," p. 100; for the Delany quote, see Letter from Delany to Garrison, May 14, 1852, in Woodson (ed.), *The Mind of the Negro as Reflected in Letters Written During the Crisis*, p. 293; for the effect of the Fugitive Slave Act, see Glasco, "Double Burden," p. 72; Bethel, *The Roots of African-American Identity*, p. 146.

encouragement to the colored race to enter our borders, but effec-
tually to protect ourselves against their entrance. Nay, more; we must
not afford encouragement to those who are already here to remain
here." Fines collected for violations of this exclusion provision were
designated for African colonization efforts. The new Indiana Constitution also provided that all contracts involving blacks migrating into
the state were void and that any person who employed a black migrant
would be fined. The Indiana Supreme Court articulated the purpose
of the law in an 1856 decision: "The policy of the state . . . is thus clearly
evolved. It is to exclude any further ingress of negroes, and to remove
those already among us as speedily as possible."[32]

Although these exclusion laws do not appear to have been widely
enforced in Illinois and Iowa where the black population significantly
increased during the 1850s, Indiana did attempt to enforce its exclusion law through both legal and extralegal means. In 1857, a white
mob in Evansville forcibly removed many blacks; similar vigilante action in New Albany in 1860 drove a group of blacks from the town. As
a result, Indiana's black population remained essentially stable during
the 1850s, while the black population of every other midwestern state
sharply increased during the same time period.[33]

Further west, antagonism toward blacks was also widespread. In
Kansas, Nebraska, California, and Oregon, legislators and constitutional convention delegates urged exclusion of African Americans
from their territories. California, at its 1848 constitutional convention,

---

[32] For black exclusion legislation, see Voegeli, *Free But Not Equal*, p. 2; Fishel, "The
North and the Negro," pp. 22–3, 29–30; Middleton, *The Black Laws in the Old North-
west*, pp. 204–5, 299–302; Robisch, "Educational Segregation and Desegregation in
Ohio," p. 22. Iowa repealed its exclusion legislation in 1860; earlier, a state trial
judge had declared the law unconstitutional. Finkleman, "Prelude to the Fourteenth
Amendment," p. 438. For the three Indiana quotes, see Thornbrough, *The Negro in
Indiana*, pp. 67–8; ibid., p. 66; ibid., p. 82. For the new Indiana constitution, see
Heller, "Negro Education in Indiana," p. 71; Thornbrough, *The Negro in Indiana*,
68–9. For the court decision, see *Barkshire v. State*, 7 Ind. 309, 310 (1856).

[33] For increases in black population, see U.S. Bureau of the Census, 1850 and 1860;
Finkelman, "Prelude to the Fourteenth Amendment," p. 439. There were, however,
at least a few prosecutions under the Illinois exclusion law. *Glenn v. People*, 17 Ill.
104 (1855) (reversing the conviction because of the state's failure to allege that "the
negro came into this State" after enactment of the law); *Nelson v. People*, 33 Ill. 390
(1864) (upholding the conviction). For enforcement in Indiana, see *Barkshire v. State*,
7 Ind. 309 (1856) (upholding the conviction under the exclusion law); *Hatwood
v. State*, 18 Ind. 492 (1862) (reversing the conviction on grounds that the statute
of limitations had already run out; the defendant had previously been convicted
under the law in 1856); *Smith v. Moody*, 26 Ind. 299 (1866) (Indiana Supreme Court
declared the exclusion law unconstitutional in violation of Art. 4, sec. 2, of the federal
constitution). For mob violence, see Thornbrough, *The Negro in Indiana*, pp. 130–1.
For the Indiana population, see U.S. Bureau of Census, 1850 and 1860; Finkleman,
"Prelude to the Fourteenth Amendment," p. 439.

initially excluded all blacks from the state due to widespread antiblack sentiment and fear of competition from black labor, but eventually reversed course so as to secure statehood. After winning statehood, one of the first issues considered by the new California state legislature was black exclusion; in 1850, the California state house adopted legislation barring the immigration of free blacks to the state but the legislation failed by one vote in the state senate.[34]

In Oregon, the territorial assembly enacted legislation during the 1840s that required the exclusion of all blacks from the territory and that barred the immigration of additional blacks. Not surprisingly, Oregon's small black population declined by almost half during the 1850s. In 1859, Congress approved Oregon's admission to the Union notwithstanding a state constitutional provision that barred blacks from settling there. Although some Republican members of Congress opposed Oregon's admission because of this exclusion law, for others Oregon's status as a free state proved more important than its exclusion of blacks.[35]

Many states imposed other disabilities on blacks during the antebellum era. Several midwestern states, including Ohio, Indiana, Illinois, and Iowa, barred African Americans from testifying against whites in court, giving rise to severe abuse of blacks who entered into contractual relations with whites. The Ohio Supreme Court explained the operation of the statute: "Let a man be Christian or infidel; let him be Turk, Jew or Mahometan; let him be of good character or bad; even let him be sunk to the lowest depths of degradation; he may be witness in our courts if he is not black. If a negro or mulatto, he must be excluded from giving evidence where a white man is a party." After the Indiana legislature enacted legislation in 1843 that forbade blacks from testifying in criminal cases involving whites, a legislative committee commented: "The track of the foot, the nail of the shoe, the bark of the dog, or the bray of the donkey, may be given in evidence to ferret out villainies; but the negro, . . . though acquainted with the villain, and cognizant to the villainy, for no reason than because he is a negro, is not even permitted to develope [sic] corroborating circumstances." In addition, several northern state constitutions or statutes during the antebellum era barred blacks from serving on juries or in state militias.[36]

---

34 Berwanger, *The Frontier Against Slavery*, pp. 5, 67–70; Hendrick, *The Education of Non-Whites in California*, p. 2.

35 La Plante, "The Negro at Jefferson High School," pp. 42–3, 49. McElderry, "The Problem of the Color Line," pp. 17–18; U.S. Bureau of Census, 1850 and 1860; Finkelman, "Prelude to the Fourteenth Amendment," p. 439; Foner, *Free Soil, Free Labor, Free Men*, pp. 289–90.

36 For bans on testimony, see Middleton, *The Black Laws in the Old Northwest*, pp. 245–7, 315; Gerber, *Black Ohio and the Color Line*, p. 4; Pease and Pease, *They Who Would Be Free*,

During the first half of the nineteenth century, most blacks in the North were denied the right to vote even as the franchise for white men expanded. Moreover, black men lost the right to vote that they had previously enjoyed in several northern states, including New Jersey (1807), Connecticut (1814), Rhode Island (1822, though the right was restored in 1842), and Pennsylvania (1838). Additionally, New York removed the property qualification on white voters in 1822 but restricted the right of black men to vote to those who owned at least $250 worth of property. This property condition served to disfranchise most of the state's black population.[37]

Of the states that joined the Union between 1800 and 1860, only Maine permitted African Americans to vote. Some of these denials were by overwhelming margins; for example, the Indiana constitutional convention of 1816 rejected the franchise for African Americans by a vote of 122 to 1. Subsequent black efforts to gain the franchise failed; Michigan, Iowa, and Wisconsin all rejected proposals to give black men the right to vote during the 1850s. Blacks did manage to vote in elections for directors of black schools in Ohio and Michigan during the 1850s, but these were exceptions. By the end of the antebellum era, black men enjoyed the legal right to vote only in New York (if they met the property requirement that did not apply to whites) and in five of the six New England states (excluding Connecticut). In 1865, as the Civil War came to a close, Connecticut, Wisconsin, and Minnesota considered granting the franchise to blacks, but each declined to do so. Historian Robert Cottrol has appropriately described much of the antebellum North as a "Herrenvolk democracy" in which political culture was "egalitarian and democratic for superordinate groups and undemocratic for subordinate groups."[38]

---

p. 156; Johnson, *The Development of State Legislation*, p. 96. For the Ohio Supreme Court decision, see *Jordan v. Smith*, 14 Ohio 199, 201 (1846). In upholding the exclusion provision, the court did concede its harshness. As Justice Hitchcock explained for the court: "In all my experience, both at the bar and as a member of this court, I cannot recollect a single case in which this law has been found subservient to the ends of justice. On the contrary, its uniform effect has been to prevent justice, both public and private." Ibid., p. 204. For the Indiana legislative committee, see Thornbrough, *The Negro in Indiana*, p. 122. Indiana did provide in 1861 that if a black person who was a party to a case was excluded from giving testimony, then his opponent in the litigation, even if white, would also be excluded from testifying. Middleton, *The Black Laws in the Old Northwest*, pp. 246–7. For state militia bans, see ibid., pp. 14, 197–8, 279, 363.

37 Williams, *Strangers in the Land of Paradise*, p. 17.

38 For black voting rights, see Cottrol, "Race, Politics and Law," p. 509, n. 176 (Maine); Thornbrough, *The Negro in Indiana*, p. 121 (Indiana); Voegeli, *Free But Not Equal*, p. 2 (Iowa, Wisconsin); Katzman, *Before the Ghetto*, pp. 33, 35 (Michigan); Fishel, "The North and the Negro," pp. 25–6 (New York and New England); Quillin, *The Color*

This denial of the franchise undermined black efforts to secure access to a common school education. First, without the franchise, blacks could not exercise political power to gain education rights. Second, since many promoters of the common school justified education as essential to equipping citizens to participate in self-government, the exclusion of blacks from the political process eliminated this imperative for black education.

To be sure, the situation for northern blacks was not entirely bleak. Every northern state prohibited slavery during the antebellum era and fiercely resisted the extension of slavery into new federal territories. Most northern states, either by statute or judicial decision, provided for the emancipation of slaves brought into northern states by their masters. And most northern states enacted personal liberty laws that offered some protection for free blacks from seizure by southern slave catchers. Nevertheless, for many northern blacks, particularly those residing outside of the New England states, racial discrimination was a deep and abiding concern throughout the antebellum era.[39]

The Common School Movement and Black Education

As northern states established public schools during the first half of the nineteenth century, African Americans were initially excluded from the overwhelming majority of local school districts. In much of the North, particularly in the lower Midwest, black children would remain excluded from the public schools until the 1850s and, in some instances, the late 1860s. Indeed, by the eve of the Civil War, a substantial majority of black children living in the lower Midwest attended no school whatsoever.

On the other hand, in many northern communities, particularly in New England, black children gained access to public schools during the 1820s and 1830s, although initially on a racially segregated basis. In some northern communities, particularly in areas with few blacks or strong abolitionist sentiment, blacks attended school alongside white children. But the overwhelming majority of northern black children who attended school prior to the Civil War, whether public or private, did so on in racially separate schools.

The outright exclusion of black children from public education was striking in light of the articulated purposes of the common schools. As noted, among the primary purposes of the common school movement

Line in Ohio, p. 9 (Ohio). For the Cottrol quote, see Cottrol, "Law, Politics and Race," p. 510, n. 189 (citing van den Berghe, *Race and Racism: A Comparative Perspective*, p. 18 [1967]).

39 For personal liberty laws, see Morris, *Free Men All.*

were the preservation of republican government through the creation of a literate and thoughtful electorate and the prevention of social disorder, but these goals did not lead to the education of black children in much of the North. The 1851 Indiana Constitution, for example, although it stated that "[k]nowledge and learning generally diffused throughout a community" are "essential to the preservation of a free government," expressly limited the public schools to white children.[40]

In fact, many northern whites, particularly in the Midwest, did not consider blacks worthy of assimilation or participation in the governing process so as to warrant inclusion in the common school system. The contrast between the treatment of the children of African Americans and those of Irish immigrants is striking. Though African Americans embraced the dominant religion of antebellum America (Protestantism), had lived in America for generations, and had ancestors who had toiled for freedom during the Revolutionary War, antebellum educators looked more favorably on educating Irish immigrant children than black children. To be sure, many northern whites regarded immigrants from Ireland and their "Popish" religion with profound disdain. Such hostile feelings occasionally exploded into violence, as with the burning of the Ursuline convent in Boston in 1834. But the Irish had never been degraded by slavery and had white skin, and hence were viewed as favorable candidates for acculturation in the Protestant-dominated common schools of the antebellum North. As Yale President Timothy Dwight said of the Irish: "The evils which I have specified are not, however, derived from the native character of these people. . . . Give them the same advantages which are enjoyed by others, and they will stand upon a level with any of their neighbors."[41]

But many northern whites did not hold such a generous assessment of the ability of African Americans to assimilate. As one nineteenth-century scholar commented: "Irishmen, Germans, Frenchmen, etc., come here, settle down, become citizens, and their offspring born and raised on American soil differ in no appreciable or perceptible manner from other Americans. . . . [But the Negro] is absolutely and specifically unlike the American as when the race first touched the soil and first breathed the air of the New World." In fact, for many northern whites, assimilation of African Americans was highly undesirable. One Indiana legislator commented on his state's decision to exclude black children from public schools: "it is even better for the weaker party that no privilege should be extended to them, the tendency of which might be to induce the vain belief that the prejudices of the dominant

---

[40] For the Indiana constitution, see McCaul, *The Black Struggle for Public Schooling*, p. 8.
[41] Quoted in Earhart, "Boston's 'Un-Common' Common," p. 178.

race could ever be so mollified as to break down the rugged barriers that must forever exist between their social relations."[42]

Most midwestern states excluded black children from public schools by law for most if not all of the antebellum era. Indiana and Illinois, for example, expressly limited the public schools to white children by state statute until 1869. Although the Illinois state constitutional convention of 1847 considered providing some type of education for black children, a majority of the delegates feared that such a provision might somehow be interpreted to permit racial mixing in the schools and defeated it. Iowa limited its public schools to white children until 1857, when, in the wake of the ascendancy of the Republican Party, a new state constitution directed the state board of education to provide "for the education of *all the youths of the State*." Ohio, which initially limited its public schools to white children, finally permitted separate black schools in 1848, although most Ohio communities would not establish schools for black children until after the Civil War.[43]

White opposition to black education in the Midwest also manifested itself in resistance to the establishment of black private schools. In a few instances, white mobs destroyed private schools established to teach black children. In Zanesville, Ohio, for example, a young woman opened a school for blacks but whites destroyed the school's books and furnishings, forcing the school to close. In Troy, Ohio, white residents also destroyed a private school for black children.[44]

To be sure, some midwestern black children did attend public schools in defiance of state law, typically in communities with abolitionist sensibilities. For example, in Chicago, pro-black abolitionists secured approval of local ordinances in 1849 and 1851 that opened the city's public schools to black children and by 1861, two Chicago schools had black enrollments of 5.2 and 3.8 percent. Although in 1862 the new Democratically controlled state legislature enacted legislation authorizing a new city charter for Chicago that barred black children from attending school with whites, when Republicans regained control of the state legislature in 1864, they repealed that legislation mandating segregation in Chicago. By the mid-1860s, a few other Illinois communities also permitted black children to attend public schools. Moreover, a few Indiana communities, particularly those settled by antislavery Quakers, and some communities in the Western Reserve of

---

[42] For the first quote, see Jacobson, *Whiteness of a Different Color*, p. 44; for the second quote, see Reynolds, "Politics and Indiana's Public Schools," pp. 265–6.

[43] For Illinois, see McCaul, *The Black Struggle for Public Schooling*, p. 5; for Iowa, see *Clark v. Board of Directors*, 24 Iowa 266, 270–1 (1868) (italics in the original).

[44] For mob violence directed at schools, see Quillin, *The Color Line in Ohio*, pp. 47–8; McGinnis, *The Education of Negroes in Ohio*, p. 38; Litwack, *North of Slavery*, p. 122.

northeast Ohio, also allowed black children to attend public schools along with white children during the antebellum era.[45]

These exceptions to the ban on black education frequently provoked white opposition. In Wayne County, Indiana, home to a large Quaker population and antislavery sentiment, a white parent filed a lawsuit during the late 1840s challenging the admission of black children to white schools in violation of state law. A Wayne County circuit court judge dismissed the suit, but in 1850 the Indiana Supreme Court reversed, holding that the Wayne County integration violated the state ban on public education for black children. Similar objections to black children in Hancock County, Indiana, attending a public school led to their exclusion. (In 1854, however, the Indiana Supreme Court rejected a white parent's legal challenge to a racially mixed *private* school, holding that the statutory exclusion of black children applied only to public schools.) On two occasions during the 1840s, litigation or the threat of litigation forced the removal of black children from schools in Ohio, while in Illinois, a black child in the late 1840s attended a white school until the complaints of some of the white parents forced his exclusion.[46]

Some mulatto children also attended public schools in the antebellum Midwest, which frequently provoked contentious efforts to retain the color line. For example, in one instance, a mulatto child in Indiana who attended a white school was prosecuted "for disturbing a common school." Conflicts about mulatto school attendance inevitably raised the vexing question of racial definition. Antebellum courts, confronted with efforts to bar mixed-race schoolchildren, were forced to construe the meaning of whiteness in the context of state statutes that limited public schools to "white" children. In one such case, the Ohio Supreme Court in 1834 determined that a mulatto child who was only one-eighth black was "white within the meaning of the law" and could attend public school. The court concluded that "the term

---

[45] For Chicago, see Homel, *Down from Equality*, pp. 1–4; for other Illinois communities with blacks attending school, see McCaul, *The Black Struggle for Public Schooling*, p. 45 (Alton, Decatur, Galesburg, Jacksonville, Peoria, Quincy, and Springfield); for Indiana, see Heller, "Negro Education in Indiana," pp. 79–80; for the Western Reserve of Ohio, see Horton and Horton, *In Hope of Liberty*, p. 154; Woodson, *The Education of the Negro*, pp. 329–30; Gerber, "Education, Expediency, and Ideology," pp. 3, 13; Quillin, *The Color Line in Ohio*, pp. 33, 45–7, 70; Kusmer, *A Ghetto Takes Shape*, pp. 15–16.

[46] *Lewis v. Henley*, 2 Ind. 332 (1850) (Wayne County); Heller, "Negro Education in Indiana," pp. 79–80 (Hancock County); *Polke v. Harper*, v. Ind. 253 (1854) (litigation challenging a racially mixed private school); *Chalmers v. Stewart*, 11 Ohio 386, 387 (1842) (litigation in Greene County forcing removal of a black student); Erickson, "The Color Line in Ohio Public Schools," p. 180 (threat of litigation in Massilon forcing removal of a black student); Cha-Jua, *America's First Black Town*, p. 65 (removal of a black student in Brooklyn, Illinois).

white, as used in the law, describes *blood* and not *complexion*," and hence the children in question, with only one black great-grandparent, were white despite their appearance. The Ohio Supreme Court affirmed that view in 1843, holding that a child with "more than one-half white blood" was white and hence could attend a public school.[47]

During the 1850s, however, Ohio elected officials and courts redefined the meaning of whiteness in a manner that excluded most mulattoes. After a white teacher in Cincinnati objected to the presence in her classroom of a mulatto child who was only 1/32 black, the Cincinnati school board adopted a resolution excluding "pupils that have in whole *or in part* African blood in their organization" from white schools. In 1859, as we have seen, the Ohio Supreme Court reversed its prior definition of whiteness, holding that children "who have *any visible taint* of African blood" were nonwhite for purposes of attending school, even if they were more than half white by ancestry. But even the "visible taint" standard would prove troublesome. A challenge to mulatto school attendance in Cincinnati failed when the complaining whites could not visually identify a mulatto child in a class of white children. In a similar manner, when a white parent in Decatur County, Indiana, objected to the presence of a mulatto girl in a public school in 1861, the child's teacher responded: "Very well. We will send a man around tomorrow to pick out the negro. If he picks out the negro she goes out, and if he picks out your child, she goes out." The white parent dropped the matter.[48]

Mixed-race children were excluded from white schools in other parts of the North as well. A school board member in Lancaster,

---

[47] For the Indiana case, see *Weaver v. State*, 8 Ind. 373 (1857) (reversing a conviction because two witnesses were improperly excluded). During the Civil War, Chicago permitted mulattoes with one-eighth or less black ancestry to attend white schools. This rule required school officials to engage in the vexing task of determining the legitimacy of claims of white ancestry. Homel, *Down from Equality*, pp. 3–4. For Ohio court decisions, see *Williams v. School District*, 1 Wright 578, 580 (1834); *Lane v. Baker*, 12 Ohio 237, 241 (1843).

[48] For Cincinnati board resolution, see Montgomery, "Racial History of the Cincinnati and Suburban Public Schools," pp. 52–4 (1983), Cincinnati Historical Society (emphasis added); for the Ohio court decision, see *Van Camp v. Logan*, 9 Ohio St. 406, 408 (1859) (emphasis added). The Ohio Supreme Court took a different direction in voting cases. In 1859, the court held that a person with "a larger proportion of the blood of the white race" than of the black race was deemed white for purposes of voting. *Anderson v. Millikin*, 9 Ohio St. 568, 570 (1859). Similarly, in 1867, the Ohio Supreme Court held that men having "an admixture of African blood, with a preponderance of white blood," were deemed white for purposes of voting. *Monroe v. Collins*, 17 Ohio St. 665, 685 (1867). For unsuccessful efforts to exclude mulattoes, see Woodson, "The Negroes of Cincinnati," p. 18; Lewis Harding, *History of Decatur County, Indiana, Its People, Industries, and Institutions*, p. 86 (1915), quoted in Heller, "Negro Education in Indiana," p. 86.

Pennsylvania, commented in 1849, for example, that those children in his county "having a tinge of negro blood in their veins, would, on that account, be excluded from white schools." In the early 1850s, the Boston School Committee excluded from a white school a student who appeared to be white but was probably one-sixth black. Litigation seeking to reverse the exclusion failed.[49]

In time, a few midwestern states did enact legislation during the antebellum era that made some provision for black education. This legislation reflected the influence of political parties with abolitionist sentiments, but it did not open schoolhouse doors to all black children. For example, Ohio's Whig and Free Soil parties, which favored black education, wielded a critical balance of power in the state legislature during the late 1840s. After years of petitions from blacks urging repeal of legislation that limited the state's public schools to white children, the Ohio legislature finally enacted a law in 1848 that permitted blacks to establish their own separate schools in any school district with at least twenty black children if taxes on black-owned property could generate sufficient revenue. In 1849, the legislature amended the new statute to *require* the establishment of black schools throughout the state unless local school districts were willing to admit black children to white schools. In 1853, however, the legislature limited its 1849 legislation, requiring the establishment of black schools only in school districts in which there were more than thirty black children.[50]

These legislative changes, however, were resisted in much of the state, particularly in the state's southern counties, which were Democratic, antiblack strongholds. Many local officials refused to provide funds for separate black schools, and it took considerable effort by the black community to ensure that tax monies were made available. In Cincinnati, home to the state's largest black population, school officials refused to use tax monies for the support of black schools until the Ohio Supreme Court ordered them to do so in 1850. A few black schools were established in Cincinnati and other larger Ohio communities during the 1850s, but most school districts had a sufficiently small number of black children such that they did not establish a black school. On the eve of the Civil War, the Ohio state legislature rejected the recommendation of the Ohio commissioner of education that local school districts be *required* to admit black children to white schools if no separate schools were provided; the legislature's failure

---

[49] For Lancaster, see Hopkins, "Door to Opportunity," p. 136; for Boston, see Kendrick and Kendrick, *Sarah's Long Walk*, pp. 217–22.

[50] Middleton, *The Black Laws in the Old Northwest*, pp. 36–41. This figure was lowered to twenty-one black children in 1864. Erickson, "The Color Line in Ohio Public Schools," p. 201.

to act forced most of Ohio's black children to go without an education. An 1865 report by the Ohio commissioner of education revealed that of the state's 626 school districts with black children, only 121 operated black schools. An 1871 report found that whereas two-thirds of white school-age children in Ohio attended a public school, only about one-quarter of African-American children did so.[51]

Abolitionist forces also promoted black education in Illinois, but with less success. In 1855, the Illinois state legislature, due to the influence of the abolitionist Anti-Nebraska Party, enacted legislation providing that local school trustees should use taxes collected from blacks to fund separate black schools. This legislation, however, had limited effect, as virtually no dollars were ever made available for black education. Between 1855, the year of the statute's enactment, and 1872, the year it was dropped in a school law revision, only one state superintendent biennial report, the 1871–2 report, noted that *any* tax monies – a total of $51 in two school counties – were used for black schools. One county school superintendent noted in his 1867–8 report that the tax provision had been "practically a dead letter," as blacks were both excluded from the public schools and "they have never, as I suppose, drawn a cent from the funds they have aided to raise." Newton Bateman, state superintendent of public instruction in Illinois, described the state of black education in his 1865–6 biennial report: "For the education of . . . [black] children the general school law of the State makes, virtually, no provision. By the discriminating terms employed throughout the statute, it is plainly the intention to exclude them from a joint participation in the benefits of the free school system." The effects were apparent. The 1860 census reports that only about 600 of the state's almost 2,700 school-age black children attended some type of school – most of which were privately funded.[52]

In the upper Midwest, Michigan, Wisconsin, and Minnesota made modest provision for black education during the antebellum era. In Michigan, the territorial legislature in response to an influx of black migrants enacted legislation in 1841 permitting separate schools for

[51] *State v. Cincinnati*, 19 Ohio 178 (1850) (requiring use of tax monies for black schools); Erickson, "The Color Line in Ohio Public Schools," pp. 239–40 (absence of black schools in smaller communities); Robisch, "Educational Segregation and Desegregation in Ohio," p. 48 (legislature's rejection of the commissioner's recommendation); Gerber, "Education, Expediency and Ideology," p. 3 (1865 commissioner's report); Fishel, "The North and the Negro," pp. 232–5 (school attendance in 1871).

[52] For the superintendent quote, see McCaul, *The Black Struggle for Public Schooling*, p. 30; for the Bateman quote, see U.S. Bureau of Education, *History of Schools for the Colored Population*, p. 342; for census material, see U.S. Bureau of the Census, 1860; Finkelman, "Prelude to the Fourteenth Amendment," p. 474.

black children in Detroit. Prior to that time, blacks had been excluded from the public schools altogether. Very few blacks lived in Minnesota when the state joined the Union in 1857, but that year, the St. Paul school board determined that if thirty black children sought an education, a separate school would be established. In 1859, the board lowered that number to fifteen and established a separate school that a few blacks did attend during the 1860s; blacks were barred, however, from the city's white schools until 1869.[53]

Of the midwestern states, only Wisconsin, with almost no black population, appears to have rejected both racial exclusion and school segregation during the antebellum era. At the state's constitutional convention of 1847, the delegates overwhelming rejected a proposal that the schools be restricted to white children. Yet blacks in antebellum Wisconsin attended school in far lower percentages than did whites. According to the 1850 census, over half of the state's white school-age population attended a public or private school, whereas only about one-third of the black school-age population did so; by 1860, more than 70 percent of white children were attending a public or private school, but fewer than 30 percent of black children enjoyed the benefits of an education. There is no evidence of explicit exclusion, but the disparity in black and white school attendance and the decline in black attendance during the 1850s suggest that many blacks may have been excluded or discouraged from attending either public or private schools.[54]

In the mid-Atlantic states of New Jersey, Pennsylvania, and New York, blacks gained admission to public schools much sooner than in the Midwest but on an almost exclusively segregated basis. Only in a few New York communities did children attend racially integrated schools during the antebellum era. Although the New Jersey Constitution of 1844 provided that the public school system should be "for the equal benefit of all the people of the state," exclusion of black children from the public schools was common and almost all black children who attended public school during the antebellum era did so in ones that were racially segregated. In 1850, the New Jersey General Assembly expressly sanctioned school segregation by granting Morris Township the authority to establish separate schools for black and white children, and in 1863, the legislature gave *all* local school trustees the authority

---

[53] Reams and Wilson, *Segregation and the Fourteenth Amendment*, pp. 295–6 (Detroit); Katzman, *Before the Ghetto*, pp. 22–5 (Detroit); Green, "'Critical Mass Is Fifteen Colored's!'" pp. 303–12 (St. Paul).

[54] Jorgenson, *The Founding of Public Education*, p. 90 (Wisconsin 1847 constitutional convention); U.S. Bureau of the Census, 1850 and 1860; Finkelman, "Prelude to the Fourteenth Amendment," pp. 472–5.

to segregate their schools, thereby giving legitimacy to school segregation throughout the state.[55]

In Pennsylvania, black children were either excluded from the public schools altogether or were educated in separate schools. In Pittsburgh, for example, blacks were excluded from the public schools until they successfully petitioned the local school directors for a separate black school in 1837. Philadelphia, on the other hand, was one of the first northern cities to embrace black education, beginning in 1822; by 1850, there were eight black public schools in the city. In 1854, the Pennsylvania General Assembly legitimized the establishment of segregated schools by enacting legislation that permitted the establishment of separate black schools and that *required* school segregation in school districts with more than twenty black children. Most communities with fewer than twenty black children made no provision for black education; indeed, for the most part, few black children in Pennsylvania outside of Philadelphia or Pittsburgh attended a public school before 1870. The superintendent of common schools in Pennsylvania expressed little interest in black education, describing blacks as "destitute of either moral or intellectual culture." To be sure, some Pennsylvania educators did support black education. A school board member in Lancaster favored the support of black schools, arguing that if "we suffer these colored children to grow up in ignorance they will become vicious, corrupt, and depraved, and in the end will be a charge upon the community. . . . [W]e must either pay for their education in our schools or for their maintenance as paupers or prisoners in our almshouses or jails."[56]

In New York, the state legislature authorized the town of Newburgh to establish a separate black school in 1835, and in 1841 it expressly permitted *any* school district in the state to establish a separate black

[55] Anderson, "Negro Education in the Public Schools of Newark," p. 51; Wright, *The Education of Negroes in New Jersey*, pp. 120–48; Fishel, "The North and the Negro," pp. 33–4; Woodson, *The Education of the Negro*, p. 311; Connor, "A Comparative Study of Black and White," pp. 13, 183; Harney, "The Evolution of Public Education," pp. 60–4; Daniels, "A Case Study of Desegregation," p. 32; Wright, *The Education of Negroes in New Jersey*, pp. 141–2; *Annual Report of the Superintendent of Public Schools of the State of New Jersey, for the Year 1863*, pp. 41–2.

[56] Proctor, "Racial Discrimination against Black Teachers," pp. 29–33 (Pittsburgh); Glasco, "Double Burden: The Black Experience in Pittsburgh," p. 72 (Pittsburgh); U.S. Bureau of Education, *History of Schools for the Colored Population*, p. 374 (1854 legislation); Franklin, *The Education of Black Philadelphia*, p. 230 n. 24 (Philadelphia); Du Bois, *The Philadelphia Negro*, p. 88 (Philadelphia); Fishel, "The North and the Negro," pp. 202–5 (Philadelphia). For the superintendent quote, see Kaestle, *Pillars of the Republic*, p. 179. For superintendent reports, see Fishel, "The North and the Negro," pp. 202–3, n. 136; for the Lancaster quote, see Hopkins, "Door to Opportunity," p. 137.

school. Thereafter, the legislature enacted specific legislation *requiring* school segregation in a few cities: Buffalo (1843), Poughkeepsie (1843), New York City (1844), Rochester (1844), and Brooklyn (1845). By the late 1840s, separate black schools were in place in fifteen New York counties. Some black children in antebellum New York did attend racially mixed schools, particularly in upstate communities, but this was rare. For example, during the 1840s, black children in Albany were permitted to attend white schools under certain circumstances, but in 1850, under pressure from white parents, the Albany school board prohibited white schools from accepting black students. Syracuse also permitted black children to attend white schools during the antebellum era, and Rochester, as we shall see, closed its remaining black school in 1856, thereby ending school segregation in that city.[57]

New England was the most hospitable region of the North to black education during the antebellum era. In fact, in 1850, the states with the highest percentage of black children attending some type of school were all in New England: Maine (64 percent), Rhode Island (52.5 percent), Connecticut (52.4 percent), New Hampshire (49 percent), Vermont (41.3 percent), and Massachusetts (40 percent). No New England state enacted legislation requiring school segregation, but a few localities did establish separate schools for black children during the antebellum era.[58]

By 1830, Boston, Hartford, New Haven, Portland, Providence, and Salem all operated racially separate public schools for black children. In Boston, a few black children attended racially mixed public schools during the late 1790s, but in 1800, Boston blacks petitioned the local school committee for a racially separate school, complaining that their children had been insulted and abused by white children. When the petition effort failed, black parents opened a private school for their children. Boston public school authorities assumed control of the black private school in 1811 without ever adopting a formal policy on school segregation. By 1823, there were three publicly supported black schools in the city; Boston retained a separate black school until 1855.[59]

---

57 For New York legislation and antebellum schooling patterns, see Ment, "Racial Segregation in the Public Schools," pp. 15–16; Woodson, *The Education of the Negro*, pp. 311–12; U.S. Bureau of Education, *History of Schools for the Colored Population*, p. 361; Horton and Horton, *In Hope of Liberty*, p. 153. For Albany, see Sacks, "'We Rise or Fall Together,'" pp. 18–19; for Syracuse, see Mabee, *Black Education in New York State*, p. 195.

58 U.S. Bureau of the Census, 1850; Finkelman, "Prelude to the Fourteenth Amendment," p. 472.

59 U.S. Bureau of Education, *History of Schools for the Colored Population*, pp. 328, 334–5; Silcox, "A Comparative Study in School Desegregation," pp. 91, 94; Horton

A Rhode Island state law enacted in 1800 required towns to establish schools for white children; black communities thereafter established their own private schools in Providence and Newport. In time, local school authorities took over operation of these separate black schools – Providence in 1838 and Newport in 1842. In Connecticut, there were no statewide provisions dealing with school segregation, but New Haven began operating a black school in 1812 and by 1825 had two such schools. During the 1830s, Hartford established a separate black school. Both New Haven and Hartford retained these racially separate schools until after the Civil War. The Connecticut state legislature legitimated the establishment of racially separate schools but did not mandate school segregation.[60]

But generalizations about black education in the antebellum North are difficult. Despite its relative liberality toward the education of African Americans, New England was also home to three of the most notorious efforts to restrict black education of the entire antebellum era. This resistance was due in significant measure to fears of additional blacks migrating to New England.

Delegates to an 1831 national Negro convention resolved to establish a private college for blacks in New Haven that would train them in both academic disciplines and manual labor skills. The New Haven project was launched at a time of great enthusiasm for manual training for poor children, especially blacks, as a means of improving their social and economic status. The New Haven project, however, ran into fierce opposition from local whites. Led by the New Haven mayor and a number of Yale professors and students, whites staged riots in front of the homes of the school's supporters, claiming that "the founding of colleges for educating colored youth is an unwarrantable and dangerous undertaking...and ought to be discouraged." In the face of extensive white opposition, the plans for the New Haven school were eventually abandoned. The New York *Journal of Commerce* complained of New Haven's response to the college: "Men complain of the ignorance and vice of the colored population, and yet when a project is presented to rescue them...from their deep degradation, the same men are roused at once to the highest pitch of indignation."[61]

and Horton, *In Hope of Liberty*, pp. 151–2; Ment, "Racial Segregation in the Public Schools," p. 14.

[60] Ment, "Racial Segregation in the Public Schools," pp. 14–15; Woodson, *The Education of the Negro*, p. 317.

[61] For New Haven, see Woodson, *The Education of the Negro*, pp. 289–90 (first quote); Goodman, *Of One Blood*, p. 33; Kliebard, *Schooled to Work*, p. 13; Banks, *Black Intellectuals*, pp. 11–12; Goodman, *Of One Blood*, p. 50 (second quote).

The idea of a privately supported college for blacks came at a time of growing anxiety, north and south, over racial issues. Antiblack riots afflicted Providence, Rhode Island, in 1831, leaving several dead. The New Haven town meeting to address the issue occurred a few days after Nat Turner's insurrection in Virginia, which stirred white anxieties about black unrest. Many New Haven whites feared an influx of young black men to the town, particularly when one of the organizers mentioned that he intended to bring newly emancipated blacks from the West Indies to the school. Ironically, at the same time that the city's white leaders opposed the black college, plans to establish a local black mission school to prepare blacks to return to Africa went unopposed.[62]

Two years later, similar white opposition thwarted Prudence Crandall's efforts to operate a private academy in Canterbury, Connecticut, for black girls. In 1833, Crandall, an antislavery Quaker, admitted a local black girl to her all-white private school. After white parents withdrew their children in response, Crandall converted her school to an all-black school, using William Lloyd Garrison's *The Liberator* to advertise for students. White reaction was fierce. Local stores refused to deal with Crandall. Her students were harassed and the school was vandalized. As in New Haven, local whites feared an influx of blacks to the area, arguing that New England "will become the Liberia of America." "The colored people can never rise from their menial condition in our country," one opponent charged, and "they ought not to be permitted to rise here." A town meeting passed a resolution in opposition, citing fears of lower property values, black equality, and amalgamation of the races. The Connecticut state legislature then enacted a state law that forbade the establishment of a school that taught black children from outside the state without the consent of a majority of the local selectmen. Crandall was prosecuted, convicted, and served jail time, but the indictment was eventually quashed by the Connecticut Supreme Court of Errors. But because of repeated vandalism and mob terror, the school was abandoned.[63]

---

[62] Goodman, *Of One Blood*, pp. 47–50; Woodson, *The Education of the Negro*, p. 290.

[63] For Crandall's school, see Reid, "Race, Class, Gender, and the Teaching Profession," p. 55; Strane, *A Whole Souled Woman*, pp. 117–19. For quotes, see Goodman, *Of One Blood*, pp. 51–2. For actions of town meeting, see Fishel, "The North and the Negro," p. 37. For statute, see Johnson, *The Development of State Legislation*, p. 77 ("No person shall establish in this state any school for the instruction of colored persons not inhabitants of this state, without the consent in writing of the civil authority"). The Connecticut legislature repealed that statute in 1838. Ibid. For the Supreme Court decision, see *Crandall v. State*, 10 Conn. 339 (1834). For mob terror and abandonment of the school, see Grimsted, *American Mobbing*, p. 53; Woodson, *The Education of the Negro*, pp. 172–5; Goodman, *Of One Blood*, p. 52.

FIGURE 1 Prudence Crandall, 1834. Reprinted with permission of the
Prudence Crandall Museum, Canterbury, Connecticut.

Efforts to establish a private integrated school in New Hampshire
during the mid-1830s also provoked a violent reaction. Following
the abandonment of the New Haven labor college, proponents of a
manual labor school targeted the New Hampshire town of Canaan.
Garrison, who had been a strong proponent of the New Haven labor
college, favored an interracial school, arguing that school segregation
reinforced the racial prejudice that supported slavery: "If the prejudice against color can be kept up in the free states, then the nation
goes for slavery." In March 1835, the Noyes Academy opened its doors
in Canaan to twenty-eight white boys and fourteen black boys who
came from as far away as Philadelphia to attend. The trustees of the
Academy resolved to "afford colored youth a fair opportunity to show
that they are capable, equally with the whites, of improving themselves
in every scientific attainment, every social virtue, and every Christian
ornament." The local white reaction to the Noyes Academy, however,
was fierce, as whites feared an influx of blacks into the community.
As one of the black students later wrote, "[f]ourteen black boys with
books in their hands set the entire Granite State crazy!" On July 4, 1835,
a mob approached the academy to destroy it, but a local magistrate
dispersed them. One month later, the local town meeting resolved to
abolish the school in "the *interest* of the town, the *honor* of the State,

and the *good* of the whole community, (both black and white)." Shortly thereafter, a group of men with ninety yoke of oxen literally dragged the school from its foundations into a nearby swamp. No efforts were made to reopen the beleaguered school.[64]

Inferiority of Separate Black Schools

Not only were most northern black children excluded from schools with white children during the antebellum era, in the northern communities that did provide schooling for black children, those schools were typically inferior to their white counterparts. Black schools were often housed in cellars or sheds. The white teacher at a black school in Boston described it in 1846 as a neglected "damp, dark cellar" filled with broken equipment. The New Haven school visitors in 1853 found the city's black schools "excessively crowded and destitute of some of the first requisites of a respectable school." The Ohio commissioner of common schools commented in an 1859 report that "[m]any of the [black] schools are kept in mere sheds and basements without decent furniture." In many northern communities, such as Buffalo, Philadelphia, and several Ohio towns, black children were housed in buildings that school authorities had deemed unsuitable for white children. In 1857, a New York education society characterized white schools as "splendid, almost palatial edifices," while black children were housed in "old and dilapidated buildings."[65]

In addition to their poor physical condition, black schools during the antebellum era typically received the poorest teachers, most of whom were white. Teachers in black schools were generally paid less than their counterparts in white schools and were often deemed unacceptable to teach white children. The Ohio commissioner of common schools commented in 1859 that in black schools, the "teachers,

---

[64] For the Garrison quote, see Silcox, "A Comparative Study in School Desegregation," p. 88. For opening of the Noyes Academy, see Litwack, *North of Slavery*, p. 117; Crummell, *Africa and America*, p. 280. For the resolution of trustees of the Academy, see Litwack, *North of Slavery*, p. 118 (quoting *The Liberator*, Oct. 25, 1834). For the student quote, see Crummell, *Africa and America*, p. 280. For the town meeting resolution, see Litwack, *North of Slavery*, 119 (quoting *The Liberator*, Aug. 8, 1835); for destruction of the school, see Crummell, *Africa and America*, p. 280; Litwack, *North of Slavery*, 119; Woodson, *The Education of the Negro*, p. 291; Goodman, *Of One Blood*, p. 53; Banks, *Black Intellectuals*, p. 11; Bond, *Education of the Negro*, 371.

[65] For the Boston quote, see Fishel, "The North and the Negro," p. 35; for the New Haven quote, see Ment, "Racial Segregation in the Public Schools," p. 116; for the Ohio quote, see Mason, "The Policy of Segregation," p. 16. For schools in Buffalo, Philadelphia, and Ohio, see White, "The Black Movement against Jim Crow Education," p. 378; Licht, *Getting Work: Philadelphia*, p. 83; Franklin, *The Education of Black Philadelphia*, pp. 32–3; Horton and Horton, *In Hope of Liberty*, p. 151; Gerber, *Black Ohio and the Color Line*, p. 5. For the New York quote, see Litwack, *North of Slavery*, p. 132.

whether white or colored, are, with few exceptions, poorly qualified and are employed because they can be had at small salaries." An official school committee investigating New Haven's black schools cited the lack of "fitness both in respect of tact and of acquired information on the part of their teachers."[66]

Not only were the buildings and teachers provided black children in the antebellum North generally inferior to those provided white children, the curriculum offered was often far more rudimentary than that in white schools. Certain academic subjects such as history and geography were frequently not taught in black schools. A black national convention in 1847 charged that the instruction of black children "had been shamefully limited," consisting only of "rudimental notings, and superficial glancings.... In very deed, it has not reached the... elevation of education." One observer reported that a white teacher forbade his black students from studying grammar, explaining that the local school committee permitted only white students to receive such training. The New Haven school board conceded in 1860 that few black children graduated with sufficient knowledge of arithmetic to permit them to be clerks or conduct independent businesses. Moreover, while many white schools adopted various educational reforms such as graded classes, black schools were typically ungraded and limited to the primary level.[67]

Debate within the Northern Black Community over Integrated Schools

The primary educational goal of most northern blacks during the antebellum era was to procure some type of schooling for their children, whether integrated or segregated, private or public. In the context of such limited opportunities, insisting on an integrated education was beyond the reach of most black parents. As historian Leon Litwack has noted, "[a]lthough Negroes hoped for eventual integration, many of them agreed, in the meantime, to send their children to separate schools."[68]

But in many northern communities, no black schools were available. Many northern communities were too small to accommodate separate

---

[66] For black schoolteachers, see Litwack, *North of Slavery*, p. 133; Fishel, "The North and the Negro," p. 206. For the Ohio quote, see Mason, "The Policy of Segregation," p. 16; for New Haven schools, see Litwack, *North of Slavery*, p. 133; Warner, *New Haven Negroes*, p. 76.

[67] For curriculum, see White, "The Black Movement Against Jim Crow Education," p. 377; for the 1847 quote, see Litwack, *North of Slavery*, p. 135; for New Haven, see Litwack, *North of Slavery*, p. 134; Warner, *New Haven Negroes*, p. 77; for ungraded schools, see Ment, "Racial Segregation in the Public Schools," p. 116; White, "The Black Movement Against Jim Crow Education," p. 377.

[68] Litwack, *North of Slavery*, p. 135.

schools for both black and white children; as a result, black children frequently went without. Moreover, in those communities that did operate a black school, black children frequently lived too far away to attend. Buffalo was one such community. Buffalo school superintendent E. F. Cook conceded the problem in the 1850s: "Many [black] families reside at a great distance from the school house which renders the regular attendance of small children difficult." Another Buffalo superintendent, V. M. Rice, though a strong opponent of racially mixed schools, expressed regret for the effects of segregation on black children: "It excites one's pity, to see [the black students] in cold stormy weather often thinly clad, wending their way over a wearisome distance. Anyone possessing humane impulses, can but regret that, with all the other burdens which power and prejudice heap upon this people, their children, when so young, are doomed to suffer so much in striving to gain a little light to make their gloomy pathway through life less tedious." Buffalo did eventually permit black children who lived far away from the city's only black school to attend a nearby white school.[69]

The problem of distant black schools plagued other communities as well. The New York City board of education concluded after the Civil War: "These [black] schools labor under great disadvantage. They are scattered at very wide intervals over the city and many of the children are obliged to walk miles to attend school." Agitation in Detroit during the 1860s for integrated schools was motivated in part by the long distances black children were forced to traverse to attend a segregated black school.[70]

Black parents sometimes sought the admission of their children to white schools even if a black school was available, favoring an integrated education. The debate in the northern black community over the importance of racially mixed schools would not gain widespread prominence until after the Civil War, but a few significant struggles to procure racially mixed schools were waged during the antebellum era. This nascent controversy over segregated schools was part of a larger debate within the antebellum northern black community over the issue of the extent to which blacks should attempt to assimilate into the dominant white culture.[71]

Those blacks who urged the operation of racially mixed schools during the antebellum era argued that separate schools reinforced tortured notions of black inferiority. Frederick Douglass, for example,

---

[69] For the Cook and Rice quotes, see White, "The Black Movement Against Jim Crow Education," p. 378. For blacks in neighborhood schools, see Mabee, *Black Education in New York State*, p. 183.

[70] For the quote, see Fishel, "The North and the Negro," p. 190. For Detroit, see Katzman, *Before the Ghetto*, p. 85.

[71] Meier, "The Emergence of Negro Nationalism, Part I," p. 97.

FIGURE 2   Frederick Douglass. Reprinted from the Library of Congress, Prints & Photographs Division, LC-USZ62-15887.

repeatedly attacked separate black schools. Writing in 1848, Douglass argued: "The evils of separate colored schools are obvious to the common sense of all. Their very tendency is to produce feelings of superiority in the minds of white children, and a sense of inferiority in those of colored children; thus producing pride on the one hand, and servility on the other, and making those who would be the best of friends the worst of enemies. As we have frequently urged on the platform and elsewhere, prejudice is not the creature of birth, but of education." "With equal school rights," Douglass continued, "colored children . . . come in contact on equal terms with white children and youth, three hundred days in the year and from six to ten hours each day. And these children, in a few years become the people of the state." John Hilton of Boston argued that "all experience teaches that where a small and despised class are shut out from the common benefit of any public institutions of learning and confined to separate schools, . . . neglect ensues, abuses creep in, the standard of scholarship degenerates, and the teachers and the scholars are soon considered and of course become an inferior class." George Downing, a leading integrationist in Providence, Rhode Island, wrote in a widely republished letter to the *Providence Journal* during that state's desegregation fight of the 1860s: "There are not held out to the colored child the same incentives in a colored school that there would be in a common school; he feels that there is a wall between him and the white boy; that he is not cared for in the community as is the white boy. Why am I proscribed? he asks; he feels, . . . 'I is nothing but a nigger.' Why study: why aim to be anything? Crime and degradation is my portion." One black leader in Ohio explained that with segregation, "[t]he White child imbibes the false idea that the color of his skin makes him the colored child's superior, while the colored child grows sour under the weight of invidious distinctions made between him and the White child, and in many cases . . . loses that ambition which would be the greatest spur to his success in life."[72]

On the other hand, many blacks preferred separate schools if given the choice. Some African Americans worried that racially mixed schools would weaken the ties of black children to their community. As one critic of integrated education argued in 1853, the black child in a racially mixed setting "must either abandon his own state of things which he finds around him, and which he is pledged to change and better, or cease to receive culture from such sources, since their whole tendency is to change him, not his condition – to educate him out of his sympathies, not to quicken and warm his sympathies, for all that is of worth to him is his elevation, and the elevation of his people."[73]

One of the strongest arguments in favor of separate schools was the fact that black children in racially mixed settings frequently suffered harassment from white peers and low expectations from white teachers. As one observer wrote in 1839: "with the first principles of education, [black children] learn they are a degraded race, shunned by their school fellows, and often neglected by the master. They rarely obtain the rudiments of knowledge." A black teacher in Brooklyn argued in 1854 that when mulatto children attended white schools, if "known to be what they really are, (colored)," they "are the continual subjects of contempt and ridicule . . . [and] are ever trembling and shaking for fear of exposure." Even in communities like Boston, with a relatively liberal attitude toward free blacks, few black children took advantage of opportunities during the late eighteenth and early nineteenth centuries to attend white schools and, in fact, black parents petitioned local school authorities for a racially separate school because of the ridicule and mistreatment their children received from their white classmates and teachers. During the desegregation controversy in Boston during the 1840s, school authorities defended school segregation, arguing that white children would "vex and insult the

---

[72] For the first Douglass quote, see "Colored Churches," *The North Star*, Mar. 10, 1848; for the second Douglass quote, see Silcox, "A Comparative Study in School Desegregation," p. 298; for the Hilton quote, see Tyack, *The One Best System*, p. 113; for the Downing quote, see Ment, "Racial Segregation in the Public Schools," pp. 84–5; for the Ohio quote, see Gerber, "Education, Expediency, and Ideology," p. 14.

[73] For black support of separate schools, see Woodson, *The Education of the Negro*, pp. 318–19; Minutes of the Fourth Annual Convention of the Free People of Colour, in the United States (New York, 1834), in Bell, *Minutes of the Proceedings of the National Negro Conventions*, p. 26. For the quote, see Proceedings of the Colored National Convention (Rochester, 1853), in Bell, *Minutes of the Proceedings of the National Negro Conventions*, p. 23.

colored children." Similarly, in Rochester, harassment of black children by white peers and teachers in racially mixed schools caused many black parents to petition the school authorities for an "African school." The white school authorities in Rochester recognized that harassment was common: "it is obvious that in [racially mixed schools] the literary and moral interests of the colored scholar can hardly prosper. He is reproached with his color, he is taunted with his origin. . . ."[74]

In some racially mixed northern schools, white teachers enforced segregated seating and threatened delinquent white children with integrated seating as punishment for misbehavior. After Boston ended school segregation during the mid-1850s, a common punishment for misbehaving white children in racially mixed schools was to place the offender in the "nigger seat" next to a black child.[75]

Many blacks believed, with good cause, that black teachers would be more nurturing of their children. Alexander Crummell, for example, argued that white teachers could not effectively teach disadvantaged black students. James McCune Smith, a black physician, argued that black teachers were more likely to require greater achievement from black children than were white teachers. A supporter of black teachers argued at the inaugural meeting of the Pennsylvania State Equal Rights League in 1865 that "as we know by experimental knowledge, that colored children make greater advancement under the charge of colored teachers than they do under white teachers, therefore we consider it to be our incumbent duty, as lovers of the advancement of our race, to see to it, that our schools are under the charge of colored teachers." In fact, in Philadelphia, home to the largest number of black schools in the antebellum North, reports of white teacher hostility toward black students were widespread.[76]

But most northern school districts during the antebellum era refused to hire black teachers for any type of school – integrated or segregated. In Philadelphia, home to several black schools, the first

---

[74] For the 1839 observer, see Parillo, "Images of Blacks," p. 109 (quoting Samuel Perkins, *The World As It Is*, p. 69 [1839]). For the quote from a Brooklyn teacher, see "Letters from the People," *Frederick Douglass' Paper*, Sept. 22, 1854; Mabee, *Black Education in New York State*, pp. 191. For treatment of black children in Boston, see Daniels, "A Case Study of Desegregation," pp. 22, 84; Horton and Horton, *In Hope of Liberty*, p. 151. For the quote concerning white children insulting blacks, see Tyack, *The One Best System*, p. 114. For the quote concerning harassment in Rochester, see White, "The Black Movement Against Jim Crow Education," p. 376.

[75] Horton and Horton, *In Hope of Liberty*, p. 153; Earhart, "Boston's 'Un-Common' Common," p. 116; Schultz, *The Culture Factory*, p. 160.

[76] For the black preference for black teachers, see Pease and Pease, *They Who Would Be Free*, p. 149. For Crummell's and Smith's views, see Banks, *Black Intellectuals*, p. 26. For the 1865 quote, see Silcox, "A Comparative Study in School Desegregation," pp. 206–7; for teacher hostility in Philadelphia, see Lane, *Roots of Violence*, p. 135.

black teacher would not be hired until 1862. When the New York Public School Society assumed operation of the African Free Schools in 1834, most of the black teachers were dismissed and replaced by white ones. A few northern communities did use black teachers in black schools, but most did not.[77]

Not surprisingly, the antebellum era witnessed considerable black activism in northern communities in support of the hiring of black teachers. Boycotts were staged in New York during the 1830s to secure more black teachers for the African Free Schools. A school boycott in Albany in the late 1850s succeeded in securing a black principal for a black school. In Pennsylvania, the State Equal Rights League pushed for black teachers in black schools in the early 1860s, arguing that "colored persons, their literary qualifications being sufficient, should receive the preference; not by reason of their complection, but because they are better qualified by conventional circumstances outside of the school-house."[78]

Those blacks favoring racially separate schools in the antebellum North tended to be more prevalent in larger towns and cities where there was a sufficient number of blacks to support separate institutions. Blacks in small communities with few African Americans typically favored racially mixed schools because of the difficulty of forming and supporting alternative black institutions.[79]

Antebellum Challenges to School Segregation

During the antebellum era, those African Americans who sought racially mixed schools used petitions, school boycotts, and litigation to pursue their goals. By the 1850s, several Negro conventions, particularly in New York, urged an end to separate black schools. These efforts achieved mixed results. During the 1830s and early 1840s, black children in Buffalo boycotted the separate black school, held mass meetings, petitioned the school board, and filed litigation to challenge school segregation. A few black parents simply took their children to the local district white school. As a result, a few black children did gain temporary access to white schools, but in 1846, the superintendent of the Buffalo schools, O. G. Steele, required that black children

---

[77] Horton and Horton, *In Hope of Liberty*, pp. 151–3.

[78] For the New York boycotts, see Waller, "Holding Back the Dawn," p. 115; for the Albany boycott, see Sacks, "'We Rise or Fall Together,'" pp. 20–1; for Buffalo demands, see White, "The Black Movement Against Jim Crow Education," p. 377; for the Pennsylvania quote, see Silcox, "A Comparative Study in School Desegregation," p. 209.

[79] Silcox, "A Comparative Study in School Desegregation," pp. 300–1.

be excluded from white district schools in Buffalo, claiming that black children required "greater patience on the part of the teacher, longer training and severer discipline than are called into exercise in the district schools" and that it would be many generations before black children "possess the vigor of intellect and the power of memory and judgement" to enable them to study alongside white children. New York State Superintendent John Spencer supported Steele, arguing that "[t]he admissions [sic] of colored children is in many places so odious that whites will not attend. In such cases the Trustees would be justified in excluding them, and furnishing them a separate room." As a result, efforts to desegregate Buffalo's schools were defeated. Finally, however, in 1855, Buffalo school authorities decided to permit those black children who lived in outlying districts, far removed from the city's black school, to attend a nearby white school. As a result, by 1857, a number of black children did attend a white school in Buffalo.[80]

One of the most significant school desegregation battles of the antebellum era took place in Rochester, New York, home to Frederick Douglass. Rochester had established racially separate public schools in 1832. As in several other northern cities, the black community in Rochester divided on the issue of racially mixed schools. In 1849, two factions of the city's black community presented petitions to the school board. One petition asked for the closure of the town's one black school and the desegregation of Rochester's white schools; the second petition asked for the construction of a second black school. A committee assigned to investigate reported the inefficiency of dual schools and recommended desegregation. The Rochester school board, however, did not accept the committee's recommendations and instead opened a second black school. A boycott of the black schools proved successful, forcing the closure of one of the schools in 1851 when no black children arrived. Moreover, by 1854, school officials allowed black children to attend white schools near their homes but continued to operate the one black school. Two years later, school officials finally closed the remaining black school, thereby desegregating the entire school system. The efforts of the Rochester integrationists, such as Douglass, played a role in the board's action, but the decisive factor was the small number of black children in question and the inefficiency of operating dual schools. Significantly, all of the antebellum

---

[80] For opposition in New York to segregation, see Mabee, *Black Education in New York State*, pp. 182–3, 188, 191. For the Steele quote, see Horton and Horton, *In Hope of Liberty*, p. 153; for the Spencer quote, see White, "The Black Movement Against Jim Crow Education," p. 381; for blacks attending a white school in Buffalo, see Mabee, *Black Education in New York State*, p. 183.

agitation in New York for integrated schools took place in upstate communities, where there were few blacks and strong abolitionist sentiment.[81]

The most significant challenge to school segregation in the antebellum North took place in Boston. During the 1840s, both blacks and white abolitionists petitioned the Boston School Committee to operate all Boston schools on a nonracial basis. These petitions noted that several other Massachusetts communities – including Nantucket, New Bedford, and Salem – had already integrated their schools. In significant measure, this early desegregation was due to the small number of black children involved and the strong antislavery attitudes of many Massachusetts whites. In Salem, the town's antislavery mayor, in response to a boycott of the separate black school, procured an opinion from a local judge that segregated schools were unconstitutional. As a result, in 1844, Salem ended school segregation. Two years later, school authorities in Nantucket met the demands – and boycott – of black parents by admitting their children to a white school. Subsequently, Lowell and New Bedford desegregated their schools.[82]

Massachusetts, home to considerable abolitionist sentiment, had already taken other actions to improve the status of African Americans. In 1843, Massachusetts became the first state to repeal its miscegenation ban. Agitation during the 1840s also led the state's railroad companies to end their practice of segregating passengers by race. The campaign against segregated schools, however, would prove far more difficult.[83]

During the 1840s, the Boston School Committee operated one segregated school for black children –the Smith School – and a few racially separate classes in other schools. An 1845 committee report conceded the poor condition of the Smith School: "we have come to the conclusion that [the Smith School] is not only in an unsatisfactory, but in a deplorable condition." In response to black complaints, the Boston School Committee made some improvements to the Smith School.[84]

---

[81] For desegregation activity in Rochester, see Ment, "Racial Segregation in the Public Schools," pp. 76–81; Mabee, *Black Education in New York State*, pp. 183–7; Pease and Pease, *They Who Would Be Free*, p. 153. For upstate New York desegregation agitation, see Mabee, *Black Education in New York State*, p. 188.

[82] For Boston desegregation petitions, see Woodson, *The Education of the Negro*, pp. 320–1; Kaestle, *Pillars of the Republic*, p. 177; for desegregation in Salem, see Ment, "Racial Segregation in the Public Schools," pp. 19, 25; Meier and Rudwick, *Along the Color Line*, p. 309; for Nantucket, Lowell, and New Bedford desegregation, see Silcox, "A Comparative Study in School Desegregation," p. 121.

[83] Ment, "Racial Segregation in the Public Schools," pp. 24–5.

[84] For the Smith school, see Ment, "Racial Segregation in the Public Schools," pp. 27–32; for the quote, see ibid., p. 29.

In support of their desegregation petition, blacks launched a boycott in 1844 of the Smith School. Between 1844 and 1849, attendance at the Smith School dropped from over 100 students to 53. Yet for many in the black community, the primary defect of the Smith School was not its racial composition, but rather the fact that the children were taught by a white teacher whom they perceived as cruel and lacking in confidence in the intellectual ability of his students. Two camps thus emerged in the Boston black community: those who preferred the retention of the Smith School, but with a black teacher, and those who favored closing the school and sending black children to white schools. White school authorities used the opposition of many blacks to the closure of the Smith School to defend their actions.[85]

The black leader of the integrationists was William Nell, who had been educated in Boston's segregated schools during the 1820s. Nell was a fierce opponent of separate black activities and organizations, including the Negro convention movement. He argued that separate schools violated principles of equality and the "common rights" of blacks to attend school on the same basis as whites. In the early 1850s, Nell published *Colored Patriots of the American Revolution*, in which he extolled the virtuous participation of blacks in the Revolution. Using a theme common to other black writers, Nell linked the struggles against slavery and segregation with the campaign for freedom from English rule.[86]

Nell and other integrationists further argued that the inconvenience of segregated schools often required black children to travel long distances. In some instances, black families had to move closer to the-Smith school so that their children could receive some type of education. At the same time, white children generally attended the school closest to their homes and the integrationists asked for the same treatment for blacks.[87]

Many white abolitionists joined the demand for racially mixed schools, arguing that school segregation was inconsistent with their condemnation of slavery because it legitimated the arguments of those who believed that slavery was a necessary guardianship for blacks. William Lloyd Garrison's *The Liberator*, for example, provided support for the desegregation movement, publishing various meeting reports and resolutions. This combination of black insistence on racially mixed

---

[85] Silcox, "A Comparative Study in School Desegregation," p. 112; Tyack, *The One Best System*, p. 113; Pease and Pease, *They Who Would Be Free*, pp. 154–5; Ment, "Racial Segregation in the Public Schools," p. 43.

[86] Ment, "Racial Segregation in the Public Schools," pp. 33–4, 38; Earhart, "Boston's 'Un-Common' Common," pp. 149–50.

[87] Ment, "Racial Segregation in the Public Schools," pp. 37–9.

schools and a strong antislavery tradition combined to produce an environment favorable to desegregation efforts.[88]

Yet the Boston School Committee consistently rejected the petitions for racially mixed schools. The School Committee argued that there was a distinction "in the physical, mental, and moral natures of the two races" and that "amalgamation is degradation." One committee member commented that black children possess "physical, mental and moral peculiarities, which render a promiscuous intermingling in the public schools disadvantageous both to them and to the whites." The School Committee also cited the racist views of many white parents: "many parents would not suffer their children to associate with colored children, and these, too, from among the class who most need instruction: for the prejudices against color are strongest among the most ignorant."[89]

The Boston School Committee moved a black teacher to the Smith School in the fall of 1849, which satisfied the demands of many blacks. In response, black integrationists pled with parents and children to boycott the school. Some blacks supported the Smith School, while others supported the boycott. Nell labeled the black supporters of the Smith School "traitors" to their race, willing to give up equality for the security of a segregated school. In response, Thomas Smith, leader of the separatists, argued that separate schools afforded blacks a better opportunity to challenge claims of inferiority and to promote pride among blacks. The key to racial advancement, argued Smith, was self-help and racial solidarity, not racial mixing. With the hiring of the black teacher, the Smith School increased in popularity. Between 1850 and 1853, attendance doubled from twenty-five to fifty-one, although well below the attendance levels of the early 1840s.[90]

In the meantime, the integrationists filed a lawsuit. After being rebuffed in his attempts to enroll his daughter in a white school, several of which were closer to his home than the Smith school, black printer Benjamin Roberts filed suit against the Boston School Committee. In 1845, the Massachusetts state legislature had enacted legislation that gave "any child deprived of the equal advantages of the public schools in any town, a right of action . . . against the town." In so doing,

---

[88] Ibid., pp. 22–4, 34.

[89] For the School Committee quote see Tyack, *The One Best System*, p. 114; for the committee member quote, see Ment, "Racial Segregation in the Public Schools," p. 13 (quoting *The Liberator*, Aug. 21, 1846); for the final School Committee quote, see ibid., p. 44.

[90] For the Smith school boycott, see Silcox, "A Comparative Study in School Desegregation," pp. 113–17; Tyack, *The One Best System*, p. 113; Ment, "Racial Segregation in the Public Schools," p. 46. For views of the Smith school and attendance at school, see Silcox, "A Comparative Study in School Desegregation," pp. 118–20.

FIGURE 3   Charles Sumner. Reprinted from the Library of Congress, Prints
& Photographs Division, LC-USZ62-66840.

the Massachusetts legislature delegated to the courts the question of
whether segregation was unlawful.[91]

Prominent abolitionist Charles Sumner agreed to argue Roberts's
case. Sumner emphasized that the Massachusetts state constitutional
language, "All men are born free and equal," guaranteed equality.
Sumner elaborated: "He may be poor, weak, humble, or black; he
may be of Caucasian, Jewish, Indian, or Ethiopian race; he may be of
French, German, English, or Irish extraction; but before the Constitution of Massachusetts all these distinctions disappear." Sumner also
addressed the practical problems with segregation: the long commute
many black children faced, the limited number of black schools that required black families to live in certain neighborhoods, the caste nature
of segregated schools that humiliated black children, and the way in
which segregation undermined the notion of common schools. Citing
the Jewish ghettos of Europe, Sumner argued that segregation "is a ves-
tige of ancient intolerance directed against a despised people." Even
if black schools were conveniently located and equal in all regards,
Sumner argued that "a school exclusively devoted to one class must
differ essentially in spirit and character from that Common School
known to the law, where all classes meet together in Equality." Sumner
also appealed to anti-Irish sentiment in Boston by raising the specter
of separate schools for Irish children: "They may establish a separate
school for Irish or Germans, where each may nurse an exclusive nationality alien to our institutions. . . . The grand fabric of our Common

<hr />

[91] For filing of the lawsuit, see Silcox, "A Comparative Study in School Desegregation," p. 121. For language of the statute, see Ment, "Racial Segregation in the Public
Schools," p. 48.

Schools . . . will be converted into a heathen system of proscription and Caste."[92]

The Massachusetts Supreme Court, with Chief Justice Lemuel Shaw writing, unanimously rejected Roberts's claim in 1850, holding that the Boston School Committee had broad discretion to classify children. The court articulated a different vision of equality, claiming that all persons "are equally entitled to the paternal consideration and protection of the law, for their maintenance and security. What those rights are, to which individuals . . . are entitled, must depend on laws adapted to their respective relations and conditions." Although blacks had equal rights under the Massachusetts constitution, that did not prevent the School Committee from determining that it was in the best interest of all children to be educated separately. Significantly, the court suggested that law could not erase the social prejudice that had created the segregation in the first place: "It is urged, that this maintenance of separate schools tends to deepen and perpetuate the odious distinction of caste, founded in a deep-rooted prejudice in public opinion. This prejudice, if it exists, *is not created by law, and probably cannot be changed by law.*"[93]

The *Roberts* decision marked a profound embrace of racial segregation, and would prove to be an important precedent for various state supreme courts considering the lawfulness of school segregation as well as for the United States Supreme Court almost half a century later in *Plessy v. Ferguson*. Indeed, one of the most significant legacies of the antisegregation fight in Boston was the *Roberts* decision that postbellum courts and politicians would draw upon to justify school segregation.[94]

But the *Roberts* decision had limited impact in Massachusetts. Within five years, the state legislature had prohibited school segregation by state statute. What accounts for this legislative action that effectively reversed the *Roberts* decision? While the *Roberts* decision was still pending in the Massachusetts Supreme Court, the Massachusetts Antislavery Society pledged to petition the state legislature for desegregation legislation if the court ruled in favor of the Boston School Committee: "Should the *Bench* fail to award us justice, an appeal can and will be made to the *people* themselves." After the court issued its decision, *The*

---

[92] All quotes from Sumner's argument are from Charles Sumner, "Segregation and the Common School," in Adler (ed.), *The Negro in American History*, III, pp. 103–17; Ment, "Racial Segregation in the Public Schools," pp. 52–8; and Earhart, "Boston's 'Un-Common' Common," p. 147.

[93] *Roberts v. Boston*, 59 Mass. 198, 206, 209 (1850) (emphasis added).

[94] *Plessy v. Ferguson*, 163 U.S. 537 (1896). For examples of courts citing *Roberts*, see *State ex rel. Stoutmeyer v. Nevada*, 7 Nev. 342, 347 (1872); *Ward v. Flood*, 48 Cal. 36, 52–6 (1874); *People ex rel. King v. Gallagher*, 11 Abb. N. Cas. 187 (1882); *Wong Him v. Callahan*, 119 F. 381, 382 (N.D. Cal. 1902).

Liberator announced that the "people (who are greater than the court) will . . . remedy this injustice through the Legislature." Over the course of the next five years, integrationists petitioned the state legislature for legislation banning segregated schools.[95]

These petition efforts enjoyed success in 1855. In early 1855, the Massachusetts state legislature received eleven petitions with 1,500 signatures from various towns requesting antisegregation legislation. A legislative committee issued a favorable report on the proposed legislation, emphasizing the inherent inequality of segregation, the hardship on black families, and the success of integration in other Massachusetts communities. In April 1855, the Massachusetts state legislature enacted the antisegregation legislation almost unanimously, forbidding distinctions "on account of the race, color, or religious opinions, of the applicant or scholar" in the state's public schools. The statute also provided for a damages remedy for those whose rights were violated.[96]

The enactment of this legislation, the first in the United States, was due to a convergence of factors not easily replicable in other states. First and foremost, the political ascendancy of the Know Nothing Party in Massachusetts produced an ideal climate for antisegregation legislation. The Know Nothing Party came to power in dramatic fashion in 1854, propelled by an intense reaction in antislavery Massachusetts to the national tilt toward pro-slavery interests. Both the Fugitive Slave Act of 1850, which left blacks vulnerable to southern slave catchers, and the Kansas-Nebraska Act of 1854, which repealed the Missouri Compromise of 1820 and thereby opened the Kansas and Nebraska territories to possible slavery, invigorated the antislavery movement in Massachusetts. The political aftershocks of this legislation, along with the capture and return of fugitive slave Anthony Burns in Boston, were dramatic. In the 1854 election, the Know Nothing Party, with roots in the old Free Soil Party and representing an amalgam of antislavery, anti-Catholic nativist, and reform interests, overwhelmed the Whig Party, which was blamed for its complicity with the Fugitive Slave Act of 1850. The Know Nothing Party captured the entire state senate and all but three of the state house seats.[97]

To the Know Nothings, with their anti-immigrant and anti-Catholic sentiments, the growing Irish Catholic population of Boston was of far greater concern than the city's small black population. As one Know Nothing legislator commented during debate on the antisegregation

---

[95] For the first quote, see Ment, "Racial Segregation in the Public Schools," p. 62; for the second quote, see ibid. (quoting *The Liberator*, Apr. 26, 1850).

[96] For the legislative committee report, see Ment, "Racial Segregation in the Public Schools," p. 74; for statutory language, see ibid., p. 75. For damages remedy, see Daniels, *In Freedom's Birthplace*, p. 448.

[97] Ment, "Racial Segregation in the Public Schools," pp. 69–70.

legislation, blacks were forced to pass white schools on their way to the Smith School, while the "dirtiest Irish" were permitted to attend school along with other white children. The same year that the Massachusetts legislature enacted antisegregation legislation, it also enacted legislation requiring the reading of the King James version of the Bible in the public schools, a pointed attack on Catholic parents who preferred the Douay version of the Bible.[98]

Efforts by Irish and German immigrants to secure public funding for separate Catholic schools during the early 1850s had exacerbated Know Nothing antagonism toward school segregation. Indeed, a plank of the Know Nothing Party platform claimed that "we rebuke all attempts to appropriate the public funds to the establishment of sectarian schools." Although the Boston School Committee considered establishing a separate school for Irish children during the 1840s, the Committee declined to do so, expressing a desire to assimilate Irish Catholic children into the dominant Protestant culture. The School Committee concluded that schools were not "to favor creeds, social theories, or private prejudices," and thus rejected the notion of "establishing and supporting, at public expense, any schools except such as can be attended by all the children of our citizens." If "distinct, exclusive schools are established," the Committee concluded, "our School system which has given to our country its strength, is broken up and its glory and usefulness departed." The irony of such an assimilationist vision, given the Committee's insistence on racial separation, was apparent. In time, many Know Nothing state legislators recognized that separate schools for blacks gave legitimacy to Irish claims for separate schools for their children.[99]

As historian Amy Earhart has noted, the "Irish problem" superseded the "Negro question" for a brief time in Boston during the 1850s, contributing to the enactment of antisegregation legislation. Know Nothings did not necessarily embrace racial integration; rather, their concerns with the Irish trumped any desire they might have had to preserve racial segregation.[100]

Desegregation also served the interests of school reformers, whose compulsory education goals were undercut by Boston's insistence on

---

[98] For the Know Nothing legislator, see Earhart, "Boston's 'Un-Common' Common," p. 5. There were 46,237 Irish-born persons living in Boston in 1855. Ibid., p. 154. For legislation on the Bible, see Billington, *The Protestant Crusade*, p. 413.

[99] For the Know Nothing Party plank, see Earhart, "Boston's 'Un-Common' Common," p. 155; for the Committee's refusal to establish a separate Irish school, see ibid., p. 155; Ment, "Racial Segregation in the Public Schools," p. 63. For School Committee quotes, see Ment, "Racial Segregation in the Public Schools," pp. 64–5. For Know Nothings' views on separate schools, see Earhart, "Boston's 'Un-Common' Common," p. 156.

[100] Earhart, "Boston's 'Un-Common' Common," p. 8.

school segregation. Massachusetts enacted compulsory school legislation in 1852; this new legislation imposed a substantial burden on
many black children in Boston who lived long distances from the Smith
School. School reformers believed that more black children would enter the public schools if segregation were abolished.[101]

In addition, the dearth of blacks in Massachusetts and the fact
that racial mixing had proceeded without incident in other Massachusetts towns made desegregation less objectionable. Only two Massachusetts towns – Nantucket and New Bedford – had a black school-
age population of more than 3 percent during the mid-nineteenth
century, and in those two towns, both of which had already desegregated their schools during the 1840s, blacks constituted less than
6 percent of the school-age population. In the meantime, in 1854,
one year prior to the Massachusetts antisegregation legislation, the
Worcester school authorities eliminated school segregation, leaving
Boston as the only community in Massachusetts that maintained school
segregation.[102]

In the wake of the new legislation, black enrollment in the public
schools increased. School officials kept the Smith School open for
those blacks who wished their children to have a separate education,
but Nell and the integrationists lobbied every black parent to boycott
the Smith School. By the fall of 1855, five months after passage of
the antisegregation law, only seven students remained in the Smith
School; as a result, the School Committee closed its doors.[103]

The Massachusetts legislation marked a significant victory in the
campaign against northern school segregation, but it was a victory,
due to the particular political circumstances in Massachusetts, that
would not be immediately replicated in other states. In Rhode Island,
blacks attempted throughout the 1850s and early 1860s to build on
the Massachusetts legislative success by petitioning the state legislature for similar legislation. Those efforts failed. Throughout most of
the North, antiblack feeling remained too strong to support antisegregation legislation during the antebellum era. As the *New York Herald*
editorialized in reaction to the Massachusetts desegregation law: "Now
the niggers are really just as good as white folks. The North is to be
Africanized. Amalgamation has commenced. New England heads the
column. God save the Commonwealth of Massachusetts."[104]

---

[101] Silcox, "A Comparative Study in School Desegregation," pp. 128–32.

[102] For black school populations, see Ment, "Racial Segregation in the Public Schools,"
p. 20; for Worcester, see ibid., pp. 65, 62–3.

[103] On the effect of desegregation, see Tyack, *The One Best Sytem*, p. 114; Silcox, "A
Comparative Study in School Desegregation," pp. 135–6.

[104] On Rhode Island efforts, see Pease and Pease, *They Who Would Be Free*, p. 156. For
the *New York Herald* quote, see Kaestle, *Pillars of the Republic*, p. 179.

Black Education at the Close of the Antebellum Era

On the eve of the Civil War, almost 30,000 black children attended some type of school – public or private – in the free states of the North and West, about 35 percent of the total number of black school-age children in those states. The overwhelming majority of those children attended racially separate schools, a significant percentage of which were privately supported. By the same token, about two-thirds of the more than 6.3 million white school-age children in the free states attended some type of school.[105]

African Americans identified education as central to notions of racial improvement and hence struggled for inclusion in the common school system. By the eve of the Civil War, these aspirations had met with some success, particularly in those parts of the North most sympathetic to antislavery concerns. Black challenges to racial segregation, however, proved more difficult. By 1860, only a handful of northern communities permitted black children to attend school on a nondiscriminatory basis, almost all of which were centers of abolitionist activity such as Boston, Cleveland, and Rochester.

But black demands for racially mixed schools would continue. On the eve of the Civil War, Frederick Douglass called for a multipronged attack on segregated schools in New York. Douglass proposed that African Americans throughout the state petition local school officials for racially mixed schools, and if they were rebuffed, then file lawsuits challenging their exclusion. Douglass also proposed an organized effort to lobby the New York State legislature for legislation banning school segregation throughout the state. "An earnest, well-organized and persistent effort in this direction must succeed," Douglass wrote in 1859. After the war, African Americans throughout the North would follow Douglass's advice, petitioning local school officials, filing lawsuits, and lobbying state legislatures for an end to school segregation. Because of changed political and cultural circumstances, those lobbying efforts would meet with striking success.[106]

---

[105] U.S. Bureau of Census, 1860; Finkelman, "Prelude to the Fourteenth Amendment," p. 474.

[106] Quoted in Mabee, *Black Education in New York State*, p. 192.

3

Legislative Reform

Banning School Segregation, 1865–1890

The extirpation of inherited, deeply seated and long cherished opinions and tastes in relation to social questions and customs, cannot be accomplished by legislation, but only by reflection and time, if at all.

– Newton Bateman, Superintendent of Schools, Illinois, 1875[1]

The Civil War did not settle the educational rights of African Americans in northern states. As the war came to an end, many northern communities provided no education for black children, while others provided schooling but in racially separate schools. By 1865, Massachusetts was the only state that had abolished school segregation by statute, while Vermont, New Hampshire, Maine, and probably Wisconsin – each with a minuscule black population – also freely admitted black children to public schools without regard to race. In the rest of the free states, some communities, particularly in upstate New York, lower New England, and the upper Midwest, admitted black children to school on a nondiscriminatory basis, but most did not. The majority of black children in the North who received a common school education in 1865 did so in segregated schools.

After the Civil War, many northern blacks renewed their efforts to secure both access to public schools where access was denied and admission to public schools on a nonracial basis where segregation was common. Buoyed by the successful assault on slavery and expressing confidence that law could be used to secure black education rights, African Americans utilized a variety of tactics to press their demands, including litigation and legislative lobbying. Although Congress considered legislation during the early 1870s that would have banned school segregation throughout the nation, those legislative efforts failed. The question of school segregation in the North would be resolved on a state-by-state, community-by-community basis.

---

[1] Quoted in Fishel, "The North and the Negro," p. 216.

Over the course of the next twenty-five years, those northern states that had explicitly barred black children from public schools during the antebellum era reversed course. Moreover, by 1890, almost every northern state that had previously permitted or required racial separation in the public schools had enacted legislation prohibiting school segregation. State supreme courts, when called upon, almost uniformly enforced this antisegregation legislation by requiring local school officials to admit black children to school on a nonracial basis. By the end of the nineteenth century, significant progress had been made in the assault on segregated schools.

Yet despite this strong legal regime allied against northern school segregation, racial separation in the public schools persisted in many northern communities as recalcitrant school boards that opposed racial mixing refused to comply with the prevailing legal mandate. Reconstruction witnessed a brief ascendancy in parts of the North of whites and blacks committed to racial equality, but by the last decades of the nineteenth century those manifestations of racial liberalism had been overwhelmed in much of the North by antiblack sentiment. Long after a Pennyslvanian explained to de Tocqueville during the 1830s why laws protecting black rights frequently went unenforced, his words still rung true in much of the North: "the law lacks force when the majority does not support it. Now, the majority is filled with the strongest prejudices against Negroes, and the magistrates do not feel strong enough to guarantee the rights granted to them by the lawmakers."[2]

Black Civil Rights at the End of the Civil War

In the wake of victory in the Civil War, many white northerners, motivated by a racial idealism nurtured by the devastating war, moved to repeal some of the harsh statutory restrictions on northern blacks and to enact a variety of legal measures for their protection. At the state level, between 1863 and 1867, Indiana, Illinois, Iowa, California, and Oregon repealed their Black Laws, while Pennsylvania prohibited segregation in public transportation and Massachusetts prohibited discrimination in public accommodations. More significantly, Congress proposed and the states ratified the Thirteenth, Fourteenth, and Fifteenth Amendments to the United States Constitution that, in theory, forbade slavery, provided citizenship rights for African Americans, mandated equality, and secured the right to vote for black men. Congress also enacted significant civil rights legislation that,

---

[2] De Tocqueville, *Democracy in America*, p. 253, n. 4.

among other things, protected black rights to contract and criminalized various intrusions on the civil and political rights of African Americans.[3]

But many white northerners, particularly those living in the lower Midwest, objected to extending full civil and political rights to northern blacks. During the Civil War, tens of thousands of white Ohioans had petitioned their state legislature to take action to bar black settlement in the state. In response to Lincoln's Emancipation Proclamation, Indiana Democratic Senator Joseph Wright announced that his constituents would not accept emancipated slaves: "We tell you that the black population shall not mingle with the white population in our States. We tell you that in your zeal for emancipation you must ingraft colonization upon your measure." Republican Senator Lyman Trumbull of Illinois offered a similar observation: "There is a very great aversion in the West – I know it to be so in my State – against having free negroes come among us."[4]

After the war, antiblack sentiment continued in much of the North. Between 1865 and 1867, six northern states, including Connecticut, the only New England state that had denied blacks the franchise during the antebellum era, voted down referenda that would have permitted blacks to vote. Between 1865 and 1868, only three northern states – Wisconsin, Iowa, and Minnesota – each with a minuscule black population, extended the franchise to blacks. Indeed, supporters of black suffrage recognized that an amendment to the United States Constitution was the most efficacious way to secure the right to vote for blacks in both the North and the South.[5]

---

[3] For repeal of Black Laws, see McPherson, "Abolitionists and the Civil Rights Act," p. 495.

[4] For Ohio petition efforts, see Voegeli, *Free But Not Equal*, pp. 15–17; for Wright quote, see ibid., p. 25; for Trumbull quote, see ibid., p. 18.

[5] For post–Civil War suffrage efforts, see Klarman, *From Jim Crow to Civil Rights*, p. 28; Fishel, "The North and the Negro," pp. 117–18. Black men in Wisconsin finally won the right to vote in a curious fashion when the Wisconsin Supreme Court in 1866 determined that the voters of Wisconsin had approved black suffrage in an 1849 referendum. In that referendum, a majority of voters who cast a ballot on the issue of black suffrage voted affirmatively, but because many voters failed to cast a ballot on the suffrage issue, fewer than half of the total voters approved black suffrage. The Wisconsin Constitution, which limited the franchise to white men, provided that the franchise could be expanded if "approved by a majority of all votes cast" in a "vote of the people." Both the state legislature and local election officials had construed the 1849 referendum on black suffrage as failing since a majority of *all persons voting that day* had not voted in favor of the proposal. Moreover, subsequent referenda in Wisconsin on black suffrage in 1857 and 1865 had failed. The Wisconsin Supreme Court, however, held that the 1849 black suffrage proposal had carried since a majority of those who cast a vote *on the issue of black suffrage* had voted yes. *Gillespie v. Palmer*, 20 Wis. 544 (1866).

Even when Congress ratified the Fifteenth Amendment to the United States Constitution that forbade racial discrimination in the exercise of the franchise, a number of northern states balked at ratification. Ohio, for example, having reversed its initial ratification of the Fourteenth Amendment in 1868, refused to ratify the Fifteenth Amendment in 1869. The Ohio state legislature finally ratified the Fifteenth Amendment by one vote after the requisite number of other states had already ratified it. (Ohio would not ratify the Fourteenth Amendment until 2003.) New York rejected black suffrage in an 1869 referendum and rescinded its initial ratification of the Fifteenth Amendment in 1870. New Jersey was one of the last states to ratify the Thirteenth and Fifteenth Amendments, revoked its initial ratification of the Fourteenth Amendment, and did not remove the restriction on black voters from its state constitution until 1875. Moreover, proposals to extend the jurisdiction of the Freedmen's Bureau to northern states met with considerable resistance in the Congress, since some northern states did not permit blacks some of the civil rights that southern blacks now enjoyed.[6]

During and immediately after the war, approximately 80,000 freed slaves left the South, which further provoked antiblack sentiment. Most of the migrants headed to the Midwest. Since Missouri and Kentucky, of all the slave states, had the longest contiguous borders with free territory, the most common route was simply to cross the Ohio River into Ohio, Indiana, or Illinois or to move west into Kansas. As a result, the black population in the Midwest more than doubled during the 1860s (and increased twenty-seven-fold in Kansas). Ohio had the biggest increase in black population (more than 26,000), followed by Illinois (more than 21,000), Kansas (more than 16,000), and Indiana (more than 13,000). Blacks still constituted a fraction of the northern population in 1870, comprising no more than 1 percent of the population in the North as a whole, but the black population increase of the late 1860s contributed to an upsurge in antiblack feeling in parts of the North, particularly in the lower Midwest. Wanton violence against blacks sharply increased after the Civil War. An 1867 newspaper story on the murder of a black man at the docks in Evansville, Indiana, coldly observed: "There is no clue to the murderer and no effort to hunt him out. It was only a nigger." As the Civil War came to a close, the

---

[6] For ratification of the Fifteenth Amendment, see Fishel, "The North and the Negro," pp. 121; Grossman, *The Democratic Party and the Negro*, p. 19; Quillin, *The Color Line in Ohio*, pp. 98–102; Mohr, "New York," pp. 73–5; Gaines, "New Jersey and the Fourteenth Amendment," pp. 37, 42–3, 53–4; Wright, "New Jersey Laws," p. 189; Wright, "Extending Civil Rights," p. 93. For Freedmen's Bureau proposals, see Fishel, "The North and the Negro," p. 75.

Cincinnati Enquirer, giving voice to the antiblack feeling characteristic of many white midwesterners, starkly announced: "Slavery is dead, the negro is not, there is the misfortune. For the sake of all parties, would that he were."[7]

The Postwar Campaign for Black Education Rights

Notwithstanding resistance in parts of the North to an expansion of black rights, African Americans in the post–Civil War era were united in their insistence on inclusion in the common schools in those northern states – Indiana and Illinois – where they were still formally excluded. By 1869, education campaigns had succeeded in both states. Similar campaigns succeeded in Kansas, California, and Nevada – each of which also excluded black children from public schools. Moreover, across the North, many – but not all – blacks sought inclusion in the common school system on a nonsegregated basis. That campaign would take much longer and would be fraught with far greater difficulty.

After the Civil War, blacks stepped up their efforts to gain entry to the public schools of Indiana by petitioning the state legislature for inclusion. In 1865, a black convention in Indiana resolved that "for the encouragement of our race we will petition the Legislature of this State, at its next session to grant us access to the public school fund." For most of the thousands of newly emancipated slaves who flocked to Indiana, the desire for education was exceeded only by their desire for food and shelter. Many whites, however, opposed black education, fearing that it would attract even more freed slaves to the state. In fact, Indiana's black population more than doubled between 1860 and 1870, having shown no growth during the 1850s, with most of the population growth taking place after the conclusion of the war. At the 1865 legislative session, a group of white legislators announced their opposition to providing public funds for black education: "Now that the institution of slavery is broken up, the negroes will of necessity flock to that section, State or country which holds out the greatest inducements. The States refusing to do anything for them, will first of all be relieved of a free colored population, which we hold to be a nuisance to any community of Anglo-Saxons. We desire to ride our State of this degraded, inferior race, rather than invite it hither, which we believe would be the effect of breaking down the barriers and admitting the negroes to our common schools." Others favored black education, arguing that if blacks

---

[7] For population figures, see U.S. Bureau of Census, 1860 and 1870. For the Evansville quote, see Thornbrough, *The Negro in Indiana*, p. 272; for the *Cincinnati Enquirer* quote, see Fishel, "The North and the Negro," p. 70.

were going to settle in Indiana, they should receive schooling. Republican Governor Oliver Morton, though opposed to granting political rights to blacks, supported black education: "Surely it cannot be denied that, as we have a colored population in our midst, it is *our interest*, independent of those considerations of natural justice and humanity which plead so strongly, to educate and elevate that population."[8]

After failed attempts in 1865 and 1867, the Republican-controlled legislature finally provided for black education in 1869. Crucial to passage of the legislation was the provision that black children would be educated on a segregated basis. In response to the new legislation, a few black public schools opened in Indiana in the fall of 1869. In some communities, however, there were not enough black students to justify opening a separate school, so those children went without. The superintendent of public instruction for Indiana reported in 1870: "In some localities, there has been an evident neglect, on the part of Trustees, to secure [black children] such privileges as the law provides. The colored children – are compelled to grow up uneducated. For these the law fails adequately to provide." Some black children in Indiana continued to go without an education. The state superintendent of public instruction noted in his 1875–6 report that in some communities, the Indiana education law resulted "in sending the colored children to a private school, in others in giving the children books to read, in others, in giving the money belonging to each child to the parents to spend as they please, but in many of them it results in nothing." During the post–Civil War era, Indiana had the highest illiteracy rate in the North.[9]

In Illinois, the antebellum state education law also made no provision for black education except to provide that school taxes collected from black taxpayers should be used for black education, a provision that went unutilized. At the end of the Civil War, black children in Illinois attended public schools in a few places such as Chicago, but in most of the state they continued to be excluded from the public schools. After the war's conclusion, Illinois's black population tried, in the words of Newton Bateman, Illinois's superintendent of public

---

[8] For the black convention quote and the black desire for education, see Thornbrough, *The Negro in Indiana*, p. 317. For population data, see U.S. Bureau of Census, 1860 and 1870. For the legislators' quote, see Heller, "Negro Education in Indiana," p. 94. For the Morton quote, see Thornbrough, *The Negro in Indiana*, p. 320 (emphasis added).

[9] For the struggle to provide education to blacks in Indiana, see Heller, "Negro Education in Indiana," pp. 111–12; Reynolds, "Politics and Indiana's Public Schools," p. 303; Thornbrough, *The Negro in Indiana*, pp. 324–5. For the 1870 quote from the superintendent of public instruction, see Heller, "Negro Education in Indiana," p. 117; for the quote from the 1875–6 report, see Thornbrough, *The Negro in Indiana*, p. 326. For Indiana literacy rates, see Bigham, *We Ask Only a Fair Trial*, p. 10.

instruction, "by conventions, petitions, and appeals to reach the ears and hearts of the representatives of the people to see if anything can be done for them." Bateman, probably the most influential proponent of black education in the Midwest, repeatedly denounced the exclusion of black children from the state's public schools as the "shame of our otherwise noble system of free schools." "No state can afford to defend or perpetuate such provisions," Bateman argued, "least of all the State that holds the dust of the fingers that wrote the [Emancipation] proclamation of January First, 1863." Recognizing that many whites opposed black education due to fears of racial mixing, Bateman suggested that local school districts should be free to operate segregated schools until "wiser counsels" should prevail. Finally, the 1869 Illinois constitutional convention, with strong Republican support, included a provision in the new constitution mandating that "[t]he General Assembly shall provide a thorough and efficient system of free schools, whereby *all children* of this State may receive a good common school education." Thereafter, in 1872, the Republican-controlled state legislature enacted legislation requiring "a sufficient number of free schools for the proper accommodation of all children in the district, and shall secure to all such children the right and opportunity to an equal education in such free schools." In the wake of these actions, many black children began to receive an education for the first time in Illinois, but most did so in separate and inferior school settings. Left unclear under the new legislation was whether the state legislative mandate that there be an "equal education" for all children permitted the retention of racially segregated schools. Many observers, including Republican Governor John Palmer, construed the statutory grant of authority to local school boards to make pupil assignments as permitting segregation.[10]

A few other states also opened their doors to black children for the first time during the 1860s and 1870s. Kansas limited its public schools to white children until 1862, when the legislature determined that cities with more than 15,000 people should establish separate schools for black children. The California state legislature in 1864 mandated the establishment of separate schools for African Americans, Asian

[10] For the Bateman quote on black efforts to achieve an education, see Fishel, "The North and the Negro," p. 210; for the Bateman quote on the "shame" of excluding blacks, see McCaul, *The Black Struggle for Public Schooling*, p. 113. For the Bateman quote that no state can defend black exclusion, see Fishel, "The North and the Negro," p. 211. For the Bateman statement that schools can be segregated, see McCaul, *The Black Struggle for Public Schooling*, p. 114. For constitutional and statutory language, see *People ex rel. Bibb v. Mayor of City of Alton*, 193 Ill. 309, 314 (1901) (emphasis added); Reams and Wilson, *Segregation and the Fourteenth Amendment*, p. 140. On the reaction to the constitutional amendment and statute, see Fishel, "The North and the Negro," p. 214; McCaul, *The Black Struggle for Public Schooling*, pp. 116–18.

Americans, and Native Americans upon the petition of ten or more parents. Prior to 1864, the California state legislature made *no* provision for the education of minority children and in 1860 had enacted legislation requiring the withholding of state educational funds from those school districts that allowed minority children to attend white schools. Nevada, which received statehood in 1864, expressly excluded black children by statute from the public schools until 1872, when the Nevada Supreme Court found the exclusion to be inconsistent with the state constitution. The Colorado Territory initially required local communities to establish a separate school for blacks if there were fifteen or more black children, but the measure was not enforced, leaving many of the territory's black children without any schooling. Finally, in 1876, due in part to the lobbying efforts of Frederick Douglass's two sons, the new Colorado Constitution prohibited school segregation, thereby opening the state's schools to some black children for the first time.[11]

Challenges to School Segregation

After the Civil War, many African Americans across the North demanded an end to school segregation, emphasizing the harm of racial separation. Indeed, the decade following the conclusion of the war constituted the most intense period of northern antisegregation activity of the entire nineteenth century. Many whites joined the campaign against school segregation, particularly those who had been active in the antebellum movement for the abolition of slavery.[12]

Those African Americans who favored racially mixed schools conducted their campaign in a variety of ways: petitions, boycotts, litigation, and legislative lobbying. Many black parents who sought inclusion of their children in white schools initially petitioned local school authorities to repeal their policies of segregation. Some of these petition efforts succeeded. In New Jersey, various communities in the northern section of the state, including Newark, Jersey City, Paterson, and Elizabeth, desegregated their schools during the 1870s in response to demands from the black community. African Americans

---

[11] For the discussion of California, see Dolson, "The Administration of the San Francisco Public Schools," p. 115; Hendrick, *The Education of Non-Whites*, p. 16; Reams and Wilson, *Segregation and the Fourteenth Amendment*, pp. 35–8. For the discussion of Kansas and Nevada, see Reams and Wilson, *Segregation and the Fourteenth Amendment*, pp. 186, 371–3; *State ex rel. Stoutmeyer v. Duffy*, 7 Nev. 342 (1872). For the discussion of Colorado, see Fishel, "The North and the Negro," p. 171, n. 7; Taylor, *In Search of the Racial Frontier*, pp. 202, 217.

[12] Mabee, *Black Education in New York State*, p. 211; McPherson, "Abolitionists and the Civil Rights Act," pp. 499–510.

also successfully petitioned local school authorities for the abolition of school segregation in a few Illinois communities during the early 1870s, including Galesburg and Peoria. In Ohio, Toledo desegregated its schools in 1871, and in 1881, school authorities in Columbus responded favorably to black petition efforts, having earlier rejected such efforts. Most of these petition efforts succeeded in large measure because of the high cost of retaining dual schools. Yet many petitions for school integration filed during the post–Civil War era were rejected by white school authorities insistent on the preservation of racial segregation.[13]

When petition efforts failed, some northern blacks conducted boycotts of segregated black schools, a tactic successfully utilized in a few antebellum northern communities. As noted in Chapter 2, school boycotts in Nantucket and Salem during the 1840s and Rochester during the 1850s contributed to an end to school segregation in those communities. After the Civil War, blacks conducted school boycotts in several northern communities, including Buffalo and Lockport, New York, and Englewood, New Jersey, but none succeeded in ending school segregation. Indeed, throughout the pre-*Brown* era, boycotts unaccompanied by litigation were generally of limited effectiveness, particularly if local school officials were committed to the retention of segregated schools. As the Englewood school superintendent commented in 1879: "Many of the colored people . . . refused to send their children to the [segregated] school. But when they learned . . . there was no redress to be had in the court for their *supposed* wrongs, they were willing to quietly discuss the matter for an amicable settlement."[14]

In many northern communities, blacks turned to the courts to challenge school segregation, alleging that segregation violated the United States Constitution or some state statute or state constitutional

---

[13] For New Jersey, see Fishel, "The North and the Negro," pp. 183, 198–9 (Newark); Harney, "The Evolution of Public Education," pp. 126–7 (Jersey City); Conner, "A Comparative Study of Black and White," p. 15 (Paterson); Fishel, "The North and the Negro," p. 199 (Elizabeth). For Illinois, see Fishel, "The North and the Negro," p. 224. For Ohio, see Erickson, "Toledo Desegregates, 1871," p. 10; Gerber, "Education, Expediency, and Ideology," p. 8. In Columbus, blacks engaged in several unsuccessful petition efforts before succeeding in 1881. "School Privileges for Colored Children," *Columbus Statesman*, Sept. 3, 1878; *Ohio State Journal*, Sept. 6, 1881; *Penick v. Columbus Board of Education*, 429 F. Supp. 229, 235 (S.D. Ohio 1977). For failed efforts, see Conner, "A Comparative Study of Black and White," pp. 219–24 (New Brunswick, New Jersey); Mabee, *Black Education in New York State*, p. 197 (Lockport and Buffalo, New York).

[14] For boycott efforts, see Meier and Rudwick, *Along the Color Line*, pp. 308–9 (Buffalo and Lockport); Fishel, "The North and the Negro," p. 200 (Englewood). For the Englewood quote, see Fishel, "The North and the Negro," p. 200 (emphasis in the original).

provision. Except in states where the legislature had already banned school segregation, almost all of this litigation failed, as northern courts typically held that school segregation violated neither the United States Constitution nor state law. Only a few northern courts declared racial separation in public education unlawful absent a specific state statute so providing.

What is striking about this litigation challenging segregation is the limited usefulness to black plaintiffs of the newly ratified Fourteenth Amendment to the United States Constitution, which provided that no state shall deprive its residents "the equal protection of the law" or "the privileges or immunities of citizenship." During the nineteenth century, only two courts – both at the trial level – found that school segregation violated the Fourteenth Amendment. All other state and federal courts that considered the issue found that neither the "privileges or immunities" clause nor the "equal protection" clause of the Fourteenth Amendment barred school segregation. Most courts held that the privileges or immunities of a citizen of the United States did not encompass the right to an education, traditionally a matter of state concern, and that a racially separate education did not violate the equal protection clause. The Massachusetts Supreme Court's 1850 *Roberts* decision provided a key precedent for some of those courts sustaining the constitutionality of school segregation, even though the *Roberts* decision predated ratification of the Fourteenth Amendment by almost two decades.[15]

---

[15] The two trial court decisions finding segregation violative of the Fourteenth Amendment were in Crawford County, Pennsylvania, and Ottawa, Kansas, both in 1881. *Allen v. Davis*, 10 WNC 156 (1881); Kull, *The Color-Blind Constitution*, p. 107; Kousser, *Dead End*. Numerous courts considered but *rejected* claims that the Fourteenth Amendment barred school segregation. See, e.g., *King v. Gallagher*, 93 N.Y. 438 (1883) (but two dissenting justices held that school segregation did violate the Fourteenth Amendment); *United States v. Buntin*, 10 F. 730 (S.D. Ohio 1882); *State ex rel. Garnes v. McCann*, 21 Ohio St. 198, 209–10 (1871); *Ward v. Flood*, 48 Cal. 36, 49–51 (1874); *Cory v. Carter*, 48 Ind. 327 (1874). Moreover, Judge (and later Supreme Court Justice) David Brewer wrote separately in *Board of Education of Ottawa v. Tinnon*, 26 Kan. 1, 23–4 (1881), in which the Kansas Supreme Court reviewed the trial court decision mentioned earlier, stating: "I dissent entirely from the suggestion that under the fourteenth amendment of the constitution, the state has no power to provide for separate schools for white and colored children." For an early twentieth-century case also rejecting a challenge to school segregation on Fourteenth Amendment grounds, see *Wong Him v. Callahan*, 119 F. 381 (N.D. Cal. 1902). But the Nevada Supreme Court in *State ex rel. Stoutmeyer v. Duffy*, 7 Nev. 342, 346 (1872), concluded that the exclusion of black children from the public schools of Nevada "may be, and probably is, opposed to the spirit" of the "constitution and laws of the United States" but not the letter.

For courts relying on the *Roberts* decision in upholding school segregation, see *Wong Him v. Callahan*, 119 F. 381, 382 (N.D. Cal. 1902); *People ex rel. King v. Gallagher*, 11 Abb. N. Cas. 187 (1882); *Ward v. Flood*, 48 Cal. 36, 52–6 (1874); *State ex rel.*

Throughout the nineteenth century, the United States Supreme Court did not address the question of the constitutionality of school segregation. On at least three occasions, plaintiffs considered appealing adverse decisions on the constitutionality of school segregation to the United States Supreme Court, but no such appeals were ever filed. Morgan Kousser, the leading scholar of nineteenth-century litigation challenging school segregation, has intimated that had the United States Supreme Court considered the issue, particularly during the 1870s or 1880s, it would have struck down school segregation on Fourteenth Amendment grounds. That seems unlikely. Although the Court probably would have found that the exclusion of black children from a white school when *no* black school was available violated the equal protection clause, there is no indication in the Court's decisions that it would have struck down racially separate schools. Kousser emphasizes the Court's 1880 decision in *Strauder v. West Virginia*, in which the Court relied on the equal protection clause to reverse a murder conviction by a jury from which blacks had been excluded, but crucial to the *Strauder* decision was the *complete* ban on black participation in the jury process. To be sure, in its 1878 decision in *Hall v. DeCuir*, the Court did invalidate a state law forbidding racial segregation on an interstate steamboat. But the *Hall* decision turned on the impediments to interstate commerce caused by conflicting state regulations of interstate travel, as some states *required* segregation on steamboats traveling in their waters while others *forbade* segregation. Moreover, the Court in *Hall* implicitly conceded the legitimacy of state laws mandating racial segregation. In fact, in a concurring opinion in *Hall*, Justice Nathan Clifford cited with approval various state court decisions upholding the constitutionality of school segregation. Subsequent nineteenth-century court decisions sustaining school segregation against federal constitutional challenges relied in part on Clifford's opinion. Moreover, in its 1896 *Plessy v. Ferguson* decision, the Court made it abundantly clear that racial separation in interstate transit did not violate the Fourteenth Amendment and cited several earlier state supreme court decisions upholding the constitutionality of state statutes mandating school segregation to support its holding.[16]

Stoutmeyer v. Nevada, 7 Nev. 342, 347 (1872). Some courts concluded that the *Roberts* decision should have no application to claims that school segregation violated a state statute. See, e.g., *People ex rel. Longress v. Board of Education of Quincy*, 101 Ill. 308, 316–17 (1882).

[16] For cases where plaintiffs considered appealing to the United States Supreme Court, see Kousser, "Before *Plessy*, Before *Brown*," p. 270, n. 155. For Kousser's intimation that the Supreme Court would have struck down school segregation, see ibid., pp. 235, 263, n. 122. For relevant Supreme Court decisions, see *Strauder v. West Virginia*, 100 U.S. 303 (1880); *Hall v. DeCuir*, 95 U.S. 485, 504–6 (1878); and *Plessy v. Ferguson*,

African Americans were particularly active in Ohio, filing lawsuits challenging segregation in both state and federal courts in several towns and cities during the 1870s and 1880s. None of these lawsuits succeeded. Similar results followed in New York, California, Nevada, and Oregon. On the other hand, at least two courts – one in Pennsylvania and one in Nevada – held that the exclusion of a black child from a white school *when no separate black school was provided* did violate state law.[17]

Even when segregation meant that black children received no education, however, a few courts upheld the right of school authorities to exclude black children from white schools. In Indiana, after the state legislature in 1869 authorized racially separate public schools for black children "with all the rights and privileges of other schools," Carey Carter, a black parent in Lawrence Township in Marion County, sought to enroll his children and grandchildren in a white school because no black school was available for them – a problem in many Indiana communities with few black children. In fact, the Carter children were apparently the only black children in the school district. When a local school trustee literally stood in the schoolhouse door blocking their entry, Carter sued, alleging that the exclusion of his children and grandchildren from school violated both the federal and state

---

163 U.S. 537 (1896). By the time of *Plessy*, only two justices – Stephen Field and John Harlan – remained from the Court that decided the 1880 *Strauder* case. For those lower court cases citing Justice Clifford's opinion, see *U.S. v. Buntin*, 10 F. 730, 736 (S.D. Ohio 1882); *Bertonneau v. Board of Directors of City Schools*, 3 F. Cas. 294, 296 (D. La. 1878); *Martin v. Board of Education*, 42 W. Va. 514, 516 (1896). One court discussed Clifford's opinion, but properly held it to be irrelevant to the issue of whether school segregation violated *state* law. *People ex rel. Longress v. Board of Education of Quincy*, 101 Ill. 308, 317 (1882).

[17] For failed litigation in Ohio, see *State ex rel. Garnes v. McCann*, 21 Ohio St. 198 (1871) (Franklin County); *San Francisco Pacific Appeal*, June 28, 1873, p. 2 (Clermont County); *Ohio ex rel. Lewis v. Board of Education of Cincinnati*, *Weekly Cincinnati Law Bulletin* 139 (1876) (Cincinnati); "Colored Children in Schools," *New York Times*, Nov. 27, 1880, p. 1 (Clermont County); *U.S. v. Buntin*, 10 F. 730, 735–6 (S.D. Ohio 1882) (Clermont County); "The Gazaway Case," *Cleveland Gazette*, Feb. 16, 1884, p. 1 (Springfield); "An Outrageous Decision," *Cleveland Gazette*, June 7, 1884, p. 2 (Jackson Township).

For New York cases, see *Dallas v. Fosdick*, 40 How. 249 (1869) (Buffalo); *People ex rel. Dietz v. Easton*, 13 Abb. Pr. NS. 159 (1872) (Albany); *Williams v. Troy* (1863) (discussed in Mabee, *Black Education in New York State*, p. 194). For western cases, see *Ward v. Flood*, 48 Cal. 36 (1874) (California); *State ex rel. Stoutmeyer v. Duffy*, 7 Nev. 342 (1872) (Nevada); McElderry, "The Problem of the Color Line," pp. 21–2; McLagan, *A Peculiar Paradise*, pp. 72–3 (Oregon).

For cases striking down exclusion of black children in the absence of a separate black school, see *Commonwealth ex rel. Brown v. Williamson*, 30 Legal Intelligencer 406 (Dec. 5, 1873); *State ex rel. Stoutmeyer v. Duffy*, 7 Nev. 342 (1872).

constitutions. The local superior court ruled in favor of Carter, holding that where no separate school was provided, black children could attend their local district school. The Democratically controlled Indiana Supreme Court, however, in one of the most blatantly antiblack school decisions of the postbellum era, vehemently disagreed.[18]

The Indiana Supreme Court, in a manner reminiscent of the United States Supreme Court's much-criticized 1857 *Dred Scott* decision, concluded that blacks were not citizens of Indiana when the 1851 state constitution was ratified and hence enjoyed no legal protection under that document. In *Dred Scott*, Chief Justice Roger Taney had outrageously suggested that free blacks were "not included, and were not intended to be included, under the word 'citizens' in the Constitution, and can therefore claim none of the rights and privileges [of] . . . citizens of the United States." In *Carter*, the Indiana Supreme Court similarly concluded that "[i]n our opinion, the privileges and immunities secured by sec. 23 of article 1 [of the 1851 Indiana Constitution] were not intended for persons of the African race; for the section expressly limits the enjoyment of such privileges and immunities to citizens, and at that time negroes were neither citizens of the United States nor of this State." Indeed, the court continued, the Constitution "was made and adopted by and for the exclusive use and enjoyment of the white race." As to the argument that the equal protection clause of the Fourteenth Amendment prohibited the exclusion of black children from the public schools altogether, the Indiana Supreme Court concluded that the Fourteenth Amendment imposed no restrictions whatsoever on the conduct of state officials. The court made the outrageous claim that the Fourteenth Amendment "did not enlarge the powers of the Federal Government, nor diminish those of the states. The inhibitions [in the Fourteenth Amendment] against the states doing certain things have no force or effect. They do not prohibit the states from doing any act that they could have done without them."[19]

The Indiana Supreme Court's construction of the Fourteenth Amendment was widely derided. The state's leading Republican newspaper, the *Indianapolis Journal,* attacked the opinion as "a monstrous decision," while the *Pittsburgh Commercial* accused the Indiana Supreme Court of "nullify[ing] the provisions of the National Constitution." The

---

[18] "Colored Children: Shall They Attend Schools Not Especially for Them?" *Indianapolis Journal,* Jan. 29, 1874, p. 5; "Carey Carter's Case: Colored Children in the Common Schools," *Indianapolis Journal,* Feb. 26, 1874, p. 7; "The Corey-Carter Case," *Indianapolis Journal,* Nov. 25, 1874, p. 3; "White Schools in Indiana," *New York Times,* Dec. 3, 1874, p. 5; *Cory v. Carter,* 48 Ind. 327 (1874).

[19] *Dred Scott v. Sandford,* 60 U.S. 393, 404 (1857); *Cory v. Carter,* 48 Ind. 327, 341, 353 (1874) (quoting *State v. Gibson,* 36 Ind. 389 [1871]).

New York Times characterized the decision as barring "colored children in sparsely-settled localities from the enjoyment of the free common-school system whenever men mean enough can be found to object; and it is likely in most places [that such] a bigot will be found." The decision also caused an uproar among congressional Republicans, although no congressional action was taken to reverse its impact. Moreover, an expected appeal of the Indiana court's decision to the United States Supreme Court was never taken.[20]

In the meantime, several local school districts in Indiana, upon reading the *Carter* decision, expelled black students from their white schools, even though no black schools were available for their education. The *Indianapolis Journal* described the dismissal of a handful of black children from a white school in Brazil, Indiana, in December 1874, shortly after the *Carter* decision was announced: "One of them, a little boy of twelve, the teacher said was one of the best scholars she had.... [His teacher] hadn't the heart, or rather had too much of it, to turn him out, and keep him from learning enough to be a good and helpful citizen, so the superintendent did it. When told to go, the little fellow cried bitterly, and begged to stay. But no attention could be paid to such anti-Democratic tears, and go he must. He took up his books, ... hugged them to his breast, and again begged to be allowed to stay and study."[21]

In 1877, the Republican-dominated Indiana General Assembly did ameliorate some of the harsh effects of the *Carter* decision, providing that if a school district did not operate a separate school for black children, then they "*shall* be allowed to attend the public schools with white children." The law also provided that if a black student was eligible for promotion but no higher grade was provided, the student could attend a white school that provided the appropriate grade instruction. In response to this 1877 legislation, a few Indiana communities, particularly in the state's northern counties, abandoned their segregated schools, but school districts in the state's southern counties tended to retain separate schools for black children. On at least one

---

[20] For press coverage of the *Carter* case, see "A Monstrous Decision," *Indianapolis Journal*, Nov. 26, 1874, p. 4; "The Colored School Question: Further Press Comment on the Recent Supreme Court Decision," *Indianapolis Journal*, Nov. 30, 1874, p. 4 (quoting the *Pittsburgh Commercial*); for the *New York Times* quote, see "White Schools in Indiana," *New York Times*, Dec. 3, 1874, p. 5. For expectation of appeal to the United States Supreme Court, see Kousser, *Dead End*, p. 50, n. 70. Indiana Senator Oliver Morton presented a petition to the United States Senate protesting the ruling and seeking intervention by the U.S. attorney general, but to no effect. Ibid. Fishel, "The North and the Negro," p. 230.

[21] For expulsion of black students, see Thornbrough, *The Negro in Indiana*, pp. 328–9; for dismissal of a black student in Brazil, see *Indianapolis Journal*, Dec. 24, 1874, p. 4.

occasion, litigation seeking to *require* local school authorities to establish a separate black school in lieu of allowing racially mixed schools failed when the Indiana Supreme Court ruled that the 1877 legislation gave local school authorities broad discretion to determine whether to operate segregated schools.[22]

Litigation challenging segregation on the grounds that black schools were grossly inferior to white schools also generally failed. For example, a black child filed suit when denied admission to a white school in Richmond, Indiana, arguing that the separate black school did not provide the same facilities. The Indiana Supreme Court conceded that "it is obvious that the corps of teachers and course of instruction" at the two schools were "very different" but refused to compel admission to the white school absent a "total exclusion" of black children from the public schools.[23]

But in a few instances, black parents successfully challenged school segregation through litigation even in the absence of a state law banning segregation. The most striking example of such success was the school desegregation litigation in Iowa during the late 1860s and early 1870s. The 1846 Iowa Constitution provided that "[t]he schools shall be open and free to all *white* persons." Iowa adopted a new Constitution in 1857, however, that gave the state board of education authority to "provide for the education of *all the youths of the State*, through a system of common schools." Although the Constitution made no explicit statement about school segregation, a majority of the constitutional convention delegates who addressed the issue commented that they thought the new Constitution prohibited school segregation. The threat of substantial racial mixing, however, was minimal. The 1860 census found that only 1 of every 675 Iowans was black.[24]

In 1858, however, the Iowa state legislature enacted legislation *requiring* school segregation throughout the state absent "unanimous consent of persons sending children to school in the district." Shortly thereafter, however, the Iowa Supreme Court declared the 1858 school law, including its segregation provision, unconstitutional, holding that the state constitution gave the Iowa state board of education, not

---

[22] For the language of the 1877 statute, see Thornbrough, *The Negro in Indiana*, p. 329 (emphasis added). For the reaction to the statute, see ibid., pp. 329–32; Fishel, "The North and the Negro," pp. 320–1; Bigham, *We Ask Only a Fair Trial*, p. 43. For the Supreme Court decision, see *State ex rel. Oliver v. Grubb*, 85 Ind. 213 (1882).

[23] *State ex rel. Mitchell v. Gray*, 93 Ind. 303, 306 (1884); Thornbourgh, *The Negro in Indiana*, pp. 330–2.

[24] For the 1846 Iowa Constitution, see Johnson, *The Development of State Legislation*, p. 102 (emphasis supplied); for the 1857 Iowa Constitution, see *Clark v. Board of Directors*, 24 Iowa 266, 271 (1868). For views of convention delegates, see Kousser, *Dead End*, p. 46. For population figures, see U.S. Bureau of Census, 1860.

the state legislature, responsibility for regulation of the state's public schools. Although the Iowa Supreme Court's decision focused on the authority of the state legislature to regulate education and never actually mentioned school segregation, it was nevertheless the first court decision in the United States to strike down a state law mandating school segregation.[25]

The Iowa state legislature abolished the state board of education in 1864; in the meantime, the state superintendent of public instruction announced in both 1864 and 1866 that local school boards enjoyed discretion to decide whether to operate racially segregated schools. In 1868, the issue of school segregation again came before the Iowa Supreme Court. A local school district in Muscatine, a Mississippi River town, operated racially segregated primary schools and a white grammar school. When a black student sought to enroll in the white grammar school, she was excluded with the promise that a grammar school class would be established in the black primary school. The local Republican newspaper condemned the exclusion: "They are not animals that are thus treated – they are CHILDREN, human beings. What crime had they committed? Simply the crime of having been created by God Almighty with a colored skin. That is all." In response, the black student brought suit challenging her exclusion, securing representation from the state's Republican attorney general, who filed suit in his private capacity. After a local Republican judge ruled in favor of the black student, the Iowa Supreme Court, in one of the most sweeping decisions of the entire nineteenth century pertaining to black education, agreed, finding the Muscatine school segregation unlawful.[26]

The Republican-controlled Iowa Supreme Court conceded that local school authorities possessed considerable discretion in the operation of their schools. School authorities could, for example, "require certain qualifications, or proficiency in studies, or the like" before a student could gain admission to a particular school. But, the court emphasized, local school authorities could not interfere with the *"equality of right"* that all school-age children enjoyed, a right the court construed to prohibit differentiating between children because of "nationality, religion, color, clothing or the like." To find otherwise, the court suggested, would be to "stimulate a constant strife, if not a war of races."

---

[25] Reams and Wilson, *Segregation and the Fourteenth Amendment*, p. 174; *The District Township of the City of Dubuque v. Dubuque*, 7 Iowa 262 (1858).

[26] For the Iowa Supreme Court decision, *see Clark v. Board of Directors*, 24 Iowa 266 (1868). For the background to the decision, see Reams and Wilson, *Segregation and the Fourteenth Amendment*, pp. 174–5; Kousser, *Dead End*, pp. 16–18. For the newspaper quote, see "Man's Inhumanity to Man," *Muscatine Weekly Journal*, Sept. 20, 1867, p. 1.

The court's decision, which preceded ratification of the Fourteenth Amendment by a few months, grounded its notion of equality of right in the "spirit of our laws" and the "principle of equal rights to all, upon which our government is founded." The court conceded that this equality of right could be abrogated, but only if "some express sovereign authority" – presumably a legislative body – had clearly done so. Absent such an abrogation, the principle of equality constrained the Muscatine school district from requiring racial segregation.[27]

The Iowa Supreme Court's *Clark* decision was extraordinary in the context of nineteenth-century school desegregation jurisprudence. The court had not only found that segregated schools violated an inherent equality of right not grounded in positive law, but it had also found that standards of equality could not be satisfied by separate schools, a position at odds with that of the Massachusetts Supreme Court's 1850 *Roberts* decision and almost all subsequent nineteenth-century courts that had cause to consider the issue. Five years later, in a lawsuit challenging racial discrimination in the dining room of a steamboat, the Iowa Supreme Court offered an expansive gloss on its 1868 *Clark* decision: "The doctrines of natural law and of christianity forbid that rights be denied on the ground of race or color; and this principle has become incorporated into the paramount law of the Union [the Fourteenth Amendment]. It has been recognized by this court in a decision [*Clark*] wherein it is held that the directors of a public school could not forbid a colored child to attend a school of white children simply on the grounds of negro parentage, although the directors provided competent instruction for her at a school composed exclusively of colored children."[28]

The *Clark* decision, however, did not end school segregation in Iowa, as localities determined to retain the color line operated racially separate schools. In the Mississippi River town of Dubuque, for example, school officials continued to exclude black children from the town's white district schools despite the Iowa Supreme Court's *Clark* decision. Black parents challenged this exclusion before the local board of education during the early 1870s, winning a 5–1 vote in favor of the admission of their children. The school board president, however, refused to enforce the vote, noting that "probably a majority of our

[27] *Clark v. Board of Directors*, 24 Iowa 266, 269, 275–7 (1868) (emphasis in the original). One justice did dissent, finding that school segregation was consistent with "the principle of equal rights."

[28] For decisions at odds with *Clark*, see *King v. Gallagher*, 93 N.Y. 438 (1883); *United States v. Buntin*, 10 F. 730, 737 (S.D. Ohio 1882); *Corey v. Carter*, 48 Ind. 327 (1874); *Ward v. Flood*, 48 Cal. 36 (1874); *State ex rel. Stoutmeyer v. Duffy*, 7 Nev. 342 (1872); *State ex rel. Garnes v. McCann*, 21 Ohio St. 198, 209–10 (1871). For the gloss on the *Clark* decision, see *Coger v. North West Union Packet Co.*, 37 Iowa 145, 154 (1873).

citizens are strongly opposed to the discontinuance of the colored school." As a result, school segregation continued in Dubuque until the Iowa Supreme Court, relying on its *Clark* decision, finally forced an end to the practice in 1877. Similarly, school officials in Keokuk, another Mississippi River town, also excluded black students from white schools during the early 1870s, claiming in one instance that "the citizens of the city and district are opposed to mixed schools, and to admit colored pupils with the white would destroy the harmony and impair the usefulness of the high school." The black students filed lawsuits challenging their exclusion and prevailed when the Iowa Supreme Court in 1875 separately affirmed lower court orders directing an end of segregation.[29]

The *Clark* decision reflected the dominance of Radical Republicans on the state supreme court and was the second substantial victory for black rights in Iowa in 1868. That same year, Radical Republicans won passage of a state constitutional amendment granting black men the right to vote, making Iowa one of the first states outside of New England to do so. These successes were likely due in part to the dearth of blacks in Iowa. Although a number of blacks had migrated to Iowa after the Civil War, the 1870 census found that only 1 in every 200 Iowans was black and that fewer than ten blacks lived in almost half of the counties in the state.[30]

A few years later, the Kansas Supreme Court, expressly relying on the *Clark* decision, also disallowed racially separate schools in the absence of legislation prohibiting such segregation. In 1870, a Republican school board in Ottawa had integrated its schools, arguing that the recently ratified Fourteenth Amendment compelled such action. In the meantime, however, probably due to the influx of blacks to Kansas as part of the Exoduster migration of the late 1870s, segregated schools had been reestablished in Ottawa. In 1881, a district court judge issued an order directing the school authorities of Ottawa to admit a black child to a white school, finding that "it is evident to every mind" that school segregation violated the Fourteenth Amendment to the United States Constitution – one of only two nineteenth-century courts to so hold. On appeal, the Kansas Supreme Court agreed that the exclusion was unlawful, but did so on grounds that the state legislature had not *expressly* granted school officials in "second-class" cities (with

---

[29] For school desegregation in Dubuque, see Fishel, "The North and the Negro," pp. 239–40. For school desegregation in Keokuk, see *Smith v. Directors of the Independent School District of Keokuk*, 40 Iowa 518 (1875); *Dove v. The Independent School District of Keokuk*, 41 Iowa 689 (1875); Fishel, "The North and the Negro," p. 240.

[30] For the Iowa constitutional amendment, see Fishel, "The North and the Negro," p. 117; for population figures, see U.S. Bureau of Census, 1870.

a population less than 15,000), like Ottawa, authority to segregate schoolchildren. In 1879, the Kansas state legislature had given authority only to "first-class" cities (with a population greater than 15,000) to engage in school segregation. As to the question of whether school segregation was consistent with the Fourteenth Amendment, the court "doubted" that it was, but ultimately held that that question "can finally be determined only by the supreme court of the United States." Republican Justice Daniel Valentine, writing for the Kansas Supreme Court, made clear his distaste for school segregation: "And what good reason can exist for separating two children . . . equally intelligent, and equally advanced in their studies, and sending one, because he or she is black, to a school house in a remote part of the city, past several school houses nearer his or her home, while the other child is permitted, because he or she is white, to go to school within the distance of a block? No good reason can be given for such a thing. . . ." Justice Valentine rejected reliance on the 1850 *Roberts* decision issued by the Massachusetts Supreme Court, dismissing it as a "very old" decision "rendered before the war."[31]

Despite the Kansas Supreme Court's decision striking down school segregation in second-class cities, some Kansas communities continued to exclude black children from white schools. The city of Independence excluded black children from a white school notwithstanding the earlier decision in the Ottawa case until the Kansas Supreme Court in 1891 reaffirmed its view that second-class cities, absent statutory authority, had no right to engage in school segregation. But black children in second-class cities in Kansas did not always prevail in their legal challenges to school segregation. In 1886, a state trial court judge in South Topeka rejected a legal challenge to the exclusion of a black child from a white school, accepting the school district's argument that the white school to which black children sought admission was already full.[32]

A final successful legal challenge to school segregation in the absence of a state statute prohibiting segregation took place in Crawford County, Pennsylvania, in the northwest corner of the state. There, a black parent whose children were refused admission to a white school sought a writ of mandamus from a local county court directing the

---

[31] For the background to the Ottawa desegregation, see Kousser, "Before *Plessy*, Before *Brown*," p. 244, n. 21; Kull, "A Nineteenth-Century Precursor," pp. 1203–6. For the Supreme Court decision, see *Board of Education of Ottawa v. Tinnon*, 26 Kan. 1, 21, 23 (1881).

[32] For the Independence litigation, see *Knox v. Board of Education of the City of Independence*, 45 Kan. 152 (1891). For the South Topeka litigation, see *Daniel v. Board of Education of South Topeka*, 4 Kan. L.J. 329 (1886).

admission of his children. In May 1881, a trial judge in Crawford County granted the writ, finding in an extraordinary opinion that the 1854 Pennsylvania state statute authorizing school segregation violated *both* the Thirteenth *and* the Fourteenth Amendments to the United States Constitution. The matter was apparently never appealed to the Pennsylvania Supreme Court, where its fate was uncertain, probably because within a few weeks of the decision, the Pennsylvania state legislature abolished school segregation by statute.[33]

On at least one occasion, litigants successfully challenged school segregation alleging that it constituted a waste of public resources. In 1872, a group of white taxpayers in McLean County in Illinois sued their local school authorities to prevent the continued operation of a separate school for only two black children on the property of a white school, arguing that the children should be admitted to the white school to avoid the misuse of education monies. The taxpayers did not argue that segregation was unlawful, but rather that the construction and continued operation of the small black school constituted "a misappropriation of the public funds." The Republican-dominated Illinois Supreme Court agreed in 1874, finding that the local school authorities had committed a "fraud upon the tax-payers" by establishing a separate school to teach only four black children. The court noted in dicta that local school authorities may not "discriminate between scholars on account of their color, race or social position" but left unresolved the question of whether the provision of "a separate room for [black and white children], where the facilities for instruction were entirely equal" would violate Illinois law. In response to the Illinois Supreme Court's decision, with full recognition of the poor condition of so many of the state's black schools, the state superintendent of education in Illinois, Newton Bateman, declared as a matter of state policy that school districts with fewer than ten black children must admit these children into white schools.[34]

In some instances, litigation, though it failed to end segregation directly, did contribute indirectly to the enactment of antisegregation legislation. Litigation frequently highlighted the unfairness of the exclusion of black children from white schools, which aided the political efforts of those blacks seeking legislative or administrative action ending school segregation. Litigation also demonstrated the desire of

---

[33] For the Crawford County litigation, see *Allen v. Davis*, 10 WNC 156 (1881); Kull, *The Color-Blind Constitution*, p. 107; Silcox, "A Comparative Study in School Desegregation," p. 227; Brown, *The Negro in Pennsylvania History*, pp. 53–4. For legislation, see Lane, *William Dorsey's Philadelphia*, p. 154.

[34] For the decision, see *Chase v. Stephenson*, 71 Ill. 383, 385–6 (1874); for Bateman's action, see Fishel, "The North and the Negro," p. 215.

blacks for integration and thus helped defuse the commonly offered argument that blacks preferred racially separate schools.

For example, in Michigan, litigation contributed to the enactment of antisegregation legislation. In 1867, the former Republican governor of Michigan, Austin Blair, filed a legal action on behalf of a black child denied entry into a white school in the town of Jackson. Shortly thereafter, and before a court could hear the complaint, the Radical Republican-controlled state legislature enacted legislation providing that "*[a]ll* residents of any district shall have an equal right to attend any school therein." The litigation contributed to the legislative success. The Michigan Supreme Court explained the connection in 1869: "We might, perhaps, take notice of the fact, that immediately preceding the passage of that [1867 legislation prohibiting school segregation], an application was made to this court for a *mandamus* to compel the trustees of one of the union school districts, embracing the city of Jackson, to admit a colored pupil to the same school with white children, notwithstanding they had established a colored school within the district. If that application was not the immediate occasion of the legislation in question, it is at least highly probable that it presented one of the cases which made new legislation appear important. . . ."[35]

Similarly, in New York, although a court refused to order the desegregation of the Albany schools, litigation nevertheless indirectly contributed to a political solution to school segregation in that city. In 1872, a black parent in Albany filed suit challenging the exclusion of his children from a white school. A state trial court judge ruled that the Albany school officials could exclude black children from white schools under New York law so long as they provided black schools of equal quality. The judge, however, told the plaintiff that if Albany's black community "as a body" petitioned the Albany school authorities for desegregation, "their views . . . will doubtless have great weight with the board." Following the judge's suggestions, the black community petitioned for the right to attend white schools, and in 1873, the Albany school authorities gave them that right and closed the local black school. Twenty-seven years later, the well-publicized unsuccessful litigation efforts of a black woman in Queens seeking access to a white school for her children contributed to the subsequent enactment by the New York legislature of antisegregation legislation that overruled the adverse court decision. Similarly, in Ohio, unsuccessful

---

35 For legislation, see Katzman, *Before the Ghetto*, pp. 84–5; Reams and Wilson, *Segregation and the Fourteenth Amendment*, p. 286; Middleton, *The Black Laws in the Old Northwest*, p. 365 (emphasis added). For the court decision, see *Workman v. Board of Education*, 18 Mich. 400, 412 (1869).

desegregation litigation in Springfield helped build support in the black community for antisegregation legislation.[36]

Thus, although most northern courts rejected legal challenges to school segregation absent a state law prohibiting segregation, African Americans in communities somewhat predisposed to school desegregation were able to use litigation on a few occasions to support political efforts to procure a ban on school segregation in the legislative process.

Campaign for Antisegregation Legislation

While litigation generally failed to desegregate northern schools after the Civil War, black efforts to procure legislation forbidding school segregation enjoyed considerably greater success, as many northern states enacted antisegregation legislation during the quarter century following the end of the Civil War.

One of the most significant efforts to procure antisegregation legislation took place in Congress. Beginning in 1870, Radical Republican United States Senator Charles Sumner of Massachusetts, who had argued for an end to school segregation in Boston in the *Roberts* case, introduced legislation in each session of Congress until his death in 1875 that would have prohibited racial discrimination in public accommodations, transportation, schools, and juries throughout the country. Supporters of Sumner's bill made their case in letters to newspaper editors, in editorials, and on the lecture circuit. Many emphasized the importance of mixed schools to republican government. Wendell Phillips wrote in 1869 that "the education of all classes and conditions of children *together* is one of the most valuable elements of our School System and makes it the root of our Republicans Institutions. If you separate sects, races, or classes and educate them . . . you lose one of the finest influences of the plan." Others emphasized the stigma that segregated schools imposed on black children. *Harper's Weekly* wrote in 1874 that "[a] State which separates the colored children from the white in the public schools stigmatizes them on account of color, and denies their equality as citizens, because it declares them by reason of color unfit to associate with their fellows." Although Congress did prohibit racial discrimination in public accommodations in the Civil Rights Act of 1875, efforts to include a ban on school segregation were defeated. For many members of Congress, eliminating racial discrimination in

---

[36] For Albany, see Mabee, *Black Education in New York*, pp. 198–9, 202; Ment, "Racial Segregation in the Public Schools," pp. 145–51. For Queens, see *Cisco v. School Board of the Borough of Queens*, 161 N.Y. 598 (1900); Mabee, *Black Education in New York State*, pp. 243, 245. For Ohio, see Kousser, "'The Onward March of Right Principles,'" p. 190.

public accommodations, which would have limited practical effect on the lives of most whites, was tolerable, but the mixing of black and white children in the public schools was not. The legislative campaign against school segregation would have to be waged at the state level.[37]

Efforts to procure state antisegregation legislation enjoyed significant success. Between 1866 and 1887, *every* northern state except Indiana that had previously required or permitted school segregation by law enacted legislation that either explicitly or implicitly prohibited the continued operation of segregated schools. Some of these statutes, as in Ohio, simply withdrew prior legislative authority given to local school districts to operate racially separate schools. Other states prohibited school segregation outright. Further west, several states and territories also enacted antisegregation legislation or ratified state constitutional provisions banning school segregation between 1873 and 1901.[38]

---

[37] For legislative efforts, see McPherson, "Abolitionists and the Civil Rights Act." For the Phillips quote, see ibid., p. 498; for the *Harper's* quote, see "Civil Rights and the Constitution," *Harper's Weekly* (Oct. 10, 1874), p. 830.

[38] *Rhode Island* (1866) ("no distinction shall be made on account of the race or color of the applicant"); *Michigan* (1867, 1871) (1867: "All residents of any district shall have an equal right to attend any school therein"; 1871: "No separate school . . . shall be kept for any persons on account of race or color"); *Connecticut* (1868) ("No person shall be denied admittance to . . . any public school in the school district where such person resides, on account of race or color"); *Minnesota* (1869) ("no classification of scholars with reference to color, social position or nationality"); *New York* (1873, 1900) 1873: ("No citizen of the State shall by reason of race . . . [be] excluded from full and equal enjoyment of the accommodations . . . furnished by . . . officers of common schools and public institutions of learning"; 1900: "No person shall be refused admission into or be excluded from any public school in the State of New York on account of race or color"); *Kansas* (1873, 1874, 1876) (In 1873, the legislature repealed legislation requiring segregated schools in second-class cities; in 1874, the legislature forbade all school segregation: "If any trustees, etc., of any . . . school of public instruction . . . shall make any distinction on account of race, color, or previous condition of servitude, it shall be a misdemeanor, punishable by a fine . . . and the offender shall also be liable in damages to the person injured thereby," which it reaffirmed in 1876. Kansas subsequently amended this statute in 1879 to allow school segregation in first-class cities.); *Illinois* (1874) (boards of education "are prohibited from excluding [schoolchildren] . . . on account of the color of such child."); *Colorado* (1876) ("Nor shall any distinction or classification of pupils in public schools be made on account of race or color."); *California* (1880) ("Children of any race or nationality, from six years to twenty-one years of age inclusive, residing in the district, shall be entitled to admission to the public schools"); *New Jersey* (1881) ("No children . . . shall be excluded from any public school in the State on account of . . . color." The statute was amended in 1903 to impose a criminal sanction on school officials who excluded children from public schools on account of their race.); *Pennsylvania* (1881) ("It shall be unlawful for any school director . . . to make any distinction whatever, on account of or by reason of the race or color of any pupil . . . [in] any public or common school"); *Ohio* (1887) (repealed prior statutes that permitted school boards

Reasons for the Enactment of the Antisegregation Legislation

The enactment of antisegregation legislation throughout the North and parts of the West did not reflect a uniform and enthusiastic embrace of racially mixed schools. Rather, it reflected a combination of Radical Republican support for the abolition of racial distinctions in public education, the calculated desire of legislators in some states to secure the electoral support of black voters, and the unwelcome expense of retaining dual schools. Moreover, every northern state had a minuscule – and unevenly distributed – black population during the nineteenth century, allowing many white legislators to support legislation knowing that it would have a limited impact on their constituents.

Many Radical Republicans during the postbellum era opposed virtually all racial distinctions in public life, including school segregation, and sought legislative prohibitions on racial discrimination in schools and public accommodations at both the national and state levels. In four northern states, Radical Republican-dominated state legislatures pushed through antisegregation legislation during the first four years of Reconstruction. In 1866 and 1868, Republican-controlled legislatures in Rhode Island and Connecticut, the only New England states where a few communities continued to operate racially separate schools, enacted antisegregation legislation. In Connecticut, the legislation forced two Democratic cities, Hartford and New Haven, both of which were underrepresented in the state legislature due to

to segregate schools); *Washington Territory* (1889) ("It is the paramount duty of the state to make ample provision for the education of all children residing in its borders, without distinction or preference on account of race, color, caste or sex"); *Idaho* (1889) ("No distinction or classification of pupils in schools shall be made on account of race or color"); *Montana* (1889) ("The public free schools of the State shall be open to all children and youths"); *New Mexico Territory* (1901) ("Any teachers, school directors, or members of any board of education . . . who shall refuse to receive any pupil at a school on account of race or nationality . . . shall be guilty of a misdemeanor and punished by a fine . . . and imprisonment . . . and shall be forever barred from teaching school . . . in this territory." New Mexico amended its school law in 1923 to permit school segregation.); *Arizona Territory* (1901) ("No child shall be refused admission to any public school on account of race or color." The Arizona territory amended its antisegregation law in 1909 to permit segregation.). Johnson, *The Development of State Legislation*, pp. 33, 68, 74–5, 95–6, 100, 105, 126–8, 143–5, 156, 150, 152, 164–5, 174; Appendix to the Supplemental Brief for the United States on Reargument, 185, *Brown v. Board of Education*, 347 U.S. 483 (1954); Taylor, *The Forging of a Black Community*, p. 181; Stephenson, *Race Distinctions*, pp. 186–7; Kousser, "Before *Plessy*, Before *Brown*," pp. 222–4; Oak and Oak, "The Illegal Status of Separate Education in New Jersey," p. 671; Murray, *States' Laws on Race* and Color, pp. 290, 524; Green, "Race and Segregation in St. Paul's Public Schools," p. 147. Maine, New Hampshire, Vermont, and Wisconsin allowed the few black children who lived in those states to attend public schools on a nondiscriminatory basis, and hence antisegregation legislation was deemed unnecessary.

malapportionment, to close the only remaining black schools in the state.

Michigan was the first state outside of New England to enact antisegregation legislation in 1867 when the Radical Republican-dominated legislature enacted a School Integration Act over the dissent of the Democratic Detroit Board of Education, which operated segregated schools. When school authorities in Detroit maintained that their statutory right to operate segregated schools, granted in 1841, had not been explicitly revoked by the 1867 legislation, the Republican legislature enacted additional legislation in 1871 that expressly barred the operation of racially separate schools throughout the state – including Detroit. The two states outside of New England most reliably Republican during the early 1860s – Iowa and Minnesota – were the next two states to abolish segregated schools: Iowa by judicial decision in 1868 and Minnesota by statute in 1869. Shortly after the voters of Minnesota approved a Republican-sponsored referendum granting black men the right to vote in November 1868, Minnesota's Republican Governor William Marshall addressed the newly enfranchised black residents of St. Paul, where most of the state's black population lived, welcoming them "to liberty and equality before law." Within weeks, in early 1869, the Republican-dominated state legislature not only enacted legislation prohibiting school segregation, it also took the additional step of requiring the withholding of state educational funds from school districts that failed to comply, an action other state legislatures failed to take. This Republican effort targeted the only city in the state that operated segregated schools: the heavily Democratic St. Paul.[39]

Five years later, in 1874, despite strong opposition from Democratic legislators in the state's southern counties where support for school segregation was strongest, the Republican-dominated Illinois state legislature enacted legislation that prohibited any local school official "from excluding, directly or indirectly, any ... child from school on account of the color of such child." The legislature also imposed fines on "[a]ny school officer who shall exclude, or aid in excluding from the public schools, on account of color, any child who is entitled to the benefits of such school" and on private persons "who shall by threats, menace, or intimidation, prevent any colored child entitled to attend a public school, from attending such school." Although many

---

39 For Michigan, see Katzman, *Before the Ghetto*, p. 85. For Minnesota, see Green, "Race and Segregation in St. Paul's Public Schools," pp. 147–9; Green, "'Critical Mass Is Fifteen Colored's!'" p. 313. During the Civil War, the Republican Party captured a higher percentage of the vote in Minnesota and Iowa than in any other state outside of New England. Dykstra, "Iowa," pp. 167–70.

contemporaries, including proponents of racially mixed schools, believed that this legislation merely prohibited the exclusion of black children from the public schools and did not proscribe segregated schools, the Illinois Supreme Court interpreted this legislation in 1882 as banning school segregation. Throughout the North, a Republican-dominated legislature did not guarantee the enactment of antisegregation legislation, but as historian Morgan Kousser has noted, such legislation was enacted only when Republicans enjoyed legislative control.[40]

The efforts of congressional Republicans to secure federal legislation banning school segregation favorably influenced efforts in some states to secure state antisegregation legislation. For example, Republicans in the New York General Assembly argued that their party could not pursue antisegregation legislation in Congress while opposing similar legislation at home. In 1873, the New York state legislature considered legislation providing that children could not be "excluded from full and equal enjoyment" of the schools because of their race. Republicans, who held about 80 percent of the seats in the New York General Assembly, voted overwhelmingly for the legislation, clearly influenced by the antisegregation efforts of their Republican colleagues in Congress. One black proponent of school desegregation in Geneva, New York, for example, argued that "the North should practice the racial equality it was trying to force on the South." After the New York Court of Appeals, with a majority of Democratic judges, construed the legislation as permitting the retention of separate but equal schools, the Republican-dominated legislature enacted additional legislation providing that no person could "be excluded from any public school in the state of New York on account of race or color."[41]

Congressional efforts to enact antisegregation legislation also favorably influenced legislative efforts in Illinois, where the state legislature enacted antisegregation legislation in 1874, and Pennsylvania,

[40] For Illinois legislation, see Johnson, *The Development of State Legislation*, p. 96; Squibb, "Roads to *Plessy*," pp. 131–2. On conflicting understandings of the meaning of the statute, see McCaul, *Black Struggle for Public Schooling*, pp. 127–41; Cha-Jua, *America's First Black Town*, p. 108. For the Supreme Court decision, see *People ex rel. Longress v. Board of Education of Quincy*, 101 Ill. 308 (1882). For Kousser, see Kousser, "'The Onward March of Right Principles,'" p. 190.

[41] For the effect of federal legislative efforts on New York, see Silcox, "A Comparative Study in School Desegregation," p. 211; Ment, "Racial Segregation in the Public Schools," p. 111; Kousser, *Dead End*, p. 42, n. 41; Mabee, *Black Education in New York State*, p. 201. For the quote from Geneva, see Mabee, *Black Education in New York State*, p. 196; for subsequent legislation, see Ment, "Racial Segregation in the Public Schools," p. 199.

where the state senate approved antisegregation legislation in 1874. Pennsylvania Republicans specifically sought to make their state's laws conform to the school desegregation legislation then pending in Congress, which would have banned school segregation throughout the nation. The Republican-controlled Pennsylvania legislature finally enacted antisegregation legislation in 1881.[42]

In a similar manner, congressional antisegregation efforts had a favorable impact on desegregation efforts in Kansas. During the 1860s, the Kansas state legislature had permitted first-class cities (with a population of more than 15,000) and second-class cities (with a population of less than 15,000) to establish segregated schools. But in 1873, the Republican-dominated state legislature prohibited school segregation in second-class cities, and in 1874 it prohibited racial discrimination in the operation of *any* school in the state.[43]

At the same time, the Republican campaign for the abolition of school segregation converged with the Republican embrace of public education as an important political issue during the Reconstruction era. Senator Henry Wilson of Massachusetts, chair of the Republican National Committee, published an essay in January 1871, "New Departure of the Republican Party," in which he called for education to be the centerpiece of a new Reconstruction for the entire country. To Wilson, given the enfranchisement of millions of blacks, as well as the arrival of scores of European immigrants, public schools were needed to protect social stability. President U.S. Grant's education commissioner, John Eaton, wrote in 1874 that unless the nation "elevated and harmonized" its citizenry – including blacks and poor immigrant whites – by education, the "existence of the republic" would be an "impossibility." The following year, 1875, President Grant proposed a federal constitutional amendment guaranteeing a free education to all Americans.[44]

One manifestation of this embrace of public education was the enactment of compulsory education laws. Massachusetts had enacted the first and only compulsory attendance law of the antebellum era in 1852; by 1880, fifteen additional northern states had enacted such

---

[42] Kousser, *Dead End*, p. 41, n. 39; Evans, *Pennsylvania Politics*, p. 125.

[43] But in 1879, in response to the significant black Exoduster migration to Kansas of the late 1870s, the legislature again permitted segregated elementary schools in first-class cities. Thereafter, Kansas would continue to permit first-class cities to retain segregated elementary schools until the 1950s. Kousser, "Before *Plessy*, Before *Brown*," pp. 222–3; Reams and Wilson, *Segregation and the Fourteenth Amendment*, pp. 183, 186–7; Taylor, *In Search of the Racial Frontier*, p. 216.

[44] For the Wilson statement, see Wilson, "New Departure of the Republican Party," pp. 108–12. For the Eaton quote, see Smith, *Civic Ideals*, p. 322; for the Grant amendment see ibid., p. 321.

legislation. This embrace of compulsory education was due in part to Republican animus toward Democratic-voting Irish Catholics who favored parochial school education. Proponents of antisegregation legislation frequently linked their concerns to those of the compulsory education movement, arguing that segregated schools deprived many black children of an education because of the long distance from their home to the nearest black school.[45]

In many northern states, other factors dominated legislative considerations of antisegregation legislation. Every northern state outside of New England and New York had prohibited blacks from voting prior to the Civil War, but black males throughout the North were enfranchised following ratification of the Fifteenth Amendment to the United States Constitution in 1870. Moreover, the northern black population sharply increased following the Civil War, particularly in the Midwest, outpacing the growth in white population. Between 1860 and 1870, the black population increased in Kansas (2,629 percent), Iowa (439 percent), Illinois (277 percent), Minnesota (193 percent), Indiana (115 percent), Wisconsin (80 percent), Michigan (74 percent), and Ohio (72 percent), although in each of those states except Kansas, the black population remained less than 2.5 percent of the total population.[46]

Most northern blacks were inclined to support the antislavery Republican Party, but some prominent black leaders, such as Peter Clark of Cincinnati and George Downing of Providence, openly questioned the unfaltering allegiance of African Americans to the party of Lincoln, shrewdly recognizing that as long as Republicans took the black vote for granted, they would be less willing to grant legislative and patronage benefits to African Americans. Although blacks still comprised only a fraction of the northern population, closely contested elections in some northern states during the 1870s and 1880s gave black voters some electoral influence, as did the concentration of blacks in certain urban centers. Indeed, by the 1870s, even some Democrats, who had long been openly hostile to African Americans, courted the black vote in parts of the North. Black votes were particularly important in postbellum elections in Connecticut, Indiana, New Jersey, New York, Pennsylvania, and Ohio. As historian Lawrence Grossman has noted: "the evidence of increased Negro [political] independence, though impressionistic rather than statistically verifiable, cannot be ignored. Politicians at the time took it seriously, Democrats seeing opportunity, Republicans fearing danger." This competition for the

---

[45] McAfee, *Religion, Race, and Reconstruction*, pp. 71–2; Lieberson, *A Piece of the Pie*, p. 136.
[46] U.S. Bureau of the Census, 1860 and 1870. In Kansas, blacks comprised 4.7 percent of the state's population in 1870.

black vote played into the hands of those blacks seeking antisegregation legislation.[47]

The results were particularly striking in Ohio, one of the three northern states (along with Illinois and Indiana) most resistant to black education during the antebellum era. In Ohio, many African Americans during the post-Civil War era sought to enroll their children in white schools through school board petitions and lawsuits. Only a few school districts responded favorably to these petitions, and all of the litigation failed. But those black Ohioans who favored integrated schools exercised their newly won franchise to elect legislators sympathetic to their concerns.[48]

Beginning in 1873, many Ohio blacks began to openly question their unwavering support for the Republican Party since Republicans had failed to deliver patronage appointments and to repeal the state's Black Laws. During the 1873 election, Ohio Democrats for the first time made a direct appeal for black votes, abandoning an earlier decision to campaign on the evils of racial mixing. For the next several years, Ohio Democrats actively recruited black political support, sponsoring the development of black Democratic clubs and supporting the establishment of a black Democratic newspaper. By the early 1880s, both Democrats and Republicans, anxious to secure black votes, supported a variety of desegregation initiatives in Ohio. Even though blacks comprised less than 3 percent of the Ohio population during the last three decades of the nineteenth century (the second highest percentage in the North behind New Jersey), in the closely contested elections of the 1870s and 1880s their vote proved crucial, often providing the margin of victory. For example, in the Ohio gubernatorial election of 1883, a contest of two Cincinnati attorneys, Democrat George Hoadly defeated Republican Joseph Foraker by 12,529 votes. Hoadly believed that he won the election by capturing the votes of a significant portion of the state's 16,000 black voters, many of whom were upset that Foraker had recently defended the Springfield (Ohio) school board's efforts to keep a black child out of her white neighborhood school.[49]

Governor Hoadly took office in 1883 shortly after the United States Supreme Court in the *Civil Rights Cases* declared unconstitutional the

[47] For black political influence, see Gerber, "A Politics of Limited Options," p. 236; Grossman, *The Democratic Party and the Negro*, pp. 38, 41, 60, 99, 105 (including quote); Evans, *Pennsylvania Politics*, p. 199.

[48] Kessen, "Segregation in Cincinnati," p. 132; McGinnis, *The Education of Negroes in Ohio*, p. 59.

[49] For Democrats and blacks, see Grossman, *The Democratic Party and the Negro*, pp. 80–1; for population data, see U.S. Bureau of Census, 1870, 1880, 1890, 1900. Blacks in Kansas comprised a slightly higher percentage of total population than in Ohio or New Jersey. For the 1883 election, see Gerber, *Black Ohio and the Color Line*, p. 232.

federal Civil Rights Act of 1875, which had prohibited racial discrimination in public accommodations. The Court's decision outraged blacks throughout the North and prompted the establishment of approximately 200 equal rights organizations in Ohio alone. In response to the Court's decision, twelve northern and western states enacted legislation banning discrimination in public accommodations within two years – Massachusetts, Rhode Island, Connecticut, New Jersey, Ohio, Indiana, Illinois, Iowa, Michigan, Minnesota, Nebraska, and Colorado. This legislative success was attributable in significant measure to the demands of northern blacks and the desire of white politicians to win black political support. Analyses of voting patterns suggest a positive correlation between support for the legislation and the number of black constituents in a legislator's district.[50]

But for many northern white legislators, the commitment to civil rights did not go deeper than the desire to capture black votes. As had been true with the Civil Rights Act of 1875, these state antidiscrimination measures contained weak enforcement provisions and were widely underenforced. Northern legislators, even Democrats generally hostile to black rights, could support antidiscrimination legislation, recognizing that such legislation would have little impact on levels of interracial contact.

The campaign for public accommodations legislation in Ohio reveals the ambivalence of many northern legislators about the elimination of racial discrimination. In early January 1884, the Ohio state legislature began consideration of legislation banning discrimination in public accommodations in reaction to the Supreme Court's decision in the *Civil Rights Cases* a few months earlier. Most Democrats in the legislature opposed the bill but were reluctant to voice opposition for fear of antagonizing black voters. When forced to go on record, Democrats supported the legislation, hoping that it would die in committee. Republican legislators kept the antidiscrimination bill alive, although Democrats voted along party lines to block a Republican-sponsored amendment that extended coverage to eating establishments. In early February 1884, the more limited Democratic version of the legislation passed unanimously. After blacks objected to the exclusion of

[50] For the Court decision, see *Civil Rights Cases*, 109 U.S. 3 (1883); for the black reaction to the decision, see Weaver, "The Failure of Civil Rights," pp. 374–5. Prior to the Court's decision, only Massachusetts (1865), New York (1873), and Kansas (1874) had enacted antidiscrimination legislation. Pennsylvania enacted similar legislation in 1887, and the Washington Territory (1889), California (1893), and Wisconsin (1895) followed suit during the 1890s. Leskes, "State Law Against Discrimination," pp. 155–251; Johnson, *The Development of State Legislation*, pp. 55, 74, 202, 207; Taylor, *The Forging of a Black Community*, p. 21. For voting patterns, see Grossman, *The Democratic Party and the Negro*, pp. 75, 99.

eating establishments, the legislature subsequently voted, with only two dissenting Democratic votes in each chamber, to include a ban on discrimination in eating establishments.[51]

But the Ohio antidiscrimination law did not reflect widespread support for black civil rights. Significantly, Ohio's civil rights legislation (as well as similar legislation in Massachusetts, Rhode Island, Connecticut, Indiana, Illinois, Michigan, and California) provided for monetary penalties but with no specified minimum. In the hands of unsympathetic judges and jurors, the penalties tended to be minimal, often little more than "a registration fee for discriminatory practices." For example, one lawsuit in Ohio challenging the exclusion of blacks from a roller skating rink resulted in a damages award of one cent. Small damages awards, coupled with the cost of retaining counsel and pursuing litigation, severely undermined the efficacy of the antidiscrimination legislation.[52]

Moreover, many courts construed the legislation very narrowly, reflecting the lack of commitment to black rights particularly when those rights collided with the autonomy of private business operators. Virtually every statute prohibiting discrimination in public accommodations listed specific businesses as well "other places of public accommodation." But many courts refused to extend coverage to any business not *specifically* mentioned in the statute, rendering superfluous the language "other places of public accommodation." Other courts denied liability on the basis of a technicality. An Ohio circuit court, for example, reversed a finding that a theater had refused to sell a ticket to a black man, concluding that the plaintiff had not proven that the theater had specifically authorized the ticket seller to refuse him a ticket. In so doing, the court sidestepped established principles of agency law.[53]

---

[51] Grossman, *The Democratic Party and the Negro*, pp. 85–6.

[52] Weaver, "The Failure of Civil Rights," p. 381. In time, some states, including Colorado, Connecticut, Massachusetts, Minnesota, New York, and Ohio, did impose a minimum monetary penalty on violators. Ibid., p. 376.

[53] For court decisions refusing to extend coverage, see *Kellar v. Koerber*, 61 Ohio St. 388 (1899) (saloon); *Cecil v. Green*, 161 Ill. 265 (1896) (soda fountain); *Rhone v. Loomis*, 74 Minn. 200 (1898) (saloon); *Burks v. Bosso*, 180 N.Y. 341 (1905) (boot black stand); *Humburd v. Crawford*, 128 Iowa 743 (1905) (boarding house); *Brown v. J. H. Bell Co.*, 146 Iowa 89 (1910) (merchant's booth at a food show); *Faulkner v. Solazzi*, 79 Conn. 541 (1907) (barbershop).

Some courts did allow suits to go forward despite the fact that the specific entity was not named in the statute. *People v. King*, 42 Hun. 186 (N.Y. Sup. 1886) (skating rink deemed to fall within the meaning of "other places of public amusement"); *Kopper v. Willis*, 9 Daly 460 (N.Y. Com. Pl. 1881) (restaurant deemed to fall within the meaning of "inn"); *Youngstown Park & Falls St. Ry. v. Tokus*, 4 Ohio App. 276 (1915) (dancing hall is a "place of public amusement"); Weaver, "The Failure of Civil Rights," p. 379.

92 Jim Crow Moves North

As a result, in the wake of the enactment of this civil rights legislation, racial discrimination in public amusements and accommodations remained widespread. For example, during the roller skating craze of the 1880s, many skating rinks throughout Ohio either barred blacks or held special skating nights for blacks while excluding them the rest of the week. While some blacks successfully challenged this discrimination through litigation, these successes did not eliminate skating rink discrimination. As a result, many blacks simply gave up and patronized only those rinks that served blacks. Both barbershops and hotel proprietors also widely disregarded the antidiscrimination legislation. When the Fisk University Jubilee Singers traveled throughout the North during the mid-1880s, they met with exclusion or discriminatory treatment from hotels in city after city despite laws prohibiting such behavior. The *New York Age*, writing in 1890, captured the unwillingness of courts to enforce the antidiscrimination legislation: "People of Afro-American extraction who live here [in New York City] or who pass through this city, need not be told that there are keepers of restaurants, saloons, theatres, etc., who almost daily kick Afro-Americans out of their places, when the latter happen to go there for accommodation; and that these same persons, knowing the inadequacy of the law for any redress, laugh in your faces and tell you to sue and do your best."[54]

In addition to supporting a statutory ban on discrimination in public accommodations, Ohio Republicans took action in 1884 to shore up their support among black voters by introducing legislation that would ban school segregation. Black Ohioans had sought such a statutory ban since the early 1870s, but those efforts had repeatedly failed. In 1878, the Ohio legislature did amend its school segregation law, making it permissive rather than mandatory, but separate schools persisted in much of the state. By the 1880s, however, many Democrats perceived the political benefits of supporting legislation that prohibited school segregation. Democratic Governor Hoadly, a strong proponent, joined

---

For the Ohio theater decision, see Quillin, *The Color Line in Ohio*, p. 118. Other courts dismissed suits on technicalities, such as the plaintiff's failure to allege that he was a citizen. *Messenger v. State*, 25 Neb. 674, 41 N.W. 638 (1889). See also *State v. Hall*, 72 Iowa 525, 34 N.W. 315 (1887) (indictment claiming that the defendant refused service to a black customer was insufficient); *Bowlin v. Lyon*, 67 Iowa 536, 25 N.W. 766 (1885) (unlicensed skating rink is not a public accommodation).

54 For continuation of discrimination, see Weaver, "The Failure of Civil Rights," pp. 377–9; Bigham, *We Ask Only a Fair Trial*, p. 38; Price, *Freedom Not Far Distant*, p. 132; Wright, *Afro-Americans in New Jersey*, p. 54; Wright, "New Jersey Laws and the Negro," pp. 192–3; "From the Queen City: Roller Rink for Colored People, *Cleveland Gazette*, Feb. 21, 1885, p. 1. For the quote, see *New York Age*, Apr. 12, 1890, quoted in Fishel, "The North and the Negro," p. 386.

the effort to secure its enactment. Hoadly had had a long history of involvement in issues pertaining to black education. A member of the Free Soil Party and later of the Republican Party during the antebellum era, Hoadly had successfully sued the Cincinnati school authorities on behalf of a group of black parents in 1849 to force the release of tax monies to support black schools.[55]

Securing antisegregation legislation, however, proved to be much more difficult than enacting legislation prohibiting discrimination in public accommodations. The mixing of children aroused white fears of racial amalgamation. Hence, many Ohio legislators, particularly Democrats from the state's racially conservative southern counties, drew the line with school desegregation and narrowly defeated pro- posed antisegregation legislation in both 1884 and 1885. One house Democrat had attempted to persuade his colleagues to support the antisegregation legislation in 1885, arguing that if they opposed it, they would lose crucial black support that might cost them the 1885 election. Though his efforts secured enough Democratic votes to gain passage in the house, the measure failed in the senate.[56]

Competition for the black vote during the 1885 Ohio gubernato- rial election was particularly fierce. Although Democratic incumbent Hoadly sought black support based upon the enactment of the public accommodations antidiscrimination legislation of 1884, the Republi- can U.S. Supreme Court's adverse decision in the *Civil Rights Cases* in 1883, and his extensive granting of patronage to black office seekers, the Republicans countered by raising the issue of the oppression of southern blacks by the Democratic Party. The Republican candidate, Joseph Foraker, won the closely contested election, and the Republi- cans recaptured both houses of the state legislature. Commenting on the importance of the black vote to his success, Foraker noted that "[t]he Negro vote was so large that it was not only an important but an essential factor in our consideration. It would not be possible for the Republican party to carry the state if that vote should be arrayed against us." Accordingly, in his inaugural address, Governor Foraker

55 For Ohio efforts to secure antisegregation legislation, see Erickson, "The Color Line in Ohio Public Schools," pp. 339–53; Montgomery, "Racial History of the Cincinnati and Suburban Public Schools," p. 61 (1983), Ohio Historical Society; Kousser, "'The Onward March of Right Principles,'" p. 198. For 1878 legislation, see Williams and Ryan, *Schools in Transition*, p. 24. For Hoadly, see Gerber, *Black Ohio and the Color Line*, pp. 232–3; *State v. City of Cincinnati*, 19 Ohio 178 (1850).

56 Grossman, *The Democratic Party and the Negro*, pp. 87–8; Mason, "The Policy of Seg- regation," pp. 18–20; Washington, "The Black Struggle for Desegregated Quality Education," pp. 45–7; Montgomery, "Racial History of the Cincinnati and Suburban Public Schools," p. 74 (1983), Ohio Historical Society; Gerber, *Black Ohio and the Color Line*, p. 240.

urged an end to the harsh Black Laws, including the law permitting
school segregation. A black Republican legislator from Cleveland, Jere
Brown, explained the importance of the repeal legislation to Ohio's
black community. "Defeat this bill," he counseled his legislative colleagues, "and the wrath of the colored voters will bury you beneath
their ballots." Such sentiment seemed unfounded given that only 1 in
40 Ohioans was an African American. The narrow electoral margins in
Ohio's state elections during the 1880s, however, gave the black vote
particular importance.[57]

Although antisegregation legislation failed in 1886, in 1887 the long
struggle against school segregation came to fruition as the Ohio state
legislature, with broad Republican and some Democratic support, repealed earlier legislation that permitted segregated schools and prohibited miscegenation. Concern for the black vote was undeniably a
critical factor in the enactment of this legislation.[58]

The black vote played an important role in the enactment of antisegregation legislation in other states as well. Black votes were critical to
Republican electoral victories in Pennsylvania throughout the 1870s.
For example, Republican Governor John Hartranft won reelection in
1875 by about 12,000 votes; the black Republican vote in Philadelphia
that year was estimated at 15,000. Republicans overwhelmingly supported the 1881 antisegregation legislation – 99 of the 102 Republican
house members supported the measure – but 8 of the 59 Democrats
in the house voted in favor of the legislation as well. Some Democrats
emphasized that the antisegregation legislation would have little impact on patterns of racial mixing and hence urged support for the
measure so as not to alienate black voters. One year earlier, in 1880,
Benjamin Chew, a black barber whose four children were required to
walk a long distance past white schools to attend a black school, had
filed suit challenging school segregation in Philadelphia. The local
Court of Common Pleas ordered the school board to show cause why
it should not grant relief to Chew. In response, the Democratic *Record*
supported Chew, arguing that there were too few black children in
Philadelphia to cause any problems.[59]

---

[57] For the 1885 election, see Grossman, *The Democratic Party and the Negro*, pp. 91–2; for
the Foraker quote, see Dabney, *Cincinnati's Colored Citizens*, p. 84; for the Brown quote,
see J. A. Brown, "The Black Laws!", p. 27 (1886), in Daniel A. P. Murray Collection,
Ohio Historical Society.

[58] Squibb, "Roads to *Plessy*," pp. 173–5; McGinnis, *The Education of Negroes in Ohio*, pp. 30–
4, 57–63.

[59] For the Pennsylvania elections, see Evans, *Pennsylvania Politics*, p. 198–9; Kousser,
"'The Onward March of Right Principles,'" p. 198. For the Chew litigation (the final
results of which are unknown), see Lane, *William Dorsey's Philadelphia*, p. 154; for the
1887 legislation, see Grossman, *The Democratic Party and the Negro*, p. 75.

But vigorous competition between Democrats and Republicans for the black vote did not aid antisegregation efforts in all northern states. In Indiana, for example, gubernatorial elections were close throughout the 1870s and 1880s – with margins consistently less than 2 percent – and yet, because of the state's particularly intense anti-black feeling, the state legislature consistently refused to enact anti-segregation legislation. Republican loss of control of the state senate beginning in the mid-1870s contributed to the dim prospects of anti-segregation legislation in the Hoosier state.[60]

During the 1890s, the close electoral competition in many northern states between Democrats and Republicans came to an end as many northern states entered an era of Republican ascendancy that would last until the 1930s. The absence of closely contested elections and a declining commitment to black rights in the Republican Party combined to weaken black political influence. As legal scholar Michael Klarman has noted, the hegemony of northern Republicans during the 1890s "eliminated the party's need to bid for the votes of northern blacks, which in earlier decades had sometimes been the deciding factor in closely fought elections." In Illinois, for example, neither political party captured more than 51 percent of the statewide vote in any presidential contest between 1876 and 1892, but during the 1890s Republicans dominated Illinois state politics. This political shift harmed black interests. The town of Cairo, in southern Illinois, had been remarkably favorable toward black rights during the quarter century following the Civil War, as both parties competed for black electoral support. But when Republicans came to dominate the city's politics during the late 1890s, they turned on their former allies. In the late nineteenth and early twentieth centuries, racial discrimination and segregation in Cairo significantly increased and black voters were effectively disenfranchised. This change in Republican attitudes toward blacks did not pass unnoticed. In 1896, *The Nation* lamented the fact that for the first time in party history, Republican state nominating conventions, with only one exception, "omitted all reference" to the protection of black rights, a topic that had been a staple of Republican politics since 1856.[61]

Another factor contributing to the enactment of northern antiseg-regation legislation during the nineteenth century was the inefficiency

---

[60] Grossman, *The Democratic Party and the Negro*, p. 100; Thornbrough, *The Negro in Indiana*, pp. 260–1; Kousser, "'The Onward March of Right Principles,'" pp. 199–200.

[61] For the Klarman quote, see Klarman, *From Jim Crow to Civil Rights*, p. 15; for Cairo, see Wheeler, "Together in Egypt," pp. 122–7; for the *Nation* quote, see "One Issue Disposed Of," *The Nation* 62 (May 21, 1896), p. 392.

of dual schools. Most northern communities, particularly outside of urban areas, had very few black children during the postbellum era. As a result, in many northern school districts, maintaining racially separate schools proved to be extraordinarily burdensome. As a result, legislators in states like Pennsylvania that *required* racially separate schools supported antisegregation legislation in order to relieve school districts with few black children of the burden of operating separate schools. These economic concerns were exacerbated during and after the Panic of 1873, which further strapped local school authorities.

In fact, in several northern states, many school districts had already abolished segregated schools even before the enactment of state antisegregation legislation. The Pittsburgh Board of Education, for example, voted in 1874 to forward a bill to the state legislature repealing the 1854 legislation that required segregated schools because of the cost of maintaining the city's one black school. When the legislature failed to act, the Pittsburgh school board simply closed its black school and reassigned those children to white schools in violation of the state's segregation law. It would be another seven years before the Pennsylvania state legislature banned school segregation throughout the state.[62]

During the fifteen years prior to the enactment of New Jersey's 1881 antisegregation legislation, several school districts in northern New Jersey abandoned school segregation. In most of these school districts, there were few black schoolchildren and the continued operation of a dual school system proved both expensive and inefficient. By the time New Jersey enacted its antisegregation legislation in 1881, about half of New Jersey's segregated schools in the state's northern counties had been eliminated.[63]

In Ohio, several communities including Columbus had already desegregated their schools prior to the enactment of the 1887 antisegregation legislation in part because of the cost of dual schools. Although Cincinnati did not close its separate black schools until after 1887, one observer estimated in 1882 that Cincinnati could save 90 percent of the annual $50,000 cost of its separate black schools if they were merged with the city's white schools. Earlier, in 1863, when the Ohio General Assembly had reenacted legislation *requiring* school systems to provide separate black schools when there were a certain number of black children in the district, many Clevelanders complained of the economic burden of establishing separate black schools. The *Cleveland Leader*, for example, argued that "[t]o establish separate schools

<hr />

[62] Proctor, "Racial Discrimination Against Black Teachers," pp. 33–4; Glasco, "Double Burden," p. 73.

[63] Wright, *Education of Negroes*, pp. 154–7; Fishel, "The North and the Negro," pp. 199–201.

for colored children will be to entail upon taxpayers the additional expense of new school buildings and new teachers."[64]

In the west, the city of San Francisco decided to end school segregation in 1875, one year after prevailing in a legal challenge to school segregation and five years before the state legislature banned school segregation because of the cost of maintaining a separate black school for the city's few black children. Oakland had already integrated its schools in 1872 because the dearth of black children in the city – eight – rendered the continued operation of a separate school economically infeasible. Similarly, several communities in Oregon and Montana during the postbellum era abandoned school segregation because of the cost of maintaining a separate black school.[65]

The fact that blacks comprised only a fraction of the northern population throughout the nineteenth century also contributed to the enactment of antisegregation legislation. Maine, New Hampshire, and Vermont, the three New England states that generally admitted black children to public school by custom on a nondiscriminatory basis by the end of the antebellum era, had a black population of only 0.2 percent at the onset of the Civil War, and Massachusetts, the first state to abolish school segregation by statute in 1855, had a black population at the time of less than 1 percent. Rhode Island and Connecticut, which enacted antisegregation legislation during the late 1860s, had black populations at the time of about 2 percent. Moreover, the northern migration of emancipated slaves following the end of the Civil War left New England largely unaffected; the black percentage of the total population declined in Connecticut and remained essentially stable in Rhode Island during the 1860s.[66]

Those midwestern states that abolished school segregation during the late 1860s or that appear to have never operated segregated schools had the fewest blacks and the lowest percentage of the black population in the region at the time: Wisconsin (0.2 percent), Minnesota (0.2 percent), Iowa (0.5 percent), and Michigan (1 percent). In each of these states, the black percentage of the total population, already

---

[64] For desegregation efforts in Ohio, see Gerber, "Education, Expediency, and Ideology," p. 8; Squibb, "Roads to *Plessy*," p. 179; Kessen, "Segregation in Cincinnati," p. 134; Gerber, *Black Ohio and the Color Line*, p. 195; Corr, "Black Politics and Education in Cincinnati," p. 103. For the quote from the *Cleveland Leader*, see Goliber, "Cuyahoga Blacks," p. 125.

[65] For desegregation in California, see *Ward v. Flood*, 48 Cal. 36 (1874); Tyack, *The One Best System*, p. 115; Hendrick, *The Education of Non-Whites*, pp. 21–4. For desegregation in Montana and Oregon, see Taylor, *The Forging of a Black Community*, p. 21; Johnson, *The Development of State Legislation*, pp. 137–8; McLagan, *A Peculiar Paradise*, pp. 72–4, 86.

[66] U.S. Bureau of the Census, 1860 and 1870.

minuscule, *declined* between 1870 and 1890. On the other hand, two of the northern states in which blacks comprised the largest percentage of the total population in 1870 – New Jersey (3.4 percent) and Ohio (2.4 percent) – were two of the last two northern states to enact antisegregation legislation during the nineteenth century. Between 1870 and 1890, the black percentage of the total population in most northern states remained both low and stable, factors that contributed to white tolerance of legislation prohibiting racial segregation in the public schools. Significantly, when the black percentage of the total population increased in many northern states during the 1890s in response to black migration, white resistance to racial mixing in the public schools noticeably hardened in many communities.[67]

Moreover, many northern legislators supported antisegregation bills recognizing that the legislation would have little effect on patterns of racial segregation. Many legislators understood that laws prohibiting school segregation would grant those school districts that preferred to eliminate dual schools the right to do so by removing statutory mandates requiring segregation but would, in all likelihood, allow those districts that favored the retention of separate schools to keep them. Many northern whites argued that blacks were far more interested in eliminating the stigma of legally mandated segregation than they were in actually attending white schools. For example, one supporter of antisegregation legislation in North Providence, Rhode Island, argued that "[black parents] do not contemplate any inconsiderate or sudden change.... [V]ery many of the children now attending the colored schools, will, because residing in their vicinity, continue to go to the same, if made equal in all respects to others."[68] In fact, as we shall see, following the enactment of antisegregation legislation, many northern blacks favored the retention of racially separate schools.

Moreover, most of the antisegregation statutes imposed no sanction on a school district that continued to segregate its students in violation of the state mandate, leaving enforcement to the vagaries of private litigation. A few antisegregation statutes did provide for fines for school officers who persisted in maintaining segregated schools (as in Illinois and Kansas) or the withholding of educational monies that retained segregated schools (Minnesota), but there is scant evidence that these enforcement provisions were ever utilized. The weak enforcement provisions of the antisegregation legislation undermined compliance in some states and probably reflected a lack of commitment on the part

[67] U.S. Bureau of the Census, 1870, 1890, and 1900. In 1870, blacks in Kansas comprised a larger percentage of the total population (4.7 percent), than either New Jersey or Ohio.

[68] Quoted in Ment, "Racial Segregation in the Public Schools," p. 89.

of many northern legislators to the elimination of school segregation as well as respect for the decentralized nature of nineteenth-century public education. In a similar fashion, as noted earlier, laws prohibiting racial discrimination in public accommodations, the other significant civil rights legislative accomplishment of the late nineteenth century, were also severely undermined by minimal penalties and weak enforcement.[69]

The Effect of Northern Antisegregation Legislation

The results of this nineteenth-century antisegregation legislation widely varied. In communities where school segregation was already on the decline, the legislation helped accelerate the trend toward racial mixing. For example, by the early 1870s, integrated school systems were the norm in New England. In Rhode Island, most of the remaining black schools in the state were closed within a year of the 1866 antisegregation legislation, although Providence retained one all-black school, the Meeting Street School, until 1887. By the mid-1870s, the last remaining black school in Connecticut had closed, even though local school authorities in New Haven had urged black parents to accept segregation after the enactment of that state's antisegregation legislation. Schools in Massachusetts generally operated on a nondiscriminatory basis after enactment of the 1855 statute prohibiting school segregation, although Boston established a "colored school" in the latter years of the nineteenth century to serve the growing black population in the city's South End and Lower Roxbury. Contributing to the maintenance of integrated schools in New England was the small size of the region's black population. Between 1870 and 1900, the black percentage of the total population declined in every New England state except Massachusetts.[70]

In other northern communities with a small black population and a general commitment to school integration, desegregated schools remained the norm for the last three decades of the nineteenth

---

[69] Grossman, *The Democratic Party and the Negro*, pp. 105–6; Buni, *Robert L. Vann*, pp. 81–2; Fishel, "The North and the Negro," pp. 378–82.

[70] For Rhode Island, see Ment, "Racial Segregation in the Public Schools," pp. 113–14. Racially gerrymandered school district lines did, however, contribute to the continuation of two black schools in Providence, and evening school classes at Providence's Meeting Street School separated students into racially homogeneous classrooms. Perlmann, *Ethnic Differences*, p. 182. For Connecticut, see Ment, "Racial Segregation in the Public Schools," pp. 128–9; Warner, *New Haven Negroes*, pp. 118–20. For Massachusetts, see Allen, "Segregation and Desegregation," p. 109; Fishel, "The North and the Negro," pp. 316–17. For population data, see U.S. Bureau of Census, 1870 and 1900.

century. In New York, most upstate and Hudson River communities, including Albany, Buffalo, Geneva, Newburgh, Poughkeepsie, Schenectady, and Troy, moved to desegregate their schools either prior to or immediately following the enactment of the 1873 antisegregation legislation. Similarly, in the upper midwestern states of Michigan, Wisconsin, and Minnesota, school segregation remained minimal with a few exceptions. In Wisconsin, which never enacted antisegregation legislation, the superintendent of public instruction reported in 1868 that "I do not know of a separate school for [black children] – no one from which they are excluded anywhere in this state." In Minnesota, the 1869 antisegregation legislation led to the closure of the only black school in the state within a couple of years. Compliance was less complete in Michigan; in 1880, Michigan still had eighteen black schools and Ypsilanti would retain segregated schools until well into the twentieth century.[71]

But some northern communities resisted desegregation despite the enactment of antisegregation legislation. Particularly in areas contiguous with southern states where segregationist sentiment remained strong and black enrollments were significant, many local school boards retained separate schools in open violation of the new antisegregation laws.

In Philadelphia, for example, which was home to one of the largest black populations in the North, some black children entered the city's white schools in the wake of the new legislation, but many who presented themselves for enrollment in the white schools were turned away. White school authorities in Philadelphia were clearly unsympathetic to the new antisegregation legislation. Within days of the enactment of the 1881 law, members of the Philadelphia Board of Education went to considerable lengths to allay white concerns that the legislation would trigger an influx of black children into white schools. Board Secretary Henry J. Halliwell explained that the school board had endorsed the new state statute "cause we had to, but it won't make no difference cause we all know that Negroes are lazy and shiftless and avoid hard work.... [T]hat will help keep them out of the schools." Another board member suggested that only light-skinned mulatto children would attend racially mixed schools: "the colored children who go into the regular schools are generally about as white as the other pupils and generally much better dressed." Another argued that few black children would be able to keep pace in white schools: "I think

---

[71] For New York, see Mabee, *Black Education in New York State*, pp. 202–6; Ment, "Racial Segregation in the Public Schools," p. 2; for the Wisconsin quote, See Fishel, "The North and the Negro," pp. 238, n. 124; for Minnesota, see ibid., p. 240; for Michigan, see Katzman, *Before the Ghetto*, p. 90.

it very doubtful if there are many colored children who can submit to the course of studies and discipline of the regular public schools. For one thing, they have not the same mental oversight at home and by nature they are not partial to restraint." Philadelphia would continue to maintain officially designated colored schools and urge the establishment of additional such schools. W. E. B. Du Bois described the city's schools in his landmark 1899 study of Philadelphia's black population: "[The 1881] enactment was for some time evaded, and even now some discrimination is practiced quietly in the matter of admission and transfers. There are also schools still attended solely by Negro pupils and taught by Negro teachers, although, of course, the children are at liberty to go elsewhere if they choose." Some smaller Pennsylvania communities, such as Lancaster, also maintained segregated schools in violation of state law.[72]

Similarly, although New Jersey's antisegregation legislation accelerated the trend toward integrated schools in the state's northern and central counties where school segregation was already in decline, communities throughout southern New Jersey retained segregated schools and established new ones in defiance of the new state statute throughout the latter years of the nineteenth century. For example, Paul Robeson, in his autobiography, *Here I Stand*, described attending the segregated black school in Princeton during the first decade of the twentieth century. Even in the town of Fair Haven, where objections to the poor condition of the separate black school had triggered the 1881 legislative fight resulting in antisegregation legislation, schools remained segregated. One month after enactment of the antisegregation legislation, Fair Haven built a new separate school for black children to the satisfaction of the local black community. School segregation would continue in Fair Haven until well into the twentieth century.[73]

---

[72] For Philadelphia, see Silcox, "A Comparative Study in School Desegregation," pp. 231–2; Mohraz, *The Separate Problem*, pp. 86–7; Lane, *William Dorsey's Philadelphia*, p. 155. For the Halliwell quote, see Silcox, "A Comparative Study in School Desegregation," p. 231; for board member quotes, see ibid., p. 230; for the Du Bois quote, see Du Bois, *The Philadelphia Negro*, p. 89; for Lancaster, see Hopkins, "Door to Opportunity," p. 147.

[73] For communities that desegregated, see Wright, *The Education of Negroes*, pp. 171–2, 175–6, 198 (New Brunswick, Morristown); Conner, "A Comparative Study of Black and White," pp. 287–9 (New Brunswick, 1881); Crew, *Black Life in Secondary Cities*, p. 135 (Rahway, 1882; Elizabeth, early 1880s); Fishel, "The North and the Negro," p. 200 (Englewood, 1884).

For communities that retained separate schools, see Wright, *The Education of Negroes*, pp. 160–1; 169–71, 175–6, 198 (Salem County, Long Branch, Fair Haven); Crew, *Black Life in Secondary Cities*, pp. 129–31 (Camden); Robeson, *Here I Stand*, p. 18 (Princeton); "The Color Line in Schools," *New York Times*, Nov. 13, 1883, p. 1 (Burlington). For the discussion of Fair Haven, see "The Fair Haven School,"

In New York, upstate school districts moved quickly after enactment of antisegregation legislation to integrate their schools, but the downstate communities of Amityville, Flushing, Jamaica, Rosyln, and Stapleton, each with a relatively sizable black population, refused to allow black children to attend white schools. Moreover, in Brooklyn, local school authorities retained their black schools, although a few white schools in Brooklyn did admit black children.[74]

Opponents of school integration in New York argued that the 1873 statute that prohibited the denial to any school child of "full and equal enjoyment" of school facilities did not require racially mixed schools, only equal educational benefits that could be provided in racially separate schools. Moreover, because the 1873 legislation had not *explicitly* repealed the 1864 legislative reauthorization of racially separate schools, segregationists argued that school segregation remained lawful so long as equal school privileges were provided in black and white schools.

These arguments appeared specious. Both opponents and supporters of the 1873 legislation agreed at the time that the law would ban school segregation. In fact, several Democratic members of the legislature argued that the law would require racially mixed schools and hence lead to "amalgamation" of the races. African-American supporters of the legislation widely understood that the law forbade school segregation. Nevertheless, some local school officials and Democratic judges called upon to interpret the language of the statute took the opposing view.[75]

For example, in 1875, the principal of a white school in Brooklyn refused to allow a black child who lived nearby to enroll, which triggered litigation. A local trial judge ruled that the 1873 antisegregation law merely forbade "discrimination against" black children, not "discrimination between" black and white children. The judge concluded that requiring black children to attend a separate black school constituted no discrimination "against" them because, the court argued, it might be "highly conducive to the welfare" of black children to attend a separate school.[76]

During the early 1880s, another black parent brought a legal challenge to the exclusion of his child from a white school in Brooklyn.

Monmouth Democrat (Freehold, New Jersey), May 5, 1881, p. 2; "The Fair Haven School Meeting," *Monmouth Democrat* (Freehold, New Jersey), Apr. 7, 1881, p. 2; "Fair Haven School Troubles," *New York Times*, Apr. 6, 1881, p. 5.

[74] Mabee, *Black Education in New York State*, pp. 206–7; Ment, "Racial Segregation in the Public Schools," pp. 161–3.

[75] Mabee, *Black Education in New York State*, pp. 201–7; *King v. Gallagher*, 93 N.Y. 438 (1883); "Civil Rights in Public Schools," *Brooklyn Daily Times*, Sept. 13, 1875.

[76] "Civil Rights in Public Schools," *Brooklyn Daily Times*, Sept. 13, 1875; Mabee, *Black Education in New York State*, p. 208.

Again, a local trial judge upheld the exclusion on the grounds that the 1873 statute did not bar segregation. This time, however, an appeal was taken to the New York Court of Appeals, the state's highest court. In a 3–2 decision, the three Democratic judges rejected the challenge to segregation, ruling instead that the statute guaranteed only "equal facilities and advantages for the colored race," not racially mixed schools. The two Republican judges dissented.[77]

Despite the New York Court of Appeals decision, the Brooklyn school board eventually adopted a plan requiring all principals to accept black children on the same basis as whites but retaining separate black schools for those blacks who preferred such schools. By the mid-1890s, the overwhelming majority of black children in Brooklyn were attending integrated schools.[78]

The Jamaica community in Queens was one of the most resistant to racial mixing in the entire state. During the 1890s, seventy-five black children were educated in a one-room schoolhouse in Jamaica with a single teacher. A group of black parents challenged this segregation, utilizing both a school boycott and litigation. In response, school officials threatened to incarcerate those parents who withheld their children from school, but the boycotted persisted. The New York Court of Appeals ultimately sustained this school segregation in Jamaica, but the controversy led to additional antisegregation legislation as supporters of racial mixing turned to the New York General Assembly for a legislative solution. In 1900, with the support of Governor Theodore Roosevelt, the General Assembly enacted legislation that provided that "No person shall be refused admission into or be excluded from any public school in the state of New York on account of race or color." Thereafter, all remaining separate black schools in Queens were closed. The new law, however, contained an ambiguity: it expressly repealed an earlier education law that had permitted separate black schools in towns and cities, but it did not repeal an earlier law that permitted separate black schools in certain rural school districts. Three rural school districts – Rosyln, Hillburn, and Goshen – would thereafter contend that they had a right to retain segregated schools. This legislative loophole would not be closed until the late 1930s.[79]

In the midwestern states of Ohio and Illinois, the results of the antisegregation legislation were mixed. In the wake of Ohio's

---

[77] *King v. Gallagher*, 93 N.Y. 438 (1883).

[78] Ment, "Racial Segregation in the Public Schools," pp. 181–6; Fishel, "The North and the Negro," pp. 333–6.

[79] For Jamaica desegregation, see Waller, "Holding Back the Dawn," pp. 119–20; *Cisco v. School Board of the Borough of Queens*, 161 N.Y. 598 (1900). For legislation, see Mabee, *Black Education in New York State*, pp. 243, 245. For closure of Queens schools, see Ment, "Racial Segregation in the Public Schools," p. 199. For legislative loophole, see Mabee, *Black Education in New York State*, pp. 243, 245.

antisegregation legislation, many school districts abolished their segregated schools. Many others, however, particularly in the southern
counties of the state, simply refused to comply with the new law. A
few communities, such as Chillicothe and Xenia, utilized racially gerrymandered attendance zones to preserve racial separation. Other
Ohio communities opened a few white schools to black students but
retained black schools as well. Cincinnati, home to the state's largest
black population and strong black opposition to the antisegregation
legislation, closed most but not all of its black schools. A Cincinnati
black educator commented during the early twentieth century about
the 1887 antisegregation legislation: "Because of the success of the
bill, [most blacks] thought race prejudice was at an end. But race prejudice cannot be superficially cured." An early twentieth-century study
of Ohio race relations aptly noted that "legal provisions intended to
establish racial equality are either observed or ignored according as
the white element in the several communities may determine." Efforts
to repeal the Ohio antisegregation legislation persisted for the next
few years after its enactment.[80]

School segregation also remained common in parts of Illinois following the enactment of antisegregation legislation. School districts
in the northern section of the state had generally abolished their segregated schools by 1880. The situation was quite different, however,
in the state's southern counties, as school districts in twenty-six southern Illinois counties maintained separate, undistricted black schools.
Most of these school districts tended to have significant black populations. For example, in Illinois's three most southern counties – Pulaski,
Massac, and Alexander – African Americans comprised 30 percent of
the population by 1900, probably the highest percentage in the North.

---

[80] Following the legislative repeal of the Ohio statute, schools in Bellefontaine, Cir-
cleville, Crestline, Dayton, Findlay, Marietta, Marion, Piqua, Rendville, Springfield, Steubenville, Troy, and Wooster were desegregated. Squibb, "Roads to *Plessy*,"
pp. 173, 179; McGinnis, *The Education of Negroes in Ohio*, p. 47. Moreover, the legislation strengthened recently integrated schools in Athens, Lancaster, Mt. Vernon,
Marysville, and Upper Sandusky. Squibb, "Roads to *Plessy*," p. 179. But schools in
Avondale, Bainbridge, Chillicothe, Gallipolis, Hillsboro, Lockland, New Richmond,
Oxford, Wilmington, Xenia, and Yellow Springs remained segregated. Gerber, *Black
Ohio and the Color Line*, p. 266; Squibb, "Roads to *Plessy*," p. 180; Fishel, "The North
and the Negro," pp. 323–4; Quillin, *The Color Line in Ohio*, pp. 94, n. 11, 95. For
Chillicothe and Xenia, see Gerber, *The Color Line in Ohio*, pp. 265–6 (Chillicothe);
Quillin, *The Color Line in Ohio*, p. 96 (Xenia); David, *Social Effect of School Segregation*,
pp. 14–15, 23–4 (Xenia). For Cincinnati, see Washington, "The Black Struggle for
Desegregated Quality Education," p. 50. For the Cincinnati quote, see Porter, "The
Problem of Negro Education," p. 131; for the second quote, see Quillin, *The Color Line
in Ohio*, p. 125. For repeal efforts, see Fishel, "The North and the Negro," pp. 322–3;
Brown, "The History of the Negro," pp. 67–8.

These three counties would remain among the most resistant to school integration until the 1950s.[81]

In the West, compliance with California's 1880 antisegregation law was also not complete. For example, in Sacramento, many black elementary schoolchildren continued to attend a segregated school for the remainder of the century. In Visalia, located in California's cental valley, the school board retained its colored school and continued to send all black children to it. A black parent in Visalia whose child was denied admission to a white school in 1888 filed suit, challenging the violation of California's antisegregation law. The offending school administrator testified: "I refused to admit [the black child] to the [white] public school because he was colored, and because this public colored school was established by the board of education, who had instructed me to send the colored children to that colored school. These were my only reasons for refusing to admit him to the [white] public school." A lower court upheld this action, but the California Supreme Court struck it down as inconsistent with the 1880 antisegregation legislation.[82]

Using Litigation to Enforce Antisegregation Legislation

Given the mixed record of compliance with these state antisegregation statutes, supporters of racially mixed schools turned to the courts to enforce the new legal mandate against racial separation. What is striking about this litigation is the strong enforcement record of northern state courts. Every state supreme court, with the exception of the New York Court of Appeals (the highest court in that state), and numerous lower courts, when called upon to enforce state antisegregation legislation, did so. In part, this success was due to the significant presence of Republican judges on state appellate courts. The one exception to this enforcement record, the New York Court of Appeals, was dominated by Democratic judges, with Republican judges bitterly dissenting from

---

[81] For Illinois, see Fishel, "The North and the Negro," p. 319; Hamblin, "Drive the Last Nail," pp. 85–8. By 1874, of the sixty-seven Illinois counties that had a black population, ten provided only segregated schools, forty-one provided only integrated schools, and sixteen provided both integrated and segregated schools. Fishel, "The North and the Negro," p. 217, n. 32; Tyack, *The One Best System*, pp. 115–16. Carlson, "The Black Community in the Rural North," p. v. One southern Illinois school superintendent suggested in 1874 the provision of black education in Illinois through the establishment of "asylums . . . the same as for the blind and other unfortunates." Quoted in Fishel, "The North and the Negro," p. 220, n. 43.

[82] For California, see Hendrick, *The Education of Non-Whites*, p. 78. For the quote, see *Wysinger v. Crookshank*, 82 Cal. 588 (1890).

their colleagues' refusal to enforce that state's 1873 antisegregation legislation.[83]

One could easily infer from this powerful legal attack on school segregation – the enactment of antisegregation legislation throughout the North and the strong enforcement record of northern state supreme courts – that government-mandated racial separation in northern public education ended during the nineteenth century. Yet despite these legislative and litigation victories, school segregation, as we have seen, persisted in much of the North. Why did the litigation seeking to enforce the antisegregation legislation fail to end patterns of school segregation despite its remarkable success rate?

First of all, African Americans filed relatively few lawsuits seeking to enforce the antisegregation legislation until well into the twentieth century. For example, in Pennsylvania and New Jersey, two states where school segregation persisted in many communities in open violation of state law, only two reported decisions – one in each state – reflect litigation filed by African Americans to enforce the state antisegregation legislation during the last two decades of the nineteenth century. Although blacks used the courts more extensively in other northern states, particularly Illinois and Ohio, the overall level of litigation enforcing antisegregation legislation was still quite limited.[84]

The reasons for the dearth of litigation challenging violations of the state antisegregation legislation are several. First, litigation, which frequently required appeals to more sympathetic appellate courts, was

---

[83] For courts that enforced antisegregation legislation, see *Workman v. Board of Education*, 18 Mich. 400 (1869); *Kaine v. Commonwealth ex rel. Manaway*, 101 Pa. 490 (1882); *People ex rel. Longress v. Board of Education of Quincy*, 101 Ill. 308 (1882); *State ex rel. Pierce v. Union District School Trustees*, 46 N.J.L. 76 (1884); *Board of Education of Oxford v. State ex rel. Gibson*, 45 Ohio St. 555 (1888); *People ex rel. Peair v. Board of Education*, 127 Ill. 613 (1889); *Wysinger v. Crookshank*, 82 Cal. 588 (1890); *People ex rel. Bibb v. Mayor*, 179 Ill. 615 (1899); *People ex rel. Bibb v. Mayor*, 193 Ill. 309 (1901); *People ex rel. Bibb v. Mayor*, 209 Ill. 461 (1904); *People ex rel. Bibb v. Mayor*, 221 Ill. 275 (1906); *People ex rel. Bibb v. Mayor*, 233 Ill. 542 (1908). For the two New York Court of Appeals decisions, see *King v. Gallagher*, 93 N.Y. 438 (1883), and *Cisco v. School Board of the Borough of Queens*, 161 N.Y. 598 (1900). See generally Kousser, *Dead End*.

[84] In New Jersey, the first lawsuit came shortly after the enactment of the 1881 antisegregation legislation. In that case, the New Jersey Supreme Court held that in accord with the new legislation, a black child could not be excluded from a white school that was the nearest to his residence. *State v. Union District School Trustees*, 46 N.J.L. 76 (1884); "Colored Children in the Public Schools," 6 *New Jersey Law Journal* 286 (1883). A second lawsuit was filed in the early twentieth century. *Stockton v. Board of Education*, 72 *New Jersey Law Journal* 80 (1905). In Pennsylvania, black parents apparently filed only one legal challenge. *Kaine v. Commonwealth*, 101 Pa. 490 (1882). A few blacks did agitate against segregated schools – as in Chester and Uniontown during the 1890s – but no additional legal challenges were apparently filed. Fishel, "The North and the Negro," p. 319.

expensive and beyond the means of many black parents. Although in some instances fund-raising efforts assisted black plaintiffs, many potential litigants could not afford to file suit or take a case to an appellate court. Few organizations financially able and institutionally committed to challenging school segregation, such as the NAACP, existed in the nineteenth-century North to spearhead a litigation campaign to enforce the antisegregation laws.[85]

Second, few African Americans practiced law in the North until the twentieth century, which exacerbated the difficulty of bringing litigation. For example, Pennsylvania and New Jersey – two of the northern states with the largest black populations during the nineteenth century – had only four and three black attorneys, respectively, in 1890. In fact, black attorneys filed very few lawsuits during the nineteenth century challenging school segregation. Although prominent white lawyers did sometimes represent black plaintiffs seeking enforcement of antisegregation legislation, and although on a few occasions state attorneys general interceded on behalf of black litigants, the dearth of black lawyers likely contributed to the lack of enforcement efforts.[86]

Third, many African Americans favored the retention of segregated schools and hence expressed no interest in enforcing the newly enacted antisegregation legislation. Blacks in many northern communities, including Brooklyn, New York City, Camden, New Brunswick, Trenton, Philadelphia, Cincinnati, and Dayton, petitioned local school authorities for the retention of separate black schools and opposed efforts to procure integrated schools.[87]

For many African Americans, fears of mistreatment of black children in racially mixed schools by white teachers and classmates, common in the antebellum era, remained widespread. An 1865 school committee

[85] See, for example, Kousser, *Dead End*, p. 50, n. 70 (no appeal in an Ohio case because of lack of funds).

[86] For population data, see U.S. Bureau of Census, 1870, 1880, 1890, 1900. In New Jersey and Pennsylvania, at no time during the pre-*Brown* era did black lawyers account for more than one-half of 1 percent of the bar. Several distinguished white lawyers did represent black litigants in desegregation litigation, including former Illinois Governor and United States Senator John Palmer of Illinois, Illinois state senator John Brenholdt, and former Michigan Governor Austin Bair.

[87] Meier and Rudwick, "Early Boycotts of Segregated Schools: The Case of Springfield," pp. 291–2 (Springfield, Ohio); Kessen, "Segregation in Cincinnati," p. 135 (Cincinnati); Gerber, "Education, Expediency, and Ideology," p. 11, 22; (Dayton); Mohraz, *The Separate Problem*, p. 87 (Philadelphia); Wright, *The Education of Negroes*, pp. 170–2 (Brown's Point, Matawan, and Fair Haven, New Jersey); Crew, *Black Life in Secondary Cities*, pp. 130–1 (Camden, New Jersey); Conner, "A Comparative Study of Black and White," pp. 284, 287 (New Brunswick, New Jersey); "Separate Schools," *Cleveland Gazette*, Mar. 15, 1890, p. 2 (Ohio); "Mixed Schools," *Cleveland Gazette*, Mar. 15, 1890, p. 2 (Ohio).

report in Providence reported: "It is deeply to be regretted that one of the most popular amusements for the young at the present day, consists in caricaturing and holding up to ridicule, the peculiarities and eccentricities of a long-neglected and downtrodden race. Our children are taught to be merry and indulge in hilarity over the weaknesses and follies of a people that have the strongest claim for sympathy." In New York City, an 1871 school board report found that "[i]n some parts of the city these [black] children have been greatly annoyed, and often abused and seriously injured by the persecution of ruffian boys, who, in spite of the police, . . . waylay and assail the children on their way to and from school. This necessarily alarms many parents, and prevents a regular attendance of pupils." Such harassment led many blacks in New York City to prefer segregated schools. Similarly, those black parents who petitioned for the reopening of a black school in nearby Brooklyn in 1875 claimed that "sending our children to other Public Schools . . . [would be] placing them in conflict with troubles of aggravating circumstances, the nature of which your Honorable Board are in all probability cognizant." In Cincinnati, 700 blacks signed a petition in 1897 complaining of the mistreatment of their children in the city's racially mixed schools. The mistreatment was so severe that by 1901, after most of Cincinnati's separate black schools had been closed, only about half of the city's school-age black children still attended the public schools. An Indianapolis newspaper urged separate schools due to the harassment black children would likely receive in mixed schools: "No teacher and no law could secure them just treatment, or a fair chance of improvement [in white schools]. It would be sheer cruelty to put them there. In schools of their own they would escape such annoyances and obstructions, and deterred neither by the superiority nor enmity of the white pupils, they would have a fair opportunity to try their full powers."[88]

In addition, some African Americans worried that their children who were ill dressed because of family poverty would suffer embarrassment in racially mixed schools. One black teacher in Cincinnati explained: "Colored people, as a rule, are poor, and their children are not as well clad as the white children with whom they would be compelled to associate in mixed schools and the colored children will

---

[88] For the Providence quote, see Fishel, "The North and the Negro," p. 176; for the New York City quote, see ibid., p. 190, n. 80; for the Brooklyn quote, see Ment, "Racial Segregation in the Public Schools," p. 156; for Cincinnati, see "School Board Reappoints Superintendent Morgan," *Cincinnati Enquirer*, May 11, 1897, p. 6; "Stormy Meeting of School Board Occasioned by Petition from Colored People," *Cincinnati Enquirer*, Apr. 27, 1897, p. 5; Washington, "The Black Struggle for Desegregated Quality Education," pp. 52–4; for the Indianapolis quote, see *Indiana State Journal*, Jan. 22, 1867, quoted in Heller, "Negro Education in Indiana," p. 101.

feel they are not wanted. These things will seriously embarrass colored children – in fact, many will absent themselves entirely."[89]

Many blacks favored segregation in order to ensure that their children were taught by black teachers. In some northern cities, including Boston, Chicago, and Cleveland, a few black teachers did teach in racially mixed schools during the 1880s and 1890s, but these were exceptions and frequently involved only one or two teachers. Because most northern school districts refused to permit black teachers to teach in racially mixed schools, integration almost invariably denied black children access to black teachers.[90] Those northern blacks who favored the retention of segregated schools placed great weight on the presence of black teachers.

Many blacks complained that white teachers did not properly nurture the educational aspirations of their children. As *The Christian Recorder*, a black publication in Philadelphia, noted in 1882, one year after enactment of Pennsylvania's antisegregation legislation: "It constrains us more than ever to adhere to our motto of 'Colored teachers for colored schools'.... [W]hite teachers take no real interest in [black children's] work nor of the scholars but teach and tolerate them only in order to enable them to draw the money they receive at the end of each month." In some racially mixed schools, white teachers punished white children by making them sit next to black children.[91]

Moreover, many African Americans recognized the important role that black teachers played in the social and political fabric of the black community and feared that the loss of black teachers would strip the community of many of its natural leaders. Teaching was one of the few professions open to African Americans in the nineteenth century, and it tended to attract some of the most educated members of the community. One black teacher offered this assessment of the antisegregation legislation: "I know of no better scheme to reduce the most intelligent classes of colored people to penury and want, or to drive them from the state to become the victims of southern cruelty and barbarism."[92]

Not surprisingly, many black teachers were firm opponents of school desegregation. Black teachers in Ohio, for example, mounted a fierce campaign in opposition to the antisegregation campaign of the 1880s.

[89] "Mixed Schools," *Cleveland Gazette*, Feb. 14, 1885, p. 2.

[90] For cities that did permit black teachers, see Fishel, "The North and the Negro," pp. 343–4. For exclusion of black teachers, see ibid., p. 319; Mohraz, *The Separate Problem*, p. 87; Grossman, *The Democratic Party and the Negro*, p. 87.

[91] For quote, see Silcox, "A Comparative Study in School Desegregation," p. 293; for school punishments, see "Outrage!" *Cleveland Gazette*, Oct. 3, 1885.

[92] For the importance of black teachers, see Tyack, *The One Best System*, p. 118; for the quote, see Gerber, "Education, Expediency, and Ideology," p. 11.

Their opposition helped kill the proposed legislation until its eventual enactment in 1887. As one Ohio black teacher explained: "To mix the schools will be virtually dismissing all the colored teachers from the profession. We have many teachers who have labored hard to make themselves proficient in the art of teaching. To repeal [the segregation law] will bring upon them an unjust hardship." Ohio Governor George Hoadly, who supported antisegregation legislation, conceded in 1885 during the debate over integrated schools that the elimination of segregated schools "would result in the dismissal of some [black] teachers." Black teachers also actively opposed school integration at the local level. When the Dayton school board considered abolishing segregated schools in 1884, the opposition of black teachers helped defeat the proposal.[93]

In Indiana, the only northern state not to ban school segregation during the nineteenth century, black teachers lobbied vigorously against antisegregation legislation. After the Indiana state house voted for legislation in 1897 that would have allowed all children to attend the school closest to their home – which would have desegregated many schools – a group of black teachers in Indianapolis urged its defeat in the state senate: "If such a Bill becomes a Law, we believe that it will be detrimental to the colored people of the State; that it will deprive not only ourselves but many colored men and women of their livelihood; and that it will remove the opportunity that colored men and women now have to strive after and obtain honorable employment in our public schools." Indiana's black teachers were well aware that no black teacher taught white children in their state.[94]

Some African Americans bitterly attacked those black teachers who favored segregated schools, accusing them of being more interested in their own job security than in the education and advancement of black children. The *Cleveland Gazette*, a black newspaper edited by Harry Smith, was a consistent and strong voice against school segregation and castigated those in the black community, including black teachers, who favored the retention of segregated schools. The *Gazette* labeled such blacks "a nuisance to the community in which they live" and

---

93 For opposition of black teachers, see "The School Question," *Cleveland Gazette*, Feb. 14, 1885, p. 2; "Mixed Schools," *Cleveland Gazette*, Feb. 16, 1884, p. 2; Kessen, "Segregation in Cincinnati," p. 133; Gerber, *Black Ohio and the Color Line*, pp. 200–1; Washington, "The Black Struggle for Desegregated Quality Education," pp. 29–30; Grossman, *The Democratic Party and the Negro*, p. 88; Gerber, "Education, Expediency, and Ideology," p. 19. For the black teacher quotes, see "Mixed Schools," *Cleveland Gazette*, Feb. 14, 1885, p. 2; for the Hoadley quote, see Grossman, *The Democratic Party and the Negro*, p. 88. For Dayton, see Gerber, *Black Ohio and the Color Line*, p. 206.

94 For the quote from black teachers, see Thornbrough, *The Negro in Indiana*, p. 338; for lack of black teachers in Indiana, see Tyack, *The One Best System*, p. 116.

claimed that "Negroes who oppose mixed schools . . . should be treated as enemies to their race."[95]

But fears of black teacher loss were real. Following the enactment of antisegregation legislation in Ohio in 1887, hundreds of black teachers lost their jobs and left the state to pursue teaching opportunities in segregated southern school systems. In Springfield, Ohio, school authorities discharged *every* black teacher after enactment of the 1887 antisegregation legislation. In fact, after 1887, Cleveland, Columbus, and Youngstown were the only communities in Ohio to use black teachers in integrated classrooms. As one Ohio school superintendent explained: "Negroes gave up their teachers when they gave up separate schools."[96]

Similarly, after Pittsburgh closed its one black school in 1875, no black teacher would teach in Pittsburgh again until the 1930s. Efforts to secure a black teacher in Pittsburgh during the 1880s failed, causing many blacks in that city to support the reestablishment of segregated schools. In Philadelphia, school officials also did not permit black teachers to teach white children. An 1896 report on black teachers in Philadelphia concluded: "No matter how well qualified [black teachers] may be to teach, directors do not elect them to positions in the schools. It is taken for granted that only white teachers shall be placed in charge of white children. The colored Normal School graduates might be given a chance by appointments in the centre of some colored population, so that colored people might support their own teachers if so disposed, as they support their own ministers in their separate colored churches." When New York enacted antisegregation legislation in 1873, several black teachers in New York City either retired, were released, or moved to other school systems with a need for black teachers, such as Brooklyn, Philadelphia, or Washington, D.C. In fact, the comparisons between Brooklyn, which resisted school integration during the 1870s, and New York City, which generally did not, are striking. In Brooklyn, the number of black teachers increased by 50 percent during the 1870s, while in New York City, the number of black teachers declined by over 38 percent during the same time period. One southern state superintendent boasted in the late 1880s that Missouri, with racially segregated schools, employed "more [black

---

95 For the quote, see "Mixed Schools," *Cleveland Gazette,* Jan. 12, 1889, p. 2. For other articles, see "The School Question," *Cleveland Gazette,* Sept. 22, 1883, p. 2; "Springfield," *Cleveland Gazette,* Mar. 22, 1884, p. 1; "The Democrats Sanction the Black Laws," *Cleveland Gazette,* Apr. 12, 1884, p. 2; "Mixed Schools," *Cleveland Gazette,* Feb. 14, 1885, p. 2.

96 For teacher job loss, see Squibb, "Roads to *Plessy,*" p. 195; Meier and Rudwick, *Along the Color Line,* p. 291; Gerber, *Black Ohio and the Color Line,* p. 265. For quote, see Squibb, "Roads to *Plessy,*" p. 195.

teachers] than are employed in the public schools of all the old free states."⁹⁷

Another factor contributing to the limited efficacy of antisegregation litigation was the procedural context of this litigation. Most nineteenth-century school desegregation litigants sought a writ of mandamus compelling the appropriate school authorities to admit a black child to a white school. On most occasions, losing school boards would grant relief only to the student specifically named in the writ, since the writ technically commanded the admission of only the petitioner child and no one else. As a result, all other black children in the community were forced to file their own lawsuits. On a rare occasion, as in Detroit in 1869 and Queens in the late 1890s, African Americans filed scores of lawsuits to overcome this procedural impediment, but in most communities they simply gave up. Class action litigation to challenge racial discrimination and segregation would not be fully available to black litigants until the second half of the twentieth century. Moreover, litigants seeking a writ of mandamus were required in some states to pay a substantial deposit for courts costs, a hurdle that in some instances either delayed or prevented litigation.⁹⁸

In some northern communities, African Americans who insisted on school integration faced retaliation or even violence. Some whites used economic pressure – terminations at work or refusals to renew leases – to discourage desegregation efforts. For example, in Providence, white employers threatened pro-integration blacks with a loss of jobs during the campaign for desegregated schools in that city during the 1860s. In Oxford, Ohio, a white merchant fired all of his black employees when a black parent filed a lawsuit to end school segregation. Some white landowners in Ohio refused to renew leases to black tenants in the wake of the enactment of antisegregation legislation, forcing black families to abandon communities in danger of school integration. In several communities in Ohio and Illinois, violence accompanied efforts to integrate schools during the late nineteenth century. A contemporary

---

97 For black teachers in Pittsburgh, see Proctor, "Racial Discrimination Against Black Teachers," p. 39; Glasco, "Double Burden," p. 73; Fishel, "The North and the Negro," pp. 345–6. For the Philadelphia quote, see Du Bois, *The Philadelphia Negro*, 94–5, n. 11. Many black parents in Philadelphia preferred that their children attend separate black schools after the enactment of the 1881 antisegregation legislation because of their preference for black teachers. Ibid., p. 89. For New York City and Brooklyn, see Tyack, *The One Best System*, p. 120; Mabee, *Black Education in New York State*, pp. 209–10. For the superintendent quote, see Fishel, "The North and the Negro," pp. 342–3.

98 For Detroit and Queens, see Kousser, *Dead End*, p. 36, n. 18; for a history of class action litigation, see Yeazell, *From Medieval Group Litigation to the Modern Class Action*, pp. 220–66; for limits of the writ of mandamus and the requirement that the plaintiff pay a deposit for court costs, see "The Illinois Race War," *New York Times*, Jan. 15, 1890, p. 5.

news report described the white reaction to black efforts to desegregate the Felicity, Ohio, schools: "The white people . . . kept colored
children out of the schools by force, and beat and maltreated the colored parents, destroying their property in some cases, and established
a boycott against all colored people, to drive them out."[99]

Finally, in many instances, school authorities ignored or evaded
court orders mandating desegregation, further undermining the efficacy of litigation. In Ohio, although several African Americans successfully challenged the retention of segregated schools, some recalcitrant school boards found ways of avoiding compliance with adverse
court decisions and leaving segregated schools intact. For example,
after litigation forced the integration of the Xenia schools, the local
school board racially gerrymandered the school district to preserve
segregated schools. The school boards in New Richmond and Felicity,
Ohio, simply closed schools following a court decision requiring desegregation. Both communities also used racially segregated classrooms
to evade court-ordered desegregation.[100]

Litigation in Detroit to enforce antisegregation legislation illustrates
the difficulty that black plaintiffs faced in securing enforcement of favorable court orders. Detroit had operated segregated schools since
the 1840s. During the 1860s, antiblack animus remained strong in
Detroit, particularly among Irish immigrants who feared black competition for jobs. Irish–black conflict led to race riots in various northern cities during the Civil War; Detroit was home to the worst riot
in the Midwest, which destroyed hundreds of black homes. When
the Republican-controlled state legislature enacted antisegregation
legislation in 1867, the Democratic Detroit Board of Education refused
to comply. Detroit city attorney William Gray advised the Detroit Board
of Education that the new antisegregation law was binding on Detroit
and that the school board could no longer segregate black children.

---

99 Whites in some areas used economic pressure to force African Americans out of the
community and hence out of the public schools. Squibb, "Roads to *Plessy*," pp. 183–
4. For retribution in Ohio and Illinois, see "The White Caps Warn Us," *Cleveland
Gazette*, Jan. 12, 1889, p. 2; *Cleveland Gazette*, Dec. 8, 1888, p. 2; Gerber, *Black Ohio and
the Color Line*, p. 264; Weinberg, *A Chance to Learn*, p. 68; Quillin, *The Color Line in
Ohio*, pp. 94–5; Fishel, "The North and the Negro," pp. 217–19. For the news report
quote, see Quillin, *The Color Line in Ohio*, pp. 94–5.

100 For successful challenges in Ohio, see *Board of Education of Oxford v. State ex rel. Gibson*,
45 Ohio St. 555 (1888) (Oxford); "Mixed Schools," *Cleveland Gazette*, Apr. 6, 1889,
p. 2 (New Richmond); "Another Victory for Equal Rights," *Cleveland Gazette*, Dec.
24, 1887, p. 2 (Yellow Springs); "School Board Case," *Cleveland Gazette*, Dec. 17, 1887,
p. 2 (Xenia). For racial gerrymandering see Quillin, *The Color Line in Ohio*, pp. 96–7;
David, *Social Effect of School Segregation*, pp. 14–15; for school closures and segregated
classrooms, see "Mixed Schools," *Cleveland Gazette*, Apr. 6, 1889, p. 2; Squibb, "Roads
to *Plessy*," pp. 182–3.

The board, however, comprised primarily of Democrats unsympathetic to racial mixing, ignored Gray's recommendation and engaged in the legal fiction that because the Detroit public schools had been created by a special legislative act in 1842 that gave the Detroit school board "full power and authority" to regulate that city's schools, the 1867 anti-segregation law did not apply to Detroit.[101]

The situation for black children in Detroit was bleak. Whereas the Detroit Board of Education offered twelve years of instruction in white schools, it offered black children only six years. Moreover, many black children did not live near a black school, forcing them to walk, in some instances, several miles to attend school or else go without. Forty percent of the black children in Detroit lived in wards that had no school for their race. The black schools in operation were admittedly in poor condition.[102]

Black parents complained of both the poor condition of the black schools and of their exclusion from the white schools. The Detroit school board, however, persisted in its defiance. In response, Joseph Workman, a black laborer, brought suit in 1868 to compel the school board to admit his child to a white school. The school board defended its policy of racial segregation, arguing that "there exists among a large majority of the white population of Detroit a strong prejudice or animosity against colored people, which is largely transmitted to the children in the schools, and that this feeling would engender quarrels and contention if colored children were admitted to the white schools." The matter reached the Michigan Supreme Court, which held in an 1869 decision written by Chief Justice Thomas Cooley that the state's antisegregation legislation did indeed apply to Detroit. Four years later, Cooley, in his 1873 revision of Joseph Story's *Commentaries on the Constitution*, expressed doubt whether under the equal protection clause of the Fourteenth Amendment, "*any* distinction whatever, either in right or in privilege, which has color or race for its sole basis, can either be established in the law or enforced where it has been previously established." As we have seen, however, most nineteenth-century jurists did not agree with Cooley in the context of public schools.[103]

The Detroit school board, however, though it admitted Workman's child to his white neighborhood school as the writ of mandamus issued by the court required it to do, continued to deny other black

---

[101] Katzman, *Before the Ghetto*, pp. 44–7, 86; *People ex rel. Workman v. Board of Education*, 18 Mich. 400 (1869).

[102] Katzman, *Before the Ghetto*, pp. 85–6.

[103] Ibid., p. 87; *Workman v. Board of Education of Detroit*, 18 Mich. 400 (1869). For the Cooley quote, see Kousser, *Dead End*, p. 10 (Cooley, ed., Story, *Commentaries*, pp. 676–7) (emphasis supplied).

children entry to white schools. In response to the exclusion of their children from white schools, black parents filed approximately forty new lawsuits during the fall of 1869 challenging the failure of the Detroit school board to comply with the Michigan Supreme Court's *Workman* decision and seeking writs of mandamus ordering the school board to admit their children to their district school. In an effort to forestall litigation, the school board announced that it would abide by the *Workman* decision. The change of heart, however, was not sincere. When one black parent presented his child for enrollment at a nearby white school, the school, with the support of the school board, denied his child entry, stating that the term had begun and all seats in the white school were now filled.[104]

Met with this rebuff, blacks called a general meeting to protest the school board's discriminatory actions and to seek legislative assistance. In 1871, the Republican-controlled state legislature responded by enacting additional legislation that made it clear that Detroit was included in the antisegregation mandate: "All persons, residents *of any school district* and five years of age, shall have an equal right to attend school therein; and no separate school or department shall be kept for any person on account of race or color." The Detroit school board continued to protest that white parents would not accept racial mixing in the schools, but finally pledged full compliance with both the antisegregation legislation and the various court orders mandating an end to racial segregation. To placate white parents, the school board replaced the school system's double desks with single desks that provided a modicum of separation between children.[105]

Enforcing court orders mandating the admission of black children into white schools proved even more difficult in Illinois. Indeed, the Illinois Supreme Court enforced antisegregation legislation on almost every occasion that it was called upon to do so, but in several instances the order was circumvented by local school authorities who refused to comply. For example, in 1878, the school board of Quincy, Illinois, divided the town into eight districts, each with its own school. The board excluded all of the town's black children from these district schools, requiring them instead to attend the all-black Lincoln School even though many lived much closer to one of the district schools than to Lincoln. Securing representation from the Republican attorney general and the former Republican governor, John Palmer, a local blacksmith brought suit on behalf of his five children who were excluded

[104] Katzman, *Before the Ghetto*, pp. 87–90; Fishel, "The North and the Negro," pp. 242–3; Kousser, *Dead End*, p. 36, n. 18.

[105] Reams and Wilson, *Segregation and the Fourteenth Amendment*, pp. 287 (emphasis added); Katzman, *Before the Ghetto*, pp. 87–90.

from their district school. The school board defended its action on the grounds that segregation was necessary to the good order and efficient operation of the school system. Although the local trial court ruled in favor of the school board (as frequently happened in the post–Civil War North), the Republican-dominated Illinois Supreme Court reversed, claiming that both the 1874 antisegregation legislation *and* the 1870 state constitution forbade school segregation. The court's construction of the state constitution was particularly generous and reflected its commitment to enforcing a no-segregation principle.[106]

Notwithstanding that decision, local officials resisted implementation of the Illinois Supreme Court's mandate. One month after the court's decision, Quincy's school authorities redistricted the town into nine school districts, gerrymandered the district lines such that a majority of the town's black students were in the Lincoln School district, and assigned only black teachers to the Lincoln School. White children who lived in the Lincoln School district were then permitted to transfer to another school. The Quincy superintendent of schools defended these actions on the grounds that the Illinois Supreme Court's decision had attempted to impose "social equality" between the races and that "law cannot interfere with such social questions." Although blacks in Quincy initiated litigation challenging the racial gerrymandering, a trial court found that the plaintiffs had not established a violation of the state's antisegregation law, in significant measure because those few black students living outside the Lincoln School district were not required to attend the Lincoln School. The Illinois Supreme Court refused to disturb that ruling. Consistent with other northern courts, the Illinois Supreme Court did not find racially gerrymandered school district lines in violation of the state's antisegregation legislation.[107]

Blacks in Upper Alton, a Mississippi River town near St. Louis, also confronted difficulties in enforcing Illinois's antisegregation legislation. Prior to 1886, Upper Alton operated three schools for white children and one for black children. In 1886, however, Upper Alton school authorities erected a new school building large enough to accommodate all of the town's children. Although school officials closed the three white schools, they kept the black school open and denied black children admission to the newly constructed school. In response, several black children boycotted the black school and one parent filed suit, arguing that the exclusion of his children from the new school violated the 1874 antisegregation legislation. But the trial judge

---

[106] *People ex rel. Longress v. Board of Education of Quincy*, 101 Ill. 308 (1882); Squibb, "Roads to *Plessy*," pp. 144–7.

[107] *People ex rel. Hunt v. McFall*, 26 Ill. App. 319 (1886), *aff'd*, 124 Ill. 642 (1888); Squibb, "Roads to *Plessy*," pp. 147–50 (superintendent quote, pp. 148–9).

instructed the jury that it should find a statutory violation only if the black children were excluded from *all* the public schools of Upper Alton – which they were not – and if their assignment to the black school did not constitute an "exercise of a reasonable discretion" by the school board. In response, the jury ruled in favor of the school board. On appeal, the Illinois Supreme Court found that the verdict was "so manifestly the result of misdirection by the court as to be entitled to no consideration" and hence determined that the petitioner was entitled to a writ of mandamus requiring the admission of his children to the new school. The issuance of the writ, however, was delayed for several months, as the plaintiff could not pay the $75 court deposit required before the writ could be issued. Following the Illinois Supreme Court decision and the subsequent issuance of the writ, about twenty black children appeared at the local white school seeking entry, but were turned away since technically the writ applied only to the petitioner's children. To be sure, the Illinois Supreme Court had suggested that the rights of *all* black children in Upper Alton had been violated: "the right claimed by the [petitioner] is not merely a personal right. . . . It is the public, – the community at large, – that is most deeply interested in the enforcement of this and all other laws enacted for the wise and humane purpose of educating the children of the State. While it was natural and appropriate that the father should become the relator, *we entertain no doubt that any citizen of the school district might, with equal right of law, have done so,* and maintained the petition." But the school district clung to the technicality that the writ of mandamus commanding the board of education to take action applied only to the petitioner's children and that other black children seeking entry to the white school must procure their own writs. Thereafter, racially gerrymandered school attendance zones and violence contributed to the maintenance of segregated schools in Upper Alton. Shirley Portwood, an historian of school desegregation in southern Illinois in the late nineteenth century, has suggested that Upper Alton's "success in maintaining separate schools" emboldened other communities to do likewise.[108]

One of the most dramatic instances of white defiance of judicial authority took place in nearby Alton, a southern Illinois town across the Mississippi River from St. Louis, where newspaper publisher Elijah

---

[108] *People ex rel. Peair v. Board of Education,* 127 Ill. 613 (1889) (quotes on p. 623 and pp. 625–6; emphasis added); "The Illinois Race War," *New York Times,* Jan. 15, 1890, p. 5; "Race in Education," *New York Times,* Jan. 16, 1890, p. 4; "Upper Alton," *Alton Daily Telegraph,* Dec. 28, 1886, p. 3; Hamblin, "Drive the Last Nail," p. 96; Morgan Kousser, "The Trials of Scott Bibb," (unpublished paper, 2004). For the Portwood quote, see Portwood, "The Alton School Case," p. 5.

Lovejoy had been murdered in anti-abolitionist violence in 1836. In
May 1897, the Alton school board decided to segregate the town's
elementary school children by assigning all black children to one of two
newly established black schools. Although Alton, unlike most southern
Illinois communities, had operated racially integrated schools since
the early 1870s, an influx of southern whites and the pressure of real
estate interests who sought to attract white residents from St. Louis
helped push the community toward segregation.

Local political leaders supported school segregation. The Republican mayor of Alton, Henry Brueggemann, announced that "I pro-
pose to keep the niggers out of school . . . with the white children
of Alton, if I have to use every policeman I have got in the city to
do it." Mayor Brueggemann used his opposition to racial mixing in
the Alton schools to bolster his reelection efforts, garnering support
from white Democrats as well as white Republicans. Brueggemann's
deliberate alienation of the black community reflected the decline in
black political influence and the increase in antiblack feeling in Illinois
during the late 1890s, which manifested itself in lynchings, violence
against black strikebreakers, and segregated schools. Many Illinois
Republicans embraced this antiblack sentiment, prompting African
Americans to label the Republican Party the "Grand Old Lilly White
Party."[109]

Most of the black community of Alton, which comprised about 6 percent of the town's population, vigorously protested the segregation,
although some blacks, including the teachers at the two black schools,
supported racial segregation. Those Alton blacks favoring integration
sharply criticized these teachers, condemning them as "part of the
worse Niggers in Alton" and suggesting that they "should go to the
mirror and take a look at themselves, for they must have forgotten
that they are Negroes by birth."[110]

When schools opened in September 1897, many black parents
took their children to their local district school, where they were rebuffed. The town's entire police force was dispatched to keep the black
children out of white schools. A few black children slipped into a white
school but were promptly expelled. In response, Scott Bibb, securing the legal assistance of two prominent Illinois Republicans – John

[109] Portwood, "The Alton School Case," pp. 3–7; Weinberg, *A Chance to Learn*, p. 34;
Hamblin, "Drive the Last Nail," p. 97; Meier and Rudwick, "Early Boycotts of Segre-
gated Schools: The Alton, Illinois Case," p. 395; Squibb, "Roads to *Plessy*," p. 151;
"The Illinois Race War," *New York Times*, Jan. 15, 1890, p. 5; "Minnie Bibb in White
School," *New York Age*, Oct. 1, 1908, p. 1; Cha-Jua, *America's First Black Town*, pp. 133–4.
Quote from *People ex rel. Bibb v. Mayor*, 179 Ill. 615, 629 (1899).
[110] Portwood, "The Alton School Case," p. 3; quote from ibid., p. 13.

Palmer and John Brenholdt, the former mayor of Alton and future state senator – filed a legal action on behalf of his two children to compel their admission to their district school in accord with the state's antisegregation statute. Other than the plaintiffs' lawyers, few white people in Alton – Republican or Democrat – publicly supported racially mixed schools.[111]

In addition to the litigation, blacks in Alton organized a boycott of the town's black schools coupled with an attempted sit-in at the white district schools. Although the sit-in was thwarted by local police, the boycott would continue for eleven years until 1908. Initially, the boycott enjoyed broad support. During the first few months, only 10 of the approximately 300 school-age black children in Alton attended one of the two all-black schools. Those numbers would gradually increase over the next eleven years, such that by 1908, 144 black children attended one of the separate black schools in Alton. During the boycott, many of Alton's black children, including Bibb's, were educated privately, although many went without any schooling.[112]

The Alton school fight became a *cause celebre* throughout the state and the region as African Americans established special committees, held rallies, and raised funds in support of the Alton school struggle. As one black supporter in Venice, Illinois, commented: "We hope to be of some benefit to the citizens of Alton though the conflict does not reach us directly as individuals, but it does indirectly as a nation." Black newspapers, particularly the *Illinois Journal* in Springfield, gave the school fight extensive coverage; some black newspapers outside of Illinois also covered the controversy. Monies in support of the desegregation effort came in from as far away as St. Paul, Minnesota. The *New York Times* gave front-page coverage to the Alton school conflict, fearing that it might trigger a "race war" in Illinois.[113]

Despite a clear violation of the Illinois antisegregation law, the litigation failed to integrate the Alton schools. Seven times over the course of ten years, the plaintiffs presented their case to a jury. Twice the

[111] "Race War in Alton, Ill.," *New York Times*, Sept. 25, 1897, p. 1; Portwood, "The Alton School Case," pp. 10–11; Hamblin, "Drive the Last Nail," p. 98; Meier and Rudwick, "Early Boycotts of Segregated Schools: The Alton, Illinois Case," pp. 397–8.

[112] Portwood, "The Alton School Case," pp. 12–14, 18; Meier and Rudwick, "Early Boycotts of Segregated Schools: The Alton, Illinois Case," pp. 396–7.

[113] For the quote, see Portwood, "The Alton School Case," p. 18. Some complained that blacks did not support the Alton case because of their preference for segregated schools. See *The Forum* (Springfield, Illinois), Feb. 15, 1908, p. 1. For black newspapers, see Portwood, "The Alton School Case," pp. 15, 17–18; Cha-Jua, *America's First Black Town*, pp. 134–5. For the *New York Times*, see "May Have a Race War," *New York Times*, Sept. 23, 1897, p. 1; "Race War in Alton, Ill.," *New York Times*, Sept. 25, 1897, p. 1.

jurors could not agree and five times they rendered verdicts upholding school segregation. The Illinois Supreme Court reversed all five
jury verdicts on the various grounds that the trial judge refused to
admit evidence of the exclusion of black children from the Alton
schools other than the two Bibb children, that the trial judge had
merely asked the jury to determine whether the separate black schools
were equal – not whether the plaintiffs had been excluded from the
white schools because of their race, and that the jury verdicts finding
no segregation were contrary to the evidence. Four times the Illinois
Supreme Court ordered a new trial, rejecting on technical grounds
the petitioner's request that the court issue a "peremptory" writ of
mandamus in light of the overwhelming evidence of a statutory violation. Finally, in 1908, the court – exasperated with the unwillingness of
the trial court to follow the law – did issue a peremptory writ of mandamus requiring the admission of the black plaintiff children into
the white schools. The court characterized the actions of the Alton
trial court as "a deplorable disregard for the law and for the rights of
citizens."[114]

Some scholars have criticized the Illinois Supreme Court for not taking corrective action sooner in response to the trial court's continued
obstruction. There is merit to this charge. In 1889, in the Upper Alton
case, the court had issued a peremptory writ of mandamus – instead
of remanding the case to the trial court for additional proceedings –
upon finding that the trial court had misinstructed the jury. The court's
failure to issue a peremptory writ of mandamus sooner in the Alton
case may have been motivated in part by its declining enthusiasm for
racial integration. In its 1899 opinion, the court noted that "the wisest
of both races believe that the best interests of each would be promoted by voluntary segregation." Moreover, two of the court's justices
dissented from the court's eventual issuance of the writ, announcing that they refused "to join in the criticisms" of the trial court's
actions.[115]

---

[114] For court decisions, see *People ex rel. Bibb v. Mayor*, 179 Ill. 615 (1899); *People ex rel.
Bibb v. Mayor*, 193 Ill. 309 (1901); *People ex rel. Bibb v. Mayor*, 209 Ill. 461 (1904);
People ex rel. Bibb v. Mayor, 221 Ill. 275 (1906); *People ex rel. Bibb v. Mayor*, 233 Ill. 542
(1908) (quote at p. 547). The court justified its initial refusal to issue a writ on the
grounds that the petitioner had failed to secure either a jury verdict or a directed
verdict by the trial judge in his favor – as arguably required under Illinois law. When
the trial court explicitly refused to direct a verdict in the petitioner's favor, the court
concluded that it had grounds to issue a peremptory writ of mandamus.

[115] For critics of the court, see Meier and Rudwick, "Early Boycotts of Segregated
Schools: The Alton, Illinois Case," p. 402. For the first quote, see *People ex rel. Bibb v.
Mayor*, 179 Ill. 615, 632 (1899); for the second quote, see *People ex rel. Bibb v. Mayor*,
233 Ill. 542, 549 (1908).

Despite a delay of more than a decade since the onset of the litigation, African Americans greeted the Illinois Supreme Court's 1908 decision with great enthusiasm. A black newspaper in Springfield characterized the court's decision as "the greatest blow against caste prejudice and jury bribing in many a day." The Illinois Colored Historical Society resolved that "the thanks of the colored people, and all others who love justice in a free country, are hereby tendered the honorable Supreme Court of our great state."[116]

But the Supreme Court's writ had little impact. Consistent with the practice of many northern school boards confronted with an adverse court order, the school board determined that the writ of mandamus applied only to Bibb's two children specifically named in the lawsuit – now aged twenty-one and nineteen – and refused to allow any other black children, including Bibb's three younger children not named in the original lawsuit, to attend the white district schools. In fact, after the court issued its writ, about twenty-five other black children sought entry to white schools in September 1908 but were turned away by police. One such student was Bibb's nineteen-year-old daughter Minnie, who sought to enter the local white high school. The Alton school superintendent, however, insisted that she attend third grade since she had been absent from school for the past eleven years and her private tutoring had, in his view, been deficient. Bibb refused and left school. Scott Bibb tried to organize another boycott of the separate black schools and threatened additional litigation on behalf of his three younger children, but eventually gave up and enrolled his children in one of the colored annexes the school board had established to accommodate those black children who lived a considerable distance from the two black schools. The bloody Springfield, Illinois, riot of August 1908 and white threats to use violence in Alton undoubtedly put a chill on black protest. The Bibbs would eventually leave Illinois, and the schools of Alton would remain thoroughly segregated until 1950.[117]

The Alton experience underscored the limits of litigation to secure segregated schools in the face of virulent white opposition. Notwithstanding the work of some of the best legal talent in Illinois, five favorable state supreme court decisions, and strong black support for

---

[116] For the first quote, see "Supreme Court's Decision Sweeping," *The Forum* (Springfield, Illinois), May 2, 1908, p. 2; for the second quote, see "Resolutions," *The Forum* (Springfield), May 9, 1908, p. 1.

[117] On the school board's refusal to admit black students and Minnie Bibb, see Portwood, "The Alton School Case," pp. 19–20; Meier and Rudwick, "Early Boycotts of Segregated Schools: The Alton, Illinois Case," pp. 400–2; "Minnie Bibb in White School," *New York Age*, Oct. 1, 1908, p. 1. Scott Bibb ultimately left the state for Ohio. Meier and Rudwick, "Negro Boycotts of Jim Crow Schools," pp. 58–9; Ming, "The Elimination of Segregation," p. 269.

the integration fight, the white community successfully dodged school integration in Alton and throughout southern Illinois until the middle of the twentieth century. The increasingly hostile racial climate of the late nineteenth and early twentieth centuries, accompanied by racial violence, made challenges to racial segregation increasingly difficult. Moreover, the dismal results of the Alton litigation discouraged further challenges to school segregation; for more than forty years, no African American would file a lawsuit seeking school integration in southern Illinois. As one black supporter of the school fight had bitterly commented in 1898 of Alton's refusal to obey Illinois's antisegregation law: "Those who put their trust in legislation as a sure means of receiving good and preventing evil are no wiser than those of today who have implicit confidence in the saving power of corporations, trusts and monopolies."[118]

By the end of the nineteenth century, African Americans in the North seemed to have secured a significant legal victory in the form of antisegregation legislation and judicial decisions enforcing that legislation. This altered legal status of northern school segregation was striking, but it did not reflect a widespread shift in northern white attitudes toward racial mixing in the public schools. To be sure, the racial idealism of many Republican legislators did contribute to the enactment of this antisegregation legislation, particularly during the late 1860s and early 1870s. But most of the state antisegregation legislation enacted after the mid-1870s was attributable to a combination of factors such as political expediency and the cost of dual schools that went well beyond claims of racial justice.

As a result, those legislative victories did not translate into the eradication of school segregation, as many northern communities retained racially separate schools in defiance of state law. Northern black schoolchildren had won the legal right to attend their local school along with white children during the last quarter of the nineteenth century, but it would be years before that legal right had meaning for many northern blacks.

---

[118] Quoted in Cha-Jua, *America's First Black Town*, p. 135.

4

The Spread of Northern School
Segregation, 1890–1940

Some of us went to some of the influential Negroes and told them, conditions being as they were, we thought it would be better to establish some separate schools for the colored people in the lower grades. That would give some of the colored people positions as teachers in the colored schools. They agreed to this and they were established.

— A white school official in Chester, Pennsylvania, 1922[1]

The political influence that African Americans enjoyed in most northern states following the end of the Civil War that resulted in antisegregation legislation had begun to fade by the end of the nineteenth century. White insistence on racial separation in northern schools increased in response to the northern migration of southern blacks that began during the last decade of the nineteenth century and exploded during and after World War I. This influx of southern blacks exacerbated racial tensions, and many white school officials who had tolerated school integration when the number of African Americans was relatively small began to insist on racial separation. By the late 1930s, northern school segregation was considerably more extensive than it had been at the turn of the century. Although much of this racial separation was due to residential segregation, in many communities school officials engaged in explicit racial assignments. For much of the North, the antisegregation legislation of the nineteenth century was long forgotten.

Growing White Hostility in Response to Migration of Southern Blacks

Northern commitments to racial equality deteriorated during the late nineteenth and early twentieth centuries, contemporaneous with increasing white hostility to blacks in southern states. During the last

---

[1] Quoted in Duncan, *The Changing Race Relationship*, pp. 38–9.

decade of the nineteenth century and the first decade of the twentieth century, many northern whites began to insist on racial separation
in various aspects of public life, including education. In 1890, the
New York Times, which had previously championed black school desegregation efforts, criticized – in extraordinary fashion – a black parent in southern Illinois for seeking the admission of his children to a
white school: "Some of the negroes insist that their children shall ... be
taught in the same schools [as white children.] The Constitution [of
Illinois] seems to uphold this pretension, but the negroes are none
the less foolish and ill advised to make it.... Whoever insists upon
forcing himself where he is not wanted is a public nuisance, and his
offensiveness is not in the least mitigated by the circumstance that
he is black." In 1906, the *New York Commercial* commented on the
growing trend toward segregation across the country: "Northern sentiment on the race question is not at bottom a million miles away from
Southern sentiment." In 1916, Seth Low, a former mayor of New York
City and president of Columbia University, wrote to Robert Moton,
Booker T. Washington's successor as president of Tuskegee Institute:
"race purity is as strong an instinct at the North as it is at the South."
Racist southern educator Thomas Bailey, in his 1914 study *Race Orthodoxy in the South*, noted, in a self-serving manner, the decline in
northern opposition to southern racism: "Is not the South being *encouraged* to treat the negroes *as aliens* by the growing discrimination
against the negro in the North, a discrimination that is social as well as
economic? Does not the South perceive that all the fire has gone out of
the Northern philanthropic fight for the rights of man? *The North has
surrendered!*"[2]

The migration of tens of thousands of southern blacks to northern
cities during the late nineteenth and early twentieth centuries exacerbated white hostility toward African Americans. Migration northward
began in significant numbers during the 1890s. Whereas only 88,000
blacks left the South during the 1880s, 185,000 departed during the
1890s and 194,000 during the first decade of the twentieth century.
Between 1890 and 1910, about 2.5 percent of the South's black population moved north. Of the five northern states with the largest black
populations in 1910 – Pennsylvania (191,000), New York (120,000),
Ohio (110,000), Illinois (109,000), and New Jersey (88,000) – each
experienced an increase in black population between 1900 and 1910

---

[2] For the *New York Times* quote, see "Race in Education," *New York Times*, Jan. 16, 1890,
p. 4; for the *New York Commercial* quote, see "Jim Crow School in New Jersey," *Raleigh
Daily News and Observer*, Feb. 18, 1906, p. 4; for the Low quote, see Fairclough, *Teaching
Equality*, p. 21; for the Bailey quote, see Woodward, *The Strange Career of Jim Crow*, p. 113.

of over 25 percent. Urban population increases were even more dramatic. During the decade of the 1890s, the black populations of Chicago, Cleveland, and Pittsburgh doubled, while the populations of Detroit, New York, and Philadelphia also sharply increased. In 1903, W. E. B. Du Bois noted that "the most significant economic change among Negroes in the last ten or twenty years has been their influx into northern cities." This trend would continue. Between 1900 and 1910, the number of African Americans living in Chicago and New York increased by about 50 percent.[3]

Given the correlation between the enfranchisement of northern blacks and the increase in political influence that African Americans enjoyed in much of the North during the 1870s and 1880s, one might have expected this increase in black population during the 1890s and the first decade of the twentieth century to have positively affected the status of northern blacks. With a few exceptions, however, the status of northern blacks declined with the onset of the migration of southern blacks into northern cities. The special conditions of the 1870s and 1880s – Radical Republican commitments to removing legal disabilities imposed on African Americans, closely contested elections, and the paucity of black residents in much of the North – had faded by the early twentieth century. The growth of the northern city, populated by northern-born whites and blacks alongside growing numbers of European immigrants and southern blacks, produced an array of tensions that led to the diminishment of the status of African Americans. As historian Judy Mohraz has noted: "the rising percentage of Negroes in northern cities in the last decades of the nineteenth century altered the previous obscurity of the black residents and triggered varying degrees of racial hostility and tension. Heightened friction followed the greater visibility of Negroes in the early twentieth century city – on the streets, in residential areas, on the job, and in the schools."[4]

The migration of southern blacks during the late nineteenth and early twentieth centuries accompanied a rise in racist ideology across the country grounded in white supremacy. In the South, this racist ideology manifested itself in segregation laws and disfranchisement. In the North, many whites also began to embrace white supremacist views that dismissed blacks as inferior and unfit for full participation in white civilization. Leading scholars during the 1890s and the first decade of

---

[3] For population data, see U.S. Bureau of Census, 1890, 1900, 1910; Diner, *A Very Different Age*, p. 131; Department of Interior, Bureau of Education, *Negro Education*, pp. 677–89. For the Du Bois quote, see Meier and Rudwick, *From Plantation to Ghetto*, p. 215.

[4] Mohraz, *The Separate Problem*, pp. 3–4.

the twentieth century, particularly in the field of anthropology, offered scientific justifications for racial separation, rejecting notions that the poorer social outcomes of many blacks were due to environmental influences. University of Chicago anthropologist Frederick Starr, in an 1897 essay "The Degeneracy of the American Negro," emphasized inherent racial differences between blacks and whites: "[I]t is certain that race differences are real and persistent.... Study of criminality in the two races gives astonishing results. Of the total prisoners in the United States in 1890, nearly 30 per cent were colored; the negro, however forms but 11 per cent of the population.... Conditions of life and bad social opportunities cannot be urged in excuse.... The difference is *racial*." Starr held little optimism that education would improve the situation for African Americans: "What can be done? Not much. But faith in school-book education as a means of grace must die.... Recognition of difference between white men and black men is fundamental. The desire and effort to turn bright black boys into inefficient white men should cease.... [W]e may expect the race here to die and disappear; the sooner perhaps the better." Economist Frederick Hoffman, writing in 1896, agreed: "In marked contrast with the frequent assertions... that race is not important and that environment or conditions of life are the most important factors in the final result of the struggle for life,... we have here abundant evidence that we find in race and heredity the determining factors in the upward or downward course of mankind.... [T]he colored race is shown to be on the downward grade, tending toward a condition in which matters will be worse than they are now.... Neither religion nor education nor a higher degree of economic well-being have been able to raise the race from a low and anti-social condition...."[5]

At the same time, many white Americans applied Darwinian notions of "survival of the fittest" to social relations, arguing that weaker groups, such as blacks, would fail while others would prosper. The burgeoning new "science" of eugenics lent support to notions of racial superiority. Two leading educational theorists of the early twentieth century, G. Stanley Hall and G. E. Partridge, articulated a "genetic philosophy of education" pursuant to which "[e]ach race must be educated and governed according to the stage of culture and development to which it belongs": "The greatest mistakes have been made in trying

---

[5] For the rise of racist ideology, see Spear, *Black Chicago*, p. 8; Hatfield, "The Impact of the New Deal," p. 20; Woodward, *The Strange Career of Jim Crow*, p. 70; Fishel, "The North and the Negro," p. 370; Baker, *From Savage to Negro*, p. 3. For the Starr quotes, see Starr, "The Degeneracy of the American Negro," pp. 17–18. For the Hoffman quote, see Hoffman, *Race Traits and Tendencies*, pp. 310, 312.

to cope with the negro question, in not understanding the nature of the negro, who is so different from the white man, both in body and mind, that the two races should not be treated alike in any particular.... [The negro] must be trained according to his own nature.... His whole training must centre in industry rather than in mental development disconnected from motor expression.... Given the proper conditions, the negro will make progress naturally toward a higher stage of civilisation, but he cannot be hurried by imitating the white man's nature."[6]

As the northern black population grew, so did opportunities for interracial conflict, as many whites began to fear competition for jobs, housing, and political influence. The immigration of millions of southern and eastern Europeans to northern cities during the 1880s had already triggered fears of job loss among native whites and anxieties about dilution of the "Anglo Saxon racial stock." The northward migration of southern blacks beginning during the 1890s provoked additional resentment among many white workers and exacerbated racial hostility. The Supreme Court's 1896 *Plessy v. Ferguson* decision, which legitimated "separate but equal," gave voice to what was already becoming the dominant mood throughout the country. Not surprisingly, the *Plessy* decision provoked minimal coverage in the nation's leading newspapers.[7]

This growing racial antagonism manifested itself in a variety of ways. Lynchings sharply increased in some midwestern states during the 1890s. The governor of Georgia, one of the nation's leaders in lynchings, attempted to condone his state's record by citing the large number of lynchings in Indiana. During the first decade of the twentieth century, a number of northern communities such as New York City, Philadelphia, Akron and Springfield (Ohio), Belville and Springfield (Illinois), and Evansville and Greensburg (Indiana) were torn by race riots. In several of these riots, white mobs destroyed homes and drove blacks out of the community. The Evansville riot, for example, triggered in part by white working-class apprehensions about economic competition from African Americans, left many dead or wounded, inflicted substantial damage on black homes and businesses, and caused

---

[6] Partridge, *Genetic Philosophy of Education*, pp. 378, 379–80.

[7] For immigration fears, see Klarman, *From Jim Crow to Civil Rights*, p. 12. For dilution of Anglo-Saxon stock, see Walker, "Restriction of Immigration," pp. 828–9 (arguing in the *Atlantic Monthly* that these new European immigrants, "degraded below our utmost conceptions" and "representing the worst failures in the struggle for existence," posed "great danger to the health and life of the nation"). For the reaction to *Plessy*, see Lofgren, *The Plessy Case*, pp. 196–7.

the evacuation of many blacks from the city. The Springfield, Illinois, riot of 1908 captured nationwide attention for its brutal attacks on black lives and property. William English Walling, a distinguished white writer who would later help found the NAACP, commented about the Springfield riot: "Either the spirit of the abolitionists, of Lincoln and of [Elijah] Lovejoy, must be revived...or [James K.] Vardaman and [Ben] Tillman will soon have transferred the race war to the North." Mississippi Governor Vardaman, for his part, commented that the Springfield riot would "cause the people of the North to look with more toleration upon the methods employed by the Southern people."[8]

Discrimination in public accommodations significantly increased during the late nineteenth and early twentieth centuries. Indeed, as early as the 1890s, many communities in the racially liberal Western Reserve of Ohio began, for the first time, to experience racial discrimination in public accommodations. By the onset of World War I, many hotels and restaurants in Cleveland that had once freely served black customers had implemented a color line. At the same time, many northern state legislatures considered or enacted legislation banning interracial marriage during the first decade of the new century, as did Congress during the second decade of the century.[9]

Blacks who migrated north during the late nineteenth and early twentieth centuries were confronted with increasing residential segregation. Indeed, many scholars have labeled the late nineteenth and early twentieth centuries as "the formative years of the black ghetto" in northern cities. For example, in Cleveland, which enjoyed considerable residential integration for most of the nineteenth century, an influx of blacks during the late nineteenth century and the first decade of the twentieth century brought residential segregation, as restrictive real estate practices forced blacks into the Central Avenue area of the city.[10]

---

[8] For lynchings, see, for example, "An Illinois Lynching," *Cleveland Gazette*, June 13, 1903, p. 1; for the Georgia governor, see Thornbrough, *The Negro in Indiana*, pp. 179–80. For race riots, see Franklin, *From Slavery to Freedom*, pp. 443–4; Woodward, *Origins of the New South*, p. 351; Bigham, *Towns and Villages*, pp. 234–5. For the Walling and Vardaman quotes, see Walling, "The Race War in the North," p. 534.

[9] For Cleveland segregation, see Washington, "The Black Struggle for Desegregated Quality Education," p. 79; Moore, "The Limits of Black Power," p. 13; "Euclid Ave. Store Tries Out Segregation," *Cleveland Advocate*, Sept. 25, 1920, p. 4; for interracial marriage bans, see Taylor, *In Search of the Racial Frontier*, p. 212; Moore, *Leading the Race*, p. 206.

[10] For the black ghetto quote, see Kusmer, *A Ghetto Takes Shape*, p. 35; for Cleveland segregation, see Moore, "The Limits of Black Power," p. 12; Mosey, "Testing, Tracking, and Curriculum," pp. 17–18.

Chicago also experienced an increase in segregationist pressure during the early twentieth century. White property owners urged real estate agents and property owners in white neighborhoods to sell or rent only to whites. The Hyde Park Improvement Protective Club in Chicago was especially aggressive in its efforts to keep blacks out, threatening to blacklist real estate firms that sold or rented housing to blacks and to boycott white merchants who did business with blacks. The Hyde Park club also attempted to buy property or leases from blacks who had purchased or rented property in white neighborhoods. Black families that resisted experienced vandalism. These efforts were successful: most of Hyde Park remained white until the middle of the twentieth century.[11]

A few northern communities did more than insist on residential segregation. Some communities, such as Syracuse, Ohio, Lawrenceburg, Salem, and Ellwood, Indiana, simply forbade blacks to settle within their limits. One writer described the Syracuse practice in 1913: "When a colored man is seen in the town during the day he is generally told of these traditions and is warned to leave before sun-down. If he fails to take heed, he is surrounded at about the time that darkness begins, and is addressed by the leaders of the gang in about this language: 'No nigger is allowed to stay in this town overnight. . . . Get out of here now, and get out quick.' . . . The command is always effective, for it is backed by stones in the ready hands of boys none too friendly."[12]

Employment discrimination also increased throughout the North during the early twentieth century as blacks in many northern cities were pushed out of skilled labor positions. Between 1870 and 1910, the percentage of blacks in Cleveland working in skilled trades declined from 32 percent to 11 percent. In Gary, Indiana, the community's white leaders sponsored a "clean out the Negro" campaign in 1909 aimed at removing those black workers that U.S. Steel had brought to the city to build new factories. In 1911, the *Gary Evening Post* reported that "any Negro in Gary who hasn't got a job had better lose no time in getting one" and reported that fifty blacks had been run out of the city in the prior two days. Many industrial employers simply excluded blacks from employment, while union apprenticeship programs – essential for learning necessary job skills – were typically closed to blacks, as labor unions were frequently hostile to black workers.[13]

---

[11] Spear, *Black Chicago*, pp. 21–3.

[12] For exclusion of blacks from certain communities, see Thornbrough, "Segregation in Indiana," p. 596; Franklin, *From Slavery to Freedom*, p. 443; for the quote, see Quillin, *The Color Line in Ohio*, p. 160.

[13] For Cleveland, see Moore, "The Limits of Black Power," p. 13; for Gary, see Betten and Mohl, "The Evolution of Racism," p. 53 (quote, p. 54).

As a result, domestic work emerged as the most promising line of work for many northern blacks during the late nineteenth and early twentieth centuries. A survey in Philadelphia during the late 1890s found about 60 percent of all black working men and about 90 percent of black working women employed as low-paid domestics; these figures would hold constant for the next forty years. By comparison, fewer than 30 percent of white immigrants and about 10 percent of native-born white workers in Philadelphia were employed as domestics during this time period.[14]

Strikebreaking provided the best opportunity for blacks to secure higher-paid jobs during the early twentieth century. Such work was short term, however, as white workers generally reclaimed these jobs with the resolution of the strike. Moreover, the strikebreaking activities of African Americans provoked bitter antagonism from white workers. The hiring of black strikebreakers during the 1904 stockyards strike and the 1905 teamsters strike in Chicago, for example, triggered "the most serious racial conflicts" in that city's history.[15]

A dramatic example of this increasing racist sentiment in the North took place at Oberlin College in Ohio. Founded by abolitionists, Oberlin had been one of the first colleges in America to admit students without regard to race during the 1830s. Moreover, the town of Oberlin was one of the few northern communities during the 1830s and 1840s to admit black children to the public schools on a nonsegregated basis. Both the town and college were important antislavery outposts, serving as a stop on the Underground Railroad and as a training ground for teachers in the Freedmen's schools after the Civil War.[16]

By the end of the nineteenth century, however, the racial idealism at Oberlin had faded. As early as 1882, white Oberlin students began to protest having to eat at the same dining hall tables with black students. Although the college president forbade racial segregation, pressure from white students for racial separation continued. In 1905, literary societies, a critical element in the Oberlin education, formally excluded black male students from membership, and in 1909 the college established separate housing for black female students. One white Oberlin student justified the exclusion of blacks from the literary societies in 1910 by citing larger patterns of societal discrimination: "[E]ven if he had been taken in and made one of us in every way, many of you older men know full well how small a degree of any such treatment he could receive outside Oberlin walls. Would you

[14] Licht, *Getting Work*, p. 48.
[15] Trotter, *Black Milwaukee*, pp. 13–14; Spear, *Black Chicago*, p. 36 (quote).
[16] Waite, "Permission to Remain among Us," pp. 3–4, 38–9.

tantalize a human soul with the vision of a promised land from which an impassable gulf will soon shut him off?" The *Cleveland Plain Dealer*, no friend of Oberlin, reported the white students' position, noting that "the feeling against the African is shifting from the south to the north more and more, and the ultimatum of Oberlin's students is but added proof of that." Oberlin's president agreed: "I think the attitude of the students towards the colored question as a whole is merely a representative of the attitude of the whole north toward the question." Oberlin's president announced in 1914 that "I do not . . . see how we can avoid having some separate colored boarding houses for colored students." Mary Church Terrell, one of the school's most distinguished alumnae, replied: "I try to be optimistic in this wicked and cruel country . . . [but] nothing has come so near forcing me to give up hope, and resigning myself to the cruel fate which many people are certain awaits us, than the heartbreaking backsliding of Oberlin College."[17]

The Great Migration

During the First World War, hundreds of thousands of southern blacks moved north, launching what would become over the course of the next four decades the most significant internal migration in American history. This increase in the number of African Americans living in the North would further intensify antiblack sentiment among many whites.

Between 1915 and 1920, about 500,000 blacks left the South, moving to northern cities. Another 800,000 to 1 million southern blacks migrated north during the 1920s. All told, about 10 percent of blacks living in the South moved to the North between 1915 and 1930. Whereas in 1910 90 percent of the country's black population lived in the South, those demographics would dramatically shift over the course of the next half century. By 1960, half of the nation's black population lived outside the South.[18]

Those states receiving the largest number of black migrants during World War I were, in descending order, Pennsylvania, Illinois, Ohio,

[17] For a discussion of the increasing segregationist sentiment at Oberlin, see Waite, "Permission to Remain among Us," pp. 86–98, 117–18, 132–5. For quotes, see ibid., pp. 121, 126, 128, 139, 142. See also letter from William Pickens to Frances J. Hosford, May 1, 1919, NAACP Papers, Box I-C-271 (efforts to exclude black students from Oberlin dormitories).

[18] For demographic changes, see Trotter, *River Jordan*, p. 95; Hardy, "Race and Opportunity," p. v; Anyon, *Ghetto Schooling*, p. 61; Meier and Rudwick, *From Plantation to Ghetto*, p. 213. Between 1910 and 1940, approximately 1.8 million blacks left the South for the North in pursuit of better jobs. McAdam, *Political Process and the Development of Black Insurgency*, p. 80.

New York, and Michigan. Most black migrants settled in cities. Indeed, by 1920, almost 40 percent of northern blacks resided in just eight cities – New York, Philadelphia, Chicago, Detroit, Pittsburgh, Cleveland, Cincinnati, and Columbus – each of which experienced a dramatic increase in its black population as a result of the migration. For example, between 1910 and 1930, New York City's black population increased from 91,700 to 327,700; Chicago's from 44,100 to 233,900; Philadelphia's from 84,500 to 219,600; Detroit's from 5,700 to 120,100; and Cleveland's from 8,400 to 71,900. Smaller cities experienced sharp increases in their black population as well. The black population of Buffalo, for example, more than doubled between 1910 and 1920 and then doubled again between 1920 and 1925.[19]

Several factors contributed to the Great Migration of southern blacks to northern cities during and after World War I. Economic concerns were highly significant. First of all, sharp declines in southern agriculture due to the devastations of the boll weevil – that "ashy-colored rascal" – the reduction in cotton prices in 1913 and 1914, and the floods of 1915 and 1916 forced southern blacks to look elsewhere for work. These economic problems were coupled with the lure of employment opportunities in the North created by sharp declines in foreign immigration, the labor needs of wartime industry, and the loss of American workers to the battlefields of Europe. Immigration declines were particularly dramatic. Whereas 1,200,000 foreign immigrants entered the United States in 1914, only 110,000 arrived in 1918.[20]

Desperate for labor, many northern industries during World War I sent labor agents to the South to recruit black workers. These recruitment efforts were aided by numerous northern black newspapers and journals that relentlessly promoted job opportunities in northern cities and devoted considerable time and space to the lives and wages of northern blacks compared to their southern counterparts. The most vigorous promoter of northern work opportunities was the *Chicago Defender*, which had become the most widely read and influential black newspaper in the nation. In response, many southern communities banned the sale of the *Chicago Defender* and tightened labor agent restrictions. Moreover, many migrants wrote or returned home for visits and encouraged their friends and families to come North, spreading tales of abundant work and good wages. Following the conclusion of

[19] U.S. Bureau of Census, 1910, 1920, 1930; Spear, *Black Chicago*, p. 139; Mosey, "Testing, Tracking, and Curriculum," p. 13; Hine, "Black Migration to the Urban Midwest," p. 242; Robisch, "Educational Segregation," p. 24.

[20] Phillips, *AlabamaNorth*, p. 43 (quote); Waller, "Holding Back the Dawn," p. 127; Spear, *Black Chicago*, p. 131.

World War I, the northern migration continued, fueled by the postwar industrial boom and restrictions on foreign immigration.[21]

Yet economic factors were not the only ones that accounted for the Great Migration. Many African Americans left the South to escape the region's racial oppression. In letters to the *Chicago Defender*, migrants cited hope for better treatment as a reason for departing as well as the lure of higher wages. As one black Alabamian wrote the *Chicago Defender* during World War I: "I am in the darkness of the south.... [P]lease help me to get of this low down country [where] I am counted as no more than a dog." Lynching also increased during World War I in parts of the South, almost doubling between 1917 and 1918 alone.[22]

Some migrants were drawn northward by the promise of better educational opportunities, as southern black schools were grossly underfunded. Both migrants and northern black newspapers cited better schools as a major draw for migration. One Georgia migrant commented: "My children I wished to be educated in a different community than here. Where the school facilities are better and less prejudice [is] shown and in fact where advantages are better for our people in all respect." Studies of the Great Migration show that a very high percentage of migrant children quickly found their way into the public schools. The *Chicago Defender*, with some exaggeration, trumpeted "the splendid unrestricted system of learning in the northern cities," in comparison with southern schools, "where Jim-Crowism is to be the first lesson taught."[23]

Racial integration, however, was not foremost on the minds of southern black migrants. As historian James Grossman has written of the migration to Chicago: "There is little evidence that black southerners coming to Chicago were especially interested in integration per se; most were more concerned about legal protection, political rights, and access to the paths of security or mobility.... In some aspects of everyday life, many newcomers looked forward to freedom from whites; they evinced little desire to attend integrated churches or spend leisure time with white people."[24]

---

[21] Buni, *Robert L. Vann*, p. 72; Barnett, "The Role of the Press," p. 479; Phillips, *AlabamaNorth*, p. 46; Spear, *Black Chicago*, pp. 184–5; Grossman, "Blowing the Trumpet," pp. 90–6; Diner, *A Very Different Age*, p. 153; Miller, "The Black Migration to Philadelphia," p. 316.

[22] For the letter to the *Chicago Defender*, see Fultz, "'Agitate Then, Brother,'" p. 24; for the increase in lynchings, see Phillips, *AlabamaNorth*, pp. 44–5.

[23] For the importance of schools to migrants, see Waller, "Holding Back the Dawn," pp. 137, 145; Miller, "The Black Migration to Philadelphia," p. 346. For the quote from a Georgia migrant, see Marks, *Farewell – We're Good and Gone*, p. 77; for the quote from the *Chicago Defender*, see Homel, "The Politics of Public Education," p. 179.

[24] Grossman, *Land of Hope*, p. 161.

Impact of the Great Migration on White Hostility toward Blacks

The black migration during World War I and the postwar era dramatically increased racial tensions in the North and accelerated the racial separation that had already begun during the early twentieth century. "It is a gentle conceit of northern people that race prejudice is a vice peculiar to the south," Detroit minister Reinhold Niebuhr observed in 1927. "The tremendous migration of southern Negroes into the industrial centers of the north is rapidly dispelling this illusion." The arrival of southern blacks provoked profound anxiety in many northern whites. Cleveland City Manager W. R. Hopkins announced in 1925 that "I don't know of any problem confronting the city that contains more potential menace than the fact that 40,000 southern Negroes have been dumped into Cleveland within the last few years." White demands for segregation in public accommodations, housing, and education sharply increased during the 1920s. As Harvard Sitkoff has written of the Great Migration: "Some who followed the North Star looking for the Promised Land found hell instead: educational and residential segregation, dilapidated housing milked by white slumlords, discrimination by labor unions and employers, brutality by white policemen, and liquor and narcotics the only means of escape."[25]

Public accommodations discrimination sharply increased in the wake of the Great Migration, as many restaurants, hotels, stores, and theaters employed a variety of tactics to discourage black patronage. As W. E. B. Du Bois noted in 1934, in the early twentieth century "not a single hotel in Boston dared to refuse colored guests," but after the Great Migration, there remained "few Boston hotels where colored people are received." This reversal was not confined to Boston. Du Bois also noted that "[i]n 1910, colored men could be entertained in the best hotels in Cleveland, Detroit and Chicago. Today [in 1934], there is not a single Northern city, except New York, where a Negro can be a guest at a first-class hotel." Black leader George Schuyler made a similar observation in 1937: "Literally thousands of hotels, theaters, tourist camps, restaurants, amusement parks, swimming pools, soda fountains and even some stores either completely bar or jim crow Negroes in hundreds of cities and towns in the 'free' North." Confronted with white hostility, many northern blacks simply gave up. The leading black newspaper in Indianapolis, the *Freeman*, commented: "We have learned to forego some rights that are common, and because we know the price. . . . We have not insisted that hotels should entertain our race, or the theaters, rights that are clearly ours." In fact,

---

[25] For the Niebuhr quote, see Niebuhr, "Race Prejudice in the North," p. 583; for the Hopkins quote, see "Hopkins, Schrembs and Jones," *Cleveland Gazette,* Jan. 31, 1925, p. 2; for the Sitkoff quote, see Sitkoff, *The Struggle for Black Equality,* p. 8.

FIGURE 4   Sign in restaurant window, Lancaster, Ohio, 1930s. Reprinted from
the Library of Congress, Prints & Photographs Division, FSA/OWI Collection,
LC-USF33-6392-M4.

blacks would be excluded from most theaters, public hospitals, and
public parks in Indianapolis, except on a segregated basis, until after
World War II.[26]

Although most northern states had enacted laws during the 1880s
prohibiting racial discrimination in public accommodations, those
laws were frequently disregarded during the 1920s and 1930s. Some
states, like New Jersey, weakened their nineteenth-century public accommodations statutes in the wake of the migration of southern blacks.
Moreover, prosecutors were reluctant to enforce the criminal aspects
of public accommodations legislation, as juries frequently refused to
convict despite clear violations. Private plaintiffs were dissuaded from
filing suit by restrictive court decisions and the fact that successful litigation typically resulted in nominal damages, often not enough to
cover court costs.[27]

[26] For the first Du Bois quote, see Du Bois, "William Monroe Trotter," *The Crisis* (May
     1934), p. 134; for the second quote, see Du Bois, "Postscript," *The Crisis* (Apr. 1934),
     pp. 115–17; for the Schuyler quote, see Schuyler, "Do We Really Want Equality?"
     p. 103; for the quote from the *Freeman*, see Thornbrough, "Segregation in Indiana,"
     p. 597. For exclusion of Indianapolis blacks, see *United States v. Board of Commissioners*,
     332 F. Supp. 655, 661 (S.D. Ind. 1971).
[27] For New Jersey, see Price, *Freedom Not Far Distant*, p. 142; for other limitations of these
     statutes, see Spear, *Black Chicago*, pp. 41–3, 207; Russell H. Davis, "Civil Rights in
     Cleveland 1912 through 1961," p. 15 (1973), Russell Howard Davis Papers, Container
     9; for restrictive court decisions, see, for example, *Chocos v. Burden*, 74 Ind. App. 242
     (1920), and *Harvey v. Sissle*, 53 Ohio App. 405 (1936).

One of the most striking effects of the Great Migration was a significant increase in northern urban residential segregation. As southern blacks settled in northern cities, they were segregated into certain neighborhoods through a series of private and public tactics. With the exception of Indianapolis, northern cities did not promulgate local ordinances requiring residential segregation, a tactic the Supreme Court declared unconstitutional in 1917, but did so with equal efficacy through racially restrictive covenants and discriminatory real estate practices, zoning regulations, and neighborhood associations. Throughout the North, local real estate agents steered black families away from white neighborhoods. In Cincinnati, for example, the local real estate board during the 1920s instructed its employees that "no agent shall rent or sell property to colored people in an established white section or neighborhood and this inhibition shall be particularly applicable to the hill tops and suburban property." White realtors in Indianapolis refused to show blacks homes in white neighborhoods and used a two-tier pricing structure: "a realistic market price to whites and a ridiculously inflated price to Negroes." Indianapolis newspaper want ads would continue to describe certain property "for colored" until the mid-1960s. In Chicago, the local real estate board took action in 1917 to restrict black migrants to certain blocks in the city, resolving that "each block . . . [in black neighborhoods] be filled solidly and that further expansion . . . be confined to contiguous blocks," and that "owners' societies . . . [be created] . . . in every white block for the purpose of mutual defense." Other cities, like Pittsburgh, followed suit. From 1924 until 1950, realtors throughout the nation subscribed to a national code that provided that "a realtor should never be instrumental in introducing into a neighborhood . . . members of any race or nationality, or any individual whose presence will clearly be detrimental to property values in the neighborhood."[28]

In many parts of the North, vigilante violence accompanied black attempts to move into white neighborhoods or their refusal to vacate homes in white neighborhoods. One such incident provoked murder charges against Ossian Sweet, a black doctor in Detroit who confronted a white mob seeking to drive him from his home. Legal scholar John Frank has persuasively argued that the explosion of violence in racially

---

[28] For the Supreme Court decision, see *Buchanan v. Warley*, 245 U.S. 60 (1917); for other residential segregation tactics, see Trotter, *Black Milwaukee*, p. 233. For the Cincinnati quote, see Trotter, *River Jordan*, p. 106; for the Indianapolis discussion, see *United States v. Board of Commissioners*, 332 F. Supp. 655, 662–3 (S.D. Ind. 1971); for the Chicago discussion, see Mosey, "Testing, Tracking, and Curriculum," p. 16; *The Chicago Real Estate Board Bulletin*, Apr. 25, 1917, pp. 315–17; for Pittsburgh, see Buni, *Robert L. Vann*, p. 62; for the realtor code quote, see Lipsitz, *The Possessive Investment in Whiteness*, pp. 25–6.

mixed neighborhoods during the 1910s and early 1920s helped persuade courts to uphold racially restrictive covenants.[29]

Some governmental officials also played a role in the preservation of residential segregation. For example, in 1923, the mayor of Johnstown, Pennsylvania, ordered all black southern migrants to leave his town. Moreover, with the onset of federal loan programs in the 1930s, racial discrimination in housing continued. A 1933 report of the Federal Home Owners Loan Corporation stated that the presence of "Russian Jews of lower class, South Italians, Negroes, and Mexicans" caused declining property values and that in these neighborhoods no mortgages should be financed. Federal loans, available under the National Housing Act of 1934, encouraged residential segregation, as the Federal Housing Administration (FHA) rated the presence of blacks in a neighborhood a risk that factored into the availability of mortgages.[30]

The effect of these various public and private acts of discrimination was dramatic. In 1910, only 30 percent of Chicago's African Americans lived in predominantly black neighborhoods; by 1920, a majority did so. In Cleveland, the number of census tracts with no black residents more than doubled between 1910 and 1920, from seventeen to thirty-eight. Racially restrictive covenants in San Francisco caused one black newspaper in that city to announce in 1927: "Residential Segregation is as real in California as in Mississippi. A mob is unnecessary. All that's needed is a neighbor[hood] meeting and agreement in writing not to rent, lease, or sell to blacks, and the Courts will do the rest." Even in Minnesota, neighborhoods embraced racially restrictive covenants during the 1920s despite having a paucity of African Americans.[31]

The Great Migration also triggered increasing violence toward blacks, particularly during and after World War I. Race riots erupted in several northern cities – including East St. Louis, Chicago, Philadelphia, and Syracuse, New York – sparked in part by white–black competition for jobs and housing. In East St. Louis, the hiring of black workers triggered mass destruction in the black community in 1917 by

---

[29] For vigilante violence, see "In Henry Sweet Trial," *Cleveland Gazette*, May 15, 1926, p. 1; "Three Telling Victories," *Cleveland Gazette*, June 13, 1925, p. 1; *Cleveland Gazette*, Feb. 20, 1926, p. 2; Meyer, *As Long as They Don't Move Next Door*, pp. 38–45. See also Frank, "Can the Courts Erase the Color Line?", p. 309 ("the cases of the 1920's appearing to condone restrictive covenants were a direct retreat because of the racial violence which shortly preceded them").

[30] For Johnstown, see *Cleveland Gazette*, Sept. 29, 1923, p. 2; for the 1933 report, see Anyon, *Ghetto Schooling*, pp. 62–3.

[31] For Chicago, see Spear, *Black Chicago*, p. 17; for Cleveland, see Reid, "Race, Class, Gender and the Teaching Profession," p. 39; for the 1927 quote, see Taylor, *In Search of the Racial Frontier*, p. 236; for Minnesota, see Delton, "Forging of a Northern Strategy," p. 118.

a white mob that left 125 blacks dead and hundreds of others maimed. Some of the worst violence took place in Chicago. Between 1917 and 1921, fifty-eight racially inspired bombings took place there, most directed at the homes of black families in racially mixed neighborhoods. The most significant outbreak in Chicago was the July 1919 riot that took 38 lives and injured more than 500; blacks bore the brunt of the violence. Historian John Hope Franklin has called the last six months of 1919 "the greatest period of interracial strife the nation had ever witnessed." As a result of the violence, white demands for segregation increased. As the *Chicago Tribune* editorialized: "Despite the possible justice of Negro demands, the fact is that the races are not living in harmony. . . . How long will it be before segregation will be the only means of preventing murders?"[32]

Employer and labor union discrimination against black workers increased in the wake of the Great Migration, particularly in skilled labor positions. White workers opposed hiring black workers, and employers readily acceded to this opposition. A survey by the Cincinnati Chamber of Commerce between 1925 and 1930 found that the most frequent reason employers gave for their failure to hire black workers was that they were "unable or unwilling to mix white and Negro workers." White employers in Minneapolis refused to hire black workers except for certain jobs; as a result, 80 percent of the black men in Minneapolis in 1926 worked as porters, janitors, and night watchmen. White workers in an integrated munitions factory in Chicago during World War I placed a sign in the factory lavatory: "Niggers not allowed to use this toilet." Although the number of blacks employed in skilled and semiskilled work had dramatically increased during World War I, racial discrimination among both northern employers and northern unions sharply curtailed these advances after the conclusion of the war.[33]

Increase in Northern School Segregation in Response to the Migration of Southern Blacks

One important manifestation of this growing racial antagonism was a sharp increase in white insistence on school segregation. Despite state antisegregation laws, school segregation increased in much of

---

[32] For East St. Louis, see Baker, *From Savage to Negro*, p. 138; for Chicago, see Spear, *Black Chicago*, pp. 211–16; for the Franklin quote, see Franklin, *From Slavery to Freedom*, p. 480; for the *Chicago Tribune* quote, see Spear, *Black Chicago*, p. 217.

[33] For the Cincinnati quote, see Trotter, *River Jordan*, pp. 101–2; for Minneapolis, see Delton, "Forging of a Northern Strategy," pp. 120–2; for the Chicago quote, see "Judge John Richardson Gives 'Jim Crow' Decision," *Ohio State Monitor*, Sept. 14, 1918, p. 4; for union discrimination, see Trotter, *Black Milwaukee*, pp. 46–7.

the North during the two decades prior to World War I, and then increased even more dramatically following the onset of the Great Migration.

A number of local school boards introduced school segregation between 1897 and 1910 – even in states that expressly prohibited such segregation – including Alton, Illinois (1897), Brooklyn, Illinois (1901), Sheffield, Massachusetts (1904), East Orange, New Jersey (1905), and Oxford, Pennsylvania (1909). Other northern school boards with a tradition of integrated schools fought to preserve racial mixing in the face of intense segregationist pressure. For example, Chicago schools had been desegregated since 1865, but white insistence on school segregation dramatically increased during the early twentieth century in response to the arrival of thousands of African Americans. One black Chicago attorney noted in 1910 of the growth of the city's black population since 1890: "Colored children have appeared in numbers in many schools. . . . [T]hese things have a tendency to cause whites to resort to jim crow tactics." Chicago whites sought both school board action and a city charter amendment to reverse a half-century history of integrated schools. A leader of the antiblack Hyde Park Improvement Protective Club announced in 1909 that "[i]t is only a question of time when there will be separate schools for Negroes throughout Illinois." Many white students joined the struggle for racial separation. In 1905, a group of white students in Chicago rioted when they were transferred to a predominantly black school, and in 1908 over 150 white students staged a boycott when they were transferred to an integrated school. Moreover, in 1909, when two black children were transferred to a white school, they were beaten by their new classmates. Although black resistance prevented explicit segregation during the first decade of the twentieth century, the Chicago school board did allow white children to transfer out of mixed schools and racially gerrymandered school attendance zones to increase racial cohesion.[34]

During the first decade of the twentieth century, a few state legislatures altered their laws to permit segregation. In 1900, the Kansas

[34] For the increase in school segregation, see Meier and Rudwick, "Early Boycotts of Segregated Schools: The Alton, Illinois, Case"; Meier and Rudwick, "Early Boycotts of Segregated Schools: The East Orange, New Jersey, Experience"; Cha-Jua, *America's First Black Town*, p. 135; "Arson Follows Race War," *New York Times*, Jan. 1, 1904, p. 7; "Bay State 'Jim Crow' School," *New York Times*, Jan 6, 1904, p. 1; "Negroes Win School Fight," *New York Times*, Feb. 12, 1906, p. 2. For the Chicago attorney quote, see Spear, *Black Chicago*, p. 48; for the Hyde Park quote, see Mohraz, *The Separate Problem*, p. 100; for school riots in Chicago, see Spear, *Black Chicago*, pp. 44–5; for Chicago school board policies, see Mohraz, *The Separate Problem*, pp. 98–100; Spear, *Black Chicago*, pp. 204–5.

state legislature, in response to the murder of a white boy by an African American, enacted legislation permitting school segregation in the high schools of Kansas City. Thereafter, pressure for school segregation in other parts of Kansas increased. In 1906, the superintendent of the public schools of Kansas wrote his counterpart in North Carolina requesting information about North Carolina's school segregation statute: "There is a movement in Kansas looking toward the segregation of the races in the public schools, where the per cent of colored population will warrant the separation. . . . Have you any laws on the subject?" In 1909, the Kansas state legislature, in response to overwhelming demand, enacted special legislation allowing Wichita to segregate its schools, reversing a decision of the Kansas Supreme Court that had declared school segregation in Wichita unlawful. Arizona also enacted legislation in 1909 *permitting* school segregation throughout the state; in 1912, the Arizona legislature *mandated* segregation in all elementary schools and permitted local school officials to decide whether to segregate high schools. Specifically, if an Arizona high school had at least twenty-five black students, the local school board was obliged to hold a referendum on segregated schools if 15 percent of the electorate called for such an election. New Mexico enacted legislation permitting school segregation in 1923. In 1911, the Ohio legislature considered but ultimately declined to enact legislation that would have again permitted school segregation in the Buckeye state, while segregationists in New York sought similar legislation the same year.[35]

In the wake of the Great Migration, school segregation sharply increased throughout the North, even in communities that had long enjoyed a tradition of racially mixed schools. As Kelly Miller of Howard University noted in 1929: "The issue of separate schooling is moving Northward with the rising tide of Negro migration. The color line in public education is vigorously asserting itself across the continent." Much of this increase in segregation took place in the southern portions of those states bordering the South. As a 1922 study of northern race relations aptly noted: "There is . . . along the Southern border of Pennsylvania, Ohio, Indiana, Illinois, and Kansas a semi-legal

---

[35] For Kansas legislation, see Duncan, "The Changing Race Relationship," p. 37; for the quote, see "Segregation of Races: Kansas Superintendent of Schools Wants Information," *Raleigh Daily News and Observer*, Aug. 24, 1906, p. 5; for 1909 legislation reversing *Rowles v. Board of Education*, 76 Kan. 361 (1907), see Van Meeter, "Black Resistance to Segregation," pp. 73–4, 77; for Arizona and New Mexico statutes, see Murray, *States' Laws on Race and Color*, pp. 35–6, 290. For proposed Ohio legislation, see Montgomery, "Racial History of the Cincinnati and Suburban Schools," p. 95 (1983), Cincinnati Historical Society; for New York, see "To Demand Separate Schools for Negroes," *New York Times*, Jan. 18, 1911, p. 3.

segregation in the schools in force. At least, it amounts to a tacit understanding, in some of the towns, that the colored children must go to the colored schools, and that they will not be admitted to the schools attended by white children. In fact, in any Northern town where they are proportionately numerous, there is just the same tendency and desire to have them separated from the whites that there is in the South."[36]

Northern school segregation during the post–World War I era took many forms. Although some racial separation was due to the burgeoning residential segregation of northern cities, much of it resulted from specific actions taken by local school officials to preserve racial separation. The most explicit form of school segregation was the establishment of separate schools for black and white children, with pupil assignments conducted on a racial basis. School segregation in New Jersey, for example, already widespread in the state's southern counties by the end of the nineteenth century, substantially increased during the first four decades of the twentieth century as school officials in many communities formally established dual school systems – sometimes by local ordinance – in which school assignments were explicitly based on race rather than geography. A 1925 report found: "[f]rom the university town of Princeton, including the capital city of Trenton, southward to Cape May, every city or town with a considerable Negro population supports the dual educational system, with a building for its white and a building for its Negro pupils of the grammar grades." A few southern counties in New Jersey segregated black students not only at the elementary school level but also at the high school level. A study published in the early 1950s noted striking similarities between segregation in southern New Jersey and the South throughout the first half of the twentieth century: "While most of New Jersey is geographically above the Mason-Dixon line, the history of its public school education, especially at the elementary and junior high school levels, has had more in common with states below than above the line. In the [state's] southern counties both basic policies and prevailing practices have been essentially similar to those of the Southern states."[37]

But this increase in school segregation in New Jersey was not confined to the state's southern counties. During the two decades

---

[36] For the Miller quote, see Miller, "Is the Color Line Crumbling?," p. 284; for the 1922 study, see Duncan, "Changing Race Relationship," p. 37.

[37] For the 1925 study, see Granger, "Race Relations and the School System," p. 327. For other sources on the increase of segregation in New Jersey, see Crocco, Munro, and Weiler, *Pedagogies of Resistance*, p. 67; Payne, "Negroes in the Public Elementary Schools," p. 227; Weinberg, *A Chance to Learn*, p. 75; Mumford, "Double V in New Jersey," p. 25. For the 1950s study, see Williams and Ryan, *Schools in Transition*, p. 121.

following World War I, a few northern New Jersey communities, most of which had integrated their schools during the 1870s, reintroduced racially separate schools in response to the increase in black population. A 1939 report to the state legislature found that "in recent years...many communities in northern New Jersey have either instituted or plan to institute experiments of their own in separate school facilities." Across the state, the number of separate schools for African-American children increased by 35 percent between 1919 and 1935, and by 1940 there were more segregated schools in New Jersey than at any time since the enactment of the 1881 antisegregation legislation. This increase in school segregation clearly violated New Jersey law. As one lawyer noted, New Jersey engaged in the "theoretical admission of colored children to white schools by terms of legislation and simultaneously actual exclusion by method of administration."[38]

School boards in other northern states also engaged in explicit racial assignments, rejecting the practice of assigning children to school based on geography. Many small towns in eastern Pennsylvania established racially separate schools during the 1910s and 1920s. Chester, for example, which had segregated its elementary schools in 1912, established a separate black junior high school in 1929 and a separate black senior high school in 1934. The Chester school board assigned all of the town's black children to Frederick Douglass High School and all of the white children to Chester High School. School authorities in Lower Oxford maintained a black and a white school across the street from each other, justifying such segregation on the grounds that black children are "not as bright as whites." Some Pennsylvania and New Jersey school districts retained geographic assignments, but nevertheless assigned white children who lived in "black" school districts to the closest white school and black children living in "white" school districts to the closest black school. Philadelphia engaged in this practice after the city experienced a fourfold increase in black population during and after World War I. The Philadelphia school superintendent explained in 1926 that "whenever the colored element was in predominance [at a given school] it was deemed wise to transfer all of the white students and faculty members and install a colored faculty." As a result, by the mid-1920s, almost one-third of Philadelphia's black students attended single-race schools, due in

---

[38] For the increase in New Jersey segregation, see Wright, *The Education of Negroes*, pp. 185, 194; Oak and Oak, "The Development of Separate Education in New Jersey," p. 110; Wright, "Racial Integration in the Public Schools," p. 282. For the 1939 report, see *Report of the New Jersey State Temporary Commission*, p. 41. For the lawyer quote, see Satterthwait, "The Color-Line in New Jersey," p. 395.

significant measure to the race-conscious assignment policies of the school board.[39]

In some communities, school officials placed black children in a separate building on the grounds of a white school or in separate classrooms in an otherwise racially mixed school. For example, in Gary, Indiana, school officials established racially segregated elementary schools – East Pulaski and West Pulaski – on the same parcel of land, with separate teachers, classrooms, and American flags. The two schools operated on slightly different schedules to reduce racial interaction. In many counties in southern New Jersey, school buildings were divided into white and black sections, with white teachers for white children and black teachers for black children. Some Pennsylvania and New Jersey school districts established racially separate classrooms, with "Union Rooms" for black children of all ages and graded classrooms for whites. Although the Pennsylvania state legislature enacted legislation in 1925 prohibiting racially separate classrooms, the new legislation was frequently ignored.[40]

---

[39] For segregation in eastern Pennsylvania, including Carlisle, Chester, Coatesville, Frankford, Germantown, Lansdown, Lower Oxford, Sharon Hill, Swarthmore, West Chester, and York, see "World War II Brought Change in Jim Crow School Pattern," *York Gazette and Daily*, July 1, 1954, NAACP Papers, Box II-A-228; Letter from S. B. Randolph to National Office of the NAACP, July 1944, NAACP Papers, Box II-B-146; Duncan, "The Changing Race Relationship," pp. 39–40; Hatfield, "The Impact of the New Deal," pp. 205–6; Kennedy, *The Negro Peasant Turns Cityward*, p. 194. For Chester, see "Chester Creates First Jim Crow High School in State," *Philadelphia Tribune*, Feb. 22, 1934, p. 1; Mohraz, *The Separate Problem*, p. 92; *Murray v. School District of the City of Chester*, Bill of Complaint, May 29, 1934, Arthur Spingarn Papers, Box 33. For Lower Oxford, see "Say Negroes 'Not Bright,'" *Houston Informer*, July 31, 1948, NAACP Papers, Box II-B-146; for assignment policies, see Kennedy, *The Negro Peasant Turns Cityward*, p. 194; Pennsylvania Department of Public Welfare, "Negro Survey of Pennsylvania," p. 58; Henri, *Black Migration*, p. 181; Mosey, "Testing, Tracking, and Curriculum," pp. 13–14; "Annual Report of the Urban Colored Population Commission, State of New Jersey" (1945), Lett Papers. For the school superintendent quote, see Franklin, *The Education of Black Philadelphia*, p. 82. For Philadelphia patterns, see Franklin, *The Education of Black Philadelphia*, p. 66; Licht, *Getting Work*, p. 84; Daniels, "Schools," pp. 178–82; "How Separate Schools Menace!" *Cleveland Gazette*, July 21, 1928, p. 1.

[40] For separate buildings and classrooms, see New Jersey Conference of Social Work, *The Negro in New Jersey*, p. 37; Granger, "Race Relations and the School System," p. 329; Devore, "The Education of Blacks in New Jersey," pp. 101–2, 144–5; Johnson, *The Negro in American Civilization*, pp. 268–9; *Report of the New Jersey State Temporary Commission*, p. 40; Henri, *Black Migration*, p. 181; Tyack, *The One Best System*, p. 124; Pennsylvania Department of Public Welfare, "Negro Survey of Pennsylvania," pp. 58–9; Kennedy, *The Negro Peasant Turns Cityward*, pp. 193–5. For Gary schools, see Tipton, *Community in Crisis*, p. 21; Millender, *Yesterday in Gary*, p. 57; for fenced playgrounds, see Payne, "Negroes in the Public Elementary Schools of the North," p. 227; for failed legislation banning separate classrooms, see Letter from Theodore O. Spaulding

Several Ohio cities, including Cincinnati, Cleveland, Columbus, and Dayton, also established racially separate classrooms in the wake of the Great Migration. Dayton, for example, established separate classrooms for black children in racially mixed schools in 1912, a practice it had previously used prior to the 1887 antisegregation legislation in Ohio. During World War I, a number of southern black families migrated to Dayton, many of whom settled in the attendance area of the Garfield elementary school, a white school. In 1917, the Dayton school board assigned these newly arrived black students to a poorly heated and maintained frame building behind the Garfield School to keep them separate from the white children educated inside the main building. These black students were crowded into classrooms with more than twice as many pupils as the classrooms in the main building that housed the white children. Even black children at Dayton's racially mixed orphanage were assigned across town to black classes at Garfield, whereas white orphans went to a nearby school, a practice that continued until after the 1954 *Brown* decision.[41]

Cleveland reversed its long-standing commitment to racially integrated schools during the 1920s by assigning black children to racially separate classrooms, prompting a local black newspaper, the *Call and Post*, to comment in 1928: "Daily it becomes more apparent that the virus of southern race prejudice is bearing its malignant fruit in this cosmopolitan city of Cleveland. With amazing rapidity it is spreading through the very arteries of this city – once famous for its liberality to minority groups." The trend towards segregation increased during the 1930s as the Cleveland school board began to assign most of the city's black high school students to Central High School, even those who lived closer to other high schools, and to permit white students who lived near Central High School to transfer to other schools.[42]

Where there were too few black children to justify a racially separate classroom, some teachers insisted on racial separation within the classroom. Prior to the establishment of a separate black senior high

to Roy Wilkins, Mar. 25, 1940; Letter from W. M. Gilmore to Constance Baker Motley, Feb. 22, 1950, NAACP Papers, Box II-B-146; Untitled and undated article on Segregation in Northern Schools, NAACP Papers, Box II-B-137.

[41] For racially separate classrooms in Ohio, see "'Jim Crow' School Rooms," *Cleveland Gazette*, May 22, 1937, p. 1; "Is the Ohio Supreme Court K.K.K.?" *Cleveland Gazette*, Apr. 4, 1925, p. 1; Porter, "The Problem of Negro Education," p. 124. For Dayton, see *Brinkman v. Gilligan*, 583 F.2d 243, 249, n.19 (6th Cir. 1978); *Board of Education v. State ex rel. Reese*, 114 Ohio St. 188 (1926); Watras, *Politics, Race, and Schools*, p. 85; Appendix to Brief in Opposition to Petition for Writ of Certiorari, pp. 3a, n.3, 5a, n.6, *Brinkmann v. Gilligan*, United States Supreme Court, 1979.

[42] For integrated schools in Cleveland, see "Cleveland's Schools," *Cleveland Advocate*, Sept. 18, 1915, p. 4; Kusmer, *A Ghetto Takes Shape*, pp. 182–4, 187 (quote, p. 187).

school in Chester, Pennsylvania, for example, some teachers required segregated seating. A white teacher in Dayton in the 1920s told a black student that "even though I was a good student I was not to sit in the front of the class because most of the colored children sat in the back." One Arizona school teacher went to an even greater extreme, placing a screen around the desk of a black student to shield him from his white classmates.[43]

In some racially mixed schools, black and white children were segregated during recreational activities. For example, some New Jersey schools, as in Asbury Park, fenced their playgrounds to keep black and white children apart. A Wichita school also designated a specific part of the school playground for black children. Several school districts throughout the North, including districts in New Jersey, New York, Ohio, Illinois, Indiana, and Kansas, excluded black students from high school swimming pools or else forced them to swim on Friday afternoons, after which the pools would be drained. Many northern school districts with racially mixed schools excluded black children from a variety of extracurricular activities such as athletics, the school band, and ROTC, forcing the black community to organize private extracurricular activities for their children. For example, during the early twentieth century, blacks in Portland, Oregon, used churches to stage plays and oratorical contests to provide black children with opportunities denied them in the public schools. Students at high school graduation ceremonies in Montclair, New Jersey, marched in a racially segregated fashion until the NAACP petitioned for an end to the practice in 1925.[44]

---

43 For racially separate seating, see "Girl Fought 'Jim-Crow,'" *Cleveland Gazette*, Apr. 4, 1931, p. 1 (Chester); Appendix to Brief in Opposition to Petition for Writ of Certiorari, p. 4a, n. 4, *Brinkmann v. Gilligan*, United States Supreme Court, 1979 (Dayton – quote); Taylor, *In Search of the Racial Frontier*, p. 217 (Arizona).

44 For separate playgrounds, see Granger, "Race Relations and the School System," p. 329 (New Jersey); Payne, "Negroes in the Public Elementary Schools of the North," p. 227 (New Jersey); Taylor, *In Search of the Racial Frontier*, p. 218 (Wichita). For separate swimming pools, see *Patterson v. Board of Education of Trenton*, 11 N.J. Misc. 179 (1933), *aff'd*, 112 N.J.L. 99 (1934) (Trenton); "Court Upholds Ban on Race Segregation," *New York Times*, Jan. 6, 1934, p. 17 (Trenton); Thomas, "Schooling as a Political Instrument," p. 587 (Buffalo); "Our Student Strike!" *Cleveland Gazette*, Sept. 27, 1930, p. 1 (Sandusky, Ohio); "Atlantic's 'Jim Crowists,'" *Cleveland Gazette*, June 7, 1924, p. 1 (Atlantic City); Tipton, *Community in Crisis*, pp. 25–6 (Gary); "Along the N.A.A.C.P. Battlefront," *The Crisis* 43 (June 1936), p. 182 (Kankakee, Illinois); "Victory against School Segregation," *Cleveland Gazette*, Apr. 26, 1924, p. 1 (Wichita). Other districts required black and white children to swim at separate times. Interview with Robert Carter, Aug. 7, 2003 (East Orange, New Jersey); Robisch, "Educational Segregation and Desegregation," p. 71 (Dayton, Ohio). For example, in Gary, school authorities during the early 1940s finally permitted black boys to swim in the school pool, but only on Fridays, and then required that the pool be thoroughly cleaned over

Some local school authorities preserved racial separation through racially gerrymandered school district lines accompanied by discriminatory transfer policies that permitted only white students to transfer to a school in another district. The experience in New Rochelle, New York, illustrates this practice. In 1889, school authorities closed New Rochelle's one black school, which dated from the antebellum era, and assigned the town's black children to white schools. Thereafter, black children in New Rochelle attended racially mixed schools. But in 1930, faced with a growing black population, the New Rochelle school board opened a new school, the Webster School, and racially gerrymandered its attendance zone lines so that it would be a predominantly white school, while the nearby Lincoln School would be a predominantly black school. The New Rochelle school board permitted all white children who lived in the Lincoln school district to transfer to the Webster School but denied black children living in the Lincoln district the same right. The effect of these actions was dramatic. Between 1930 and 1933, black enrollment at Lincoln increased from 25 to 75 percent, and by 1949 Lincoln was an all-black school. Finally, in 1949, confronted with the inequities of its transfer policy, the school board ceased to allow transfers, although it did not redraw its racially gerrymandered district lines.[45]

Other school districts also used racial gerrymandering to preserve racial separation. The Columbus Board of Education – which had desegregated its schools and used racially mixed faculties during the 1880s – resegregated many of its schools during the early twentieth century through racially gerrymandered school district lines and the assignment of teachers on a racial basis. In 1909, the Columbus school board established a new elementary school in the middle of a black neighborhood and gerrymandered the school's attendance zone to preserve its character as a black school. As a result, the new school – Champion Elementary – was more than 90 percent black, whereas two other elementary schools, each about three blocks away, were less than 4 percent black. Many African Americans, fearing that the Champion

---

the weekend before white children used it again. Tipton, *Community in Crisis*, pp. 25–6. For exclusion of blacks from school activities, see Homel, "Two Worlds of Race?" pp. 241–2 (Chicago); Betten and Mohl, "The Evolution of Racism," pp. 54–5 (Gary); Wallis, *All We Had Was Each Other*, p. 6 (Madison County, Indiana); McElderry, "The Problem of the Color Line," p. 67 (Portland). For Montclair graduation ceremonies, see "Alter Graduation March," *New York Times*, June 13, 1925, p. 6.

45 "Protest to Governor on 'Jim Crow' Schools," *New York Times*, Sept. 10, 1930, p. 22; *Taylor v. Board of Education of New Rochelle*, 191 F. Supp. 181, 184–6 (S.D.N.Y. 1961); United States Commission on Civil Rights, *Civil Rights U.S.A.: Public Schools Cities in the North and West*, pp. 46, 48, 68; Ment, "Racial Segregation in the Public Schools," pp. 264–73.

School's placement would lead to school segregation, had petitioned the school board – unsuccessfully – to build the school elsewhere, claiming that "the boundary lines of certain school districts in this city [had already] been drawn as to segregate colored children." During the 1920s, the Columbus school board grew bolder in its segregation efforts, expanding its use of gerrymandered school districts and racially explicit teacher assignments to preserve the racial integrity of the city's schools. In addition, in 1925, the school board established a "portable school" to house black students living in a predominantly white neighborhood in the northern section of the city, rather than assign these children to a nearby white elementary school. A 1931 report from the Ohio director of education to the governor found that 1,269 black children in Columbus attended "special schools for colored children." A 1937 report on the Columbus schools concluded that the problem of black education "seems to be met satisfactorily with separate schools wherever possible." School district lines would remain racially gerrymandered in Columbus until after the 1954 *Brown* decision.[46]

Chicago racially gerrymandered its school district lines as well. Prior to the Great Migration, Chicago school officials had largely resisted school segregation in the face of white pressure. But as the number of blacks living in Chicago sharply increased during and after World War I, pressure for school segregation mounted, as many whites argued that "white children should not be compelled to sit with colored children." In response, school authorities racially gerrymandered school district lines and liberally granted white children transfers from predominantly black schools to which they had been assigned based on residence. Black children were denied such transfer rights. The effect of these practices was dramatic. Whereas in 1916, only one Chicago school – Keith Elementary – was 90 percent black and it enrolled only about 8 percent of the city's 4,500 black students, by 1930, 26 of the city's schools were at least 90 percent black and they enrolled about 82 percent of the city's 34,000 black students. These shifting patterns were due in significant measure to residential segregation caused by an

[46] For the discussion of Columbus, see "Would Draw a 'Color Line' in the Public Schools," *Cleveland Gazette*, Sept. 26, 1903, p. 1; Columbus Board of Education Minutes, Sept. 30, 1907, May 11, 1908, June 8, 1908, cited in Testimony of W. A. Montgomery, Appendix, pp. 368–71, *Columbus Board of Education v. Penick*, 443 U.S. 449 (1979); Gerber, *Black Ohio and the Color Line*, pp. 266–7; Minor, "The Negro in Columbus," pp. 147–53. For the black petition quote, see Brief for Respondents, p. 14, n. 12, *Columbus Board of Education v. Penick*, 443 U.S. 449 (1979); for the 1931 report, see *Penick v. Columbus Board of Education*, 519 F. Supp. 925, 929 (S.D. Ohio 1981); for the 1937 quote, see Robisch, "Educational Segregation and Desegregation," p. 69.

FIGURE 5 Students at Keith Elementary School, Chicago, 1936. National
Archives photo, no. 69-N-5442-C (Works Progress Administration photo).

array of practices by realtors, mortgage lenders, and local politicians in
response to the Great Migration that led to the creation of a rigid, permanent black ghetto in Chicago, but racially gerrymandered district
lines also played a role. In 1945, the president of the Chicago NAACP
would declare with some exaggeration: "We have segregated schools
outright.... They are as much segregated as the schools in Savannah,
Georgia, or Vicksburg, Mississippi."[47]

Where racial gerrymandering could not preserve school segregation, some local school boards established "undistricted" attendance
zones; white children living in these zones were permitted to attend
certain designated white schools, but black children were required
to attend a black school. Gary, Indiana, followed this strategy. Other
northern school districts deployed undistricted attendance zones but
only encouraged, not required, black children in those areas to attend
separate black schools. Cincinnati, for example, had eliminated most
of its separate black schools after the enactment of antisegregation

---

[47] For the discussion of Chicago, see Homel, "Two Worlds of Race?" pp. 241–2; Spear,
    Black Chicago, pp. 201–2, 204; Homel, *Down from Equality*, pp. 27–8. For the quote
    concerning whites sitting with blacks, see Spear, *Black Chicago*, p. 205; for the quote
    from the NAACP president, see Homel, "Two Worlds of Race?" p. 242.

legislation in 1887, but the school board reestablished several black schools during the first three decades of the twentieth century. In residentially integrated areas of the city, the school board did not utilize geographic attendance zones; rather, the board maintained both white and colored schools. In theory, black children could choose the school they wished to attend, but frequent mistreatment in the white schools caused most to choose one of the colored schools. The Cincinnati school board would continue to exclude several black elementary schools, designated "Separate Schools," from the city's general geographic assignment plan until the early 1950s. By the same token, in the 1920s, the Cincinnati school board introduced a disciplinary policy pursuant to which black children in racially mixed schools who misbehaved were transferred to one of the separate colored schools.[48]

Patterns of racial segregation varied between elementary schools and high schools. In many northern cities, such as Atlantic City, Camden, Trenton, Cincinnati, and Philadelphia, elementary schools were segregated, while high schools were integrated. However, some communities, such as Dayton, Ohio, and Chester, Pennsylvania, maintained segregated elementary schools and high schools. Some northern school districts provided elementary schools for black children but no high schools. Several school districts in southern Illinois, for example, excluded black children from all local high schools, requiring them to travel to segregated high schools in neighboring counties or, more typically, to go without.[49]

In a few instances, black children were excluded from public schools altogether. For example, during the 1920s, as southern blacks moved to Oregon to work in the lumber industry, their children were denied entry into public schools in some communities. In the town of Maxville in eastern Oregon, the public schools barred black children, instead hiring a black woman to teach them in her home during the evenings. Some black children in Maxville traveled to other towns to attend school.[50]

---

[48] For Gary, see Tipton, *Community in Crisis*, p. 22; for Cincinnati, see Washington, "The Black Struggle for Desegregated Quality Education," pp. 83, 101, 103; Montgomery, "Racial History of the Cincinnati and Suburban Public Schools," pp. 125–6 (1983), Cincinnati Historical Society.

[49] For variations in segregation, see Homel, "Two Worlds of Race?" p. 242; for exclusion of blacks from high school, see Valien, "Racial Desegregation," p. 304 (Illinois); "Gallipolis School Situation," *Ohio State Monitor*, Oct. 19, 1918, p. 8 (Ohio); Letter from William Hastie to Walter White, Oct. 2, 1933, Hastie Papers, Box 102-2 (New Jersey).

[50] McLagan, *A Peculiar Paradise*, pp. 111, 115, 123, 131, 135, 141, 165; see also letter from "Non de plume" to W. E. B. Du Bois, Apr. 9, 1914, NAACP Papers, Box II-L-14 (exclusion of blacks from public schools in Nogales, Arizona).

FIGURE 6   New York City school, 1937. National Archives photo, no. 69-N-9609 (Works Progress Administration photo).

To be sure, in some parts of the North, school segregation was minimal in the wake of the Great Migration. New England experienced the smallest increase in school segregation due in significant measure to the fact that relatively few southern blacks migrated to New England during and after World War I. New Haven, Connecticut, for example, experienced minimal school segregation during the first three decades of the twentieth century; during those years, black students comprised less than 3.5 percent of the New Haven student population. Both Boston and Providence, each of which also received relatively few black migrants during the Great Migration, also retained racially mixed schools. In fact, the black population in Rhode Island increased only slightly during the 1910s and actually *declined* during the 1920s.[51]

Patterns of segregation were also less rigid in New York City even though many blacks did migrate there during and after World War I. In fact, New York City is somewhat unique among northern cities,

[51] For New Haven, see Homel, "Two Worlds of Race?" p. 241; Warner, *New Haven Negroes*, pp. 275–8; Ment, "Racial Segregation in the Public Schools," pp. 275–6; for Boston, see Daniels, *In Freedom's Birthplace*, p. 188; for Providence, see Perlmann, *Ethnic Differences*, pp. 182–3; for the Rhode Island black population, see U.S. Bureau of Census, 1910, 1920, 1930.

FIGURE 7   New York City school, 1930s. National Archives photo, no. 69-N-9597 (Works Progress Administration photo).

as it experienced a large black influx but generally declined to engage in deliberate efforts to segregate its schools during the 1910s and 1920s. A 1913 study of black education in New York City revealed that assignment patterns in the city's elementary schools were generally consistent with residential patterns. Another 1913 study found black students present in every school in the city. After World War I, black students in New York City were increasingly concentrated in certain schools due to residential segregation, but the NAACP made few claims of intentional segregation during the 1920s and 1930s and offered the New York City elementary schools as a model for other cities to emulate. Similarly, the biracial Mayor's Commission on Conditions in Harlem, appointed in 1935, made no mention of school segregation even though by 1934, Harlem had thirteen virtually all-black schools due to residential segregation. Alain Locke, upon reviewing the Mayor's Commission report, commented that "the comparative absence of racial discrimination in the school system is one of the bright features of the report." A 1939 report of the New York State Temporary Commission on the Condition of the Colored Urban Population, created by the state legislature, also found no intentional segregation in New York City's elementary schools, although it did find that high school district lines had been gerrymandered in and around Harlem to preserve racial segregation.[52]

In Indiana, the one northern state that expressly permitted school segregation by local option until the middle of the twentieth century, the number of racially separate schools sharply increased during the 1920s due to a variety of segregationist tactics. Indeed, by the 1930s, most of Indiana's larger cities had partial or complete school segregation, as did several smaller towns and cities, particularly in the southern counties of the state. Moreover, in 1935, the Indiana General Assembly took action in further support of school segregation. In 1907, the state legislature had provided for the closure of any public school with a daily average attendance of fewer than twelve students – a provision that led to integration in a few rural communities. In 1935, however, the legislature provided that that closure provision did not apply to separate black schools and ordered all school districts that had previously closed black schools pursuant to the 1907 statute to reopen them. As a federal judge later characterized the 1935 statute, the state legislature ordered local school authorities "to furnish a separate school building and teacher for the instruction of . . . one Negro child attending primary school rather than permit that child to attend a white school." Despite the gross inefficiency of school segregation in certain areas, many Indiana school authorities retained their separate black schools. During the 1948–9 school year, for example, nine counties in Indiana averaged five or fewer students per grade in their separate black schools.[53]

Indianapolis, though most of its black elementary schoolchildren had always attended racially separate schools, had never segregated its public high schools. In 1922, however, several white groups, including the Indianapolis Chamber of Commerce, petitioned the school board for the establishment of a separate black high school; thereafter, the board agreed to build such a school. The *Indianapolis Recorder*, a black newspaper, bemoaned the board's decision: "The Colored High School is to be a reality. Jim-Crowism is rapidly encroaching the colored citizens of Indianapolis. Color-phobia is rampant. First

---

[52] For the first 1913 study, see Blascoer, *Colored School Children in New York*; for the second 1913 study, see Henri, *Black Migration*, p. 181; for New York schools after World War I, see Stern, "Jim Crow Goes to School in New York," pp. 201–2; Ment, "Racial Segregation in the Public Schools," pp. 228–9, 235–51; Thompson, "The Negro Separate School," p. 242; Homel, "Two Worlds of Race?" p. 241. For the Locke quote, see Ment, "Racial Segregation in the Public Schools," p. 245, n. 1.

[53] For the discussion of Indiana, see *United States v. Board of Commissioners*, 332 F. Supp. 655 (S.D. Ind. 1971) (quote, pp. 664–5); Reynolds, "The Challenge of Racial Equality," p. 177.

came segregation in the theatres, department stores, and other public places. Next our own city park. Now . . . the Negroes' only weapon of defense has failed, the ballot. . . . Politicians no longer fear the wrath of the Negro vote."[54]

As racial separation in northern public schools increased in response to the Great Migration, ignorance of the illegality of school segregation under state law remained widespread. One of the leading education texts of the period, Stanford Professor Ellwood Cubberley's *State and County Educational Reorganization*, published in 1914, noted that "[a]ny county or city school-district may also establish separate schools for children of the negro race, when there are enough to make such separate instruction advantageous," advice that ran directly contrary to the antisegregation legislation in most northern states. The same year, Cubberley wrote "an ideal state school code" that noted, again contrary to the law of most northern states, that school officials may set up separate schools for "defective, delinquent, or . . . negro" children. Finally, Cubberley erroneously advised local school districts that they could either provide separate secondary schools for their black students or else contract with a neighboring school district to educate them. Even the United States Bureau of Education displayed ignorance of the nineteenth-century antisegregation legislation. In a 1917 report, the Bureau made the preposterous claim that Pennsylvania and Illinois had "no law governing separation of the races in the public schools" – ignoring the fact that both of those states clearly prohibited school segregation by statute.[55]

Reasons for the Increase in Northern School Segregation

This impetus toward increased school segregation in the early twentieth century had many causes. Central to white insistence on segregation was the influx of southern black children into northern school districts. Indeed, white insistence on school segregation was generally strongest in those cities that received the largest number of southern migrants and generally increased in proportion to the number of black children in the school district. A 1932 study of New Jersey schools, for example, found that when the black population in

---

54 For Indianapolis segregation, see Thornbrough, "Segregation in Indiana," pp. 601–4; Williams and Ryan, *Schools in Transition*, p. 50. For the quote, see "Jim-Crow High School Reality, To Build in April," *Indianapolis Recorder*, Nov. 29, 1924, in NAACP Papers, Box I-D-58.

55 For the first quote, see Cubberley, *State and County Educational Reorganization*, pp. 83–4; for the second quote, see ibid., p. 4; for erroneous advice, see ibid., pp. 83–4. For the final quote, see Department of the Interior, Bureau of Education, *Negro Education*, pp. 677, 683, 688.

a given community reached 10 percent, pressure to segregate black children substantially increased.[56]

Many white principals, teachers, and school boards justified school segregation on the grounds that the newly arrived southern migrant children were not equipped to engage in studies alongside white children because of their poor educational backgrounds. In the South, black children had typically attended school for only a few months a year, and the quality of southern black education was vastly inferior to that available in most northern schools. The Chicago Commission on Race Relations concluded in 1922 that "the great majority of the retarded Negro children were from southern states" and that their retardation was due in significant measure to their poor educational backgrounds. A 1926 survey of the Detroit Bureau of Governmental Research also found that most black children who had fallen behind their grade level were migrant children with inferior educational backgrounds.[57]

As a result of their educational deficiencies, many black children were placed in classrooms in which they were considerably older than their peers. These age gaps, coupled with cultural differences, produced socialization problems that adversely affected the attitudes of white school administrators toward the migrant children. Black sociologist Charles Johnson reported in 1932 that when southern black children "come into northern schools . . . the usual problems of overage children develop. Truancy, delinquency and incorrigibility are expressions of this and require special and concerted efforts to correct."[58]

Under the best of circumstances, the assimilation of poorly educated southern black children into northern schools would have required patience and care from teachers, most of whom were white. But many white teachers were neither prepared nor willing to assist these students in making the necessary adjustment to their new school. Instead, the limited academic preparation of the southern migrant children gave way to racist stereotypes about the deficiencies of

---

[56] For white insistence on segregation, see Henri, *Black Migration*, p. 182; Kennedy, *The Negro Peasant Turns Cityward*, p. 193; for the New Jersey study, see Wright, *The Education of Negroes*, p. 192.

[57] For justifications of segregation, see Spear, *Black Chicago*, p. 204; Woofter, *Negro Problems in Cities* pp. 175–6; "The Segregation of Negro Children at Toms River, N.J.," 25 *School and Society* 365 (Mar. 26, 1927); Meier and Rudwick, "Early Boycotts of Segregated Schools: The East Orange, New Jersey, Experience," pp. 23–4; Johnson, *The Negro in American Civilization*, p. 270; Kennedy, *The Negro Peasant Turns Cityward*, pp. 196–8; Chicago Commission on Race Relations, *The Negro in Chicago*, pp. 239, 256 (quote, p. 260). For Detroit survey, see Kennedy, *The Negro Peasant Turns Cityward*, p. 199.

[58] For socialization problems, see Mosey, "Testing, Tracking, and Curriculum," p. 64; for the Johnson quote, see C. S. Johnson, "The Need of Social Work in Cities – in the North," January 30, 1932, p. 4, Johnson Papers, Box 166, Folder 16.

African Americans. Many white administrators openly urged school segregation, notwithstanding state laws that prohibited such action.

For example, a survey of educational attitudes among New Jersey school superintendents found widespread support for segregation. The superintendent of Trenton schools explained his support in 1927: "The problem of retardation is more serious among colored children than among any other racial group. I am inclined to believe that the further extension of segregation . . . is the only real practical solution." Philadelphia's school superintendent also urged separate schools in the early twentieth century: "[Segregation] has given to the colored child better opportunity to move at its [sic] own rate of progress through the materials of the curriculum, which rate of progress is in some respects different from the rate of progress of other children."[59]

At the same time, many northern white teachers preferred school segregation. In a 1921 survey in Columbus, Ohio, 115 out of 130 school teachers reported that they favored school segregation. A majority of these teachers stated that black children were "backward" and impeded the progress of white children. Many of these teachers also believed that black children were inherently inferior to white children. When asked about the wisdom of racial mixing, one Columbus high school teacher remarked that "their capacities are not the same, thus one retards the possible progress of the other." Another Columbus school teacher commented that "[t]he very make-up of the races are different, and one race is repulsive to the other. Thus the teacher if she be of the white race cannot and will not give the attention to the negro that he should have."[60]

Other northern educators shared these views. The assistant principal of a predominantly black school in Buffalo commented that "other children should not be mixed-up with the colored as their standard of morals is so much lower." In Gary, Indiana, most of the white teachers in a racially integrated school (but with segregated classrooms) petitioned their principal in 1918 to remove the black children from their school: "The promiscuous association of the white and colored pupils is a terrible thing. It should not be allowed, particularly in a school with a large number of foreign pupils. They will soon lose sight of the color line." The Gary teachers also complained that black children posed discipline problems due to their poor educational

---

[59] For racial stereotypes, see Frazier, *The Negro in the United States*, pp. 440–1; for the New Jersey survey, see *Report of the New Jersey State Temporary Commission*, pp. 38–42. For the Trenton superintendent quote, see Payne, "Negroes in the Public Elementary Schools," p. 230; for the Philadelphia superintendent quote, see Tyack, *The One Best System*, p. 227.

[60] Harshman, "Race Contact in Columbus," pp. 19–20.

backgrounds and the age disparity between many black and white children.[61]

Many white education scholars argued that black children would fare better in separate schools under the tutelage of black teachers.[62] Louis A. Pechstein, dean of the University of Cincinnati School of Education and a prominent northern white educator, wrote in 1929: "While all would prefer to have democracy in education, this goal has not been reached and is not likely to be reached in the northern cities studied, since the separation of the races in all walks of life is operating and seems likely to continue.... [T]he ideal separate public school for negroes in northern cities will, under a staff of well-trained negro teachers, function in providing a closer parent-pupil-teacher relation as well as a clearer insight into the treatment of mental deficiency, social maladjustments, special disabilities, and irregularities in behavior."[63]

Many northern school officials were blatantly racist in their resistance to pupil integration, arguing that black children were inherently inferior and not fit to associate with white children. A white principal in Atlantic City, New Jersey, explained his support for school segregation: "I believe in segregation.... [Black children] are like little animals. There is no civilization in their homes. They shouldn't hold up white children who have had these things for centuries. They are not as clean. They are careless about their bodies. Why should we contaminate our race?" Another white school principal in Toms River, New Jersey, dismissed an objection by black parents to the midyear removal of thirty black students from their racially mixed school to a poorly equipped church: "I've just returned from a trip to Texas, and, believe me, they know how to treat colored people down there.... Why, if these people had done in Texas what they've done here, or had done it in any of the Southern states, they'd have been lynched. They would have gone to whatever school the whites told them to and be mighty glad to have the chance." The president of the Westhampton Township, New Jersey, Board of Education announced in 1939 that "[o]ur plan is to have a separate school for colored children from the first grade through high school. The reason is because the colored children are objectionable." Not surprisingly, many black leaders called New Jersey the "Mississippi of the north."[64]

---

[61] For the Buffalo quote, see Mosey, "Testing, Tracking, and Curriculum," p. 63; for the Gary discussion and quote, see Cohen, *Children of the Mill*, p. 69.

[62] Frazier, *The Negro in the United States*, p. 441.

[63] Pechstein, "The Problem of Negro Education," pp. 197–8.

[64] For the Atlantic City quote, see Johnson, *Background to Patterns of Negro Segregation*, p. 198; for the Toms River quote, see Wilson, "Citizens Protest to Governor," *Pittsburgh*

Such racist attitudes were prevalent among school administrators in other parts of the North as well. In Madison, Indiana, one student recalled the white school superintendent visiting his black school: "[He talked] to us like we were just something that came in from darkest Africa or somewhere. He told us that we were worthless, dumb, that we couldn't learn anything, that we would never learn. I will never forget it." Upon hearing a white student comment that "if Negroes should ever try to enroll in our school, we'll get machine guns and see that they leave as quick as they came," a white principal in Gary replied: "I wouldn't blame them either, might even help them."[65]

Many white parents also opposed school integration. When a teacher in Flushing, New York, in 1911 required a white girl to dance with a black boy, provoking taunts from her white classmates that she was a "nigger's partner," white parents demanded a return to separate schools. A 1921 study in Columbus, Ohio, found that a majority of white parents surveyed objected to racially mixed schools on the grounds that black children were backward and that their presence in the classroom retarded white children in their school work. Such parental attitudes were widespread. One white man in Gary urged school segregation: "After all, they came from Africa quite recently, and as slaves at that. They have no tradition of civilization and education as we have. . . . They are still dirty, lazy, loud and not too pleasant to have living nearby."[66]

Many white students also expressed strong opposition to the presence of black children in their classrooms. White high school students in Cincinnati engaged in an unsuccessful strike to exclude their black classmates in 1916. In 1919, white students in Gallipolis, Ohio, conducted a boycott to protest a court decision that black children could not be excluded from their school. White high school students in Darby, Pennsylvania, unsuccessfully protested the announcement of a black student as their valedictorian in 1924 and threatened to hold separate commencement exercises. White students in Gary engaged in a massive walkout in 1927 when a few black students were assigned to their school; eventually, school authorities did reassign most of the

Courier, Apr. 2, 1927, p. 1; for the Westhampton quote, see *Report of the New Jersey State Temporary Commission*, p. 41; for the Mississippi quote, see Morse, "New Jersey, New Laboratory in Race Relations," p. 156. The *New Jersey Herald News* reported in 1941 that white teachers in Trenton "have a reputation for gross prejudice against colored children." "Little Hitlers in School System," *New Jersey Herald News*, Feb. 22, 1941, p. 8.

[65] For the Madison quote, see Wallis, *All We Had Was Each Other*, p. 65; for the Gary quote, see Tipton, *Community in Crisis*, p. 99.

[66] For Flushing, see "To Demand Separate Schools for Negroes," *New York Times*, Jan. 18, 1911, p. 3; for the Columbus study, see Harshman, "Race Contact in Columbus, pp. 16–18; for the Gary quote, see Tipton, *Community in Crisis*, p. 16.

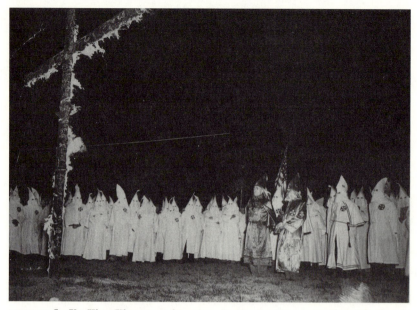

FIGURE 8   Ku Klux Klan cross burning, Indianapolis, 1920s. Reprinted with permission of the Indiana Historical Society, Indianapolis Recorder Collection, P0303, Box 81, Folder 14.

black students to another school. To be sure, some northern white students did oppose racial segregation, particularly when the numbers of black children were quite small. In 1929, more than 400 white students in Dorchester, Massachusetts, refused to hold their high school prom at a hotel that announced that it would exclude the school's sole black student.[67]

Moreover, the Ku Klux Klan experienced a striking resurgence throughout much of the North and West during the 1920s and 1930s that led to increased pressure for school segregation. In many northern communities, newly energized Klan groups pressured school officials to establish or maintain segregated schools. The Grand Dragon of the Indiana Klan urged support in 1924 for a variety of positions including "White American supremacy and the segregating of Negroes, especially in schools." Klan support contributed to the establishment of

[67] For the Cincinnati strike, see "No Racial Lines for Cincinnati Schools," *New York Age*, Feb. 3, 1916, p. 1; for the Gallipolis boycott, see "Court Refuses to Stand for Segregation in Public Schools," *Colorado Statesman*, Jan. 25, 1919, in NAACP Papers, Box I-C-405; for the Darby protest, see *Cleveland Gazette*, July 26, 1924, p. 2; for the Gary walkout, see Betten and Mohl, "The Evolution of Racism," p. 55; for the Dorchester prom, see "400 White Hi Grads Loyal," *Cleveland Gazette*, July 27, 1929, p. 2.

the first segregated high school in Indianapolis. In Ohio, the Klan waged a public campaign for both school segregation and a ban on interracial marriage throughout the 1920s and early 1930s. George McCord, superintendent of the Springfield, Ohio, schools during that city's reestablishment of segregated schools during the early 1920s, along with two members of the local school board, were Klan members. The Columbus, New Jersey, school superintendent during the 1920s was also a local Klan leader. In 1922, the rare hiring of a black teacher to teach white children in Hackensack, New Jersey, prompted a Ku Klux Klan parade in opposition and a barrage of threats. Similarly, in 1936, the Klan threatened to intervene in a school segregation dispute in East Orange, New Jersey. The Oregon Klan used death threats to drive the only black resident out of Oregon City and threatened blacks who moved into white neighborhoods in Portland.[68]

At the same time, many educational theorists of the 1920s urged a "scientific basis for educational policy" that included ability groupings, intelligence tests, and a differentiated curriculum for slower learners. White educators used intelligence testing, which became increasingly popular during the 1910s, to support their notions of the intellectual inferiority of blacks and to justify school segregation. Indeed, African Americans migrated north in large numbers at a time when prevailing social science described blacks as a "social problem" and many educational researchers made scientific claims of black intellectual inferiority. For example, Lewis Terman, a prominent professor of psychology at Stanford and an important figure in the eugenics movement, concluded in an influential 1916 book, *The Measurement of Intelligence*, that low levels of intelligence were "very, very common among Spanish–Indian and Mexican families of the Southwest and also among negroes" and that these deficiencies were "racial, or at least inherent in the family stocks from which they come." Terman also believed that intelligence tests could be used to forecast a child's later station in

---

[68] For resurgence of the Klan, see Trotter, *River Jordan*, p. 105; for the Indiana quote, see Proclamation of Grand Dragon of Ku Klux Klan, Realm of Indiana, Nov. 1924, NAACP Papers, Box I-G-63; for the Klan in Indianapolis, see Press Release, "N.A.A.C.P. Contributes $200 to Fight Indianapolis School Segregation," Mar. 20, 1925, NAACP Papers, Box I-D-58; for the Klan in Ohio, see "Kluxers Out in the Open," *Cleveland Gazette*, Oct. 3, 1931, p. 1; *Cleveland Gazette*, Feb. 21, 1925, p. 2; "The Dayton School Fight," *Cleveland Gazette*, June 20, 1925, p. 2; "Ku Klux Klan Victory!" *Cleveland Gazette*, June 13, 1925, p. 2; for the Klan in New Jersey, see Moore, "Full Citizenship in New Jersey," p. 272; Morrow, *Way Down South Up North*, pp. 94–5; "Black Legion Shows Hand in New Jersey School Teacher Campaign," *Norfolk Journal and Guide*, Aug. 22, 1936, p. 10; for the Klan in Oregon, see McLagan, *A Peculiar Paradise*, pp. 138–40.

life, which would "be of great value . . . in planning the differentiated curriculum here recommended."[69]

The wartime intelligence tests given to Army recruits provided further fodder for those who believed in the intellectual inferiority of black children, as the scores of white soldiers were, on average, higher than the scores of black soldiers. Many white psychologists concluded that the lower test scores of certain racial and ethnic group members were due to their inherent inferiority. For example, University of Oregon psychologist Kimball Young, a protege of Lewis Terman, concluded that the poorer test results of Latin American and southern European children were due to a "considerable negroid strain" in their population and that "amalgamation of inferior with average and superior" groups must be avoided. Schools were encouraged to separate children accordingly.[70]

Black scholars attacked this reliance on intelligence testing to justify school segregation. *Opportunity*, the journal of the National Urban League, emerged as a leading voice of black scholars during the 1920s, including Horace Mann Bond, E. Franklin Frazier, Howard H. Long, Ira de A. Reid, Alain Locke, Joseph St. Clair Price, and Charles Johnson, the last of whom served as the publication's editor from 1925 until 1928. *Opportunity* published a number of articles attacking the use of intelligence testing to suggest that black children were intellectually inferior. Johnson published a major critique of the Army intelligence testing in 1923, arguing that the tests did not support a theory of inherent black inferiority, but rather demonstrated that blacks had had poorer educational opportunities. Johnson noted that black recruits from northern states, on average, scored significantly higher than did white recruits from southern states due to better educational opportunities in northern schools. In another article in *Opportunity*, Long concluded that "extreme advocates of race superiority who are also devotees of mental tests" would "be put to their wit's end" in trying to harmonize their point of view with "the state of affairs revealed by the army tests."[71]

---

69 For the use of intelligence tests, see Priest, "A Historical Study of the Royal Elementary School," p. 39; Du Bois, "Literacy Tests in the Army," p. 86; for claims of black inferiority, see Tyack, *The One Best System*, p. 217. For the first Terman quote, see Terman, *The Measurement of Intelligence*, p. 91; for the second quote, see Terman, et al., *Intelligence Tests and School Reorganization*, p. 28.

70 For psychologist views, see Thomas, "Black Intellectuals," p. 477; for Young's views, see Hendrick, *The Education of Non-Whites*, p. 88; Mosey, "Testing, Tracking, and Curriculum," p. 23.

71 For *Opportunity*, see Fultz, "'Agitate Then, Brother,'" pp. 213–14; for Johnson's views, see Johnson, "Mental Measurements of Negro Groups," pp. 21–5; for the Long quote, see Long, "Race and Mental Tests," p. 28.

In fact, in some northern states, such as Ohio, black recruits scored on average higher than white recruits from almost every southern state. As one contemporary noted sarcastically: "A [white] southerner can still boast of being above a 'n–r,' as long as he is certain that the latter is not a New York or Ohio Negro." Black educator Horace Mann Bond conducted a study of the Army intelligence tests, correlating the test results with various educational data such as teachers' salaries, state funding, length of the school term, and school attendance. Bond concluded: "the indisputable truth [is] that Alpha [the Army test] measures environment, and not native and inherent capacity. Instead of furnishing the material for racial propagandists and agitators, it should show the sad deficiency of opportunity which is the lot of every child, white or black, whose misfortune it is to be born and reared in a community backward and reactionary in cultural and educational avenues of expression."[72]

Other contemporary data supported the view that educational success was influenced significantly by educational opportunity. A study of Chicago schoolchildren in 1920 found "relatively little difference between the reading accomplishments of . . . [Chicago-born] colored pupils and white pupils who have had the advantages of the same method of instruction and environment." This same report, however, found that the reading scores of southern black migrant children were considerably lower than those of both whites and blacks born in Chicago. Subsequent tests would also show the effect of cultural factors such as educational opportunities and parents' vocation on pupils' achievement test scores.[73]

Some white psychologists rejected the notion that differing educational opportunities accounted for the differences between northern and southern black intelligence scores. When confronted with the sharp variations in test results between southern and northern blacks, Princeton's Carl Brigham in his 1922 analysis of the World War I Army intelligence test data, *A Study of American Intelligence*, claimed, with no apparent support, that the higher scores of northern blacks were due

[72] For black recruit scores, see C. S. Johnson, "Mr. Waring and the Lonely Crowd," Jan. 10, 1954, p. 6, Johnson Papers, Box 166, Folder 10; for the "boast" quote, see "Boasted 'Bunk,'" *Cleveland Gazette*, Dec. 8, 1923, p. 1 (reprint of an article in *Pearson's Magazine* by Herbert Alexander); for the Bond quote, see Bond, "What the Army 'Intelligence' Tests Measured," p. 201.

[73] For the Chicago study, see Daniel, "A History of Discrimination Against Black Students," p. 151. The 1922 Chicago Commission on Race Relations, charged with investigating the 1919 riot, found that "Negro children born in the North had, as a rule, no higher rate of retardation" than white children. Chicago Commission on Race Relations, *The Negro in Chicago*, p. 261. For other tests, see Thomas, "Black Intellectuals," pp. 482–5.

in part to their "admixture of white blood" and that "the more intelligent negro" had migrated north. Brigham dismissed the notion that the dramatic differences in educational opportunities between North and South could fully explain the test score differences.[74]

But many other psychologists during the 1920s and 1930s challenged this notion of black inferiority. In fact, during this period, social scientists increasingly argued that culture and environment were largely responsible for observable differences between social groups. Sociologists Franz Boas, E. Franklin Frazier, Robert Park, and Edward Reuter would be particularly influential in their assault on widely held assumptions that the poor social outcomes of many blacks were due to innate inferiority. For example, in 1927, Reuter, a University of Iowa sociologist, published a book, *The American Race Problem*, in which he concluded that the intelligence test score gap was due not to "any innate intellectual difference" between whites and blacks but to "a difference in education and in educational opportunity."[75]

Moreover, during the 1930s, Columbia University psychologist Otto Klineberg found that blacks who migrated north were no more intelligent than those who remained behind, but that their length of residence in the North did positively influence their test scores – confirming the positive impact of superior northern education. Klineberg's *Race Differences*, published in 1935, found no compelling evidence of inherent race differences and concluded that social and cultural environment accounted for test scores differences. In particular, Klineberg, who administered intelligence test scores to more than 3,000 Harlem blacks, found that the longer southern-born black children remained in the North, the higher their intelligence scores were. Klineberg would later offer testimony in one of the cases that comprised *Brown v. Board of Education* that blacks had the same learning abilities as whites. Other studies supported Klineberg's conclusions. For example, studies of children in Los Angeles during the early 1930s found that black students had slightly higher IQs than white students; contemporaneous studies in New York City found the test scores of the two racial groups to be roughly equivalent.[76]

At the same time that many northern white educators insisted on separate schooling for African Americans, assimilation of white

---

[74] Brigham, *A Study of American Intelligence*, p. 192.

[75] For social scientists, see Scott, *Contempt and Pity*, pp. 19–70; for the Reuter quote, see Reuter, *The American Race Problem*, p. 89.

[76] For Klineberg, see Klineberg, "The Question of Negro Intelligence," pp. 361–7; Klineberg, *Race Differences*, pp. 184–9; Pettigrew, *Negro American Intelligence*, p. 18; Kluger, *Simple Justice*, p. 439. For other studies see Klineberg, *Race Differences*, pp. 183, 185–9; Hendrick, *The Education of Non-Whites*, p. 89.

immigrant children remained a central imperative of contemporary educational theory. Though many white immigrant children came from poor backgrounds, experienced dismal living conditions, and spoke no English, white administrators and teachers were generally confident in the ability of the public school to assimilate them. They deplored the isolation of white ethnic groups in their own neighborhoods and communities and urged assimilation into the American mainstream. As one New York educator noted: "In a commonwealth such as the United States social inequalities are largely the result of difference in up-bringing, and to this extent the problem of assimilation is one of *education* in the broadest sense of the word. In all progressive communities the school is recognized as the chief instrument of socialization and civilization." Although this assimilationist perspective played a central role in urban educational theory in the early twentieth century, in many northern communities it did not include the black southern migrant.[77]

Curricular Variations for White and Black Children

In addition to school segregation, many northern white school authorities during the first four decades of the twentieth century urged separate "tracks" for black (and, in some instances, certain immigrant) children with different curricula on the grounds that they were intellectually ill-equipped to engage in rigorous academic study. Proponents of separate tracks also argued that the reality of employment discrimination rendered certain educational pursuits superfluous for black children. This sorting out of students into separate tracks, an early twentieth-century educational innovation, frequently placed black students in the lowest curricular levels. In many school districts, such as that of Buffalo, psychological and intelligence tests were used during and after World War I for the purpose of placing certain students – typically black children who had recently migrated from the South – in dead-end special classes or schools that emphasized low-skill training, such as broom- and rug-making. Black girls in Buffalo were frequently placed in the Domestic Arts Curriculum, which the director described in 1926: "The girls, most of them Negro and many of them strangers to our gates, are divided into small working groups.... The actual sewing is but a medium for putting over much necessary instruction in hygiene of person and clothing and worthy home membership." Another school administrator described these special programs as designed to teach children "habits of industry,

---

[77] For the quote, see Tyack, *The One Best System*, p. 233.

accuracy, promptness, loyalty to superiors, obedience, courtesy, patience, respect for the rights of others and care of equipment." Preparing black children to assume a particular social and economic role in society emerged as an important educational goal in many northern school districts during the 1920s. Many immigrant children from southern and eastern Europe also landed in these separate tracks.[78]

Many of these vocational schools tended to be in dismal condition. Buffalo's vocational school for black children was housed in a building that had been closed in 1918 due to "intolerable conditions." A 1931 United States Office of Education survey of the Buffalo schools found in the city's "development" school "loose and broken boards on landings, dark corners with no means of lighting and an old, inefficient boiler system. Loose plaster threatened the safety of children and the lavatory arrangements were totally unsanitary and unworthy of any modern school system."[79]

Other northern cities followed similar patterns. In Cleveland, school administrators reduced elective courses such as foreign languages in black schools during the 1920s and increased vocational courses such as cooking, sewing, and manual shop work. A 1933 study found that in the predominantly black Central High School in Cleveland, the majority of students studied no math, and home economics courses placed primary emphasis on laundry procedures. In Providence, Rhode Island, the percentage of black students at the city's Technical High School, which provided basic vocational training, sharply increased between 1915 and 1925. As historian Joel Perlmann has noted, "by 1925, when the Tech program had become clearly identified as the less academically elite and less socially elite program, and the more likely to prepare students for manual work, black males were concentrated there." Black girls were also concentrated in the Tech program, where they were taught cooking and sewing rather than typing and stenography.[80]

By the same token, black children were frequently excluded from those technical schools that provided training for skilled labor

---

[78] For the discussion of tracks, see Tyack, *The One Best System*, p. 221; for the discussion of Buffalo vocational education, see Thomas, "Urban Schooling for Black Migrant Youth," p. 282. For the first quote, see Mosey, "Testing, Tracking, and Curriculum, pp. 65, 68–71, 76–7; for the second quote, see ibid., p. 72 (quoting Principal James Farrell).

[79] For Buffalo vocational education, see Mosey, "Testing, Tracking, and Curriculum," p. 66; for the Survey quote, see ibid., pp. 91–2.

[80] For Cleveland, see Homel, "Two Worlds of Race?" p. 252; Kusmer, *A Ghetto Takes Shape*, pp. 182–4; Lieberson, *A Piece of the Pie*, pp. 236–7; Mosey, "Testing, Tracking, and Curriculum," pp. 28–9. For the Perlmann quote, see Perlmann, *Ethnic Differences*, p. 183.

positions. Such exclusions were justified in part on the grounds that skilled labor jobs would not be available to black workers. Buffalo was one such city. Members of the Buffalo Board of Education concluded that vocational education in skilled trades made no sense for black students because no employer would hire them. Accordingly, the Buffalo Technical High School, which offered training in skilled trades and which was located across the street from a black school, had only 10 black students out of 1,400 in 1923. During the 1930s, black students in Buffalo were not allowed to attend classes in aircraft construction because the Curtiss-Wright and Bell Aircraft Corporations publicly announced that they did not employ black workers. The Buffalo Urban League, noting the discrimination among Buffalo's labor unions, reported in 1939: "The complete absence of Negroes in the vocational schools was striking. Vocational instruction, undoubtedly, holds the greatest opportunity for the minority race in the community to improve their social position." In Cleveland, the school board operated a trade school to train the city's youth for skilled labor positions. Local unions, however, controlled admission to the program, which led to the exclusion of most black children from the school. This racial discrimination continued until at least the mid-1950s; in 1956, the local school board finally adopted a policy of nondiscrimination for the trade school.[81]

Blacks confronted barriers to vocational training for skilled labor positions in New York City as well. The Mayor's Commission on Conditions in Harlem found in its 1936 report extensive channeling of black students into low-skill vocational courses, such as domestic science, while discouraging enrollment in academic courses or high-skill vocational courses. The Mayor's Commission explained: "These [school] advisers, often reflecting the traditional belief concerning the capacity of the Negro for purely academic pursuits, direct these girls into vocational courses. But there are restrictions concerning vocational courses. These educational advisers discourage the Negro girls from taking the commercial courses on the ground that opportunities are not open to Negro girls in the commercial field." In 1933, a counselor at the Girls' High School in Brooklyn discouraged a black girl from taking courses that would prepare her to study medicine, stating erroneously that "they weren't allowing Negroes to study medicine." The Mayor's Commission found that school authorities placed many black girls in the "dumping ground" of the Harlem annex to the Straubmuller Textile High School, where there were no

---

[81] For Buffalo, see Thomas, "Urban Schooling for Black Migrant Youth," pp. 276–81 (quote, p. 281); Mosey, "Testing, Tracking, and Curriculum," pp. 106–8; for Cleveland, see Moore, "The Limits of Black Power," pp. 61–3.

facilities for training in meaningful work, and excluded black boys from "real vocational training" at the Manhattan Trade School for Boys. The Commission blamed this exclusion in part "on the principals who make the selection and partly on the American Federation of Labor's policies in regard to the Negro in certain trades." The 1939 report of the New York State Temporary Commission on the Condition of the Colored Urban Population concluded that school officials, encouraged by trade union discrimination, shunted black students into courses with limited vocational opportunities. As one city official conceded: "Let's not mince words; let's be practical about this matter; the Negro is not employed in certain trades, so why permit him to waste his time taking such courses." The Mayor's Commission indicted the policy as "narrow in outlook and vicious in consequence. It is the completion of a vicious cycle in that Negroes cannot find jobs without training and they are refused training because they might not be able to find the jobs."[82]

Blacks understood the effects of these exclusions. An investigator in New York reported that the exclusion of black children from skilled vocational training programs "was sapping the ambition of colored boys and girls, and that they were not making the effort put out by their parents and grandparents to secure an education." A 1940 study of black high school graduates found that the more education black persons received, the more job dissatisfaction they experienced because so many higher-level jobs were foreclosed to blacks.[83]

African Americans had made substantial strides toward full inclusion in the public education systems of the North during the late nineteenth century, but the migration of hundreds of thousands of southern blacks into northern cities during the early twentieth century provoked renewed white insistence on racial separation in much of the North. Stung by this growing web of racial separation, the northern black community divided on the appropriate response. The 1920s and 1930s would bring the greatest turmoil around the issue of northern school segregation since Reconstruction.

[82] For vocational schools in New York City, see Stern, "Jim Crow Goes to School in New York," p. 202; Ment, "Racial Segregation in the Public Schools," pp. 251–2 (first quote, ibid., p. 252; second quote, ibid., p. 250; third quote, ibid., p. 253; fourth and fifth quotes, ibid., p. 254).

[83] Quote in Blascoer, *Colored School Children in New York*, pp. 18–19; 1940 study in Tyack, *The One Best System*, p. 222.

5

Responding to the Spread of Northern School Segregation

Conflict within the Black Community, 1900–1940

A girl with [a] brown and serious face, came to me after a lecture. She was not satisfied with what I had said, nor to my answer to her questions from the floor. She said: "It seems to me you used to fight Segregation, and that now you are ready to compromise." I answered: I fight Segregation with Segregation, and I do not consider this compromise. I consider it common sense.

— W. E. B. Du Bois, 1934[1]

In the face of increasing white insistence on school segregation during the first four decades of the twentieth century, the northern African-American community divided over the appropriate response. This divergence of views on how best to respond to the increase in northern school segregation revealed competing visions for black uplift and empowerment.

Many African Americans, particularly those associated with the NAACP, argued that the eradication of racial separation in all of its forms was critical to black efforts for political and economic improvement. Others favored the development of separate black institutions, including schools, recognizing the depths of white racism and the benefits of black-controlled institutions. This division in the northern black community over the importance of integration and assimilation would hamper the efforts of those seeking to resist the trend toward greater school segregation.

Although a number of civil rights groups, including most prominently the NAACP, emerged during the first three decades of the twentieth century committed to challenging the trend toward greater racial separation, the struggle to resist the spread of northern school segregation enjoyed mixed results until the 1940s. Most of the litigation filed during the first four decades of the twentieth century seeking to enforce the nineteenth-century antisegregation legislation succeeded, but this litigation campaign failed to stem the tide toward racial separation as northern school boards continued to find ways

---

[1] Du Bois, "Postscript" (May 1934), p. 147.

to avoid racial mixing. Integrationists would learn that lawsuits alone were insufficient to overcome white resistance to racial integration in the public schools.

Competing Black Responses to the Increase in Antiblack Sentiment

The increasing racial discrimination of the late nineteenth and early twentieth centuries provoked a variety of responses within the northern black community. Many African Americans, particularly those who had lived in the North for many years, continued to insist upon racial integration and resistance to the rising tide of segregationist sentiment. During the early twentieth century, this integrationist perspective would find a voice in the biracial Niagara Movement of 1905 and then, in 1909, in the formation of the NAACP, which from its founding expressed a deep commitment to resisting racial segregation. Indeed, for the first half of the twentieth century, the NAACP would serve as the leading integrationist organization in the United States committed to challenging northern school segregation.

During the early twentieth century, however, many new black leaders articulated a competing ideology that challenged this insistence on racial integration. In the face of increasing discrimination and the hardening of racial caste, this new group of leaders emphasized black economic and cultural development through separate civic organizations, businesses, and political groups, and urged group solidarity and racial pride. They established a broad array of black-operated community service organizations and institutions, thereby meeting the increase in racial discrimination with self-help rather than protest. By World War I, involvement in organizations committed to community self-help had become, for many, an important aspect of elite status in the black community.[2]

At the national level, this impulse toward separation and self-help manifested itself in a variety of organizations, such as the National Negro Business League founded in 1900. But this separatist impulse played out across the North at the local level as well. In Cleveland, for example, a group of blacks under the leadership of J. Walter Wills established the Cleveland *Journal* in 1903 to counteract the integrationist views of Harry C. Smith, editor of the *Cleveland Gazette*. Wills and his supporters established the Cleveland Association for Colored Men to further their objective of creating separate black institutions that would be patronized by the black community. Similarly, Jane Edna Hunter founded the Phyllis Wheatley Association in Cleveland during

---

[2] Spear, *Black Chicago*, pp. 54, 71, 83, 91, 167; Meier, "The Emergence of Negro Nationalism, Part II," pp. 100–1; Moore, *Leading the Race*, p. 8; Trotter, *River Jordan*, p. 109.

the first decade of the new century as an all-black training school in the racial uplift tradition of Booker T. Washington and in response to the exclusion of black women from the local YWCA. These endeavors provoked mixed responses in Cleveland's black community. Smith criticized the Phyllis Wheatley Association for capitulating to the trend toward greater racial segregation, while other Cleveland blacks lauded her association for providing important support for young black women. In other northern cities, separate black institutions, including YMCAs, YWCAs, and fraternal organizations, were also established during the early twentieth century to provide a variety of educational and social services for the African-American community.[3]

The Impact of World War I on Developing Black Consciousness

World War I produced great optimism in the northern black community about an end to racial oppression. More than 360,000 blacks entered military service, eager to fight in the war for the preservation of democracy in Europe, with the hope that their participation would bring democracy to America's shores as well. In fact, in some southern states, black enlistment exceeded white enlistment. As Emmett Scott noted in 1919: "[T]he thought uppermost in the minds of 12,000,000 colored Americans was that the Teutonic allies should be brought to their knees, and that the war should result in the downfall of *all* kinds of tyranny and oppression." Noting black aspirations for better treatment, Scott further observed that "[i]f . . . Negroes do not get these things (equal justice, abolition of Jim Crow, discrimination and segregation, improved economic conditions) the war would have been fought in vain."[4]

Many black leaders, hoping that participation in the war would secure racial gains upon the war's conclusion, urged black men to fight, even in a segregated army. W. E. B. Du Bois, in his famous and controversial 1918 "Close Ranks" editorial, wrote: "Let us not hesitate. Let us, while this war lasts, forget our special grievances and close our ranks shoulder to shoulder with our own white fellow citizens and the allied nations that are fighting for democracy." Similarly, a May 1917 conference of African Americans resolved: "We . . . earnestly urge our colored fellow citizens to join heartily in this fight for eventual world liberty; we urge them to enlist in the army; . . . to labor in all ways by hand and thought in increasing the efficiency of our country. We urge this

---

3 Meier and Rudwick, *Along the Color Line*, pp. 209–12; Moore, "The Limits of Black Power," pp. 14–16.

4 For the Scott quotes, see Clark, "Morale of the Negro," pp. 423–4 (emphasis added); for black enlistment, see Barnett, "The Role of the Press," p. 480.

despite our deep sympathy with the reasonable and deep-seated feeling of revolt among Negroes at the persistent insult and discrimination to which they are subject and will be subject even when they do their patriotic duty."[5]

Yet the question of accepting wartime segregation for the sake of long-term goals divided the black community. For example, the Milwaukee branch of the NAACP split in 1919 over a War Camp Community Service proposal to establish a segregated black Soldiers and Sailors Club in Milwaukee for veterans of World War I. The vice president of the local NAACP branch vigorously opposed the establishment of the segregated facility, but the branch overcame his objections and supported the establishment of the club, in part because of the support of black veterans.[6]

Hopes that black support for the war would reduce racial discrimination at home were quickly dashed. Postwar race riots, lynchings, and increasing white insistence on racial segregation stood in marked contrast to the wartime slogan of "fighting to make the world safe for democracy." The nation's failure to deliver on its wartime promise of democracy provoked a variety of responses in the northern black community.[7]

Many African Americans responded to the continued mistreatment of blacks by demanding a breakdown of racial segregation patterns and the inclusion of African Americans in the full range of American institutions, including the public schools. A heightened sense of militancy enveloped the black community after World War I that Franklin Frazier described as reflecting a "new type of negro." In particular, the national office of the NAACP, which enjoyed sharp membership increases during the war, urged an assault on racial segregation during the 1920s and offered assistance to those interested in challenging separate schools.[8]

On the other hand, many African Americans continued to embrace black separation. Northern blacks developed an array of new separate institutions during the postwar era – businesses, political entities, and social welfare organizations. At the same time, many northern blacks embraced black nationalism. The central figure of the World War I era promoting a black nationalist vision was Marcus Garvey, founder of the United Negro Improvement Association (UNIA). Garvey, a

---

[5] For the Du Bois quote, see Du Bois, "Editorial – Close Ranks," *The Crisis* 16 (July 1918), p. 111; for the second quote, see Du Bois, "Editorial – Resolutions of the Washington Conference," *The Crisis* 14 (June 1917), p. 59.

[6] Trotter, *Black Milwaukee*, pp. 124–5.

[7] Clark, "The Morale of the Negro," p. 420.

[8] Frazier, "The American Negro's New Leaders," p. 56.

FIGURE 9   Marcus Garvey, 1924. Reprinted from the Library of Congress, Prints & Photographs Division, George Grantham Bain Collection, LC-USZ61-1854.

Jamaican who emigrated to the United States in 1916, founded the UNIA for the purpose of creating a racially proud and economically self-sufficient black America. The UNIA encouraged the development of separate black institutions in lieu of integrating into existing white institutions. Garvey combined Booker T. Washington's notions of black self-help and separate economic development, with the pan-African ideals championed by W. E. B. Du Bois. Garvey's emphasis on self-help, personal empowerment, racial separation, and formal pageantry had tremendous appeal for many blacks, particularly southern migrants to northern cities who were beleaguered by increasing white hostility. By 1919, Garvey claimed 2 million members in his organization, although that estimate was probably on the high side.[9]

Garvey's widespread appeal underscored the division in the black community over racial integration versus racial separation. The Baltimore *Afro-American* captured the conflict in a 1923 editorial following Garvey's conviction for mail fraud. According to the paper, many black leaders, including those associated with the NAACP, embraced an integrationist or assimilationist perspective popular with the black middle class, whereas the black working-class masses, trapped by economic oppression and white racism, were drawn more to Garvey's

9 Fultz, "'Agitate Then, Brother,'" p. 28; Farrar, *The Baltimore Afro-American*, pp. 145–6; Phillips, *AlabamaNorth*, p. 186.

appeals to black nationalism. Indeed, in many northern cities, Garvey's organization captured the support of lower-class blacks, while the NAACP appealed primarily to middle-class blacks.[10]

Some members of the NAACP recognized the limited appeal of their integrationist organization for many northern blacks. As one NAACP member in Cleveland commented: "if the Cleveland branch is typical of other branches, then the NAACP is in bad shape. We hold practically no mass meetings throughout the year. Consciously or otherwise, the Negro leaders take a high-brow attitude toward the Negro masses and no effort is made to interest them in the affairs of the organization. . . . What saves us is that the white people in town do not know how ineffective we really are or how poorly we are qualified to speak for the Negroes of Cleveland." In fact, in many northern cities, Garvey's followers far outnumbered those with membership in the NAACP.[11]

This divergence in the black community over the issue of separation versus assimilation would affect the struggle for integrated schools. In certain northern cities, such as Gary, Indiana, Garvey's followers urged the retention of segregated schools, while the NAACP sought to secure racially mixed schools. For example, when Gary school authorities resolved in the late 1920s to establish a separate black high school, the decision provoked deep conflict in the local black community, with the NAACP and UNIA on opposite sides of the issue. The bitterness between the integrationist NAACP and the separatist UNIA eventually led to competing accusations that the other group belonged to a black unit of the Ku Klux Klan called the "Bow-tie Amalgamation."[12]

Black Support for School Segregation

The division in the black community over how best to respond to the growing antiblack sentiment among many northern whites manifest itself in the controversy over increasing northern school segregation. In many northern communities, African Americans enthusiastically supported racially separate schools during the early twentieth century. Indeed, during the first three decades of the century, African Americans petitioned local school authorities for the establishment of separate black schools throughout the North, particularly in southern New Jersey, southeastern Pennsylvania, and Ohio. Northern school

[10] For the 1923 editorial, see "Editorial – What about Garvey?", *The Afro-American* (Baltimore), Sept. 14, 1923, p. 16; Farrar, *The Baltimore Afro-American*, pp. 147–8.
[11] For the NAACP quote, see Stein, *World of Marcus Garvey*, p. 241.
[12] Betten and Mohl, "The Evolution of Racism," pp. 61–3.

boards frequently defended their establishment of segregated schools by arguing that black parents had requested them.[13]

Those blacks who favored segregated schools continued to emphasize, as they had during the nineteenth century, the importance of their children learning under the nurturing care of a black teacher, as opposed to what was frequently the indifference or even hostility of a white teacher. Robert Vann, editor of the *Pittsburgh Courier*, though a supporter of integrated schools, articulated the value of black children learning from black teachers: "It is very necessary that [the black child's] teacher have sympathy, patience, interest and love. The teacher that can best meet these requirements is the Negro, because his sympathy, patience, interest and love for his race are qualities innate and natural and do not have to be acquired. [The black teacher] knows the peculiarities of his students, their nature; understands their modes of expression, their temper; can read their emotions far better than anyone else.... Being naturally interested, he will discern the child's tendencies in their earliest stages and provide remedies accordingly."[14]

Many African Americans viewed separate black schools as the only way to ensure that black children would receive instruction from a

---

[13] Communities where blacks petitioned for separate schools included Atlantic City, Cinnaminson, Lakewood, Ocean County, Pennsgrove, Salem County, and Swainton (New Jersey); Philadelphia and Dowington (Pennsylvania); Buffalo; and Cincinnati, Columbus, Dayton, Mansfield, Springfield, and Tuscarawas County (Ohio). "Atlantic's 'Jim Crowists,'" *Cleveland Gazette*, June 7, 1924, p. 1 (Atlantic City); Wright, *The Education of Negroes*, pp. 186–7 (Salem County and Ocean County); Devore, "The Education of Blacks," pp. 106, 149, 168, 192–3 (Salem County and Cinnaminson); Oak and Oak, "The Development of Separate Education," p. 112 (Lakewood, Pennsgrove, and Swainton); Letter from W. M. Gilmore to Constance Baker Motley, Feb. 22, 1950, NAACP Papers, Box II-B-146 (Dowington); *New York Age*, Nov. 5, 1908, p. 5 (Philadelphia); Thomas, "Urban Schooling for Black Migrant Youth," p. 278 (Buffalo); "A Sermon for All of Our People," *Cleveland Gazette*, May 1, 1927, p. 1 (Mansfield and Cincinnati); Jackson, "The Development and Character of Permissive and Partly Segregated Schools," p. 307 (Columbus); Minor, "The Negro in Columbus," p. 154 (Columbus); Kornbluh, "James Hathaway Robinson," pp. 212–13 (Cincinnati); "Springfield, Ohio, Defeats Segregated School Move," *The Crisis* 26 (May 1923), p. 25 (Springfield); "The School Strike in Springfield Ohio," *Opportunity* 1 (Feb. 1923), pp. 27–8 (Springfield); "Law Abiding America," *The Crisis* 32 (June 1926), p. 92 (Dayton); Priest, "A Historical Study of the Royal Elementary School," p. 84 (Tuscarawas County). For school boards relying on black petitions, see Jensen, "Current Trends and Events of National Importance," p. 84; Current, "Exit Jim-Crow Schools," p. 11.

[14] For nurturing black teachers, see Du Bois, "Editorial – Education," *The Crisis* 24 (1922), p. 252; Thompson, "Court Action the Only Reasonable Alternative," p. 427; Franklin, "The Persistence of School Segregation in the Urban North," p. 60; Wright, *The Education of Negroes*, pp. 160, 173–4, 200; Johnson, *The Negro in American Civilization*, p. 268; Gerber, *Black Ohio and the Color Line*, pp. 393–5; Berry, "Wendell Phillips Dabney," p. 55. For the Vann quote, see Buni, *Robert L. Vann*, pp. 67–8.

black teacher. In fact, white resistance to black teachers in racially mixed classrooms remained strong throughout much of the North during the first four decades of the twentieth century. Some school districts formally prohibited black teachers from teaching white children. The Dayton school board, for example, maintained an explicit segregation policy until 1951 pursuant to which black teachers were forbidden to teach white children. School boards in Cincinnati and Indianapolis also barred black teachers from teaching white children until the late 1940s and early 1950s, while in virtually every Pennsylvania school district, black teachers were prevented from teaching white students until the late 1940s. The school board president in Chester, Pennsylvania, spoke for many when he flatly announced in 1932: "I would never consider, under any circumstances, a colored teacher to teach white children."[15]

Some school districts employed no black teachers, even in all-black or predominantly black schools. Pittsburgh was one such city. Aspiring black teachers who sought teaching jobs in Pittsburgh were counseled by the Pittsburgh school superintendent to "go South" to look for work. One black graduate of the University of Pittsburgh was told by the director of personnel for the Pittsburgh school board in 1937: "It's too bad you're not white. I'd hire you immediately." As a result, during the mid-1930s, many Pittsburgh blacks favored the creation of a separate school system for black children in order to secure black teachers. Beginning in 1937 and continuing throughout the 1940s, the Pittsburgh school board did hire a number of black teachers, but primarily to teach nonacademic subjects such as physical education, home economics, and industrial arts in the predominantly black schools in the Hill district. Black teachers in Pittsburgh would serve almost exclusively in predominantly black schools until the 1960s.[16]

[15] For the view that separate schools were necessary to ensure black teachers, see Du Bois, "The Negro and the Northern Public Schools, Part I," *The Crisis* 25 (Mar. 1923), p. 205; Reddick, "The Education of Negroes," pp. 297–8; Woofter, *Negro Problems in Cities*, p. 181; *Report of the New Jersey State Temporary Commission*, p. 78; Mohraz, *The Separate Problem*, p. 24; "School Segregation of Negroes Holds in New Jersey's 'South,'" Sunday *Call*'s Story Relates," *New Jersey Herald News*, Apr. 7, 1945, p. 1. For the Dayton policy, see *Brinkman v. Gilligan*, 583 F.2d 243, 250 (6th Cir. 1978); *Brinkman v. Gilligan*, 503 F. 2d 684, 697 (6th Cir. 1975); for Cincinnati, see Washington, "The Black Struggle for Desegregated Quality Education," pp. 101–3; for Indiana, see Thornbrough, "Segregation in Indiana," p. 601; for Pennsylvania, see Kusmer, "The Black Urban Experience," p. 100. For the quote from Chester, see "Board of Education Head Opposes Having Negroes Instruct White Children," *Philadelphia Tribune*, Apr. 14, 1932, p. 1.

[16] For teachers going south, see "Quiz School Board Head," *Pittsburgh Courier*, May 8, 1937, pp. 1, 4; for the Pittsburgh quote, see Proctor, "Racial Discrimination Against Black Teachers," p. 46. For black support for separate schools, see ibid.,

School districts in New Jersey also deployed black teachers primarily in all-black schools. One black teacher in Trenton who was inadvertently hired during the 1920s to teach white children was promptly fired when the mistake was revealed; as of 1940, no black teacher taught white children in Trenton. Newark, with one of the state's largest black populations, employed only 11 black teachers in 1930, despite having 39,000 black residents. A 1939 survey of New Jersey schools revealed that fewer than 5 percent of the state's black teachers taught in racially mixed schools. One educator in Bordentown, New Jersey, speaking in the mid-1940s, explained the exclusion of black teachers from integrated schools in his state: "We couldn't have a colored teacher in a mixed class. . . . The people would not accept it." By 1940, many other northern cities still employed *no* black teachers at all, including Akron, Des Moines, Evanston, Flint, and Minneapolis.[17]

In addition, some northern school districts that had previously employed black teachers in racially mixed classrooms stopped doing so during the first few decades of the twentieth century. During the 1910s, the Columbus school board reassigned those black teachers who had previously taught in schools throughout the city to the all-black Champion School and thereafter stopped using black teachers in racially mixed classrooms. Beginning in 1916, the Columbus school board informed black teaching applicants that Champion was the only school to which they could be assigned. In the early 1940s, a growing number of blacks in Columbus urged the hiring of more black teachers – particularly in racially mixed schools. In 1943, the school board responded to these requests by opening a new school with an entirely black faculty and only black students. No black teacher would teach white children again in Columbus until the 1950s. Although Cleveland continued to use black teachers to teach white children longer than did most northern school districts – employing, for example, about seventy-five black teachers in racially mixed schools during the mid-1920s – the Cleveland school board finally stopped assigning black

pp. 51–4, 58–62; 100–1; Buni, *Robert L. Vann*, pp. 67–8. For black teachers in Pittsburgh, see Proctor, "Racial Discrimination Against Black Teachers," pp. 51–4, 58–62, 100–1, 120. A few black teachers may have taught in Pittsburgh prior to 1937. Homel, "Two Worlds of Race?" p. 246; Reid, *Social Conditions of the Negro in the Hill District of Pittsburgh*, p. 88.

[17] For Trenton, see "Must Pay the Teacher," *Cleveland Gazette*, Mar. 3, 1923, p. 2; Reddick, "The Education of Negroes," p. 299; for Newark, see Homel, "Two Worlds of Race?" p. 246; for the 1939 survey, see *Report of the New Jersey State Temporary Commission*, p. 72. For the quote, see "School Segregation of Negroes Holds in New Jersey's 'South,' Sunday Call's Story Relates," *New Jersey Herald News*, Apr. 7, 1945, p. 1. For districts with no black teachers, see Reddick, "The Education of Negroes," p. 299.

teachers to racially mixed schools during the 1930s, placing them instead in all-black schools. By the 1939–40 school year, only a few black teachers still taught in racially mixed schools in Cleveland.[18]

Not surprisingly, northern black teachers fared better in communities with racially separate black schools. A study by the United States Immigration Commission published in 1911 suggested that in northern and border states, black elementary school teachers enjoyed their best employment prospects in cities with segregated school systems. Similarly, a 1929 study of northern and border state cities found that no city employed black teachers and black principals in numbers commensurate with black school enrollment. Cities with a large number of all-black schools, such as Cincinnati, Gary, Indianapolis, and Trenton, hired more black teachers than did cities where integrated schools were more common, such as Boston, Buffalo, Detroit, and Pittsburgh. For example, in 1928, blacks comprised 11.8 percent of the students in Cincinnati and 6.5 percent of the teachers; 8.6 percent of the students in Gary and 12.9 percent of the teachers; 10.9 percent of the students in Indianapolis and 12.6 percent of the teachers; and 6.8 percent of the students in Trenton and 4.8 percent of the teachers. By comparison, blacks comprised 2 percent of the students in Boston but only 0.1 percent of the teachers; 1.7 percent of the students in Buffalo but only 0.1 percent of the teachers; 4.5 percent of the students in Detroit but only 0.6 percent of the teachers; and 6.2 percent of the students in Pittsburgh but 0 percent of the teachers.[19]

At a time when black teachers throughout the North were assigned primarily to black schools, there were a few exceptions, most notably New York City, where school officials tended to assign teachers on a nonracial basis. In fact, New York City employed more black teachers to teach in racially mixed schools during the 1920s and 1930s than any city in the nation. In 1930, 300 black teachers worked in New York City in both all-black and racially mixed schools. The NAACP cited the New York City experience in support of its claim that school

---

[18] For Columbus, see Minor, "The Negro in Columbus," p. 153; Brief for Respondents, p. 15, *Columbus Board of Education v. Penick*, 443 U.S. 449 (1979); Foster, "'Which September?'" pp. 14–16. For Cleveland, see "'Mixed' Schools and Teachers," *Cleveland Gazette*, Nov. 15, 1924, p. 1; Homel, "Two Worlds of Race?" p. 245; Kusmer, *A Ghetto Takes Shape*, pp. 182–4, n. 17; Jane Hunter, Letter to Editor, *Cleveland News* (1935), Russell H. Davis Papers, Box 10; Reddick, "The Education of Negroes," p. 299.

[19] For the 1911 study, see United States Immigration Commission, *Reports of the Immigration Commission*, Vol. I, pp. 128–33; Kessen, "Segregation in Cincinnati Public Education," p. 146; for the 1929 study, see Pechstein, "The Problem of Negro Education," pp. 193–4. For teacher statistics, see Homel, "Two Worlds of Race?," pp. 246, 259, n. 19; Porter, "The Problem of Negro Education," pp. 35–9.

integration did not mean the end of black teachers. But New York City was exceptional in its widespread use of black teachers in racially mixed classrooms.[20]

Blacks' fears of mistreatment of their children by white teachers and principals during the first half of the twentieth century were well founded. A few examples will suffice. A white teacher in Detroit in the 1920s humiliated black students in a racially mixed classroom by using them to illustrate the physical characteristics of "the Negro race." A white teacher in Dayton in the 1920s told a black second grader who had tried out for the part of an angel in the Christmas play that she "could not be an angel . . . because there were no colored angels." In 1930, a white principal in White Plains, New York, was convicted of assault for slapping a young black student and making an insulting reference to her race. A white principal in Chicago during the 1930s called her black students "niggers," a common grievance throughout the North, and allegedly told a class of black children, "[i]f you fool with me I will send you back to the jungle where you belong." In the 1940s, a white teacher in Portland, Oregon, explained to his students that George Washington Carver was "a rare exception for a black person" and that "for the most part, blacks are only good at dancing and athletics." A white teacher in Brooklyn in 1945 told her racially mixed class that "[c]olored people are the dumbest people on the face of the earth." A white teacher in Dayton during the late 1940s directed black students to demonstrate for their white classmates their inability to pronounce certain vowel sounds.[21]

W. E. B. Du Bois, though favoring school integration, recognized in 1923 the mistreatment of black children in racially mixed schools: "In

[20] "Editorial – Congratulations to Philadelphia," *The Crisis* 44 (Aug. 1937), p. 241; Rousmaniere, *City Teachers*, p. 51; William T. Andrews, "Report on Segregated Schools," p. 3, June 10, 1931, Arthur Spingarn Papers, Box 29; Robert W. Bagnall to Harlan M. Frost, Jan. 21, 1927, NAACP Papers, Box I-C-288; Homel, "Two Worlds of Race?" p. 245; "Assistant Principal of 'Mixed' School," *Cleveland Gazette*, Jan. 3, 1925, p. 1. A few other northen cities also used black teachers in racially mixed settings. For example, New Haven employed black teachers in racially mixed schools throughout the first four decades of the twentieth century, as did Boston. Warner, *New Haven Negroes*, pp. 176, 279; Daniels, *In Freedom's Birthplace*, p. 188.

[21] For Detroit and White Plains, see NAACP, "Battering Down the Barriers of Prejudice: Stirring Chapters from the 25-Year History of the NAACP," Apr. 12, 1934, Barnett Papers, Box 375-4; for Dayton, see Appendix to Brief in Opposition to Petition for Writ of Certiorari, p. 4a, n. 4, *Brinkman v. Gilligan*, United States Supreme Court, 1979; for Chicago, see Homel, *Down from Equality*, p. 109; for Portland, see McElderry, "The Problem of the Color Line," pp. 74–5, 106; for Brooklyn, see Biondi, "The Struggle for Black Equality," p. 206; for Dayton, see Interview with John Lee, July 23, 2002. For other instances of mistreatment, see Morrow, *Way Down South Up North*, pp. 18–19; Devore, "The Education of Blacks in New Jersey," p. 106.

some of these regions where there are mixed schools innocent colored children of tender years are mercilessly mistreated and discriminated against and practically forced out of school." Black sociologist Charles Johnson, another proponent of school integration, also noted the harassment of black children in racially mixed classroom: "Minority children in mixed schools are made to feel 'different' or 'inferior,' while there is a corresponding appropriation of superiority on the part of the majority. . . . Negro children [also experience] . . . brutal treatment from white teachers who lose no opportunity to browbeat their Negro students. Teachers often stir up a student opinion, which lends itself to the distortion of the personality of Negro children." The NAACP tried to protect black children from mistreatment by white teachers. In 1939, for example, the NAACP complained of two white teachers in Portland, Oregon, who referred to black children as "niggers," winning an apology from both teachers.[22]

Other African Americans complained that white teachers failed to nurture the aspirations of their children. In one northern school district, a black girl attending an integrated school reported the following interchange with her white teacher upon expressing her desire to some day become a teacher: "She said, 'Mosel, have you seen any colored teachers? There are no colored teachers. Have you seen any colored teachers?' I said, 'No, I haven't, but my mother and father said that I can become whatever I want to become!'. . . . So she said, 'Well, I wish you luck, but you'll never become one.'" Malcolm X, the only black student in his Mason, Michigan, school, described as a "major turning point" in his life a conversation he had with his white English teacher in 1940 about Malcolm's career aspirations. When Malcolm, one of the top students in his school, stated that he'd like to become a lawyer, his teacher replied: "A lawyer – that's no realistic goal for a nigger. You need to think about something you *can* be. . . . Why don't you plan on carpentry?" Thereafter, for Malcolm, it "became a physical strain simply to sit" in that teacher's class. Filmmaker and photographer Gordon Parks remembered his white teachers in Fort Scott, Kansas, during the 1920s telling him and his black classmates that college "would be a waste of time and money" and that they "were meant to be maids and porters."[23]

---

[22] For the Du Bois quote, see Du Bois, "The Tragedy of 'Jim Crow,'" p. 171; for the Johnson quote, see Charles S. Johnson, "Children in Minority Groups," pp. 13–14, Oct. 8, 1941, Johnson Papers, Box 158, Folder 29; for Portland, see McElderry, "The Problem of the Color Line," pp. 74–5.

[23] For the Mosel quote, see Slevin and Wingrove, *From Stumbling Blocks*, p. 71; for the Malcolm X quote, see Malcolm X, *The Autobiography of Malcolm X*, pp. 41–2; for the Gordon Parks quote, see Parks, *Voices in the Mirror: An Autobiography*, pp. 1–2.

As a corollary to the argument about the mistreatment of black children by white teachers in racially mixed schools, many black proponents of school segregation cited studies suggesting that black children attending segregated schools under the tutelage of black teachers remained in school longer and were more likely to graduate from school than their counterparts in racially mixed schools.[24] These differences were attributed to the fact that black teachers in black schools provided a more nurturing and supportive environment for their students.

Studies in Baltimore in the early twentieth century found a positive link between the presence of black teachers and black enrollment, noting a significant increase in black enrollment between 1890, when almost all black students were taught by white teachers, and 1907, when almost all black students were taught by black teachers. One observer emphasized the importance of black teachers for black students in Baltimore: "the pupil receives a different and new inspiration from his teacher; he has higher ideals set before him and begins to form new aspirations and ambitions. He is no longer content necessarily with the occupation of his father or mother. He is shown the highest and best in life and assured that he can obtain them as well as anybody else if he will only persist.... [T]eachers can stimulate and train the youth of their own race with much greater success and facility than can be had with teacher [sic] and pupils of different races."[25]

Other studies during the 1920s compared the attendance and graduation rates of black students in segregated schools in border-state cities with those attending racially mixed schools in northern cities. Black students attending segregated high schools in Washington, D.C., Baltimore, and St. Louis, for example, were found to have higher attendance and graduation rates than black students in integrated high schools in New York, Boston, and Philadelphia. Similarly, a 1925 study of New Jersey schools comparing racially mixed schools (with white teachers) in the state's northern counties with segregated schools (with black teachers) in the state's southern counties found that "Negro students enter high school in larger proportion from separate schools, and graduate in greater numbers than those who attend mixed schools." Finally, a 1929 study of northern and border state cities found that black children had higher attendance and graduation rates

---

[24] Moton, *What the Negro Thinks*, pp. 112–13. For examples of studies, see Crowley, "Cincinnati's Experiment in Negro Education"; Pechstein, "The Problem of Negro Education"; Porter, "The Problem of Negro Education"; Crowley, "Comparison of the Academic Achievements of Cincinnati Negroes in Segregated and Mixed Schools"; Prosser, "Non-Academic Development of Negro Children in Mixed and Segregated Schools."

[25] Turner, "What the Colored Teachers of Baltimore Are Doing for Their Race," pp. 36–7; Fultz, "'Agitate Then, Brother,'" p. 94.

in cities with only single-race schools than in cities with both integrated and segregated schools.[26]

But the question of whether black children fared better in segregated schools was highly controversial within the African-American community. Howard University's Kelly Miller provoked a firestorm of controversy by arguing in a 1922 article in the *Chicago Defender* that all-black schools provided certain advantages for black children. In particular, Miller cited those studies indicating that black children in segregated schools in border-state cities remained in school longer than did black children in racially mixed schools in northern cities and had "a keener incentive and zest." Robert Bagnall, director of branches for the NAACP, disputed Miller's findings, noting that schools in northern cities, with an abundance of southern migrants with poor educational backgrounds, would invariably fare worse in terms of black high school graduation rates and attendance figures than would schools in border-state cities. Bagnall also argued that some segregated schools in border-state cities had lower curricular standards and were located in communities with a stronger tradition of support for black education.[27]

One of the most forceful proponents of the view that black children fared better in racially separate schools under the tutelage of black teachers was a black principal in Cincinnati, Jennie Porter. For more than two decades until her death in 1936, Porter promoted segregated schools as vital to the development of both the black community and black children. In 1928, Porter completed a doctoral dissertation on black education at the University of Cincinnati School of Education, an important center during the 1920s and 1930s for the study of the effects of segregation on black children. Porter concluded that black students in segregated schools achieved more academic success, remained in school longer, and enjoyed a greater esprit de corps than did those in mixed schools.[28]

In addition to Porter, several other students and faculty at the University of Cincinnati School of Education lauded the advantages of school segregation. Dean Louis Pechstein argued in 1929 that "the aims of education may be best realized by Negroes in separate public schools." Pechstein claimed that "greater inspiration, greater racial

[26] For attendance and graduation rates, see Bruce, "The Stimulus of Negro Teaching," pp. 13–14; Fultz, "'Agitate Then, Brother,'" pp. 94, 207; for the New Jersey quote, see Granger, "Race Relations and the School System," p. 329; for the 1929 quote, see Pechstein, "The Problem of Negro Education," pp. 193–4.

[27] For the Miller quote, see Owen, "Mistakes of Kelly Miller: Reply to Kelly Miller on Segregation in Education," *The Messenger* 4 (June 1922), p. 422; for the Bagnall quote, see Bagnall, "Why Separate Schools Should Be Opposed," pp. 485–6.

[28] Price, "Current Literature," p. 269.

solidarity, superior social activities, greater retention, and greater educational achievement are possible for Negroes in separate public schools than in mixed schools." Despite his enthusiasm for segregated schools, Pechstein did concede that segregation "is not altogether consistent with the actual law in northern states."[29]

The University of Cincinnati School of Education would continue to examine the merits of racially separate schooling for the next several years. In 1930, Mary Roberts Crowley, in her doctoral dissertation, studied the performance of 191 black students, half in all-black schools and half in racially mixed schools. Crowley found virtually no statistically significant differences in academic achievement between the two groups. Two years later, however, another graduate student, Inez Prosser, conducted a follow-up assessment of the educational and psychological progress of the black students that Crowley had studied. Prosser concluded that "the personality traits of Negro children are developing more favorably in the environment of the segregated school than in the environment of the mixed school."[30]

These University of Cincinnati studies were used by school officials in many parts of Ohio to justify the retention of segregated schools. But they also provoked rebuttals. In 1935, Charles Thompson, dean of the School of Education at Howard, published an essay in *The Crisis* in response to the research at the University of Cincinnati in which he concluded that the attendance and graduation rates of black students attending racially mixed high schools in Cleveland during the 1930–1 school year *exceeded* those of black students attending segregated high schools in Baltimore.[31]

Those blacks who favored racially separate schools also emphasized the role that black teachers played in providing leadership to the black community. Teaching was one of the few fields open to blacks, and black teachers tended to be among the most educated members of the community, enjoyed considerable prestige, and provided leadership to their communities on an array of issues. In 1910, over half of all black college graduates were school teachers; by 1930, that figure was still over 40 percent. Some blacks persuasively argued that the antisegregation legislation of the nineteenth century had cost many black teachers their jobs and in the process had undermined an important source of black leadership. For example, black teacher James

[29] Pechstein, "The Problem of Negro Education," pp. 192, 195.
[30] For Crowley, see Crowley, "Cincinnati's Experiment in Negro Education," pp. 30–3; Crowley, "Comparison of the Academic Achievements." For Prosser, see Price, "Current Literature," p. 270; Prosser, "Non-Academic Development of Negro Children."
[31] For reliance on studies, see McGinnis, *The Education of Negroes in Ohio*, p. 70; for Thompson, see Thompson, "The Negro Separate School," p. 247.

Hathaway Robinson complained that within three decades of the enactment of Ohio's 1887 antisegregation law, Cincinnati's old generation of strong black leaders was gone. In fact, the number of black
teachers in Cincinnati declined by over 60 percent between 1886, the
year prior to the enactment of Ohio's antisegregation law, and 1908,
despite substantial increases in the city's black population during those
twenty-two years. The effects were more dramatic in other Ohio cities.
Following enactment of Ohio's antisegregation legislation in 1887, every black teacher in Springfield had been fired. When a court ordered
Springfield to end school segregation in 1922, again every black
teacher was fired.[32]

By the same token, many African Americans extolled the black
school as providing broader benefits to the black community. Cincinnati's Jennie Porter argued that "[t]he new [black] school is used as
a socializing agency, not only for the children, but also for the adults
of the community. Under its guidance and control, come parents and
children alike to engage in social recreation, literary programs, dancing, plays, and games." The Frederick Douglass School in Cincinnati
was one such school. After school hours, the Douglass School offered
supervised athletic contests such as basketball and boxing for neighborhood youths, as well as adult education, social clubs, and a community branch of the public library. Many northern blacks feared that with
school integration, this function of the black school as a community
center would be lost. Many northern whites viewed strong black schools
such as the Douglass school as a justification for segregation. A white
news reporter wrote in 1919 that the Douglass school represented "the
chance to teach the world the supreme truth that democracy means,
not the wiping out of racial personality, but rather the cherishing of
racial difference and the ennobling of diverse stocks for the enrich-
ment of us all." The irony of the Douglass school bearing the name
of one of the great nineteenth-century integrationists appears to have
been lost on Cincinnati's educators.[33]

Finally, some black educators lauded the separate black school as a
place where students would gain a better appreciation for the contri-
butions of African Americans to human development. The principal of
a black high school in Gary, for example, justified his racially separate

---

[32] For black teachers generally, see Moore, *Leading the Race*, pp. 86–7. Fultz, "'Agitate
Then, Brother,'" p. 269; for Cincinnati teachers, see Kornbluh, "James Hathaway
Robinson," p. 218; Kessen, "Segregation in Cincinnati Public Education," p. 146; for
Springfield, see Meier and Rudwick, *Along the Color Line*, pp. 291–2.

[33] For the Porter quote, see Porter, "The Problem of Negro Education," p. 144; for the
Douglass school, see Kornbluh, "James Hathaway Robinson," pp. 212–13, 215; for
the quote, see Leavell, "What Does the Negro Want?" p. 606.

school on the grounds that "every race has its own contribution to make to cultural progress. At Roosevelt we will try to teach the Negro youth to value his own background with its African overtones."[34]

Not surprisingly, throughout the first half of the twentieth century, black teachers tended to be among the most forceful proponents of school segregation in northern states. In Philadelphia, for example, the Pennsylvania Association of Teachers of Colored Children (PATCC) argued that black schools advanced "race development" and insulated students from white racism. The PATCC clashed with the *Philadelphia Tribune*, the city's leading black newspaper, and the Educational Equity League, both of which backed integrated schools. An NAACP survey of school segregation in New Jersey during the 1940s noted the influence of black teachers and principals on the retention of racially separate schools in that state. For example, William Valentine, head of the all-black Bordentown Manual Training School in New Jersey, was a particularly forceful opponent of integration efforts in his state. A. Philip Randolph accused black teachers of permitting themselves "to be used as tools to assassinate democracy in the public schools, and all for a mess of pottage," while Horace Mann Bond blamed the persistence of northern school segregation on those blacks "with sons and daughters to employ" as teachers.[35]

Much of the black support for school segregation came from southern migrants who were more accustomed to segregation and were particularly fearful of mistreatment of their children by white teachers in mixed schools. Two observers in 1937 concluded that the dearth of litigation in New Jersey seeking to enforce that state's antisegregation law was due to the fact that a significant percentage of the state's black population had recently migrated from the South, where patterns of segregation were more entrenched. The Southern Society of Chicago, composed of migrants from the South, favored segregated schools, while longtime black residents of Chicago tended to favor integrated

---

[34] Quoted in Meister, "A History of Gary," p. 71 (quoting the *Gary Post-Tribune*, Apr. 21, 1931, p. 11).

[35] For black teacher support of segregation, see Oak, "The Development of Separate Education in the State of New Jersey," pp. 32–3, 44; Price, "We Knew Our Place, We Knew Our Way," pp. 18–19; for the Pennsylvania association, see Homel, "Two Worlds of Race?" p. 247; for the New Jersey survey, see New Jersey State Conference of Branches, "A Survey of the Public School Systems in the State of New Jersey," pp. 1–2, 1947, NAACP Papers, Box II-B-144; for Valentine, see "Wonders If NAACP Pulling Punches," *New Jersey Herald News*, Feb. 16, 1946, p. 1; Adams, "The Role and Function of the Manual Training and Industrial School at Bordentown," pp. 141–2; for the Randolph quote, see Letter from A. Philip Randolph to E. Washington Rhodes, *Philadelphia Tribune*, Sept. 19, 1925, p. 1; for the Bond quote, see Frazier, *The Negro in the United States*, p. 442.

schools. In the Dayton school desegregation battle of the mid-1920s, most of the blacks favoring the retention of segregated schools were recent southern migrants. A black minister in Buffalo, whose congregation consisted in large measure of recently arrived southern blacks, justified his support for a school segregation during the 1920s on the grounds that the special educational and social needs of the southern migrant children and their lack of familiarity with an integrated setting justified racial separation.[36]

In many northern communities, sharp splits developed over school segregation between northern-born middle-class blacks who favored integration and poorer southern migrants who favored segregation. Many northern-born blacks were openly disdainful of the newly arrived black migrants, with their lack of education and embrace of racial separation, and blamed them for the increase in school segregation. Harry Smith, publisher of the widely read black newspaper the *Cleveland Gazette*, repeatedly denigrated the southern black migrant as "the loudmouthed individual of color on the streets, in the streetcars and other public places." Smith blamed southern blacks for the increasing antiblack attitudes in Cleveland, claiming that if "the loud-mouthed Negro here is not soon curbed, we may wake up some fine day and find [segregated streetcars in Cleveland]." Smith also attacked southern black migrants for petitioning the Cincinnati school board for a separate black school in 1935: "What a pity they cannot be shipped back South where they belong and which they never should have left. . . . For a 'Negro' teacher they would trade vitally essential rights and privileges of all our people . . . of Cincinnati."[37]

Other northern blacks also blamed the new migrants for the increase in segregated schools. When a black woman who had recently migrated from Georgia to Chicago organized a petition drive for a separate

[36] For southern migrant support of separate schools, see Letter from Leon Harris to Arthur Spingarn, Nov. 20, 1939, NAACP Papers, Box II-L-40; "Whither Are We Drifting?" *Cleveland Gazette*, Oct. 21, 1933, p. 2; Proctor, "Racial Discrimination Against Black Teachers," p. 42. For discussion of New Jersey, see Oak and Oak, "The Illegal Status of Separate Education," pp. 672–3; Meier and Rudwick, "Early Boycotts of Segregated Schools: The East Orange, New Jersey, Experience," p. 32; for Chicago, see Mohraz, *The Separate Problem*, p. 101; for Dayton, see "Suit Filed in Dayton School Fight," *Cleveland Gazette*, Jan. 24, 1925, p. 1; "The Dayton School Fight," *Cleveland Gazette*, Jan. 24, 1925, p. 2; for Buffalo, see Thomas, "Urban Schooling for Black Migrant Youth," p. 278.

[37] For the split in the black community, see Price, "We Knew Our Place, We Knew Our Way," p. 19; Meier and Rudwick, "Early Boycotts of Segregated Schools: The East Orange, New Jersey, Experience," p. 23; Phillips, *AlabamaNorth*, p. 5. For the first and second Smith quotes, see Phillips, *AlabamaNorth*, p. 165; for the third Smith quote, see *Cleveland Gazette*, May 18, 1935, p. 2.

black school in 1910, the *Chicago Defender* urged its readers to "kill the southern viper and save Chicago. . . . When we are in touch with Mrs. Johnson we will show her the back door to Chicago and have her beat it back to her dear old southern home, where all the Uncle Toms . . . should be." An Illinois NAACP leader announced in 1923 that "I am free to say that those [blacks] who desire separate schools are invited to return at once to Alabama, Georgia, Mississippi, and Louisiana."[38]

Though blacks who had recently migrated from the South were more likely to support school segregation than were northern-born blacks, support for segregated schools did not always correlate with the length of time spent living in the North. In some northern cities, southern migrants favored school integration; moreover, in some communities, the strongest supporters of racially separate schools were northern-born black school teachers.[39]

Some observers believed that many of the recent migrants from the South did not embrace the importance of education as much as did northern-born blacks. In 1940, Edward Shils, a researcher who assisted Gunnar Myrdal in the preparation of *An American Dilemma*, commented about lower-class blacks: "The Negro lower class does not share the beliefs of the Negro upper and middle class regarding the indispensability of education and good breeding and in many instances comes to derogate them as a reaction formation." Historian Michael Fultz concluded in his study of the black press and education during the early twentieth century that "education clearly played a central role in the social, moral, and status considerations of the Black middle class and professional group of the period. . . . [But] the question of how deeply *all* Blacks were imbued with similar values is complex."[40]

But support for education among northern blacks – both native-born and southern migrants – appears to have been strong. Prior to the Great Migration, black children attended public schools in the North in large numbers, frequently exceeding the attendance rates of white immigrant children and in some instances those of white children of native-born parents. In 1910, in eight of the nation's largest cities, black children aged fourteen to sixteen attended school in higher percentages than did American-born children of white immigrant

[38] For the *Defender* quote, see "Jim Crow School in Chicago," *Chicago Defender*, Nov. 12, 1910, pp. 1–2; for the NAACP quote, see Homel, *Down from Equality*, pp. 151–2.

[39] Homel, "Two Worlds of Race?" p. 243; Meier and Rudwick, *Along the Color Line*, p. 296.

[40] For the Shils quote, see Fultz, "'Agitate Then, Brother,'" p. 275; for the Fultz quote, see ibid., p. 274.

parents. For example, in four of the nation's largest cities – Philadelphia, New York, Boston, and Pittsburgh – fifteen-year-old black children attended school in higher percentages than did children of native white parentage.[41]

These black attendance figures would remain high in the wake of the migration of southern blacks to northern cities. Black children, particularly older ones, in Buffalo, Chicago, Cleveland, New York City, Philadelphia, and Pittsburgh – each a city with a significant influx of southern blacks – attended school in higher percentages in 1930 than did the American-born children of white immigrant parents. In fact, those cities that had experienced the largest influx of southern blacks by 1930 were among the cities with the highest percentage of black school enrollment.[42]

In part, the strong black attendance figures in comparison to those of white immigrant children reflected black enthusiasm for education. But they also reflected the realities of employment discrimination, since northern black teenagers faced far greater employment restrictions than did their white counterparts. William L. Bulkley, a black high school principal in New York City, told a reporter in the early twentieth century that "the saddest thing that faces me in my work is the small opportunity for a colored boy or girl to find proper employment."[43]

Black Support for the Desegregation of Northern Schools

In the face of increasing white insistence on racial separation, many African Americans remained firm in their belief in the importance of racial integration, particularly in the public schools. Most black newspapers were vigorous supporters of school integration, including the *Chicago Defender*, the Cincinnati *Union*, the *Cleveland Gazette*, the *New Jersey Herald News*, the *Pittsburgh Courier*, and the *Philadelphia Tribune*. In addition, *The Messenger*, which described itself as "The Only Radical Negro Magazine in America," edited by A. Philip Randolph and Chandler Owen, condemned "jim crow niggers" for their support of school segregation. "As a rule," *The Messenger* opined, "the leader of the separate school drive is some ecclesiastical clown,

---

[41] Smith, "Native Blacks and Foreign Whites," pp. 309–10. These patterns held up in some smaller northern cities as well; for example, in Camden, New Jersey, black attendance rates exceeded those of the children of native-born white parents. Ibid.

[42] Ibid., pp. 328–9. These attendance figures held up in many smaller northern cities as well, such as East St. Louis, Gary, Jersey City, and Trenton. Ibid.

[43] For employment restrictions, see Smith, "Native Blacks and Foreign Whites," p. 332; Licht, *Getting Work*, pp. 44–5; Perlmann, *Ethnic Differences*, p. 171; Du Bois, *The Philadelphia Negro*, p. 111. For the Bulkley quote, see Tyack, *The One Best System*, p. 123.

some pusillanimous pedagogue, . . . long on inspiration and short on information."[44]

Many leading black educators also supported school integration. During the 1930s, Howard University became an important intellectual center in the black community for the promotion of school integration. Indeed, Howard enjoyed an extraordinarily distinguished faculty during the 1920s and 1930s, including Franklin Frazier in sociology, Rayford Logan in history, Alain Locke in philosophy, Ralph Bunche in political science, Charles Thompson in education, and Charles Houston and William Hastie in law. In 1932, Thompson, dean of Howard's School of Education, founded the *Journal of Negro Education* to study the condition of black schools, to examine the effects of school segregation, and to provide a scholarly outlet for black scholars. The *Journal of Negro Education* devoted an entire issue in 1935 to the question of school segregation. Several of the authors argued that although black children did sometimes suffer mistreatment in racially mixed schools from which black teachers were widely excluded, the advantages of integration outweighed those disadvantages. At the same time, the Howard Law School played a central role in the legal campaign against segregated schools. Charles Houston, dean of Howard's law school, helped develop a litigation strategy challenging southern school segregation. Houston challenged those African Americans who preferred segregated schools in order to secure black teachers. "Some of you want separate schools so that you can have colored teachers," Houston told an audience in Toledo, Ohio, in 1936. "Schools are made for children, not teachers."[45]

The single most significant supporter of desegregated schools in the North during the 1920s and 1930s was the NAACP. In some localities, including Cincinnati and Hartford, opponents of school segregation established a local NAACP branch for the express purpose of aiding their desegregation efforts. Founded in 1909 to fight the increase in racial oppression that characterized the first decade of the twentieth century, the NAACP recognized the growth of school

[44] "Jim Crow Niggers," *Messenger* 7 (May 1925), p. 196; Fultz, "'Agitate Then, Brother,'" pp. 183, 205. In 1922, *The Messenger* issued an indictment of black educators for their role in requesting segregated schools: "As a rule some Negro school teacher who would like to be a principal or some such high official was lending aid and comfort [to the call for segregated schools]." Owen, "Mistakes of Kelly Miller," p. 443.

[45] For Howard, see Baker, *From Savage to Negro*, p. 176; for Thompson, see Crocco, *Pedagogies of Resistance*, p. 65; for advantages of integration, see Thompson, "Court Action the Only Reasonable Alternative," pp. 427–33; Hubbard and Alexander, "Types of Potentially Favorable Court Cases Relative to the Separate School," p. 375. For the Houston quote, see Frank Marshall Davis, "World in Review," Feb. 12, 1936, Barnett Papers, Box 379-6.

FIGURE 10   Walter White, 1942. Reprinted from the Library of Congress,
Prints & Photographs Division, FSA/OWI Collection, LC-USF34-013343-C.

segregation that followed the Great Migration. In 1925, W. E. B. Du
Bois, editor of the NAACP's monthly magazine, *The Crisis*, declared:
"The issue which...has been consistently emerging in various parts
of the United States as paramount for colored people is that of
Segregation – Residential Segregation and School Segregation."
Du Bois noted that school segregation was rapidly increasing throughout the North and claimed that "of all evils, segregation in education
is one of the greatest and that this evil cannot be outweighed by the
few benefits which result from separate schools" such as jobs for black
teachers.[46]

During the 1920s and 1930s, the NAACP, with the support of several black newspapers, engaged in a multifaceted attack on northern
school segregation. The NAACP's Walter White called for an all-out
assault on school segregation in 1924: "There must be a nation-wide
agitation to launch a counter offensive not only where segregation
is now being attempted but also in those places where segregation

---

[46] For NAACP branches, see Kellogg, *NAACP*, p. 19 (Hartford); Washington, "The Black
Struggle for Desegregated Quality Education," p. 83 (Cincinnati); for the first quote
from *The Crisis*, see "NAACP," *The Crisis* 29 (Mar. 1925), p. 208; for the second quote,
see Du Bois, "The Negro and the Northern Public Schools, Part I," *The Crisis* 25
(Mar. 1923), p. 205. The NAACP, through its publication, *The Crisis*, noted the in-
crease in school segregation throughout the country, citing specifically Philadelphia;
Cincinnati, Springfield, and Dayton, Ohio; Ypsilanti, Michigan; Indianapolis, Gary,
and Terre Haute, Indiana; Camden and Toms River, New Jersey; Coffeyville and Arma,
Kansas; Las Cruces, New Mexico; and Imperial, California. "NAACP," *The Crisis* 29
(Mar. 1925), p. 208.

exists and where there is a chance of fighting it effectively – that is in brief in all northern and border states. . . . Unless we can win out in the North, we shall never be able to win in the South and the acceptance of any segregation in the North will lessen immeasurably any efforts in the future against segregation in the South." In addition to filing lawsuits to enforce the nineteenth-century antisegregation legislation, the NAACP attempted to build support in the northern black community for school integration. The NAACP recognized that black support for racially separate schools had been utilized by white school authorities to justify segregation and that strenuous efforts must be pursued to change black attitudes.[47]

Recognizing the importance of black teachers to those African Americans who favored all-black schools, and the dearth of black teachers in racially mixed schools, the NAACP and other supporters of school integration sought to defuse this issue by promoting the hiring of black teachers in racially mixed schools. Robert Vann of the *Pittsburgh Courier*, for example, initiated a campaign in 1914 for the hiring of black teachers in Pittsburgh, claiming that "we need MIXED SCHOOLS AND MIXED TEACHERS." Robert Bagnall, the director of branches for the NAACP, traveled extensively in the North during the 1920s to build black support for school integration. Bagnall urged local NAACP branches to take a variety of actions to build support for school desegregation: petitions, letters to newspapers, mass demonstrations, political pressure on local school boards, and litigation. Recognizing that support for black teachers undermined desegregation activity, Bagnall addressed this issue directly. In a 1922 speech in Philadelphia, for example, he argued that in some northern cities – Boston, Cleveland, Detroit, and New York City – black teachers were permitted to teach in racially mixed schools and that black parents should insist on teacher integration. Similarly, the *Philadelphia Tribune* and the Educational Equity League successfully urged positions for black teachers in racially mixed schools in Philadelphia during the 1930s as a means of broadening support in the black community for school integration. The NAACP engaged in a similar, but unsuccessful, campaign for teacher integration in Cincinnati during the 1930s. This emphasis on black teachers in racially mixed

---

[47] For the NAACP plan, see "Preliminary Report of the Committee on Future Plan and Program of the N.A.A.C.P." (1934), Johnson Papers, Box 24, Folder 544; for the quote, see Memorandum from Walter White to James Weldon Johnson, Oct. 16, 1924, NAACP Papers, Box I-D-58; for efforts to build support for integration, see "Thomas Thrills," *Cleveland Gazette*, May 19, 1928, p. 3 (president of the Washington, D.C., chapter of the NAACP urges a Cleveland audience to fight segregation).

schools would be important to efforts to build black support for school integration.[48]

Those northern blacks who favored integrated schools set forth a variety of reasons for their position. First, many argued, with considerable evidence, that segregated schools would invariably be inferior to white schools, as school authorities tended to favor schools with white children. Dwight Holmes of the School of Education at Howard University contended in 1932 that "segregation always means inferior accommodations for those segregated." Robert Bagnall of the NAACP repeatedly emphasized that segregated schools would be inferior: "Everywhere there is a separate school system you will find these things following: inferior school buildings, inferior equipment, smaller salaries for teachers, fewer teachers in proportion to the population, lower curricula, shorter school terms, double and triple sessions, more Negro children out of schools, greater ignorance on the part of the Negro population, more juvenile delinquency, more crime, more race friction and misunderstanding." Bagnall further noted that Pennsylvania, with some racially integrated schools, spent on average $36.20 per year on each black student, but that neighboring Delaware and Maryland, with only segregated schools, spent only $7.68 and $6.38 per black pupil, respectively (figures that also reflected the greater overall support for education in Pennsylvania than in Delaware and Maryland). Bagnall forecast that with increased school segregation, expenditures on black education would fall. According to Bagnall, those states that operated at least some racially mixed schools, such as Pennsylvania and New Jersey, had far higher rates of black literacy than neighboring states like Delaware and Maryland that mandated segregated schools.[49]

Chandler Owen, editor of *The Messenger*, also urged racially mixed schools, emphasizing the physical inequality of black schools: "Herein lies the great argument *for* mixed and *against* segregated schools. Unless Negro and white children use the same schools, here is what will

[48] For the Vann quote, see Proctor, "Racial Discrimination Against Black Teachers," pp. 40–1; for the Bagnall quote, see Letter from Robert Bagnall to Harry D. Evans (president, Indianapolis branch of the NAACP), Jan. 19, 1923, NAACP Papers, Box I-G-63; for Bagnall's speech, see Bagnall, "Why Separate Schools Should Be Opposed," p. 485; for Philadelphia, see Homel, "Two Worlds of Race?" p. 247.

[49] For inferiority of black schools, see Horace Mann Bond, "Only Way to Keep Public Schools Equal Is to Keep Them Mixed," *The Afro-American*, Mar. 5, 1932, NAACP Papers, Box II-L-40; Bond, *The Education of the Negro*, pp. 383–90; for the Holmes quote, see "Attacks Segregation!" *Cleveland Gazette*, Aug. 13, 1932, p. 2 ("First, segregation always implies inequality of status and that one group is dangerous to the other; second, segregation always means inferior accommodations for those segregated; and third, segregation prevents the races from knowing each other through the usual means of communication."); for the Bagnall quote and discussion, see Bagnall, "Why Separate Schools Should Be Opposed," p. 486.

always happen in most details: Negro children will have schools not so well equipped as the whites; the school terms for Negroes will, as a rule, be shorter than the terms for whites; the whites will have better teachers because the white teachers will be more highly paid, which means opportunity to secure more and better education." Owen further argued: "When all children sit in the same classrooms, what is taught one must be taught the other; the equipment of the white child must be the equipment of the Negro child, too; if a white child has a competent teacher, the Negro child has a competent teacher also."[50]

Horace Mann Bond, president of Lincoln University in Pennsylvania and another important supporter of school integration, agreed. Writing in 1932, Bond argued that "the separate school always means an inferior school.... This has happened in every separate system. The only possible exception is the District of Columbia, and there the money comes from the government. In Ohio, and Indiana, and Kansas, and Illinois, Philadelphia, and southern New Jersey, wherever the schools are separated, you will find after ten or fifteen years, the colored school going into decline." In 1930, the NAACP challenged racially gerrymandered school district lines in New Rochelle that created an all-black school on the grounds that "Jim Crow schools, wherever found, do not get the consideration that white schools do. Less money is spent on them, they are not so well kept up and the least efficient teachers are assigned to these schools."[51]

In fact, black schools in the North were typically older, in poorer condition, and more overcrowded than white schools. In some communities, including Elkhart, Indiana, and Morton, Pennsylvania, school authorities condemned a building used by white children, replaced it with a new school, and used the condemned building to teach the town's black children. In 1923, the black elementary school in Atlantic City, New Jersey, was described as "an antiquated frame structure, a veritable fire trap," in comparison with "the magnificent modern brick and stone structures" for the city's white children. Only one of the six majority-black elementary schools in the Hill District of Pittsburgh received a passing mark on the school board's "educational efficiency rating" in 1927. In Newark, a mid-1930s survey of the city's schools found "extreme contrasts" between the city's black and white schools. Approximately 80 percent of the city's black schools were rated as

---

[50] For the first Owen quote, see Owen, "Mistakes of Kelly Miller," p. 423; for the second quote, see *Chicago Defender*, Aug. 26, 1922, p. 15.

[51] For the Bond quote, see Horace Mann Bond, "Only Way to Keep Public Schools Equal Is to Keep Them Mixed," *The Afro-American*, May 5, 1932, NAACP Papers, Box II-L-40; for the New Rochelle quote, see "Protest to Governor on 'Jim Crow' Schools," *New York Times*, Sept. 10, 1930, p. 22.

"poor" or "inferior," and almost two-thirds of those schools earning these ratings were for black children. These results were due in significant measure to the fact that Newark's school commissioners sent the bulk of the school funds to schools in white, middle-class sections of the city at the expense of black schools in poorer neighborhoods.[52]

Chicago's black schools tended to be considerably older than the city's white schools. A 1922 study of Chicago schools found that only one of ten schools serving a majority black population had been built after 1890, whereas more than half of the white schools had been built since 1899. Another survey of Chicago schools in 1931 found that almost 40 percent of the city's black schools were "so inferior . . . that it is not advisable to expend any considerable amount of money on them." Overcrowding meant that these schools frequently operated double shifts; in 1938, thirteen of the fifteen Chicago schools running on double shifts were black schools. By the late 1930s, black schools in Chicago had higher teacher-pupil ratios, significantly lower per pupil expenditures, and far more school crowding than did white schools.[53]

Even in New York City, black schools fared worse than their white counterparts. During the 1920s and 1930s, many Harlem all-black schools were old, dilapidated, and overcrowded. During the 1930s, all but one of the Harlem black schools utilized double or triple sessions, while nearby white schools had single sessions. By 1954, 32 percent of the black or Puerto Rican elementary schools in New York City had been built prior to 1900 compared to 5 percent of the white schools.[54]

In addition to the problem of the poor condition of many all-black schools, some integrationists insisted that segregation engendered notions of racial inferiority in blacks and racial superiority in whites. Chandler Owen argued in *The Messenger*: "I submit that segregation builds caste, intensifies racial prejudice by fostering the idea of a mental difference peculiar to race, [and] results in giving Negroes inferior

---

[52] On the condition of black schools, see Morse, "New Jersey, New Laboratory in Race Relations," p. 157; Johnson, *The Negro in American Civilization*, p. 268; *Report of the New Jersey State Temporary Commission*, p. 73; Amended Petition, *Worthy v. Board of Education of Berkeley* (1927), Arthur Spingarn Papers, Box 35; Homel, "Two Worlds of Race?" p. 255. For use of condemned buildings for blacks, see Dickerson and James, "The Cheyney Training School," p. 19; Letter from Marian Wynn Perry to Earl Drye, Sept. 3, 1947, NAACP Papers, Box II-B-138. For the Atlantic City quote, see "Atlantic's 'Jim Crowists,' " *Cleveland Gazette*, June 7, 1924, p. 1. For the discussion of Pittsburgh, see Reid, *Social Conditions of the Negro*, pp. 83–4; for the discussion of Newark, see Anyon, *Ghetto Schooling*, pp. 71–3.

[53] For the discussion of Chicago, see Homel, "Two Worlds of Race?" pp. 248–9; Henri, *Black Migration*, p. 181; for the quote, see Anyon, *Ghetto Schooling*, p. 95.

[54] For Harlem schools, see "Link Old Schools to Harlem Unrest," *New York Times*, Apr. 11, 1935, p. 16; Rousmaniere, *City Teachers*, p. 119; Osofsky, *Harlem*, p. 148. For Puerto Rican schools, see Waller, "Holding Back the Dawn," p. 189.

conditions which are sure eventually to produce an inferior race." Many blacks argued that increased exposure of black and white children to one another would lead to an eventual reduction in racial stereotypes and hostilities. Frank Marshall Davis, a journalist with the Associated Negro Press, opined in 1936 that "[r]acial hatred, born of ignorance, is perpetuated because black and white have not had sufficient contact on equal terms along all walks of life." Davis explained: "It should be obvious to anybody except a professional moron that if a white person, during impressionable school days, meets Negroes in the classroom, that person through firsthand knowledge and intimate contact cannot be made to believe that all Negroes are over-sexed beasts and mental inferiors removed by only the absence of a tail from the ape class. Too many colored students have led their classes in scholarship for rabid prejudice to be thrust down the gullet of the white person who went to school with them." The *Chicago Defender* made a similar argument for mixed schools: "Nothing is better for both races than mixed schools where the children are given opportunities to know each other and dispel some of the prejudices they have which are based entirely up on ignorance."[55]

Despite these arguments in favor of school integration, many northern blacks retained a preference for separate black schools, provoking sharp divisions in the black community in many northern cities. The conflict in Cincinnati illustrates the collision of viewpoints in the northern black community over the importance of school integration. Many African Americans in Cincinnati strongly favored segregated schools and, under the leadership of Jennie Porter, had petitioned the school board for segregated schools on multiple occasions during the first two decades of the century. Porter supported racially separate schools on the grounds that children in such schools would be removed from "all feeling of discrimination and race prejudice."[56]

Other Cincinnati blacks, under the leadership of Wendell Dabney, editor of the black newspaper *The Union*, vigorously opposed school segregation. Dabney, who argued that school segregation would lead to other forms of segregation, blamed African Americans for the city's increasing school segregation: "Separate schools could neither be established nor maintained under law, were it not for the solicitation

---

55 For the Owen quote, see Owen, "Mistakes of Kelly Miller," p. 445; for the Davis quote, see Frank Marshall Davis, "World in Review," Feb. 12, 1936, in Barnett Papers, Box 379–6; for the *Defender* quote, see *Chicago Defender*, Nov. 27, 1926; Homel, *Down from Equality*, p. 151.

56 For the discussion of Porter, see Washington, "The Black Struggle for Desegregated Quality Education," pp. 57–8, 86; Porter, "The Problem of Negro Education," p. 133 (quote).

of many colored people who, through selfishness, ignorance or cowardice, submit to such conditions as the easiest method of getting colored teachers appointed." For Dabney, blacks had sacrificed their rights in order to secure "colored teachers, colored songs and colored prayers." Dabney recognized that whites were all too eager to establish segregated schools: "The whites generally favor separate schools. Regarding Negroes as being inferior, they deplore any association with them, except upon the basis of master and man, employer and servant. They are wise enough to realize that the doctrines of subserviency can not be enforced if white children are schooled with the colored, since school association and competition breed a spirit of equality.... " As a result of black acquiescence in segregation, Dabney worried that the "time seems not far distant when there will be no mixed schools here" in Cincinnati.[57]

Dabney, who founded a local NAACP branch in 1915 to fight school segregation, repeatedly locked horns with Jennie Porter over the segregation issue. When the Cincinnati school board announced plans to establish another separate black school – the Harriet Beecher Stowe School – during World War I in response to the request of Porter and other Cincinnati blacks, the local branch of the NAACP under Dabney's leadership announced its opposition and threatened litigation if the board proceeded with its plans. Both the NAACP and Porter presented the school board with counterpetitions on the segregation issue in December 1919. Porter presented a petition with over 6,000 signatures endorsing the new black school, while the local branch of the NAACP, inspired by a visit from Walter White, gathered over 11,000 signatures on a counterpetition expressing opposition. The school board ultimately sided with Porter and established the new black school. In response to complaints that establishment of the Stowe School violated the Ohio prohibition on school segregation, the board adopted a resolution that the school would "not be known distinctly as a school for Negroes" even though the Stowe School would be designated on official documents as a colored school and only black children would attend the school until its closure in 1961.[58]

---

[57] For the first two Dabney quotes, see Dabney, *Cincinnati's Colored Citizens*, p. 149; for the third Dabney quote, see Dabney, "Glendale School Troubles," *The Union*, Sept. 18, 1920, p. 1; for the fourth Dabney quote, see Dabney, "Editorial – Jim Crowism and Segregation," *The Union*, May 13, 1922, p. 2.

[58] Washington, "The Black Struggle for Desegregated Quality Education," pp. 83–6; Berry, "Wendell Phillips Dabney," p. 56; "The Negro in Cincinnati Public Schools," pp. 5–6 (1966), Cincinnati Historical Society. For the quote, see Montgomery, "Racial History of the Cincinnati and Suburban Public Schools," pp. 106, 112 (1983), Cincinnati Historical Society.

The conflict between Porter and the NAACP continued during the 1920s as the Cincinnati school board established additional separate black schools, to the delight of Porter and the consternation of the NAACP. The board's insistence that no black teacher could teach a white child continued to play an important role in the establishment and retention of additional colored schools. In time, the conflict between Porter and the NAACP grew so severe that she forbade her teachers from joining the organization. Ultimately, the NAACP reached an accommodation with Porter pursuant to which the organization did not attack school segregation directly but instead sought to secure employment for black teachers in mixed schools. In the meantime, the separate black schools remained enormously popular for many blacks in Cincinnati. In 1938, about 35 percent of the city's black children attended one of these racially separate schools.[59]

W. E. B. Du Bois and the Importance of School Integration

The conflict in the northern black community during the interwar years over school integration is perhaps best captured by a consideration of the evolving views of W. E. B. Du Bois. Du Bois, the longtime editor of the NAACP's monthly publication, *The Crisis*, and one of the dominant figures in black America during the first half of the twentieth century, underwent a public and dramatic transformation on the issue of segregated schools during the 1930s that sent shock waves through the northern black community. Du Bois's shift on the importance of integrated schools provides a fascinating look at the evolving debate on the issue in black America.

Du Bois was an early and vocal supporter of school integration. In his inaugural issue of *The Crisis* in 1910, he harshly criticized recent efforts to establish racially separate schools in northern cities, including Atlantic City, Chicago, Columbus, and Philadelphia. Du Bois spoke eloquently of the value of integrated schools: "Human contact, human acquaintanceship, human sympathy is the great solvent of human problems. Separate school children by wealth and the result is class misunderstanding and hatred. Separate them by race and the result is war. Separate them by color and they grow up without learning the tremendous truth that it is impossible to judge the mind of a man by the color of his face.... The argument, then, for color discrimination in schools and in public institutions is an argument against democracy...."

59 Montgomery, "Racial History of the Cincinnati and Suburban Public Schools," p. 128 (1983), Cincinnati Historical Society; Washington, "The Black Struggle for Desegregated Quality Education," pp. 94–8; Scates, "Cincinnati's Colored Teachers," p. 144.

FIGURE 11   W. E. B. Du Bois, 1918. Reprinted from the Library of Congress, Prints & Photographs Division, LC-USZ62-16767.

Du Bois also argued that school integration was necessary to ensure that African Americans would share in the full benefits of American life. Writing in 1915, Du Bois argued: "In social intercourse every effort is being made to-day . . . to segregate, strangle and spiritually starve Negroes so as to give them the least possible chance to know and share civilization. . . . [The Negro] must have the right to social intercourse with his fellows. . . . [S]ocial intercourse means theatres, lectures, organizations, churches, clubs, excursions, travel, hotels, – it means in short Life."[60]

Yet Du Bois did not oppose racial separation in all contexts. Contrary to the views of much of the black press, Du Bois supported the creation of a separate training camp for black officers during World War I, believing that positive war service would help foster postwar gains for African Americans. Du Bois thus expressed a willingness to countenance limited segregation in the pursuit of the larger goal of combating white racial oppression. Moreover, in 1918, Du Bois wrote his controversial "Close Ranks" editorial, in which he called

[60] For the first quote, see Du Bois, "Editorial – Segregation," pp. 10–11; for the second quote, see Du Bois, "The Immediate Program of the American Negro," p. 311.

for a moratorium on racial protest during the waning months of World War I.[61]

In 1919, Du Bois labeled the pursuit of integrated schools as central to his "program of reconstruction" for postwar black America: "At present the tendency is to accept and even demand separate schools because our children so often are neglected, mistreated, and humiliated in the public schools. This is a dangerous and inadvisable alternative and a wicked surrender of principle for which our descendants will pay dearly." Four years later, in a 1923 article in *The Crisis*, Du Bois, outlined the extraordinary costs imposed by school segregation:

(1) It plants race prejudice in children during their most impressionable years.
(2) It makes whites and blacks fail to understand or appreciate each other because of lack of mental contact.
(3) It fosters among colored children a fear of white people and a belief that Negroes are inferior.
(4) It fosters in white children a contempt for Negroes and a belief whites are superior.
(5) It increases the cost of the school system to such an extent that Negroes are bound to get inferior schools with lower standards calculated to fit them for the lowest places in society.
(6) The public school is the only real foundation for democracy.[62]

Throughout the 1920s Du Bois remained an opponent of school segregation. In 1922, he vigorously defended racial mixing in a debate with a prominent white attorney in New York City on the question "Would Negro Segregation in the United States Improve Racial Relations and Be for the General Good?" Over the course of the 1920s, however, Du Bois began to concede the profound difficulty of the issue given the mistreatment of black children in racially mixed schools at the hands of white teachers. Du Bois understood the enormous value of black teachers to black children and recognized that most school boards refused to hire blacks to teach in racially mixed schools. In the same 1923 article in *The Crisis* in which Du Bois outlined the harms of school segregation, he also defended those blacks who sought to have their children educated by a black teacher in a racially separate school: "it will not do simply to rail against the advocates for separate schools. They are not all fools or self seekers. They see a real evil and

[61] Du Bois, "Editorial – Close Ranks," p. 111.
[62] For the first quote, see Du Bois, "Editorial – Reconstruction," p. 130; for the second quote, see Du Bois, "The Negro and the Northern Public Schools, Part I," p. 205.

those who oppose them must not do so in anger, but rather must show constructive effort to overcome the present evils of Negro children in mixed schools."[63]

In 1923, Du Bois found himself in the middle of a spirited debate over the Cheyney Training School for Teachers, an all-black state-supported school near Philadelphia that trained aspiring teachers. Founded by the Quakers in 1837 to train black teachers, Cheyney had become a state-supported school in 1920. In 1923, confronted with claims that Cheyney was a "Jim Crow" institution, Leslie Pinckney Hill, Cheyney's principal, sparked controversy by publishing an article in *The Crisis* that defended his school's role in training black teachers. Conceding that the issue of separate schools had become bitterly divisive in the northern black community, Hill emphasized that Pennsylvania did not *require* aspiring black teachers to attend Cheyney. Hill further stated that he believed "completely in the right of any group of Negroes to organize, by themselves alone, or in co-operation with white friends, for any proper ends which they themselves may voluntarily choose to further. This right of self-determination is the very essence of democracy."[64]

Hill's article provoked a sharp response from the Philadelphia branch of the NAACP. Philadelphia attorney G. Edward Dickerson and the Reverend William Lloyd Imes, chair of the local NAACP's committee on public education, accused Hill in a subsequent issue of *The Crisis* of encouraging "*practical segregation*, which he knows, as well as we, leads sooner or later to *legal* segregation." Dickerson and Imes expressed the fear that Cheyney would become "the legal beginning of a complete segregated school system for the State of Pennsylvania." "The next step will be to again legalize what has been illegally done," Dickerson and Imes predicted, "and we shall have in law, as well as in fact, a complete segregated school system in the entire state."[65]

Du Bois, as the editor of *The Crisis*, was caught in the middle of the Cheyney fight. Calling the controversy a "situation bordering on tragedy," Du Bois labeled it an "amazing paradox." "[W]e must oppose segregation in schools," Du Bois concluded, but "we must [also] honor and appreciate the colored teacher in the colored school."

---

[63] For the debate, see "Du Bois Wins," *The Union*, May 20, 1922, p. 1; for Du Bois on the value of black teachers, see Du Bois, "The Negro and the Northern Public Schools. Part I," p. 205; Du Bois, "The Tragedy of 'Jim Crow,'" pp. 170–1; Du Bois, "Postscript" (Mar. 1934), p. 85; for the Du Bois quote, see Du Bois, "The Negro and the Northern Public Schools, Part I," p. 205.

[64] For the Cheyney background, see Franklin, *The Education of Black Philadelphia*, pp. 71–2; for the Hill quote, see Hill, "The Cheyney Training School for Teachers," p. 252.

[65] Dickerson and James, "'The Cheyney Training School'," pp. 18, 20.

Du Bois continued: "I am not for a moment calling in question the motives and sincerity of those in Philadelphia who are fighting segregation. In such a fight I am with them body and soul. But when this fight becomes a fight against Negro school teachers I quit. I believe in Negro school teachers. I would to God white children as well as colored could have more of them. With proper training they are the finest teachers in the world because they have suffered and endured and nothing human is beneath their sympathy." But Du Bois's defense of Hill provoked sharp criticism. Commenting on a published report of a speech Du Bois had delivered on the Cheyney controversy, Cincinnati's Wendell Dabney expressed fear that Du Bois was abandoning his commitment to integrated schools: "The news affects as would a telegram announcing the death of a loved one. As matters stand, we await some statement, some confirmation, for after these many, many years of hard fighting on his part for racial rights, a denial of that principle by him, is as though Christ should come again and disown the faith of which he is father. . . . If Dr. Du Bois has changed, . . . such transition would be an awful blow to the thousands of people who have proudly acclaimed him leader."[66]

But despite his sympathy for those blacks who sought separate schools, Du Bois in fact did not abandon his campaign for integrated schools. In a 1929 article in *The Crisis*, responding to the widely cited comments by Louis Pechstein of the University of Cincinnati that black children often fared better in segregated schools than in integrated ones, Du Bois argued that these differences did not support segregated schools but rather the elimination of mistreatment of black students in racially mixed schools: "[I]s this an argument *for* segregation, or *against* discrimination, cruelty, cheating and hate on the part of white pupils, teachers, and officials? If the success of the [all-black] Dunbar High School [in Washington, D.C.] is to be built on the lawless snobbery of Gary, what is American democracy headed for? The success of some separate Negro schools is a crushing indictment of hatred and prejudice and not a demand for further segregation." Du Bois conceded that the poor educational background of many black children born in the South gave rise to calls for segregation, but argued that "it would be a despicable yielding to reaction and cowardice to give up democracy in the public schools because of the very disadvantages which lack of democracy and opportunity have fastened upon the Negro population of the South."[67]

---

[66] For the Du Bois quotes, see Du Bois, "The Tragedy of 'Jim Crow,'" pp. 169, 170, 171–2; for the Dabney quote, see Dabney, "Du Bois for Segregation? Unthinkable!" *The Union*, July 14, 1923, p. 1.

[67] For both quotes, see Du Bois, "Postscript – Pechstein and Pecksniff," p. 313.

By the early 1930s, however, Du Bois had begun to question the integrationist focus of the NAACP. Arguing that the economic devastation of the Depression had rendered many of the NAACP's traditional civil rights activities anachronistic, Du Bois determined that a new strategy of racial uplift was needed. He urged the NAACP to develop programs and initiatives that focused on improving the economic status of blacks, even if such endeavors were racially separate. For example, Du Bois urged African Americans to organize racially based cooperatives and to patronize black businesses as the best way of dealing with the devastating effects of the Depression. Although Du Bois continued to argue that racial segregation was wrong, he also contended that "[n]o person born will live to see national and racial distinctions altogether abolished, and economic distinctions will last many a day."[68]

In a series of explosive essays in *The Crisis* in early 1934, Du Bois squarely challenged the integrationist philosophy of the NAACP, questioning whether "we can [continue to] stand on the 'principle' of no segregation and wait until public opinion meets our position." In Du Bois's view, the increase in white racism since the onset of the Great Migration meant that widespread pupil and teacher integration would not be forthcoming in the near future. Du Bois observed that segregation "is more insistent, more prevalent and more unassailable by appeal or argument" than it had been prior to the Great Migration. To those who argued that the North had made great progress in alleviating segregation, Du Bois disagreed: "This is a fable. I once believed it passionately. It may become true in 250 or 1,000 years. Now it is not true. . . . The difference between North and South in the matter of segregation is largely a difference of degree; of wide degree certainly, but still of degree." Du Bois called segregation "evil" but argued that it was "today and in this world inevitable." He further contended that without racial separation "the American Negro will suffer evils greater than any possible evil of separation: we would suffer the loss of self-respect, the lack of faith in ourselves, the lack of knowledge about ourselves, the lack of ability to make a decent living by our own efforts."[69]

Du Bois was particularly critical of the NAACP's emphasis on using the coercive power of law to eliminate segregation. He argued that such coercion could accomplish little in the face of white resistance:

[68] For Du Bois on Depression-era strategies, see Wolters, *Negroes and the Great Depression*, pp. 230–1; Reed, *W.E.B. Du Bois*, p. 74. For Du Bois on black businesses, see Du Bois, "Postscript" (Jan. 1934), p. 20. For the quote, see Du Bois, "Postscript" (Apr. 1934), p. 117.

[69] For Du Bois's 1934 essays, see Du Bois, "Postscript" (Jan. 1934), pp. 20–1; "Postscript" (Feb. 1934), pp. 52–3; "Postscript" (Mar. 1934), pp. 85–6; "Postscript" (Apr. 1934), pp. 115–17. For the quotes, see Du Bois, "Postscript" (Apr. 1934), pp. 115–16.

"Assuming for a moment that the group into which you demand admission does not want you, what are you going to do about it? Can you demand that they want you? Can you make them by law or public opinion admit you when they are supreme over this same public opinion and make these laws? Manifestly, you cannot. Manifestly your admission to the other group . . . can only be accomplished if they, too, join in the wish to have you." Du Bois concluded that the NAACP's legal assault on segregation had accomplished little: "[T]he N.A.A.C.P. has conducted a quarter-century campaign against segregation, [and] the net result has been a little less than nothing. We have by legal action steadied the foundation so that in the future, segregation must be by wish and will and not law, but beyond that we have not made the slightest impress [sic] on the determination of the overwhelming mass of white Americans not to treat Negroes as men." Du Bois continued: "Since this is true, the practical problem that faces us is not a choice between segregation and no segregation." Segregation was unavoidable.[70]

Where Du Bois parted company most strenuously with the NAACP in 1934 was with his claim that the northern black community must embrace racial separation as "necessary to our survival and a step toward the ultimate breakdown of barriers." In the face of profound white racism, Du Bois urged African Americans "by voluntary action" to separate "from our fellowmen" and to concentrate on strengthening black institutions, including schools, and pooling economic and political resources. Northern white school boards would seize on Du Bois's views to justify racially separate schools.[71]

Du Bois's comments about racial separation were highly controversial because by the 1930s, opposition to segregation had become one of the central organizing imperatives of much black political action, particularly within the NAACP. Not surprisingly, Du Bois's essays triggered a firestorm of controversy within the black community. The *Cleveland Gazette* attacked Du Bois for his "foolish and very harmful effort to encourage our people to accept segregation, especially 'jim crow' schools." Francis Grimke, a prominent black minister in Washington, D.C., claimed that if Du Bois retained his support for racial separation, then his "leadership among us is at an end; we can follow no such leader."[72]

---

[70] For the quotes, see Du Bois, "Postscript" (Apr. 1934), pp. 115–17.

[71] For the quotes, see ibid., p. 117. For northern white school boards, see Du Bois, "My Relations with the NAACP," p. 4, Oct. 2, 1948, Houston Papers, Box 163-40, Folder 3.

[72] For the Du Bois controversy, see Reed, *W.E.B. Du Bois*, p. 74. For the first quote, see *Cleveland Gazette,* July 20, 1935, p. 2; for the second quote, see Grimke, "Segregation," p. 173.

FIGURE 12 James Weldon Johnson, 1932. Reprinted from the Library of Congress, Prints & Photographs Division, Carl Van Vechten Collection, LC-USZ62-42498.

James Weldon Johnson, who had retired as general secretary of the NAACP in 1930, described the controversy in a letter to a friend in 1934: "Within the past three months or so a vital change has taken place . . . within the Negro race itself. There is now considerable confusion and something of a schism. . . . [Du Bois's] new position . . . has not only caused confusion in the Negro race but has precipitated something of a crisis in the N.A.A.C.P. The Negro newspapers are each week filled with discussions pro and con. The discussion is based on the question: shall the Negro continue to oppose compulsory segregation or shall he accept it and make the most of it? The second choice expresses roughly the new position taken by Du Bois." The controversy caused Johnson to publish his final book, *Negro Americans, What Now?*, in which he responded to Du Bois's critique of the integrationist agenda of the NAACP. In his book, Johnson acknowledged the undeniable appeal of racial separation: "There come times when the most persistent integrationist becomes an isolationist, when he curses the White world and consigns it to hell. This tendency toward isolation is strong because it springs from a deep-seated, natural desire – a desire for respite from the unremitting, grueling struggle; for a place in which refuge might be taken." Johnson conceded the rising tide of segregation across the North in response to the Great Migration and the NAACP's limited success in battling this segregationist impulse: "Those who stand for making the race into a self-sufficient unit point out that after years of effort, we are still Jim-Crowed, discriminated against, segregated, lynched; that we are still shut out from industry, barred from the main avenues of business, and cut off from free participation in national life. They point out that in some sections of the country we have not even secured equal protection of life and property under the laws. They declare that entrance of the Negro into full citizenship is as distant as it was seventy years ago." Yet Johnson urged black Americans to resist the urge to separate: "I cannot see the slightest possibility of our being able to duplicate the economic and social machinery of the country. . . . Our separate schools and some of our other race institutions, many of our race enterprises, the greater part of our employment, and most of our fundamental activities are contingent upon our interrelationship with the country as a whole."[73]

The NAACP, which had tolerated and even supported some limited forms of segregation in the past, such as separate officer training in the United States Army, issued a forceful response to Du Bois's comments on segregation, adopting a strong pro-integration resolution: "[The NAACP] is opposed both to the principle and the practice of enforced segregation of human beings on the basis of race and color. Enforced segregation by its very existence carries with it the implication of a superior and inferior group and invariably results in the imposition of a lower status on the group deemed inferior. Thus, both principle and practice necessitate unyielding opposition to any and every form of enforced segregation." A subsequent resolution made sure that by singling out "enforced segregation," the NAACP board of directors had not intended to condone "voluntary" segregation: "The resolution passed at the April meeting of the Board in opposition to 'enforced segregation' did not imply that we approve of other forms of segregation. We believe that all forms of segregation are in their origin, if not in their essential nature enforced." Walter White, who had replaced James Weldon Johnson as general secretary of the NAACP, elaborated: "The Negro must, without yielding, continue the

---

[73] For the first Johnson quote, see Letter from James Weldon Johnson to Marshall Best, Apr. 28, 1934, Johnson Papers, Box 22, Folder 511; for other quotes, see Johnson, *Negro Americans*, pp. 13–15.

grim struggle for integration and against segregation for his own physical, moral, and spiritual well-being and for that of white America and
the world at large."[74]

In the wake of the controversy over segregation, Du Bois resigned
his position as editor of *The Crisis*. The reasons for his resignation were
complicated. In part, it was triggered by the controversy over segregation, although Du Bois claimed that that was not "the main reason." In
his letter of resignation, he stated that he had resigned in large measure because the NAACP board forbade him from publishing in *The
Crisis* "criticism of the officers and policies" of the organization and
because of his lack of confidence in the organization's leadership and
direction. But larger problems with *The Crisis* likely contributed to his
resignation as well. The NAACP hit hard times during the 1930s. In
1932, the organization imposed a 15 percent pay cut on its officers and
laid off many of its staff, provoking dissension. In the meantime, *The
Crisis* suffered a steady downturn in annual revenues, from $77,000
to $14,000 between 1920 and 1933, and a decline in circulation from
95,000 to 21,000 between 1919 and 1933. In light of these problems,
the NAACP began to assert more control over *The Crisis*, to the dis-
may of Du Bois. The national office cut the budget of *The Crisis* from
$60,000 in 1928 to $38,000 in 1934. In time, a rift developed between
Du Bois and Walter White. Du Bois denigrated the light-skinned White
and claimed that part of White's embrace of integration was his own
desire to associate with white people. Du Bois spoke openly of his refusal to take direction from White. Faced with a loss of control over
The Crisis, and growing disagreement with the policies and direction
of the NAACP, Du Bois left the organization.[75]

Thereafter, Du Bois moderated his views somewhat, but he continued to insist that segregated schools were at times necessitated by the
reality of white hostility. Writing more than a decade later, in 1945, Du
Bois explained his views in the *Chicago Defender*:

> I do not believe in "jim crow" schools. They are undemo-
> cratic and discriminatory. At the same time as I have said
> from time to time, the majority of Negroes in the United
> States depend today upon separate schools for their educa-
> tion and despite everything we can do that situation will
> continue longer than any of us now living will survive. We must,
> therefore, make the best of a bad situation.... Under these

[74] For the quotes from resolutions, see Du Bois, "Postscript" (May 1934), p. 149; Ross,
J. E. Spingarn, p. 196; Aldridge, "The Social, Economic, and Political Thought," p. 27.
For the quote from White, see Wilson, *In Search of Democracy*, p. 265.

[75] For Du Bois's letter of resignation, see "Dr. Du Bois Resigns," *The Crisis* 41
(Aug. 1934), p. 245; for financial problems, see Wolters, *Negroes and the Great Depression*, pp. 266–70, 274, 277.

circumstances there is no single answer which will apply to all situations. There are cases where the establishment of a separate school would be nothing less than a crime permitted by careless-ness. There are other cases when the establishment of a separate school is not only advisable, but a bounden duty if colored chil-dren are going to get education.... What I want is education for Negro children. I believe that in the long run this can be best accomplished by unsegregated schools but lack of segregation in itself is no guarantee of education and fine education has often been furnished by segregated schools.

The NAACP would survive the Du Bois controversy with its integra-tionist vision intact. But the organization would have considerably more work to do to persuade the mass of northern blacks of the wisdom of its approach.[76]

Tactics for Challenging School Segregation

Those northern blacks who opposed school segregation during the first decades of the twentieth century utilized a variety of tactics to pursue their objectives. Some African Americans engaged in direct action – in particular school boycotts, sit-ins at white schools, or demon-strations – to challenge segregation. Others used petitions or lawsuits to enforce existing antisegregation mandates found in nineteenth-century statutes. Behind all such actions were extensive efforts to convince fellow African Americans of the importance of insisting on racially mixed public schools.

The use of school boycotts to challenge segregation was not new. During the nineteenth century, African Americans had boycotted black schools in Massachusetts, New York, and Chicago with mixed success. However, school boycotts during the first decade of the twentieth century in Alton, Illinois (1897–1908), East Orange, New Jersey (1905–6), Oxford, Pennsylvania (1909), and Wichita, Kansas (1906), had failed to secure integrated schools. Each of those early

[76] For the quote, see Du Bois, "A Question on Jim Crow Schools," *Chicago Defender*, Oct. 6, 1945, in Barnett Papers, Box 376-2. The NAACP remained firm in its oppo-sition to any type of racial separation. In 1950, the Portland branch of the NAACP sponsored a dance to honor the city's black high school graduates and to encourage these students to attend college. Gloster Current, the national NAACP's director of branches, chastised the Portland branch for its racially focused celebration: "As an or-ganization working for complete integration, we cannot . . . be a party to the isolation of an individual or group for special consideration. . . . This means that the Branch should not . . . place itself on record in seeking out the Negro students for special recognition." Quoted in McElderry, "The Problem of the Color Line," pp. 258–9.

twentieth-century school boycotts took place in communities deeply resistant to racial mixing.[77]

During the 1920s and 1930s, school boycotts and demonstrations emerged as significant forms of protest against school segregation in more than a dozen communities in New Jersey, Pennsylvania, Ohio, Illinois, and California. The boycotts varied in length from a few weeks to almost two years in Berwyn, Pennsylvania. Although these boycott and demonstration efforts reflected the intensity of feeling of many northern blacks concerning issues of school integration, most failed to alter patterns of racial segregation. In a few instances, however, they succeeded, typically when the black community used litigation to apply additional leverage on the school board. The example of Berwyn is illustrative. In 1932, all of the black elementary schoolchildren in two school districts in Berwyn were assigned to a separate ungraded school. A group of black parents sued but the court dismissed the lawsuit, ruling that a suit could only be brought by the state attorney general. In response, the black parents launched a boycott of the separate black school that continued for almost two years, during which time some of the boycotters were jailed for violating compulsory school laws. Finally, in early 1934, the black community persuaded the state attorney general to initiate litigation, and as a result, the defendant school districts agreed to operate their schools on a nondiscriminatory basis. The boycott had helped focus attention on the plight of the black schoolchildren, but the boycott likely would have failed without the litigation. In a similar manner, in 1915 black students in Roslyn, New York, marched to a white school and demanded admission; although the tactic failed, subsequent litigation successfully desegregated that city's schools.[78]

---

[77] Meier and Rudwick, *Along the Color Line*, pp. 309–10. But litigation in Wichita did temporarily end segregation.

[78] Communities with school boycotts included Dayton, Lockland, Sandusky, Springfield, and Shaker Heights, Ohio; Abingdon Township, Berwyn, Chester, and Philadelphia, Pennsylvania; East Orange, Montclair, and Toms River, New Jersey; Chicago, Illinois; and Blythe and Monrovia, California. Meier and Rudwick, *Along the Color Line*, p. 313; "Two Suits in Dayton School-Fight," *Cleveland Gazette*, Feb. 14, 1925, p. 1; "Our Student Strike!" *Cleveland Gazette*, Sept. 27, 1930, p. 1; Homel, "The Politics of Public Education," pp. 253–4. For Berwyn, see Joseph H. Rainey, "Segregation Ends in Public Schools of Two Townships," *Philadelphia Record*, May 1, 1934, p. D9; NAACP Press Release, "Two-Year Fight Against Jim Crow School Is Won," May 5, 1934; Raymond Pace Alexander, "Outline of the School Situation in Easttown and Tredyffrin Townships," Oct. 18, 1933, NAACP Papers, Box I-D-48; Franklin, *The Education of Black Philadelphia*, pp. 139–41. Both the Bryn Mawr branch of the NAACP and the national office of the NAACP supported the desegregation efforts. N.A.A.C.P. *25th Annual Report for 1934*, p. 20 (1934); N.A.A.C.P. *24th Annual Report for 1933*, pp. 19–20 (1933); "Surprise Angle Arises in School Jim-Crow Probe," *Pittsburgh Courier*,

The most significant efforts challenging school segregation during the first four decades of the twentieth century, particularly during the 1920s and 1930s, were lawsuits seeking to enforce the nineteenth-century antisegregation legislation. Throughout the North (and West), including New Jersey, Pennsylvania, Ohio, Indiana, Illinois, Michigan, Kansas, New Mexico, and California, black parents, frequently with support from either the national office or a local branch of the NAACP, filed lawsuits challenging the establishment of segregated schools.[79]

This litigation had mixed success. Suits challenging school segregation in Indiana, which expressly permitted segregation by state law, failed, including a high-profile challenge to segregation in the high schools of Indianapolis in 1925 that enjoyed the support of the national office of the NAACP. Moreover, suits challenging racially gerrymandered school district lines also failed as courts refused to find that the construction of school district lines violated state antisegregation laws. For example, in 1927, the Chicago branch of the NAACP filed litigation in the Cook County Circuit Court challenging a racially gerrymandered attendance zone that prevented black children from attending a nearby all-white school, requiring them instead to attend the all-black Shoop School. In addition to this gerrymandering, the school board liberally permitted those white children who lived in the Shoop School district to transfer to the white school. In July 1927,

Dec. 31, 1932, p. 4; Hatfield, "The Impact of the New Deal," pp. 206–7. For Rosyln, see "Along the Color Line," *The Crisis* 10 (Aug. 1915), p. 165; Meier and Rudwick, *Along the Color Line*, p. 310.

79 Lawsuits were filed in Atlantic City, Camden, Toms River, and Trenton, New Jersey; Berwyn, Brentwood, Philadelphia, and Pittsburgh, Pennsylvania; Cincinnati, Dayton, Gallipolis, Mansfield, Shaker Heights, and Springfield, Ohio; Chicago, Illinois; Ypsilanti, Michigan; Gary, Indianapolis, and Terre Haute, Indiana; Arma, Coffeyville, and Wichita, Kansas; Camden and Las Cruces, New Mexico; and Imperial and Vallejo, California. William Andrews, "Report on Segregated Schools," June 10, 1931, Arthur Spingarn Papers, Box 29; "Court Refuses to Stand for Segregation in Public Schools," *Colorado Statesman*, Jan. 25, 1919, NAACP Papers, Box I-C-405; Russell H. Davis, "Civil Rights in Cleveland 1912 Through 1961," p. 62 (1973), Davis Papers, Container 9; "Breaking Down the Barriers of Prejudice: Stirring Chapters from the 25-Year History of the NAACP," Apr. 12, 1934, Barnett Papers, Box 375-4; Fultz, "'Agitate Then, Brother,'" p. 248, n. 6; Homel, "Two Worlds of Race?" pp. 243–4; NAACP Annual Report, "Two Supreme Court Victories," pp. 4–5 (1927), NAACP Papers, Box I-A-25; Press Release, "N.A.A.C.P. Aids Fight on Segregation," Dec. 23, 1927, NAACP Papers, Box I-D-44; "Win Boro School Ban Case," *Pittsburgh Courier*, Dec. 17, 1932, p. 1; "The Pittsburgh N.A.A.C.P.," *The Crisis* 40 (Mar. 1933), p. 70; Homel, "The Politics of Public Education," pp. 252–3; Memorandum to the Directors of the American Fund for Public Service from the Committee on Negro Work, May 1930, NAACP Papers, Box I-C-196; *State ex rel. Cheeks v. Wirt*, 177 Ind. 441 (1931); *Greathouse v. Board of Commissioners*, 151 Ind. 411 (1926).

the Cook County court denied the petition for a writ of mandamus, holding that the plaintiffs had failed to prove that racial segregation was the intent of the school officials in establishing the Shoop School district lines.[80]

On the other hand, lawsuits challenging the explicit assignment of black children to racially separate schools or classrooms were generally successful in that courts found these racial assignments to be in violation of nineteenth-century antisegregation legislation. Litigation challenging racially separate schools succeeded in several communities in New Jersey, Pennsylvania, Ohio, and Kansas during the 1920s and 1930s. In a few instances, the threat of litigation led to desegregation. As we shall see, however, in many instances, these legal victories proved illusory, as local school boards managed to retain segregated schools despite losing in court.[81]

---

[80] For Indianapolis litigation, see *Greathouse v. Board of Commissioners*, 151 Ind. 411 (1926); for Gary litigation, see *State ex rel. Cheeks v. Wirt*, 177 Ind. 441 (1931); for Chicago litigation, see Homel, "The Politics of Public Education," pp. 186–7.

[81] Litigation succeeded in Atlantic City, Toms River, and Trenton, New Jersey; Dayton, Gallipolis, Shaker Heights, and Springfield, Ohio; Abington Township, Berwyn, Brentwood, and Philadelphia, Pennsylvania; and Wichita and Coffeyville, Kansas. "Negro Parents Win in Court," unidentified newspaper article, Sept. 1928, NAACP Papers I-D-44 (Atlantic City); *Hedgepeth v. Board of Education of City of Trenton*, 131 N.J.L. 153 (1944) (Trenton); *Patterson v. Board of Education of Trenton*, 11 N.J. Misc. 179 (1933), *aff'd*, 112 N.J.L. 99 (1934) (Trenton); *Raison v. Board of Education of Berkeley*, 103 N.J.L. 547 (1927) (Toms River); "Win Boro School Ban Case," *Pittsburgh Courier*, Dec. 17, 1932, p. 1 (Pittsburgh); Rainey, "Segregation Ends in Public Schools of Two Townships," *Philadelphia Record*, May 1, 1934, p. D9 (Berwyn); "School Fight Is Won by Abington Parents," *Philadelphia Tribune*, Sept. 26, 1940, p. 1 (Abington Township); "Breaking Down the Barriers of Prejudice: Stirring Chapters from the 25-Year History of the NAACP," Apr. 12, 1934, Barnett Papers, Box 375-4 (Brentwood and Vallejo); "How Separate Schools Menace!" *Cleveland Gazette*, July 21, 1928, p. 1 (Philadelphia); "School Segregation," *The Crisis* 30 (Mar. 1926), p. 230 (Shaker Heights); *Board of Education v. State ex rel. Reese*, 114 Ohio St. 188 (1926) (Dayton); "Court Refuses to Stand for Segregation in Public Schools," *Colorado Statesman*, Jan. 25, 1919, NAACP Papers, Box I-C-405 (Gallipolis); "Victory Against School Segregation," *Cleveland Gazette*, Apr. 26, 1924, p. 1 (Coffeyville); Meier and Rudwick, *Along the Color Line*, p. 310 (Wichita). Also, litigation in Highland Park, Michigan, successfully challenged the exclusion of three black students from a field trip to Washington, D.C. "Three Telling Victories," *Cleveland Gazette*, June 13, 1925, p. 1. Litigation threats ended junior high school segregation in Abington Township, Pennsylvania. "School Fight Is Won by Abington Parents," *Philadelphia Tribune*, Sept. 26, 1940, p. 1; "Parents Win School Fight," *Pittsburgh Courier*, May 12, 1940, p. 5.

Other suits were less successful. In a few instances, courts did not find a violation of state antisegregation laws, as in Philadelphia; Hamilton County and Lockland, Ohio; and Montclair, New Jersey. Franklin, *The Education of Black Philadelphia*, p. 83 (Philadelphia); "Is the Ohio Supreme Court K.K.K.?" *Cleveland Gazette*, Apr. 4, 1925, p. 1 (Hamilton County); Meier and Rudwick, *Along the Color Line*, pp. 313–14 (Lockland and Montclair).

Impediments to School Desegregation Litigation

Although most of the lawsuits challenging school board policies compelling black children to attend racially separate schools during the first four decades of the twentieth century succeeded in the sense that they resulted in a court order requiring the admission of black children to a white school, these legal efforts had a limited impact on the overall trend towards school segregation in the North. What accounts for the limited efficacy of this litigation?

First of all, these lawsuits were few in number, even in areas of the North where violations of antisegregation laws were most egregious. For example, in southern Illinois, where local school officials flouted the state's antisegregation law with explicitly racial school assignments, no litigation was filed between the unsuccessful Alton litigation of the early twentieth century (discussed in Chapter 3) and 1949. In New Jersey, where school segregation increased dramatically during the first few decades of the twentieth century, only four lawsuits were filed between 1900 and 1940.[82]

Several reasons account for this dearth of litigation. Throughout the North, many blacks remained unwilling to file lawsuits due to their ambivalence about school segregation. As noted, many northern blacks preferred segregated schools, in large measure to secure black teachers, and hence showed little interest in filing desegregation litigation. As a result, the national office of the NAACP, which was particularly interested in promoting this type of litigation, frequently had difficulty finding a local lawyer, plaintiff, or the necessary funds to support such a lawsuit. The national office followed a policy during the 1920s and 1930s of supporting desegregation litigation only if there was sufficient local support. Walter White explained this policy in 1925: "[W]e have made it a rule that we enter into cases only where local people show sufficient interest to take the initiative and then where the case was sufficiently worthy and important, the National Office would contribute a proportion of the cost. For example, our usual arrangement is to contribute $100.00 when local people have raised $400.00."[83]

But many local NAACP branches had no interest in desegregation litigation. For example, virtually every local branch of the NAACP in

---

[82] *Patterson v. Board of Education of Trenton*, 11 N. J. Misc. 179 (1933), *aff'd*, 112 N. J. L. 99 (1934) (Trenton); *Raison v. Board of Education of Berkeley*, 103 N.J.L. 547 (1927) (Toms River); "Negro Parents Win in Court," unidentified newspaper article, Sept. 1928, NAACP Papers I-D-44 (Atlantic City); *Stockton v. Board of Education*, 72 N.J.L. 80 (1905) (Burlington).

[83] For the quote, see Letter from Walter White to R. B. Ransom, Jan. 8, 1925, NAACP Papers, Box I-D-58.

Illinois resisted litigation attempts during the first half of the twentieth century. Similarly, W. E. B. Du Bois blamed the Philadelphia branch in 1934 for its failure to resist school segregation in that city: "in the city of Philadelphia a partial system of elementary Negro schools was developed with no definite action on the part of the NAACP." The Philadelphia branch also came under criticism from the national office for being "notoriously inactive" in supporting desegregation litigation in nearby Berwyn. This lack of interest in desegregation among several local branches of the NAACP reflected the support of many northern blacks for the retention of racially separate schools.[84]

Because the national office of the NAACP possessed a limited legal staff, it relied on local lawyers to shoulder the primary responsibility for litigation. As Milton Konvitz, an attorney in the national office, explained in 1944: "It is not up to the National Office but to the local branch to initiate the proceedings which may result in a case. All that we can do is render whatever assistance may be indicated." On several occasions, the NAACP could not find a local lawyer to handle a case. On other occasions, local lawyers did substandard work. Walter White explained the NAACP's initial reluctance to support litigation in 1925 challenging the construction of a segregated black high school in Indianapolis: "When the Brief in the Archie Greathouse Case was submitted to our Legal Committee some time ago, the decision was rendered by that Committee that this Brief had not been as well drawn as it might have been. We were naturally hesitant about questioning the legal ability of the [Indianapolis] attorneys already engaged but in so important a case as this where so much was at stake, we felt that we could not justifiably put money into a case where, through faulty work, the case would probably be lost."[85]

---

84 For Illinois efforts, see Memorandum from Thurgood Marshall to Roy Wilkins, Dec. 14, 1948, NAACP Papers, Box II-B-138; Letter from W. B. Beatty to C. A. Barnett, Feb. 27, 1925, Barnett Papers, Box 374-8. For the Du Bois quote, see Du Bois, "Postscript" (Jan. 1934), p. 20; for Berwyn, see Franklin, *The Education of Black Philadelphia*, p. 140.

85 For the Konvitz quote, see Letter from Milton R. Konvitz to James E. King, Apr. 6, 1944, NAACP Papers, Box II-B-144. For the White quote, see Letter from Walter White to R. B. Ransom, Jan. 8, 1925, NAACP Papers, Box I-D-58. The national office of the NAACP was also reluctant to become involved in the Indianapolis litigation because it feared the case would result in a bad precedent, given the Indiana state statute that expressly permitted school segregation. In response to a request that the NAACP support desegregation litigation in Indianapolis, Walter White replied: "the danger of the legalization of segregated schools is so serious and imminent that . . . [the Legal Committee of the NAACP] could not recommend that the National Office take up the case." Letter from Walter White to Henry, Feb. 17, 1925, NAACP Papers, Box I-D-60. The national office did eventually support this litigation, but the case was lost. *Greathouse v. Board of Commissioners*, 198 Ind. 95 (1926).

The difficulty in procuring local support for desegregation litigation was due in part to a fear of retaliation against black teachers and plaintiffs. As was true during the nineteenth century, school desegregation litigation often provoked retaliation. For example, when a group of black parents sued the Chester, Pennsylvania, school board for maintaining segregated high schools in 1934, the school board retaliated by failing to renew the contracts of fifty-eight black teachers. School authorities in Dayton and Springfield, Ohio, took similar action during the early 1920s. Moreover, some plaintiffs who filed school desegregation litigation suffered financial retribution.[86]

Another significant factor that contributed to the dearth of litigation was the determination of white school authorities to avoid compliance with court orders requiring integration. Indeed, in a number of northern communities, the recalcitrant posture of white school boards kept segregated schools intact despite court orders requiring compliance with antisegregation laws. As noted in Chapter 3, black plaintiffs in Alton, Illinois, won five victories in the Illinois Supreme Court during the late nineteenth and early twentieth centuries, but white resistance prevented the implementation of those decisions. Other white school boards also refused to comply with antisegregation judicial mandates. On several occasions, school boards, upon losing a desegregation lawsuit, granted relief only to the actual plaintiffs, leaving other black children in their segregated schools. The inability of black plaintiffs to secure relief on behalf of those who did not join the lawsuit severely undermined the efficacy of litigation efforts.[87]

The litigation in Dayton and Springfield, Ohio, illustrates the various difficulties confronting black litigants. The Dayton school board responded to the influx of southern black migrants during World War I by creating a separate school for black children in an old building located behind the Garfield School; by 1925, this annex housed

---

[86] For Chester, see "Legal Action Decides Fate of Teachers," *Philadelphia Tribune*, July 19, 1934, p. 1; "'No Turning Back,' Says Pastor, Expressing Residents' Attitude in Chester, Pa., School Fight," *Philadelphia Tribune*, July 19, 1934, p. 1. For Dayton and Springfield, see "Suit Filed in Dayton School Fight" *Cleveland Gazette*, Jan. 24, 1925, p. 1; "The Dayton School Fight!" *Cleveland Gazette*, June 20, 1925, p. 2; "The 'Jim Crow' School Fight!" *Cleveland Gazette*, June 20, 1925, p. 1; Du Bois, "Editorial – The Victory at Springfield," p. 200; "'Told Them So'!" *Cleveland Gazette*, Jan. 16, 1926, p. 2; Meier and Rudwick, *Along the Color Line*, pp. 300–3. For financial retribution, see Letter from J. E. Edwards to William T. Andrews, Oct. 20, 1928, NAACP Papers, Box I-D-44.

[87] But in a few instances, litigation did have a broader effect. When black plaintiffs successfully challenged school segregation in Coffeyville, Kansas, other Kansas towns also ended their color bar; for example, the Coffeyville decision prompted the Wichita school board to allow black children to use swimming pools for the first time. "Victory Against School Segregation," *Cleveland Gazette*, Apr. 26, 1924, p. 1.

600 black children. At the same time, Dayton school authorities moved those black students attending the racially mixed Willard School into the school's basement to separate them from their white classmates. Paul Stetson, superintendent of the Dayton schools, justified this segregation as serving the interests of the black community, explaining that segregation provided employment for black teachers, while other local school officials cited the "backwardness of some [of the black] pupils" as justification. The Dayton school board solicited black support for its actions, helping to circulate pro-segregation petitions in the black community and promising to build a new separate black school.[88]

Many African Americans in Dayton favored racial separation, particularly when the school board announced that it would not permit black teachers to teach in racially integrated classrooms. One local black leader argued that the retention of black teachers outweighed all of the disadvantages of racially separate schools. A national NAACP leader, dispatched to Dayton to build support for desegregation litigation, reported that "a number of colored people . . . are agitating for the continuance of segregation on the ground that a number of colored teachers will lose their jobs, if it is abolished."[89]

But many African Americans opposed segregation in Dayton even if it cost black teachers jobs in the short run. Harry Smith, editor of the *Cleveland Gazette*, traveled to Dayton to stir interest in desegregation litigation. He urged Dayton blacks to "[d]rop the 'Negro' teacher question and fight all the harder for mixed schools! Later on, the question of 'Negro' teachers in 'mixed classes' can be taken up and it, too, fought to a successful issue." Those Dayton blacks who favored integration did eventually initiate legal action. In 1925, Dayton school authorities learned that two black children who lived in the Garfield School attendance zone had given a false address in order to attend a racially mixed school in another neighborhood. When Dayton school officials ordered these children to attend school in the segregated Garfield annex, their father refused and filed a lawsuit instead. Unable to secure support from the local NAACP branch, which was divided over the wisdom of challenging school segregation, the father persuaded the NAACP's national office, which viewed the Dayton case as a "very important" opportunity to challenge northern school segregation, to

---

[88] "Suit Filed in Dayton School Fight," *Cleveland Gazette*, Jan. 24, 1925, p. 1; "Two Suits in Dayton School-Fight," *Cleveland Gazette*, Feb. 14, 1925, p. 1. For the quote, see "Bars 'Jim Crow' Schools!" *Cleveland Gazette*, July 11, 1924, p. 1.

[89] "A 'Jim Crow' School," *Cleveland Gazette*, July 19, 1924, p. 4; NAACP Board Meeting, Oct. 1924, in Wilson, *In Search of Democracy*, p. 54. For the quote, see "Two Suits in Dayton School-Fight," *Cleveland Gazette*, Feb. 14, 1925, p. 1.

enter the legal fight. In response to the litigation, the Dayton school board refused to renew the contracts of employment of several black teachers at the Garfield school, stating that if the desegregation lawsuit succeeded, there would be no need for black teachers.[90]

In July 1925, a local court decided that although state law gave the board of education discretion to make assignments of pupils in a manner that would "best promote the interest of education in their districts, such power cannot be exercised with reference to the race or color of the youth." Accordingly, the court declared the segregated Garfield annex in violation of Ohio law. In 1926, the Ohio Supreme Court affirmed the lower court's decision, holding that the Dayton school board had introduced unlawful racial segregation at the Garfield school by placing black children in the separate annex building.[91]

The absence of full black support for integration, however, severely hampered enforcement of the legal victory in Dayton. Following the Ohio Supreme Court's decision, school segregation continued virtually unabated as the Dayton school board, supported by a large segment of the black community, sidestepped the court decision. As so many other northern school districts had previously done, the Dayton school board permitted only the two plaintiff children to learn with whites in the main Garfield School building. All other black children were kept in the annex building.[92]

[90] "Bars 'Jim Crow' Schools!" *Cleveland Gazette,* July 11, 1924, p. 1; Appendix to Brief in Opposition to Petition for Writ of Certiorari, pp. 3a–4a, *Brinkman v. Gilligan,* United States Supreme Court, 1979; NAACP Board Meeting, Oct. 1924, in Wilson, *In Search of Democracy,* p. 54; Meier and Rudwick, *Along the Color Line,* pp. 64–6; *Board of Education v. State ex rel. Reese,* 114 Ohio St. 188 (1926); Letter from Roy Wilkins to Raymond Pace Alexander, Sept. 8, 1932, NAACP Papers, Box I-D-48; "No Legal Ohio 'Jim Crow' Schools," *Cleveland Gazette,* Jan. 16, 1926, p. 1; " 'Told Them So'!" *Cleveland Gazette,* Jan. 16, 1926, p. 2; " 'Jim Crow' Schools Again Barred," *Cleveland Gazette,* Feb. 20, 1926, p. 1; "Suit Filed in Dayton School Fight," *Cleveland Gazette,* Jan. 24, 1925, p. 1; "The Dayton School Fight!" *Cleveland Gazette,* June 20, 1925, p. 2; "The 'Jim Crow' School Fight!" *Cleveland Gazette,* June 20, 1925, p. 1. For the quote, see "Dayton School Fight!" *Cleveland Gazette,* June 10, 1925, p. 2.

[91] For the lower court quote, see "State Supreme Court with Us!" *Cleveland Gazette,* July 18, 1925, p. 1. For Supreme Court decision, see *Board of Education v. State ex rel. Reese,* 114 Ohio St. 188 (1926); Letter from Roy Wilkins to Raymond Pace Alexander, Sept. 8, 1932, NAACP Papers, Box I-D-48; "No Legal Ohio 'Jim Crow' Schools," *Cleveland Gazette,* Jan. 16, 1926, p. 1; " 'Told Them So'!" *Cleveland Gazette,* Jan. 16, 1926, p. 2; " 'Jim Crow' Schools Again Barred," *Cleveland Gazette,* Feb. 20, 1926, p. 1.

[92] Letter from Marian Smith Williams to Roy Wilkins, Jan. 18, 1946; Letter from Marian Smith Williams to W. E. B. Du Bois, Aug. 6, 1945, NAACP Papers, Box II-B-146; "Law Abiding America," *The Crisis* 32 (June 1926), p. 92; Al Dunmore, "Objectively Yours," *Pittsburgh Courier,* Jan. 5, 1946, NAACP Papers, Box II-B-146; "Dayton Kluxers Get Very Busy!" *Cleveland Gazette,* Mar. 5, 1927, p. 1; "More 'Jim Crow' Schools,"

For the quarter century following the legal victory striking down school segregation in Dayton, racial segregation in that city continued unabated. During the early 1930s, other black children in the Garfield school annex were permitted to move into the main building, but they were taught in racially segregated classrooms by black teachers. Eventually the Dayton school board allowed white students who lived in the Garfield attendance area to transfer to a white school. As a result, by 1936, Garfield had become an all-black school. Similarly, in 1935, the Dayton school board transferred all of the white teachers and children at the racially mixed Willard elementary school to white schools, leaving Willard an all-black school with only black teachers. In 1945, the Dayton school board continued this practice by transferring all white children and teachers out of the Wogaman School, thereby converting it to a black school. White students living in the Wogaman School district were transferred to white schools.[93]

In the meantime, in 1933, the Dayton school board built Dunbar Junior and Senior High School for black children, even though a white junior and senior high school was less than a mile away. The school board did not construct a geographic attendance zone for the new Dunbar School. Rather, black students throughout the city were assigned there, regardless of their proximity to another school. No white students were assigned to Dunbar; those who happened to live nearby were assigned to the nearest white school. Dayton maintained Dunbar as the high school to which all of the city's black students were assigned, regardless of their proximity to white schools, until after the 1954 *Brown* decision. In addition, Dunbar's athletic teams could not compete with other white teams in the city until 1947, required instead to play teams from black schools in other Ohio cities or from outside the state.[94]

Similar disdain for a school desegregation court order was demonstrated in Springfield, Ohio. In 1922, the Springfield school board resegregated its schools by creating an all-black elementary

---

Cleveland Gazette, May 22, 1926, p. 1; Meier and Rudwick, "Negro Boycotts of Jim Crow Schools," p. 67; *Brinkman v. Gilligan,* 583 F.2d 243, 249 (6th Cir. 1978); Watras, *Politics, Race, and Schools,* p. 85.

93 *Brinkman v. Gilligan,* 583 F.2d 243 (6th Cir. 1978); Requests for Admission, Appendix to Brief in Opposition to Petition for Writ of Certiorari, p. 54, *Brinkman v. Gilligan,* United States Supreme Court, 1979; Appendix to Brief in Opposition to Petition for Writ for Certiorari, pp. 6a–8a, *Dayton Board of Education v. Brinkman,* 443 U.S. 449 (1979).

94 Bond, *The Education of Negroes,* p. 380; Brief for the United States as Amicus Curiae, p. 25, *Dayton Board of Education v. Brinkman,* 443 U.S. 526 (1979); *Brinkman v. Gilligan,* 583 F.2d 243, 249–50 (6th Cir. 1978); Watras, *Politics, Race, and Schools,* pp. 86–7; Appendix to Brief in Opposition to Petition for Writ for Certiorari, p. 6a, n. 7, *Dayton Board of Education v. Brinkman,* 443 U.S. 449 (1979).

school – Fulton – in response to an influx of southern blacks into the city. The Springfield school superintendent, a Klansman, described the plan as an "experiment of an all-colored school" with black teachers. All black children were sent to Fulton, and white children in the Fulton attendance area were sent to white schools. Many black parents, particularly those of southern migrant children, had petitioned for the separate school to procure black teachers. In fact, the establishment of Fulton as a black school had led to the hiring of black teachers in Springfield for the first time since the 1880s. The *Cleveland Gazette* criticized these black supporters of the separate school for giving "their assistance to this vicious K.K.K. scheme to reduce our people to an everlasting condition of inferiority and servility."[95]

The national office of the NAACP offered its support for a legal challenge, dispatching Robert Bagnall to Springfield to provide assistance, but the local branch was split on the issue and hence took no action. With the local branch of the NAACP hopelessly divided, those blacks opposed to segregation formed a Civil Rights Protective League and in the fall of 1922 organized a boycott of the segregated Fulton school, picketing the entrance to the school to keep black students and teachers away. The picketing, conducted by about 100 black women, was designed to demonstrate black opposition to school segregation in Springfield. The boycott enjoyed broad support, as about 250 of the school's 300 black children stayed away from the segregated school. Thereafter, Sully Jaymes, a Springfield black attorney and co-organizer of the Civil Rights Protective League, filed suit with support from the national office of the NAACP. A local Ohio court issued a temporary injunction barring the segregation in December 1922, and in February 1923 issued a permanent injunction requiring the school board either to close the Fulton School and transfer the black children to other schools or, as an alternative, to give all of Fulton's black children the right to attend any school they chose. The *Cleveland Gazette* called the decision "Our Greatest Victory Since the War of the Rebellion!"[96]

---

95 "Fighting in Springfield," *Cleveland Gazette*, Oct. 14, 1922, p. 2; "The School Strike in Springfield Ohio," *Opportunity* 1 (Feb. 1923), pp. 27–8; "The Victory Complete!" *Cleveland Gazette*, Feb. 2, 1924, p. 1; "Ku Klux Klan Victory!" *Cleveland Gazette*, June 13, 1925, p. 2; Du Bois, "Editorial – The Victory at Springfield," p. 200; Meier and Rudwick, *Along the Color Line*, p. 294. For the quote, see "Permanent Injunction Granted! 'Jim Crow' School Closed for Good!" *Cleveland Gazette*, Feb. 10, 1923, p. 1.

96 "Springfield, Ohio, Defeats Segregated School Move," *The Crisis* 26 (May 1923), p. 25; Meier and Rudwick, *Along the Color Line*, pp. 294–5; "Negro Rioters Arraigned," *New York Times*, Apr. 10, 1922, p. 4; "That Springfield Victory!" *Cleveland Gazette*, Feb. 10, 1923; "The Victory Complete!" *Cleveland Gazette*, Feb. 2, 1924, p. 1; "Sully Jaymes, Esq.," *Cleveland Gazette*, Mar. 10, 1923. For the quote, see "Permanent Injunction Granted! 'Jim Crow' School Closed for Good!" *Cleveland Gazette*, Feb. 10, 1923, p. 1.

The Springfield school board, however, ignored the court order and refused to admit the Fulton black children to the city's white schools; in addition, it dismissed all of the black teachers at the segregated school. No black teacher would teach again in Springfield until the late 1940s. The recalcitrant school board was voted out of office in the fall of 1923 (for reasons pertaining to the dismissal of several popular white teachers), and the new board incorporated the Fulton School into the city's geographic assignment plan. But a liberal allowance of transfers for white students living in the Fulton school district coupled with a denial of transfers for black students kept the Fulton school almost completely black. These experiences in Dayton and Springfield, in which litigation successes did not translate into meaningful desegregation, were repeated across the North.[97]

Efforts to Remove Racist Textbooks

Although legal challenges to school segregation generally failed to arrest the trend toward greater school segregation, African Americans did enjoy some success removing racist textbooks from public schools. These efforts were considerably less threatening to the racial status quo in northern cities than were antisegregation efforts.

The use of textbooks containing unflattering portraits of African Americans had long been a source of irritation for northern blacks. In Oberlin, blacks in the late nineteenth century sought to remove Charles F. King's *The Picturesque Geographical Reader* from the schools due to its negative presentation of blacks. A Cambridge, Massachusetts, schoolchild wrote the editor of a Boston paper in 1903, complaining that blacks in her textbooks were described as "slaves and niggers."[98]

Such defamatory material remained common during the first half of the twentieth century. A history textbook published in New York in 1923, for example, claimed that "[i]t is becoming more and more to be believed that white and black must be kept severed socially, and that the dominant race must see to it that the negro be given a helping hand toward educating him and making him useful in industry." Another textbook, published in Philadelphia in 1920, claimed that large numbers of blacks were "ignorant, lazy and thriftless."[99]

[97] Meier and Rudwick, *Along the Color Line*, pp. 301–3; "'Told Them So'!" *Cleveland Gazette*, Jan. 16, 1926, p. 2.

[98] Fishel, "The North and the Negro," pp. 349–50.

[99] For quotes, see Pierce, *Civic Attitudes*, pp. 90–1 (quoting Andrew C. McLaughlin and Claude Halstead Van Tyne, *A History of the United States for Schools* [New York: D. Appleton & Co., 1923], and Smith Burnham, *The Making of Our Country* [Philadelphia: John C. Winston Co., 1920]).

During the 1920s and 1930s, many northern blacks challenged the use of textbooks with such negative portrayals of African Americans. William Monroe Trotter, the distinguished editor of the *Boston Guardian*, successfully requested that Cambridge remove certain history books from its public schools in 1925 that used the words "nigger," "mongrel," and "gross plantation dialect" when discussing blacks. In Chicago, Nannie Jackson Myers persuaded the school board in 1926 to have the publisher of a civics book reword a passage that characterized blacks as "shiftless and backward." The *Philadelphia Tribune* engaged in a successful campaign in 1932 to remove from the local curriculum a widely used junior high school civics book that described blacks as dirty, ignorant, and superstitious, and to blame for the paucity of black voters in the South. Finally, blacks in Hamtramck, Michigan, succeeded in 1934 in removing from the local high school a sociology book written by a white southerner that described African Americans of "pure black blood" as "incapable of leadership" and with a tendency "toward degeneracy."[100]

Efforts to challenge racist textbooks succeeded because relatively little was at stake for white school boards, particularly in comparison to simultaneous black efforts to procure racial mixing. But textbook campaigns helped build broader support in the black community for an attack on segregation. NAACP Executive Secretary Walter White, for example, acknowledged in 1932 that a textbook campaign "would be especially helpful right now when the N.A.A.C.P. Drive for Membership is on." Similarly, the successful textbook campaign in Philadelphia led to the establishment of the Educational Equality League in Philadelphia in 1932, which played a critical role in the struggle to procure black teachers in racially mixed schools in that city during the 1930s.[101]

By the end of the 1930s, northern school segregation was more prevalent than it had been at the turn of the century. Although the NAACP had attempted to fight the spread of segregation through litigation, that campaign had met with limited success. The strong opposition among both whites and blacks conspired to limit the efficacy of these

---

[100] For Trotter, see "'Fired' Insulting Books," *Cleveland Gazette*, Apr. 4, 1925, p. 2; for Myers, see Homel, "Two Worlds of Race?" p. 252. For the *Tribune* campaign, see "Negroes Plan Fight on Slanderous Text Book in City Schools," *Philadelphia Tribune*, Jan. 14, 1932, p. 1; Homel, "Two Worlds of Race?" p. 252; Franklin, *The Education of Black Philadelphia*, pp. 136–7. For Michigan, see Associated Negro Press, "School Board Discards Text Book After Protest," Dec. 3, 1934, Barnett Papers, Box 361-2.

[101] For the White quote, see Walter White, "On Racist Textbooks," Sept. 28, 1932, in Wilson, *In Search of Democracy*, p. 248; for the Philadelphia campaign, see Franklin, *The Education of Black Philadelphia*, p. 137.

litigation efforts. Ralph Bunche, writing in 1935, expressed pessimism about the possibilities of racial change without a real commitment among whites to racial integration: "Perhaps the favorite method of struggle for rights employed by minority groups is the political. Through the use of the ballot and the courts strenuous efforts are put forth to gain social justice for the group. Extreme faith is placed in the ability of these instruments of democratic government to free the minority from social proscription and civic inequality. The inherent fallacy of this belief rests in the failure to appreciate the fact that the instruments of the state are merely the reflections of the political and economic ideology of the dominant group. . . . " Before the NAACP could succeed in the courtroom, it would need to build greater public support among both blacks and whites for its integrationist agenda. That support would come. Out of the cataclysm of World War II emerged a shift in black and white attitudes toward obvious forms of racial segregation and discrimination that led to the eradication of most of the remaining vestiges of explicit northern school segregation.[102]

[102] For the quote, see Bunche, "A Critical Analysis," pp. 314–15.

6

The Democratic Imperative

The Campaign against Northern School Segregation, 1940–1954

I was teaching my children to say the pledge to the flag. It has a lot of big words in it and I was trying to help them understand its meaning. I asked, "Do you know what the words liberty and justice mean? Can you tell me what they stand for?" After a moment a child replied, "They mean this is a free country . . . and colored children ought to be able to go to any school in [Gary]."

– A kindergarten teacher at an all-white school
in Gary, Indiana, 1947[1]

For the first four decades of the twentieth century, school segregation steadily increased throughout the North as white school boards reacted to the Great Migration with a renewed insistence on racial separation. Moreover, in most northern communities, black teachers were still not allowed to teach white children. In some communities, there were no black teachers at all. A majority of northern and western whites, when polled in 1942, favored racially separate public schools.[2]

The decade of the 1940s, however, marked a watershed in the campaign against northern school segregation. By the early 1950s, almost all explicit school segregation in the North had ended. In several northern states whose legislatures had prohibited school segregation during the nineteenth century, state and local education officials took action during the late 1940s and early 1950s to eliminate the remaining race-based pupil assignments. Moreover, Indiana, the lone northern holdout, in 1949 finally repealed its earlier legislation that permitted school segregation.

During the 1940s, a number of factors converged to produce a climate more favorable to civil rights initiatives. First, the decade witnessed a significant increase in black insistence on an end to racial segregation. This increase in antisegregation activism had several causes. World War II, which Adam Clayton Powell labeled "Civil War II,"

---

[1] Tipton, *Community in Crisis*, p. 129.
[2] Erskine, "The Polls: Race Relations," p. 139; Office of War Information, "White Attitudes Toward Negroes," p. 7, Aug. 5, 1942, Hastie Papers, Box 104-7.

invigorated black protest as thousands of black soldiers who had fought to make the world safe for democracy returned home with a renewed desire to insist on democracy at home. Moreover, beginning in the 1940s, blacks began to enjoy the fruits of years of northern migration that translated into significantly greater political influence. At the same time, certain civil rights organizations with a deep commitment to racial integration – the most important of which was the NAACP – gained much greater influence during the 1940s due to exploding membership.[3]

The 1940s also marked a significant change in white attitudes toward black demands for an end to segregation. In response to the increase in black voting power, northern white politicians supported antidiscrimination and antisegregation initiatives that would have languished only a decade earlier. The war against Nazi racism brought home the fundamental conflict between the American creed of equal treatment and the country's harsh treatment of African Americans. As the world war against fascism turned into a Cold War against communism, increasing numbers of whites perceived the damage done to America's international interests through racial oppression. Moreover, civil unrest in the form of urban riots caused many white leaders to view black demands for fair treatment with greater sympathy.

But the desegregation gains of the 1940s and early 1950s were more limited than they first appeared. Though the end of racially explicit pupil assignments did mark a significant reversal of earlier white insistence on racial separation, they did not reflect a deep and widespread commitment to racial integration and did not lead to a fundamental change in patterns of racial separation in northern schools. Rather, these desegregation gains reflected a growing uneasiness with obvious and explicit forms of racial discrimination coupled with the pragmatic need to gain black political support; they also reflected, by the late 1940s, a desire to end the international embarrassment caused by America's harsh treatment of racial minorities. Moreover, the campaign to end explicit school segregation in northern schools during the 1940s and early 1950s was aided by the fact that most northern black children would remain in separate schools because of extensive residential segregation. Hence, the elimination of racial classifications in public schools came with a limited "cost" in most northern school districts. By the time of the Supreme Court's 1954 decision in *Brown v. Board of Education*, most explicit school segregation in the North had been eliminated, but racial separation and inequality in northern schools remained widespread.

---

[3] Powell, *Marching Blacks*, p. 3.

Increased Black Insistence on an End to Racial Segregation

Black insistence on an end to racial segregation sharply increased during World War II as black Americans grew increasingly frustrated with the discrepancy between America's democratic ideals and its undemocratic racial practices. As NAACP Executive Secretary Walter White later observed about the war years: "Negro militancy and implacable determination to wipe out segregation grew more proportionately during the years 1940 to 1945 than during any other period of the Negro's history in America." *Life* magazine noted this increase in black opposition to racial segregation in 1944: "Never before have Negro leaders been so outspokenly bitter about America's refusal to give them equal status . . . [and] so active on behalf of Negro rights."[4]

Initially, many African Americans were ambivalent about participation in World War II. Horace Cayton noted during the war that many blacks were "sullen and wished to see their country brought to its knees." A 1942 survey of black attitudes in Harlem by the federal Bureau of Intelligence found that 40 percent concluded that it was more important to "make democracy work at home than to beat Germany and Japan." A substantial minority of those blacks surveyed concluded that they would be no worse off under German or Japanese rule.[5]

Many African Americans initially refused to enlist. A black Philadelphian commented that "I ain't about to give [my life] to no country that treats folks like they do us. . . . You can't kick a man's behind and then tell him to go and fight for you." A black attorney in Chicago announced: "If I go, they'll have to come and get me. Why should I join a Jim Crow Army?" Early in the war, Walter White addressed a black audience and quoted a black college student who had said: "I hope Hitler wins. . . . The Army jim crows us. The Navy lets us serve only as messmen. The Red Cross refuses our blood. Employers and labor unions shut us out. Lynchings continue. We are disenfranchised, Jim Crowed, spat upon. What more could Hitler do than that?" White was about to explain that this sentiment was shortsighted when his audience burst into lengthy applause.[6]

On the eve of America's entry into the war in 1941, *Opportunity*, the publication of the National Urban League, lamented the pervasiveness

4 For the White quote, see Biondi, *To Stand and Fight*, p. 16; for the *Life* quote, see "Editorial – Negro Rights," *Life*, Apr. 24, 1944, p. 32.

5 For the Cayton quote, see Finkle, *Forum for Protest*, p. 212; for the survey see Bureau of Intelligence, "Negroes in a Democracy at War," pp. 20–6, May 27, 1943, Hastie Papers, Box 104-7. See also Anderson, *Eyes off the Prize*, pp. 9–11.

6 For the Philadelphia quote, see Finkle, *Forum for Protest*, pp. 103–4; for the Chicago quote, see ibid., p. 103; for the White quote, see Barnett, "The Role of the Press," pp. 482–3.

of racial segregation in America: "All over the world the color line is being erased as nations fight to preserve the democratic form of government – all over the world except in Hitler's Germany, Mussolini's Italy, and the United States of America." The *Pittsburgh Courier* captured the mood among many African Americans in a 1942 editorial: "In the past we have made the mistake of relying entirely upon the gratitude and sense of fair play of the American people.... Now we are disillusioned. We have neither faith in promises, nor a high opinion of the integrity of the American people, where race is involved. Experience has taught us that we must rely primarily upon our own efforts...." Another black critic asked: "[W]hy do Americans go 1,000 miles across the ocean to defend Democracy against the same evils as they are tolerating here upon our race?"[7]

The United States government sought to build black support for the war effort, but many black leaders were dismissive of its efforts. Kenneth Clark, for example, describing "The Morale of the Negro," observed of black America: "His morale today is not likely to be appreciably raised by concessions made within the framework of a rigid policy of racial segregation and discrimination. He is not as easily satisfied as he appeared to have been in 1917.... It takes more to dissipate the smouldering cumulative resentment and generalized bitterness residual of his oppression, disillusionment and disappointments.... The Negro today is more cynical, he tends to question more the meanings and realities of slogans, appeals and symbols to which he is subjected. His past disappointments and racial experiences have made him less susceptible to a positive reaction to them." Black frustration over the disparity between the rhetoric of a war for democracy and the realities of segregation in both the armed services and at home was expressed in the popular statement "Here lies a black man killed fighting a yellow man for the protection of a white man."[8]

But many black leaders urged support for the war on the grounds that black participation in the war for democracy in Europe and Asia would boost the campaign for democracy at home. The NAACP adopted as its slogan for its 1942 annual convention "Victory Is Vital to Minorities." NAACP Executive Secretary Walter White, speaking to white America, announced in 1942 that black America would support the war: "Though 13 million American Negroes have more often than not been denied democracy, they are American citizens and will as

---

[7] For the *Opportunity* quote, see "Editorial – A Negro Pursuit Squadron," *Opportunity* 19 (Apr. 1941), p. 99. For the *Courier* quote, see "Editorial," *Pittsburgh Courier*, Sept. 12, 1942, p. 6. For the third quote, see Savage, *Broadcasting Freedom*, pp. 221–2.

[8] For the first quote, see Clark, "Morale of the Negro," pp. 426–7 (italics deleted); for the second quote, see Lawson, *Running for Freedom*, p. 7.

in every war give unqualified support to the protection of their country." Kenneth Clark described many African Americans as embracing "a positive hope that the war will result in a more liberal treatment of minorities" and "a negative hope that the war will so weaken the white races that they will be unable to continue their subjugation and exploitation of the darker races."[9]

The black press enthusiastically supported the war but made it clear that it would not compromise the fight for racial equality. The *Pittsburgh Courier*, now the black paper with the largest circulation in the nation, promoted a "Double V" campaign in early 1942. As one correspondent to the *Courier* urged: "The V for victory sign is being displayed prominently in all so-called democratic countries which are fighting for victory over aggression, slavery and tyranny.... [L]et ... colored Americans adopt the double VV for a double victory. The first V for victory over our enemies from without, the second V for victory over our enemies from within." The *Courier* embraced this idea of a Double V campaign, which every major black newspaper and organization subsequently endorsed. The *Courier* also counseled black soldiers to "insist on combat duty." As one *Courier* columnist explained: "The more we put in, the more we have a right to claim." *The Crisis* similarly argued that "this is no fight merely to wear a uniform. This is a struggle for status, a struggle to take democracy off of parchment and give it life." In fact, not a single mainstream black newspaper supported draft resistance by blacks during World War II.[10]

Similarly, the NAACP refused to aid blacks who resisted war service. When Winfred Lynn refused induction into the service to protest racial segregation in the military, not only did the NAACP turn down his request for legal assistance, Thurgood Marshall persuaded the American Civil Liberties Union not to take Lynn's case. Lynn's brother, a legal counsel for a local NAACP branch in New York, was dismissed from the local when he persisted in bringing a legal challenge on behalf

---

[9] For support for war, see Finkle, *Forum for Protest*, pp. 10, 89; for the NAACP slogan, see Sitkoff, "African American Militancy," p. 74; for the White quote, see "Leaders of Race Pledge Support as War Comes," *Chicago Defender*, Dec. 13, 1941, p. 4; for the Clark quote, see Clark, "Morale of the Negro, p. 426.

[10] For the black press, see Finkle, *Forum for Protest;* Perry, "A Common Purpose." For the first use of the "Double V" emblem in the *Pittsburgh Courier*, see the Feb. 7, 1942, issue, p. 1; for the first *Courier* quote, see Letter to the Editor, "Should I Sacrifice to Live Half-American?" *Pittsburgh Courier*, Jan. 31, 1942, p. 3; for the second *Courier* quote, see Sitkoff, "African American Militancy," p. 75; for the third *Courier* quote, see "Rogers Says: Ignore Our Enemies, Support Our Friends and Buy War Bonds," *Pittsburgh Courier*, Jan. 31, 1942, p. 6; for *The Crisis* quote, see "For Manhood in National Defense," *The Crisis* 47 (Dec. 1940), p. 375. For the black press and war, see Sitkoff, "African American Militancy," p. 74.

of his brother. In 1945, shortly before the war's conclusion, fifty-four black WACs initially refused to work at a hospital in Massachusetts because, unlike white WACs, they were assigned cleaning duties rather than work commensurate with their training as technicians. Despite the obvious racial discrimination, the Boston branch of the NAACP criticized the black WACs for their refusal to work.[11]

At the same time, during the war years, many African Americans eschewed mass protest against racial discrimination, a common practice during the 1930s, hoping that such restraint would help capture white support for racial equality. After Pearl Harbor, for example, blacks conducted only one school boycott in opposition to school segregation during the war – in Hillburn, New York – even though blacks had conducted more than ten boycotts protesting northern school segregation during the 1930s. Although there were some scattered protests against public accommodations discrimination, overall the amount of direct action protest during World War II was considerably less than during the 1930s.[12]

But this relative decline in mass protest in no way signaled a decline in black commitment to ending racial discrimination. In fact, black insistence on equal treatment noticeably increased during the 1940s. Crucial to this increase were black soldiers. Upon returning home from war service, many blacks demanded an end to racial discrimination. Those protesting racial discrimination by restaurants, for example, carried signs reading "We Die Together – Why Can't We Eat Together?" One black veteran with four years of service in the war explained his support for a local ordinance banning racial discrimination in Montclair, New Jersey: "I'm tired of being kept out of places where any bum, prostitute, or criminal may go without questioning, but not a Negro. If that's democracy, then I don't want any of it." A black newspaper in New Jersey noted the ongoing fact of racial discrimination in 1945: "as the fight is made to keep without the forces of oppression as symbolized by Nazism and Fascism we find within the borders of our country enemies equally as vicious – namely prejudice, discrimination, segregation." Another black newspaper in New Jersey published a "Jim Crow Guide to U.S.A.," comparing America's race laws to those of Nazi Germany. Adam Clayton Powell commented that "[f]ifteen million blacks agreed to fight to make the world safe for democracy, but served notice that this time they were going to fight just as hard at home to make America safe, too."[13]

---

[11] Sitkoff, "African American Militancy," p. 74; Finkle, *Forum for Protest*, pp. 150–1, 179–81.

[12] Sitkoff, "African American Militancy," pp. 75–6, 88.

[13] For the first quote, see Murray, *Song in a Weary Throat*, p. 207; for the Montclair quote, see "Anti-Bias Rule Given Setback," *Newark Evening News*, Apr. 10, 1948, p. 23; for the

Mistreatment of black servicemen upon their return home contributed to growing militancy. In 1943, a white police officer in Harlem allegedly shot a black serviceman, triggering widespread rioting. Riots followed in other American cities. Mary McLeod Bethune, who characterized the Harlem riot as the modern-day equivalent of the Boston Tea Party, warned of deep unrest in the black community: "One who would really understand this racial tension which has broken out into actual conflicts in riots as in Harlem, Detroit, and Los Angeles, must look to... the growing internal pressure of Negro masses to break through the wall of restriction which restrains them from full American citizenship.... The hard core of internal pressure among the Negro masses in the United States today is undoubtedly their resentment over the mistreatment of colored men in the armed forces.... You must add to these deep-seated feelings a whole series of repercussions of the frustrated efforts of Negroes to find a place in war production ... [and] their inability to get adequate housing."[14]

During the war, NAACP membership became an outlet for black frustration. NAACP membership skyrocketed from 50,556 and 355 local branches in 1940 to more than 500,000 members and more than 1,000 local branches in 1946. In the process, the NAACP evolved from an organization largely comprised of middle- and upper-class blacks to a mass-supported group for black equality. Adam Clayton Powell, Jr., who had denounced the NAACP in 1940, called NAACP Executive Secretary Walter White "the nation's Number One Negro" in 1945. When a 1942 government survey asked black Americans "What organizations... do you think are trying hardest to get the Negroes more rights?", three times as many respondents named the NAACP as the runner-up organization, the National Urban League.[15]

After the conclusion of the war, the national office of the NAACP, spurred by the tremendous increase in its membership, became much more aggressive on a number of fronts, including northern school desegregation, and in the process became the dominant voice for racial integration in America. In 1945, for example, the national office of the NAACP urged President Harry Truman to support a permanent Fair Employment Practice Committee, arguing that it would "reassure Negro citizens that the government has not abandoned them and

New Jersey quote, see "Hits Schools at Bordentown," *New Jersey Herald News*, Apr. 14, 1945, p. 1; for the New Jersey "Jim Crow Guide," see Mumford, "Double V in New Jersey," p. 32; for the Powell quote, see Powell, *Marching Blacks*, p. 127.

[14] Quoted in Bethune, "Certain Unalienable Rights," in Logan, *What the Negro Wants*, pp. 250–1.

[15] For NAACP membership, see Sitkoff, "African American Militancy," p. 77; McAdam, *Political Process*, pp. 103–5. For the Powell quote, see Powell, *Marching Blacks* p. 140; for the 1942 survey, see Bureau of Intelligence, "Negroes in a Democracy at War," May 27, 1942, p. 4, Hastie Papers, Box 104-7.

that the democracy their soldiers fought for is at work on the home front." As Harvard Sitkoff has noted, "[n]o other African-American protest group put forth an alternative strategy of social change" during the 1940s and early 1950s. The NAACP's antisegregation program emphasized education, litigation, political action, and collaboration with whites while eschewing mass collective action. The organization's significant victories in the United States Supreme Court challenging the exclusion of black voters from political primaries in Texas in 1944 and racially restrictive covenants in 1948 gave increased legitimacy to the organization's legal redress efforts.[16]

This increased black insistence on racial integration shocked many white Americans – particularly southerners. When the University of North Carolina Press assembled a book of essays by leading black thinkers in 1944 published under the name *What the Negro Wants*, no black writer supported segregation. Flabbergasted, the press's white editor, William T. Couch, wrote an introduction to the volume in which he questioned whether these writers truly reflected "what the Negro wants." Black sociologist Charles Johnson assured Couch that they did: "There are no two schools of thought as to what the Negro wants.... Negroes... have the right and the desire to share on an absolutely equal basis in the privileges, the opportunities and the duties that are the heritage of all Americans. They know also that this will never come to pass under a system of segregation." Some whites understood the impact of the war on black demands for racial equality. "The war and its slogans," observed Richmond newspaper editor Virginius Dabney, "have roused in the breasts of our colored friends hopes, aspirations and desires which they formerly did not entertain, except in the rarest instances."[17]

The federal Bureau of Intelligence of the Office of War Information conducted an extensive study of black attitudes during the war and concluded that black Americans were unwilling to compromise their demands for equality: "During the last world war, Negro leaders such as Dr. W. E. B. Du Bois... appealed to the Negro people to 'close ranks' with the whites; they called for a suspension of grievances until the war was won. In the present war, however, no outstanding Negro leaders have urged a policy of this sort.... On the contrary, the outbreak of the present war was accompanied by an intensification of Negro demands for equality in all phases of the national effort.... [M]ost

---

[16] For the NAACP quote, see NAACP, Minutes of September 1945 board meeting, in Wilson, *In Search of Democracy*, p. 190; for the Sitkoff quote, see Sitkoff, *The Struggle for Black Equality*, p. 18. For the NAACP, see Sitkoff, "African American Militancy," p. 89.

[17] For the Johnson quote, see Dunne, "Next Steps," p. 16; for the Dabney quote, see Janken, *Rayford W. Logan*, p. 160.

[Negroes] feel that the stated purposes of this Government in the prosecution of the war can be given validity only by a greater recognition of the Negro's claims to justice and equality." But the Bureau found no widespread disloyalty in black America: "They seek no 'new order', no overthrow of established values, no supremacy of race. They desire to identify themselves as Americans and are frustrated because they are not permitted to do so."[18]

The Effect of the War on White Attitudes Toward Racial Equality

Concurrent with the increased demand among African Americans for an end to racial segregation came a greater receptiveness to such demands among many northern whites. This shift was due to several factors: an increase in black political influence, the imperatives of both the world war and the Cold War to end racial discrimination, and the desire to quell black unrest.

During the 1940s, the political power of northern blacks significantly increased due to a dramatic increase in the number of black voters. Since World War I, hundreds of thousands of African Americans had migrated to northern states. The number of black migrants sharply increased during World War II as southern blacks sought to meet the demands of wartime industry in the industrial North and West. During the 1940s, 1.6 million southern blacks moved north or west, about three times the number that had migrated north during the Great Migration of World War I. Indeed, during the 1940s, the number of African Americans living outside the South increased from 2.4 million to 4.6 million, constituting the most significant internal migration in American history.[19]

In certain parts of the North and West, the population increases were particularly dramatic. Black migrants settled primarily in six northern states – New York, Illinois, Pennsylvania, Ohio, Michigan, and New Jersey – and one western state, California. During the 1940s, New York's black population increased by 60 percent (from 571,221 to 918,191), Illinois's by 66 percent (from 387,446 to 645,446), Pennsylvania's by 35 percent (from 470,172 to 638,485), Ohio's by 50 percent (from 339,461 to 513,072), Michigan's by 112 percent (from 208,345 to 442,296), and New Jersey's by 40 percent (from 226,973 to 318,565). In each of these states, the black population as a percentage of the total population sharply increased. Population gains were particularly

---

[18] Bureau of Intelligence, "Negroes in a Democracy at War," May 27, 1942, pp. 1–3, 6, Hastie Papers, Box 104-7.
[19] Lewis, "The Origins and Causes of the Civil Rights Movement," p. 3; Delton, "Forging of a Northern Strategy," p. 157.

dramatic in urban areas. Detroit's black population almost doubled between 1940 and 1943 alone, Cleveland's increased by 67 percent during the 1940s, and New York's increased by 64 percent between 1940 and 1948.[20]

In the West, California's black population more than tripled during the 1940s (from 124,306 to 462,172), with particularly dramatic increases in San Francisco, Oakland, and Los Angeles. Between 1940 and 1950, San Francisco's black population, drawn by jobs in the defense industry and the shipyards, increased more than eightfold, Oakland's increased almost fivefold, and Los Angeles's tripled.[21]

These population increases translated into significant political gains as both political parties competed for the black vote. Particularly in urban areas, blacks built on political gains of the Depression years and wielded unprecedented political influence. Prior to the 1940s, northern blacks had generally been too small in number to play a significant role in northern politics, comprising less than 10 percent of the total population of almost every northern city. In the two northern cities in which blacks comprised the largest percentage of the population in 1940 – Indianapolis and Philadelphia – the figure was only 13 percent.[22]

To be sure, during the 1930s, black participation in politics had sharply increased as black voters joined the New Deal Democratic coalition in support of Franklin Roosevelt's economic policies. In many northern cities, Republicans had not had to compete with Democrats for the support of black voters; the New Deal helped transform the political influence of northern blacks. Black registration dramatically increased in many northern cities during the 1930s. For example, in 1932, 69,000 blacks, or 46 percent of those eligible, were registered to vote in Philadelphia. By 1940, that figure was almost 135,000, or 82 percent of those eligible. Similarly, in two Harlem voting districts, registration climbed from 43,000 to 70,000 between 1930 and 1940 after remaining virtually static throughout the 1920s. In some northern cities, such as Cleveland, the percentage of eligible blacks registered to vote during the 1930s exceeded the percentage of eligible whites registered.[23]

---

[20] U.S. Bureau of the Census, 1940 and 1950; McAdam, *Political Process*, p. xix; Finkle, *Forum for Protest*, p. 100; Moore, "The Limits of Black Power," p. 45; Biondi, *To Stand and Fight*, p. 3.

[21] U.S. Bureau of the Census, 1940 and 1950; Delton, "Forging of a Northern Strategy," p. 157; Broussard, *Black San Francisco*, pp. 133–6; Hendrick, *The Education of Non-Whites in California*, p. 98.

[22] Homel, "Two Worlds of Race?" p. 238.

[23] Weiss, *Farewell to the Party of Lincoln*, pp. 227–8; Moore, "The Limits of Black Power," pp. 33–4; Kusmer, *A Ghetto Takes Shape*, pp. 84–5.

This increased voting strength during the 1930s had translated into some political gains. During the 1930s, several northern states – including Illinois, Ohio, Pennsylvania, and Wisconsin – enacted legislation strengthening earlier prohibitions on racial discrimination in public accommodations. Moreover, four northern states – Illinois, New York, Ohio, and Pennsylvania – enacted legislation during the 1930s prohibiting racial discrimination in public employment.[24]

This increased political influence also affected in a few instances the campaign against racial discrimination in public schools. In 1937, a newly elected black state legislator in Pennsylvania, Homer Brown, secured passage of a resolution in the Pennsylvania House of Representatives calling for a formal legislative hearing on the discriminatory hiring practices of the Pittsburgh Public School Board. The resolution passed, and the legislature subpoenaed the entire school board to appear before a legislative committee. The hearings revealed extensive discrimination against black teachers going back more than a quarter of a century. In the wake of those hearings, the Pittsburgh school board hired a full-time black teacher for the first time since Reconstruction. By the same token, in 1938, a black state assemblyman in New York helped procure legislation that withdrew from the state's rural school districts the legal authority to operate racially segregated schools. Supporters of this legislation were aided by the fact that only one school district in the state – Hillburn – continued to engage in explicit race-based pupil assignments. In New Jersey, the General Assembly, at the behest of the state's black citizens, created a new state agency in 1938, the New Jersey State Temporary Commission on the Condition of the Urban Colored Population, which issued a lengthy report in 1939 detailing the extent of school segregation in New Jersey and recommending further investigation of the issue. The commission's report was highly significant. Although it led to no immediate action, it marked the first time that an official government commission in New Jersey had addressed the issue of school segregation. Most efforts to procure stronger civil rights protection in northern states would fail until the 1940s, but these early successes reflected an increase in black political power.[25]

[24] Trotter, *Black Milwaukee*, p. 198; Konvitz, *The Constitution and Civil Rights*, pp. 114–17; Mangum, *The Legal Status of the Negro*, p. 174.

[25] For Pennsylvania, see "City Fights for School Teachers," *Pittsburgh Courier*, May 1, 1937, pp. 1, 4; Proctor, "Racial Discrimination Against Black Teachers," pp. 51–4, 58–62, 100–1. By the 1939–40 school year, Pittsburgh had three black teachers. Reddick, "The Education of Negroes," p. 299. For New York, see Mabee, *Black Education in New York State*, pp. 262–3. For New Jersey, see *Report of the New Jersey State Temporary Commission*; Samford, "Anti-Discrimination Policy in New Jersey," p. 20.

During the 1940s, the growing number of northern black voters pushed civil rights issues into the political forefront. Throughout the North and California, African Americans provided critical swing votes in national, state, and local elections, causing both major political parties to seek black votes. For example, during the 1944 presidential election, in twelve northern and border states with over 40 percent of the total electoral votes, the potential black vote exceeded the margin of victory between the Democratic and Republican candidates. This increase in black political power in the North would ultimately help cause the Truman administration to embrace civil rights positions at the cost of an ideological fissure within the Democratic Party. President Harry Truman was rewarded for his support for civil rights. In the 1948 presidential election, Truman carried Illinois and its 28 electoral votes by 33,612 votes. Chicago's black Second Ward alone gave Truman a 60,000-vote margin. By the same token, Truman carried Ohio and its 25 electoral votes by 7,107 votes; black precincts in Akron, Cincinnati, Cleveland, and Dayton gave Truman a 40,000-vote margin. Truman's views on race evolved over the course of his life, undoubtedly influenced in part by the growing political strength of African Americans. Writing to his soon-to-be wife, Bess, in 1911, Truman had commented: "I think one man is just as good as another so long as he's honest and decent and not a nigger or a Chinaman."[26]

The desire of white politicians to capture black political support contributed to the enactment of a number of antidiscrimination initiatives during the 1940s as dozens of northern states and cities adopted statutes and ordinances barring racial discrimination in public accommodations, employment, and education. Fair employment legislation emerged as a particularly important goal of northern civil rights activists, especially local NAACP branches. By 1950, twelve states and scores of cities had enacted bans on racial discrimination by either private employers or labor unions, and ten states had established fair employment practice committees, eight of which enjoyed enforcement power.[27]

In February 1945, New York became the first state to enact legislation that prohibited employment discrimination by private

---

[26] For black political influence, see Biondi, *To Stand and Fight*, p. 143; Moon, *Balance of Power*, pp. 198–9; Moon, "What Chance for Civil Rights?" p. 42; Kryder, *Divided Arsenal*, pp. 239–40; Ming, "The Elimination of Segregation in the Public Schools," pp. 268–9. For the quote from Truman, see Ferrell, *Dear Bess: The Letters from Harry to Bess*, p. 39.

[27] Sitkoff, *The Struggle for Black Equality*, p. 18; McAdam, *Political Process*, pp. 77–86; Burk, *The Eisenhower Administration*, p. 92; Pesin, "Summary, Analysis and Comment," p. 3; Murray, *States' Laws on Race and Color*, pp. 64, 147, 220, 261, 267, 270, 291, 312, 380, 396, 494, 514; Biondi, *To Stand and Fight*, p. 268.

employers and established a state agency, the State Commission Against Discrimination (SCAD), to enforce the statute. Almost every large northern industrial state followed by considering state fair employment legislation. Will Maslow of the American Jewish Congress remarked in 1946: "not since the Civil War has there been so much local interest in preventing racial or religious discrimination in employment."[28]

Much of this legislation, however, promised more than it delivered. For example, civil rights groups claimed that SCAD refused to publicize the new law for fear of "stirring up" complaints. No employer was penalized in New York during the early years even though in 1946, 348 job orders were submitted to the New York State Employment Service with limitations such as "No Negroes" or "Christians Only." At the 1946 state Democratic convention in New York, Eleanor Roosevelt criticized the enforcement of the state statute: "Passing a bill, which is good in itself, is not much use unless something happens under that bill. I do not think we can boast in this state that discrimination in employment is over." In several other northern and western states that enacted fair employment statutes, complaints of lack of enforcement were also widespread.[29]

A second factor contributing to greater white receptivity to black demands for an end to racial discrimination was the wartime and postwar need to oppose racial discrimination within the United States. During the war, many whites understood that the continuation of racial discrimination undermined the American war effort, as the Axis powers used America's treatment of blacks as part of their propaganda offensive. In 1942, the federal Bureau of Intelligence concluded: "So long as inequities exist for Negroes in American life, the Axis propaganda machine possesses a powerful fulcrum upon which to rest the lever of domestic division. This fulcrum must be removed – not only for the sake of the Negroes, but also for the sake of assuring mankind everywhere of whatever race or color, that we are engaged in a people's war for freedom, justice and social security." In his State of the Union Address in 1942, Franklin Roosevelt agreed: "We must be particularly vigilant against racial discrimination in any of its ugly forms. Hitler will try again to build mistrust and suspicion between one individual and another, one group and another, one race and another." And the Axis powers did seize on America's racial problems in their propaganda efforts. When blacks clashed with Detroit police over access to a public housing project, Japanese and German shortwave broadcasts cited the riot as illustrative of American democracy. Liberal

---

[28] Biondi, *To Stand and Fight*, p. 20. For the Maslow quote, see ibid., p. 29.
[29] Biondi, "The Struggle for Black Equality," pp. 160, 165–6, 169 (quote, p. 166).

whites urged better treatment of blacks to defuse these propaganda efforts.[30]

Others feared that the continuation of racial segregation in the United States would compromise black support for the war. Pearl Buck, for example, wrote on the eve of American entry into World War II: "in many colored Americans hopelessness results . . . in a rejection of patriotism. . . . At home and abroad the white race has a choice to make – whether it will follow the totalitarian principle of ruler and subject race . . . or whether peoples of all colors will decide to work out ways of living in harmony and freedom." At the same time, a Louisiana newspaper argued that "[n]o longer can we regard race hatred and prejudice as merely a luxury of idle bigots. Today, intolerance becomes a national menace. Any attempt to deny democracy and fair play to the Negro . . . is an acceptance of the pro-Hitler forces working to undermine national unity."[31]

During the war, concern for the adverse effect of racial discrimination on the war effort continued. A 1943 CBS radio broadcast entitled "Open Letter on Race Hatred" expressed the fear that America's widespread practice of racial discrimination undermined the nation's international interests. The program, developed in response to the Detroit race riot, labeled America's "race hatred" a danger "so great that if it is not met and conquered now, even though we win this war, we shall be defeated in victory and the peace which follows will for us be a horror of chaos, lawlessness, and bloodshed." The broadcast narrator was clear about the dangers of racial friction: "We've got too tough an enemy to beat overseas to fight each other here at home. We hope that this documented account of the irreparable damage race hatred has already done to our prestige, our war effort, and our self-respect will have moved you to make a solemn promise to yourself that . . . you will never allow intolerance or prejudice of any kind to make you forget that you are first of all an American with sacred obligations to every one of your fellow citizens." The broadcast concluded with remarks by former presidential candidate Wendell Wilkie: "Two-thirds of the people who are our allies do not have white skins and they have long, hurtful memories of the white man's superior attitude in his dealing with them." *Life* magazine articulated a similar theme in 1944: "we deny

---

[30] For the Roosevelt quote, see Bureau of Intelligence, "The Negro Looks at the War," 1942, p. I, Hastie Papers, Box 104-8; for the Bureau quote, see Bureau of Intelligence, "Negroes in a Democracy at War," May 27, 1942, p. 29, Hastie Papers, Box 104-7. For the Detroit clash, see "Along the N.A.A.C.P. Battlefront," *The Crisis* 49 (Apr. 1942), pp. 138–9.

[31] Buck, "Democracy and the Negro," p. 377; "From the Press of the Nation," *The Crisis* 48 (Nov. 1941), p. 353 (quoting the *Louisiana Weekly*).

equal rights to our largest minority, and observe a caste system which we not only criticize in other nations but refuse to defend in ourselves. This makes us living liars – a psychotic case among nations."[32]

This ideological imperative of World War II proved highly useful to those Americans – black and white – seeking the eradication of racial segregation and discrimination. As black sociologist Charles Johnson commented: "One of the salutary effects of the revival of racialism and the persecution of minorities in Europe has been that of stimulating in this country a fresh concern for its own minorities. This new concern . . . is organically a part of the smoldering democratic tradition of the nation." Johnson elaborated: "The war has sharpened the issue of Negro-white relations in the United States. . . . The effect of the war has been to make the Negro, in a sense, the symbol and protagonist of every other minority in America and in the world at large." Shortly after the attack on Pearl Harbor, the NAACP argued that "the fight against Hitlerism" began in the United States, "where black Americans have a status only slightly above that of Jews in Berlin." "It sounds pretty foolish to be *against* park benches marked 'Jude' in Berlin," the NAACP's Roy Wilkins remarked, "but to be *for* park benches marked 'Colored' in Tallahassee, Florida." White students at wartime Princeton excoriated their university's refusal to admit black students: "While the United States seeks to propagate among its thousand million colored allies confidence in America's promise of universal freedom without discrimination because of race, color, or creed, . . . Princeton continues its principle of white supremacy and . . . implicitly perpetuates a racial theory more characteristic of our enemies than of an American university."[33]

Proponents of school desegregation successfully linked segregation with fascism during and after the war. In its 1943 report, New Jersey's Urban Colored Population Commission asked: "How can a teacher convincingly impart to a pupil . . . that Hitler's 'superior race' rantings are unscientific and baseless, when these same students are living daily with the school's manifestations of racism as expressed in the separate school system in the various towns of New Jersey. Unwittingly we are raising a new generation of little Fascists." Similarly, when white students at a racially mixed school in Gary, Indiana, launched a strike

[32] For the radio broadcast quotes, see Savage, *Broadcasting Freedom*, pp. 178–9. For the *Life* quote, see "Editorial – Negro Rights," *Life*, Apr. 24, 1944, p. 32.

[33] For the first Johnson quote, see Johnson, "Children in Minority Groups," p. 1 (Oct. 8, 1941), Johnson Papers, Box 158, Folder 29; for the second Johnson quote, see Dunne, "Next Steps," pp. 14–15; for the NAACP quote, see "Editorial: Now Is the Time Not to Be Silent," *The Crisis* 49 (Jan. 1942), p. 7; for the Wilkins quote, see Logan, *What the Negro Wants*, p. 130; for the Princeton quote, see Barnett, "The Role of the Press," pp. 481–2 (quoting the *Daily Princetonian*, 1942).

in 1945 to protest the presence of black classmates, supporters of desegregation decried their actions, arguing that "[w]e don't want any
fascism" and calling upon "all citizens to stand as firmly against Hitlerism in [Gary] as in Germany, Italy and Japan."[34]

As communism replaced fascism as the dominant external threat to
the United States during the late 1940s, the desire to avoid international embarrassment on account of domestic racial discrimination
helped desegregation initiatives as well. The Soviet Union repeatedly used America's racist practices to appeal to the nonwhite peoples of Asia and Africa. As a result, the Cold War effects of racism
were frequently invoked in Supreme Court arguments, congressional
speeches, and White House statements supporting civil rights positions. The Cold War imperative operated at the local level as well. In
a 1950 debate over an ordinance barring public accommodations discrimination in Portland, Oregon, one proponent put the issue in plain
Cold War terms: "the eyes of Russia are on us. If Portland does not vote
for the [antidiscrimination] ordinance, the results will be beamed by
Russia to nations around the world where color of skin is a factor."
Others expressed fears that American blacks, in frustration, would
support communism. In 1948, a local labor leader told the Elkhart,
Indiana, school board that the continuation of school segregation in
that city would cause blacks to embrace communism: "Segregation in
some areas has come so close to producing communism as to scare you
and I out of our wits. . . . If segregation is allowed to continue, communism may catch fire among these people. We should teach our people
what democracy is and the right to live as free American citizens, and
give them the right to live as such!" Shortly thereafter, the Elkhart
school board voted to "cease immediately race segregation that now
exists in the city schools."[35]

School desegregation proponents also utilized the rhetoric of
democracy, which was ubiquitous during World War II and the early
Cold War era, to promote their cause. During the war, opponents of
school segregation for the first time labeled the practice "undemocratic." The Urban Colored Population Commission in New Jersey
concluded in its 1945 report that the continuation of school segregation in that state threatened "to destroy every concept of Democracy"

---

[34] For the New Jersey quote, see "Annual Report of the Urban Colored Population
Commission, State of New Jersey" (1943), Lett papers; for the Gary quote, see Tipton,
Community in Crisis, pp. 33, 36.

[35] For the Portland quote, see McElderry, "The Problem of the Color Line," p. 153; for
the Elkhart quote, see "Board Votes to Quit Policy of Color Line in City Schools," *The
Elkhart Truth,* June 22, 1948, NAACP Papers, Box II-B-138. For excellent analysis of the
effect of the Cold War on civil rights, see Dudziak, *Cold War Civil Rights,* pp. 79–114.

among schoolchildren. Mothers of high school children in Gary told the school board in 1947 that "true democracy required that white people accept the right of Negroes to equality in the schools." An Arizona trial court struck down that state's school segregation law in 1953 on the remarkable grounds that "democracy rejects any theory of second-class citizenship." The court acknowledged that the United States Supreme Court permitted school segregation within the framework of "separate but equal," but nevertheless concluded that segregation was no longer consistent with notions of democracy. Racial segregation was also deemed "un-American." School safety patrol award winners from New York City refused to travel to Washington, D.C., in 1948 to accept their prizes because of "un-American" segregation in the nation's capital.[36]

At the same time, social scientists highlighted the inconsistency between the American creed of equal treatment and the reality of racial discrimination. In particular, Gunnar Myrdal's highly influential *An American Dilemma*, published in 1944, "helped to delegitimize racism, and provided political leaders, courts, journalists, and other opinion makers with an authoritative text with which to buttress their liberal edicts." As one scholar has noted, Myrdal's book "became a guide for an array of social policies, a standard text in university curricula, and a dominant reference in nearly every forum on race relations."[37]

As a consequence of the wartime need to oppose racism, racial liberalism, characterized by opposition to open and notorious forms of racial segregation and discrimination, achieved an unprecedented

---

[36] For the claim that segregation was "undemocratic," see "Race Segregation in Schools Is Scored," *New York Times*, May 31, 1944, p. 16; for the New Jersey quote, see "Annual Report of the Urban Colored Population Commission, State of New Jersey" (1945), Lett Papers; for the Gary quote, see Tipton, *Community in Crisis*, p. 118; for the Arizona court quotes, see Annual Report of the NAACP West Coast Region 1953, p. 22, Franklin Williams Papers, Box 4 (*Phillips v. City of Phoenix*). In 1951, the Arizona state legislature had enacted a permissive desegregation statute that provided for the elimination of segregation in elementary schools in accord with local choice. In response to this legislation, a number of school districts eliminated school segregation including Tucson, Globe, Miami, and Douglas. The school board in Phoenix, however, retained school segregation. The NAACP filed suit against the Phoenix school board, challenging the constitutionality of the statute that permitted segregation. A superior court judge struck down the state law, one of the first such decisions in the United States at the elementary and secondary school levels. The school board appealed to the Arizona Supreme Court, then subsequently voted to voluntarily eliminate segregation. As a result, that court dismissed the appeal as moot. Ibid. For school safety patrols, see "Boy Heroes Hailed for Bias Protest," *New York Times*, May 15, 1948, p. 17.

[37] For the first quote, see Steinberg, *Turning Back*, p. 67; for the second quote, see Baker, *From Savage to Negro*, p. 194. See also Klinkner and Smith, *The Unsteady March*, pp. 183–4.

degree of legitimacy across the North and West during the 1940s. Indeed, by the end of the decade, the goal of ending explicit forms of racial exclusion had won considerable support in the white North. Although the primary effect of wartime antiracist rhetoric was to legitimize the efforts of those seeking an end to racial segregation, the rhetoric of democracy and equal treatment that filled the air during the 1940s and early 1950s also had an influence on northern white attitudes toward African Americans. In June 1942, the National Opinion Research Center reported that only 42 percent of whites thought that blacks were as intelligent as whites and could learn as well as whites if given the same education. Within four years, that figure had climbed to 53 percent and would reach 78 percent by 1956.[38]

Racial unrest that beset many cities during the mid-1940s also influenced white support for racial equality. Northern whites had long feared racial unrest. For many whites, the "Negro problem" was not a problem of injustice but rather a problem of potential racial violence. Indeed, concerns about mounting racial tensions in urban America played a role in the Carnegie Foundation's support of Myrdal's study of race in America. The wartime riots, particularly in Harlem and Detroit, motivated many local officials to take actions that would avoid the outbreaks of violence in their cities. The Detroit race riot in June 1943, for example, left over thirty dead and a call for federal troops to restore order. Other cities including Oakland, Los Angeles, Chicago, Philadelphia, and San Diego also experienced wartime rioting. According to Charles Johnson, there were 242 "major incidents" involving racial conflict in the United States between March and December 1943 alone.[39]

Although these race riots were not as extensive or as deadly as they had been during and after World War I, they increased white anxiety and put pressure on state and local officials to reduce racial conflict. Some black leaders understood white fears of racial violence and used that fear to political advantage. A. Philip Randolph, for example, warned of "outbreaks such as this nation has never seen" if Congress failed to establish a permanent Fair Employment Practice Committee.[40]

Others argued that the wartime riots undermined the American war effort. One newspaper, *PM*, reported that photos of whites beating blacks during the Detroit riots had appeared in *Die Wehrmacht*, a

---

[38] McElderry, "The Problem of the Color Line," p. 114; Erskine, "The Polls: Race Relations," p. 138; Hyman and Sheatsley, "Attitudes Toward Desegregation," p. 35.

[39] Steinberg, *Turning Back*, p. 23; Jackson, *Gunnar Myrdal*, p. 17. Finkle, *Forum for Protest*, pp. 100–1.

[40] Biondi, "The Struggle for Black Equality," pp. 31–3 (quote at pp. 32–3).

magazine published by the German High Command for distribution in Axis and neutral countries. *PM* explained the propaganda value of the photos: "The implications are obvious. Goebbels is telling enslaved and neutral people, in effect: 'If you think we Nazis are brutal, look at how an American minority is treated. Maybe you won't be so badly off under the New Order.' He is also, in effect, telling German troops: 'See how cruel the cowardly American are. You must fight them harder.'" *PM* concluded by arguing that "Americans, through their race hatred . . . have handed a propaganda weapon to the enemy. For anything that frustrates our psychological warfare in other countries, we must eventually pay in the blood of American soldiers. That is why the Detroit riots will put a bullet in the heart of many a doughboy."[41]

Across the North, cities and localities took actions to prevent rioting in their communities. Most of these efforts focused on the establishment of interracial committees and councils charged with investigating claims of racial discrimination. During the war, more than 150 interracial groups organized programs examining racism and the need to confront it; by 1950, 1,350 municipal committees concerned with "intergroup relations" had been formed across the country. Although these committees generally lacked enforcement power, they did prove useful in pushing their communities toward the elimination of obvious forms of racial discrimination. Often comprised of influential business and community leaders, these committees played a vital role in building support for desegregation initiatives, particularly among white elites. Indeed, white support for an end to explicit forms of racial segregation and discrimination in many northern cities during the 1940s and early 1950s was due in large part to the work of these committees. On several occasions, they successfully urged the enactment of local ordinances and state statutes banning racial discrimination.[42]

The NAACP's Postwar Campaign against Northern School Segregation

After World War II, black insistence on an end to northern school segregation sharply increased. In the postwar climate of increased black

[41] For quotes, see "U.S. Race Riots Helped Goebbels," *PM* (undated), Barnett Papers, Box 361-3.

[42] Biondi, "The Struggle for Black Equality," p. 32; McElderry, "The Problem of the Color Line," p. 131; Lockard, *Toward Equal Opportunity*, pp. 19–20; Mumford, "Double V in New Jersey," p. 26. For an example of the work of one such committee, see the 1948 report of the Indianapolis Community Relations Council, in which the Council produced a detailed study of school segregation in Indianapolis and its adverse effects. This report helped build support for legislation banning school segregation in Indiana. Report of the Indianapolis Community Relations Council, June 23, 1948, NAACP Papers, Box II-B-138.

political power and greater white receptiveness to claims of racial injustice, African Americans sought an end to state-sponsored school segregation across the North. These efforts met with considerable success. Indiana, the one northern state that expressly permitted school segregation, finally banned the practice by statute in 1949. In several other northern states, blacks successfully challenged explicit school segregation that persisted in several communities in violation of state antisegregation laws.

Central to these desegregation successes was the NAACP. During the late 1940s, the national office of the NAACP embarked on an extensive effort to win support in the northern black community for its integrationist vision coupled with an aggressive and eventually successful political pressure and litigation campaign for the elimination of explicit school segregation throughout the North. Although the national office of the NAACP had previously concerned itself primarily with southern school segregation, beginning in the mid-1940s it devoted increasing attention to northern schools. In 1940, Thurgood Marshall, legal director of the NAACP, had told his national legal committee that "it is just as important to fight the segregated school system in the North and West as it is to fight for equal schools in the South," but the national office did not engage in a widespread attack on northern school segregation until after the war's conclusion. In 1947, Marshall issued a press release announcing that his office would henceforth expend considerable resources challenging northern school segregation: "In spite of state statutes designed to prevent discrimination or segregation of the races in its school systems, these vicious practices are put into effect in far too many Northern states, and the NAACP shall concentrate within the next few years on breaking down such practices."[43] Marshall delivered on this promise.

The NAACP's northern desegregation campaign contrasted sharply with its southern campaign. In the South, the NAACP could do little more than file lawsuits, seeking favorable judicial precedents that

---

[43] For the first Marshall quote, see Memorandum to Members of the National Legal Committee from Thurgood Marshall, July 17, 1940, NAACP Papers, Box I-D-99; for the second quote, see NAACP Press Release, Sept. 18, 1947, NAACP Papers, Box II-B-146. Franklin Williams, an attorney in the national office of the NAACP, explained to the NAACP's Indianapolis branch in 1947: "this office has as one of its major campaigns during the coming years the removal of segregation in public schools in all of our northern states.... We are very anxious to cooperate with your Branch." Letter from Franklin Williams to Flonoi Adams, President of the Indianapolis Branch, Oct. 7, 1947, NAACP Papers, Box II-B-138. See also Letter from Thurgood Marshall to James X. Ryan, Feb. 10, 1949, NAACP Papers, Box II-B-137 ("We are actively engaged in litigation to break down segregation in public schools in the South. There could be no justification for our tolerating segregated schools in the 'North' ").

FIGURE 13 Thurgood Marshall, 1950s. Reprinted from the Library of Congress, Prints & Photographs Division, LC-U9-1027B-11.

might chip away at the constitutional underpinnings of the segregationist edifice. In the North, where favorable state laws and judicial precedents were already in place, the national office of the NAACP focused much of its efforts on encouraging African Americans to insist – by petitions, boycotts, and litigation – on their legal right to attend school on a nondiscriminatory basis.

The NAACP understood that many northern blacks were either opposed to school integration or unaware that state law prohibited school segregation. A 1947 NAACP survey in New Jersey, for example, found that most black parents did not know their state had enacted antisegregation legislation and that they had a right to send their children to school on a nonracial basis. As a result, the NAACP engaged in considerable efforts to inform northern blacks of their legal right to have their children attend racially mixed schools and to persuade them of the importance of doing so. As part of these efforts, the NAACP devoted considerable attention to the preservation of black teachers' jobs, recognizing that black teachers were crucial to the goal of winning black support for racial integration. In many northern communities, black newspapers aided the NAACP's attempts to build black support for school integration. In 1944, Myrdal called the black press "the greatest single power in the Negro race."[44]

In addition, the NAACP sought to use the increased political power of northern blacks to procure assistance from state officials in enforcing antisegregation legislative mandates. Since the nineteenth century, enforcement of antisegregation legislation had been largely left to the vagaries of private litigation. Accordingly, the NAACP and other black leaders sought new legislation that would bring the power of the state to bear on those school districts that persisted in their failure to comply with state antisegregation legislation.

The desegregation efforts of the post–World War II decade demonstrated the critical importance of meaningful government enforcement of antisegregation mandates. Efforts to eliminate the remaining vestiges of explicit racial school segregation enjoyed their greatest success in those states – New Jersey and Illinois – where the black community procured new legislation providing for the withholding of state education monies from recalcitrant school districts. Significantly, although Indiana did finally enact antisegregation legislation for the first time in 1949, the failure of the Indiana legislature to include an enforcement mechanism made implementation of that legislation more difficult.

Antisegregation efforts in New Jersey illustrate the efficacy of the NAACP's multipronged attack that involved educating the black community about the need to challenge school segregation, filing lawsuits, and securing additional legislation that brought the power of the state to bear on recalcitrant school districts. The national office of the NAACP had not played an active role challenging school desegregation in New Jersey prior to the mid-1940s, despite the presence of widespread segregation in the state's southern counties. Some observers speculated that this failure was due to the considerable influence in the state of William Valentine, head of the segregated Bordentown Manual Training School. In the mid-1940s, however, the national office of the NAACP made the eradication of the remaining vestiges of explicit school segregation in New Jersey a priority.[45]

---

44 For the survey, see New Jersey State Conference of Branches, "A Survey of the Public School Systems in the State of New Jersey," p. 2 (1947), NAACP Papers, Box II-B-144. For the role of the black press, see Perry, "A Common Purpose," pp. 32–41. For the Myrdal quote, see *An American Dilemma*, p. 924 (quoting *Edwin Mims, The Advancing South*, p. 268).

45 For Valentine, see "Wonders if NAACP Pulling Punches," *New Jersey Herald News*, Feb. 16, 1946, p. 1; *New Jersey Herald News*, Nov. 23, 1945. The challenge to school segregation in New Jersey was aided by the work of Marion Thompson Wright, who completed an influential dissertation in 1941 outlining the extent of school segregation in New Jersey. See Wright, *The Education of Negroes*. Both the NAACP and the *New*

In 1944, the NAACP supported successful litigation in state court challenging an assignment policy in Trenton pursuant to which virtually all of the city's black children had been assigned to a segregated junior high school since 1922. In the wake of that litigation, the NAACP helped persuade the Trenton school board to establish geographic districts for all of the city's schools. In 1946, Trenton, for the first time in its history, assigned all children to school on the basis of residence, not race, and also for the first time assigned black teachers to white schools. This successful assault on segregation in New Jersey's capital city marked an important early victory for desegregation.[46]

In the meantime, the enhanced political power of black voters in New Jersey led to specific governmental action on school segregation. In 1944, the state Commission on the Condition of the Urban Colored Population helped force the desegregation of dormitories at Glassboro Teachers College, a state-supported college. Thereafter, state NAACP leaders lobbied state government officials to take additional action on school segregation, noting that noncompliance with the 1881 antisegregation law was widespread, particularly in the state's southern counties. These lobbying efforts succeeded, as the New Jersey General Assembly, with the strong support of Democratic Governor Alfred Driscoll, enacted legislation in 1945 establishing a state administrative agency, the Division Against Discrimination, to investigate various complaints of racial discrimination, including segregation in the public schools.[47]

The newly established Division Against Discrimination joined the NAACP in urging the adoption of a constitutional provision at the state's 1947 constitutional convention prohibiting racial discrimination in all aspects of public life, including education. These efforts succeeded, as the constitutional convention ratified a new provision that expressly prohibited school segregation. Shortly thereafter, the General Assembly enacted legislation that provided for the withholding

---

Jersey Herald News, a prominent black newspaper that championed the cause of school desegregation in New Jersey, used Wright's work to assist their campaign against New Jersey's segregated schools. Crocco, *Pedagogies of Resistance*, p. 69.

[46] For desegregation efforts in Trenton, see *Hedgepeth v. Board of Education*, 131 N.J.L. 153 (1944); Letter from Henry J. Austin to Thurgood Marshall, Oct. 13, 1943; Letter from James King, President of Atlantic City Branch of the NAACP to Roy Wilkins, Mar. 18, 1944, NAACP Papers, Box II-B-144; Wright, "New Jersey Leads in Struggle for Educational Integration," p. 403; Daniels, "A Case Study of the Desegregation in the Public Schools of Trenton," pp. 45, 65–6, 70–1, 76, 114–16; "Integration in Trenton," *Survey* 83 (1947), p. 56; "Annual Report of the Urban Colored Population Commission, State of New Jersey" (1943), Lett Papers.

[47] For Glassboro integration, see Brown, "The State We're In," *New Jersey Herald News*, Dec. 15, 1945; for 1945 legislation, see Samford, "Anti-Discrimination Policy in New Jersey," pp. 20–70; Tifft, "A Report of the Activities," pp. 11–13.

of state education monies from school districts that continued to engage in segregation. Governor Driscoll directed the Division Against Discrimination to take aggressive action to enforce this new legislation. Given the long failure of private litigation to secure compliance with New Jersey's 1881 antisegregation statute, the ability to withhold state funds from recalcitrant school districts proved highly significant. Moreover, in 1948, the New Jersey state legislature enacted additional legislation that forbade the dismissal of any teacher in New Jersey because of his or her race. This legislation had a significant impact on black teachers's jobs – the number of black teachers in the state *increased* by almost 75 percent between 1943 and 1954 despite extensive school desegregation in the state's southern counties. This preservation of black teachers' jobs helped build support for school integration among the state's black population. In fact, the NAACP would use New Jersey's retention of black teachers following desegregation to support its integration efforts in other states.[48]

Two decades earlier, in 1927, blacks had urged another New Jersey governor, Harry Moore, to take action to eradicate school segregation. Moore, however, had refused. But Driscoll, in the mid-1940s, cognizant of the importance of the black vote and of a significant change in white attitudes toward racial segregation, fully embraced the desegregation issue. When Driscoll won reelection in 1948, many observers credited the black vote as playing an important role in his victory.[49]

---

[48] For efforts of the Division Against Discrimination, see Crocco, *Pedagogies of Resistance*, p. 71. The relevant constitutional provision provided that:

> No person shall be denied the enjoyment of any civil or military right, nor be discriminated against in the exercise of any civil or military right, nor be segregated in the militia or in the public schools, because of religious principles, race, color, ancestry or national origin.

Murray, *States' Laws on Race and Color*, p. 268. For fund-withholding legislation and its impact, see Williams and Ryan, *Schools in Transition*, pp. 22–3, 29; Samford, "Anti-Discrimination Policy in New Jersey," pp. 84–6; Greenwood, "How History Was Made in the State of New Jersey," p. 278; Wright, "Extending Civil Rights in New Jersey," pp. 104–5. For legislation preserving black teachers' jobs, see Pamphlet, NAACP, "Do Integrated Schools Threaten Jobs of 113,000 Negro Teachers?" (1954), Moon Papers, Box 8; Thompson, "Editorial Comment: The Negro Teacher," pp. 95–6; Bustard, "The New Jersey Story," p. 284; "Negro Teacher in East Orange," *Newark Evening News*, June 10, 1948, p. 49; Crocco, *Pedagogies of Resistance*, p. 71; Williams and Ryan, *Schools in Transition*, pp. 259–60; Tushnet, *The NAACP's Legal Strategy*, p. 113; "Racial Fairness Widens in New Jersey," *New York Times*, June 19, 1949, p. 52. For data on the increase in black teachers' jobs, see "Changes in Racial Policies in New Jersey's 549 School Districts – 1943 to 1954" (undated), Lett Papers.

[49] For efforts with Moore, see NAACP Press Release, "Two Supreme Court Victories" (1927), NAACP Papers, Box I-A-25; for Driscoll's reelection, see Associated Negro

In addition to lobbying for new legislation, the national office of the NAACP encouraged its New Jersey branches to take action by encouraging black parents to insist on desegregated schools and by soliciting the support of churches, labor unions, and other local organizations likely to be sympathetic to the cause of integrated education. These tactics succeeded.

In Camden, a city with a significant black population, the local branch of the NAACP lobbied the school board to end that city's long tradition of segregated schools. When the school board disingenuously responded that segregation persisted because black parents had not requested transfers to white schools, the Camden branch of the NAACP used newspaper advertisements and sermons by sympathetic ministers to persuade black parents to enroll their children at the school nearest their home. The national office of the NAACP supported these efforts by offering legal assistance to any student whose efforts were rebuffed. As a result of this multifaceted effort, several hundred black children attended racially mixed schools for the first time in Camden in 1946 and 1947. Although Camden neither eliminated its separate black schools nor established a race-neutral geographic attendance plan, this admission of many black children to white schools constituted an important first step toward the eradication of explicit school segregation in Camden.[50]

Similar tactics succeeded in the town of Long Branch, which had maintained an all-black elementary school that it had excluded from the town's general geographic assignment system since the 1880s. The local NAACP branch urged parents to withhold their children from this school and to send them to white schools. When about 60 percent of the black parents boycotted the all-black school in the fall of 1947, the school board included the black school in the town's geographic assignment plan.[51]

In 1947, the New Jersey state conference of the NAACP conducted a survey of all New Jersey school districts and found that more than

Press, "Trenton, New Jersey Shows Some Progress for Negroes," Oct. 15, 1952, Barnett Papers, Box 361-10.

[50] For NAACP lobbying efforts, see Letter from Gloster Current to All New Jersey Branches, April 21, 1947; Report of New Jersey School Desegregation, NAACP Papers, Box II-B-144; Current, "Exit Jim-Crow Schools in New Jersey," p. 11. For desegregation efforts in Camden, see Letter from Juanita Dicks to Gloster Current, Nov. 11, 1948, NAACP Papers, Box II-B-144; Current, "Exit Jim-Crow Schools in New Jersey," p. 12.

[51] Memorandum from Franklin Williams to Thurgood Marshall, Sept. 15, 1947; Letter from Stanford Welker to Franklin Williams, Sept. 8, 1947, NAACP Papers, Box II-B-144; "Long Branch Asked to End 'Segregation'," *Asbury Park Press*, Sept. 4, 1947, NAACP Papers, Box II-B-144; Current, "Exit Jim-Crow Schools in New Jersey," p. 11.

fifty of them still operated explicitly segregated schools, most of which were in the state's southern counties. This segregation took various forms. Some local school districts continued to exclude black schools from geographic assignment plans, while others segregated students into racially separate classrooms, and still others used racially gerrymandered school district lines to preserve racial separation.[52]

One year later, in 1948, the NAACP urged the state Division Against Discrimination to conduct its own survey of school segregation in New Jersey. The Division did so and found that forty-three school districts still operated racially segregated schools as a result of officially sanctioned segregation policies. Armed with the ability to withhold funds, the Division met with recalcitrant school districts during the spring and summer of 1948 to urge desegregation. The Division's conciliation efforts enjoyed significant success. By September 1948, thirty of the forty-three recalcitrant school districts decided to comply with the state's antisegregation law and end their explicit segregation practices. Even though the state provided less than 6 percent of local school budgets, less than that in most states, this threatened withdrawal of funds proved significant. Between 1948 and 1951, the Division persuaded ten more school districts to eliminate school segregation, leaving only three school districts operating officially sanctioned segregated schools – although several other districts maintained all-black schools through racially gerrymandered school attendance zones. In the meantime, many school districts began for the first time to use black teachers in integrated schools.[53]

---

[52] For results of the NAACP survey of New Jersey schools, see New Jersey State Conference of Branches, A Survey of the Public School Systems in the State of New Jersey (1947); Memorandum from Franklin Williams to Thurgood Marshall, Sept. 15, 1947; Report of New Jersey School Desegregation, NAACP Papers, Box II-B-144; Jensen, "Current Trends and Events of National Importance," p. 84; Current, "Exit Jim-Crow Schools in New Jersey," p. 11.

[53] For the Division's work, see Bustard, "The New Jersey Story," pp. 275, 278, 280; Wright, "Racial Integration in the Public Schools of New Jersey," p. 283; Williams and Ryan, Schools in Transition, p. 125. These desegregation efforts were aided by the substantial cost savings that resulted from the elimination of wasteful dual schools. Williams and Ryan, Schools in Transition, p. 124; Bustard, "The New Jersey Story," p. 281. For the percentage of local school budgets obtained from the state, see Anyon, Ghetto Schooling, p. 45. Recalcitrant school districts included Cinnaminson Township, which initially voted to end segregation but under public pressure relented and decided to retain segregated schools for another few years, and East Berlin, which retained segregated schools until a fire in 1953 destroyed its black school, forcing integration. "Report on School Segregation in New Jersey," NAACP Papers, Box II-B-144; Wright, "Racial Integration in the Public Schools of New Jersey," p. 284. At the time of the 1954 Brown decision, twelve New Jersey school districts operated all-black schools. "Racial Policies in New Jersey School Districts, 1953–1954" (undated), Lett Papers. For racial gerrymandering to preserve segregated schools in New Jersey,

The Division ultimately declined to exercise its power to withhold state funds to force pupil mixing, believing that such action might engender bitterness in local communities. But the threat of withholding funds nevertheless proved effective. Moreover, on a few occasions, the NAACP used litigation to compel the Division to withhold funds from districts that retained segregation. For example, in 1948, the NAACP filed litigation asking the Division to withhold funds from the Camden schools, since the Camden school board still refused to establish a unitary geographic assignment plan that included all students. The threat of losing all state education monies proved decisive; shortly after the NAACP filed its complaint, the Camden school board voted to establish a unitary pupil assignment plan. [54]

For almost seventy years, the African-American community of New Jersey had the law on its side in the form of favorable legislation and judicial precedents but could not use it to overcome segregationist sentiment in many of the state's southern school districts. The changed political imperatives of the 1940s – manifested in the willingness of Governor Driscoll and the state General Assembly to withhold funds from recalcitrant school districts – coupled with the organizational commitment of the NAACP created what had been lacking since the late nineteenth century: the political strength to enforce the 1881 antisegregation legislative mandate.

The ability of the black community to capture political support for its antisegregation agenda also proved decisive in southern Illinois, where many school districts had never complied with that state's 1874 antisegregation legislation and had continued to operate segregated schools. In 1949, the Illinois School Directory, which continued to list black and white schools separately for those school districts that maintained segregation, found racially segregated schools in twenty-nine districts in the state's southern counties educating about 10,000 black children. These school districts varied as to whether they required segregation in all twelve grades, as did Cairo and East St. Louis, or whether they required segregation only for students below the high school level,

see Blaustein, *Civil Rights U.S.A.*, pp. 42–3; Wright, "Racial Integration in the Public Schools of New Jersey," pp. 283, 286; *Walker v. Board of Education*, 1 Race Rel. L. Reptr. 255 (1956); "Englewood School Bias Charges," *The Crisis* 61 (Dec. 1954), p. 608.

54 For refusal to withhold funds, see Williams and Ryan, *Schools in Transition*, pp. 124–5. Although the Camden school board had permitted black students to enroll in white schools in 1946 and 1947, it had retained a dual assignment system. The Camden litigation sought to force the board to establish one assignment plan encompassing all schools. Letter from Juanita Dicks to Gloster Current, Nov. 11, 1948; "School Desegregation Efforts in Camden," undated document; NAACP Statement on Camden School Case, Aug. 25, 1948, NAACP Papers, Box II-B-144; Current, "Exit Jim-Crow Schools in New Jersey," pp. 12–13.

FIGURE 14 Segregated black school in southern Illinois, 1937. Reprinted from the Library of Congress, Prints & Photographs Divisions, FSA-OWI Collection, LC-USF34-010646-D.

as did communities such as Alton, Edwardsville, and Harrisburg. In the meantime, the Illinois superintendent of public instruction continued to employ a black special assistant to deal with the state's separate black schools.[55]

Since the time of the infamous Alton desegregation litigation of the early twentieth century, in which white school authorities resisted five desegregation orders from the Illinois Supreme Court, no desegregation litigation had been filed in southern Illinois. Thurgood Marshall complained in 1939 that many blacks in Illinois "foolishly believ[e] that segregation benefits Negroes." Even in northern Illinois, some blacks complained of complacency about school segregation. In 1930, a Chicagoan commented to Walter White about the Chicago chapter of the NAACP: "With regard to the local branch, it does not seem to function to any noticeable extent. . . . The schools are rapidly being segregated, but the Branch seems to take no note of anything."[56]

---

[55] Weinberg, *A Chance to Learn*, p. 71; Ming, "The Elimination of Segregation in the Public Schools," pp. 268–9; Current, "Segregated Schools – on Trial in East St. Louis," p. 79; Valien, "Racial Desegregation of the Public Schools," p. 304.

[56] For the Marshall quote, see Letter from Thurgood Marshall to Leon Harris, Nov. 30, 1939, NAACP Papers, Box II-C-40; for the Chicago quote, see Homel, "The Politics of Public Education," p. 190. On the limited interest of Illinois NAACP branches in desegregation, see Letter from W. B. Beatty to C. A. Barnett, Feb. 27, 1925, Barnett Papers, Box 374-8. In a few instances, however, local NAACP branches did take action. In 1936, the Chicago branch successfully lobbied local school and city officials in nearby Kankakee to allow black children to swim with white

But black resistance to desegregation initiatives was strongest in the state's southern counties. Marshall complained to NAACP Executive Secretary Roy Wilkins about the situation in 1948: "The segregated schools in South Illinois are not only illegal but they have been declared illegal by Illinois cases. They are a disgrace to the state and even more so a disgrace to the NAACP and especially the Illinois State Conference of Branches. The Legal Department has repeatedly tried to get started on these cases and has never been able to move to first base because of the practically non-existent State Conference. Unless and until we can get the State Conference willing to cooperate, there is nothing the Legal Department can do." Because the national office relied on local plaintiffs and attorneys to file desegregation lawsuits, the lack of support for pupil mixing among local NAACP leaders was a major blow to the national office's litigation campaign. Marshall expressed frustration at the unwillingness of local branches to take on school segregation. "I am beginning to doubt that our branch officers are fully indoctrinated on the policy of the NAACP in being opposed to segregation," Marshall wrote Wilkins in 1947. "It is therefore obvious that we need to educate our branch officers and in turn the membership, and finally, the people in the need for complete support in this all-out attack on segregation."[57]

In 1947, the national legal department of the NAACP directed Gloster Current, the organization's national director of local branches, to build support for desegregation among southern Illinois's local NAACP leaders. Franklin Williams, an attorney with the national legal department charged with fighting northern school segregation, told Current that he "would like to be able to file [desegregation litigation] . . . as quickly as possible" and directed Current to work with the state conference of the Illinois NAACP to build support for such litigation. The NAACP's efforts, however, bore little fruit until the Illinois General Assembly took action.[58]

children at a high school swimming pool. "Along the N.A.A.C.P. Battlefront," *The Crisis* 43 (June 1936), p. 182. Moreover, in Moline, the local branch of the NAACP successfully negotiated school integration in 1940 without litigation. Letter from Leon R. Harris to Thurgood Marshall, Jan. 3, 1940, NAACP Papers, Box II-B-138.

57 For the first quote, see Memorandum from Thurgood Marshall to Roy Wilkins, Dec. 14, 1948, NAACP Papers, Box II-B-138; for the second quote, see Memorandum from Thurgood Marshall to Roy Wilkins, Oct. 28, 1947, NAACP Papers, Box II-B-137.

58 For Current's work, see Proposed Community Action Research in Harmonious Desegregation, NAACP Papers, Box II-B-137; Press Release, "Cairo Public Schools Open Second Year of Integration," Sept. 10, 1953, NAACP Papers, Box II-A-229. For Williams's quote, see Memorandum from Franklin Williams to Gloster Current, July 10, 1947, NAACP Papers, Box II-B-137.

In 1945, the Illinois General Assembly amended its earlier antiseg-regation law by expressly providing that "[n]o pupil shall be excluded from or segregated in any such school on account of his color, race, or nationality." Lacking an enforcement provision, however, that legislation had little impact on patterns of school segregation in southern Illinois. In 1949, at the behest of a longtime Republican black representative from Chicago, Charles Jenkins, the Illinois General Assembly enacted legislation requiring the withholding of state education funds from any school district in which children were excluded from a school because of race. Jenkins explained the importance of his legislation: "[B]y tying the antidiscrimination angle to the state's purse strings we can eliminate the racial problem in Illinois in another generation." Two years earlier, the Illinois Commission on Human Relations in 1947 had urged the Illinois superintendent of public instruction to take action against school segregation in southern Illinois by withholding state monies from these school districts. The state superintendent, however, had no legal authority to withhold state funds, which led Jenkins to seek fund-withholding legislation.[59]

This was not Jenkins's first challenge to racial discrimination. During the 1933 Chicago World's Fair, blacks experienced open discrimination at eating establishments in clear violation of the state's antidiscrimination law. When the Cook County state's attorney refused to enforce the antidiscrimination law, Jenkins and two other black state representatives threatened to block passage of legislation designed to promote the World's Fair. In response and with almost no dissent, the Illinois General Assembly enacted legislation providing that any operator of a public accommodation at the Fair who discriminated against blacks would be deemed a public nuisance and subject to being shut down. Later, in 1945, Jenkins persuaded the University of Illinois to abandon its long-standing practice of barring black students from the university's dormitories.[60]

The legislative success of Jenkins, one of five black Assembly members and later chair of the powerful Illinois House Appropriations Committee, in procuring fund-withholding legislation reflected the increase in black political power in Illinois fueled by an almost sixfold increase in Illinois's black population since the onset of the Great Migration. Moreover, the fact that blatant school

---

[59] For the 1945 statute, see Williams and Ryan, *Schools in Transition*, pp. 27, 258; for the 1949 legislation, see Valien, "Racial Desegregation of the Public Schools," p. 303; Williams and Ryan, *Schools in Transition*, pp. 27, 93; Weinberg, *A Chance to Learn*, p. 71; for Jenkins's quote, see McCaul, *The Black Struggle for Public Schooling*, p. 155.

[60] For the World's Fair, see Meier and Rudwick, "Negro Protest at the Chicago World's Fair," pp. 220–2; for the University of Illinois, see Cobb, "Race and Higher Education," pp. 46–8.

segregation – characterized by separate schools and classrooms for black children – was primarily a problem in Illinois's rural southern counties facilitated efforts to win support for the legislation. Urban legislators could support the fund-withholding legislation, recognizing that it would have no effect on their districts' schools. Although many urban schools were becoming increasingly segregated in the late 1940s, most of this segregation was due to residential patterns and hence was unaffected by the new legislation. Supporters of fund-withholding legislation could take credit for taking action against segregation knowing that the legislation would have no impact on most Illinois school districts.[61]

The new legislation offered a significant opportunity for challenging school segregation, as many southern Illinois school boards would not wish to run the risk of losing substantial state support for public education. Indeed, thirty-three southern Illinois school districts were at risk for a loss of state funds as a result of the new law. The fund-withholding legislation had an immediate impact in East St. Louis. In January 1949, a handful of black students, frustrated by their failed efforts to garner additional resources for their inferior black school, attempted to enroll in two white secondary schools in East St. Louis, prompting a walkout out of over 400 white students in protest. The president of the East St. Louis school board announced that his school district's long-standing policy of racial segregation would continue. In response, the local NAACP branch, with assistance from the national office, filed the first lawsuit challenging school segregation in southern Illinois since the early twentieth century. Reflecting the importance of this litigation, the national office of the NAACP dispatched several prominent NAACP officials to East St. Louis to assist in the litigation, including Gloster Current, Roy Wilkins, Robert Carter of the national legal department, and Robert Ming, a law professor at the University of Chicago and a member of the NAACP national legal committee. In the meantime, Thurgood Marshall took pains to assure the East St. Louis branch of the NAACP that "[t]he Branch will, of course, get full credit for the case."[62]

---

[61] The Illinois black population increased from 109,000 in 1910 to 646,000 in 1950. U.S. Bureau of the Census, 1910 and 1950; Associated Negro Press, "Pupils Enroll in Cairo Schools without Incidents," Sept. 10, 1952, Barnett Papers, Box 350–6; Associated Negro Press, "Illinois Towns Score One For, One Against Segregated Schools," Jan. 30, 1950, Barnett Papers, Box 350-5.

[62] For East St. Louis desegregation, see Associated Negro Press, "Illinois Has Separate Schools Too; South End of State Like Dixie," July 25, 1949; Associated Negro Press, "400 White High School Pupils 'Walk Out' as Negro Children Attempt to Enroll," Feb. 9, 1949, Barnett Papers, Box 350-5; Memorandum from Gloster Current to Henry Moon, Feb. 10, 1949, NAACP Papers, Box II-B-137; Current, "Segregated Schools – On Trial in East St. Louis," pp. 77–9. For the Marshall quote, see Letter

In July 1949, the new fund-withholding legislation took effect and the state announced that an adverse judicial determination would cost the city of East St. Louis almost $700,000 in education monies in accord with the new law. As a result, the East St. Louis school board experienced difficulty selling education bonds to finance new schools. The financial pressure caused the school board to capitulate. In December 1949, the school board unanimously agreed to integrate its schools, ending eighty-five years of school segregation, a decision that captured national attention. One year later, in nearby Edwardsville, the school board voted to end eighty years of school segregation. The reasons were clear. As one local official explained: "It is unwise to prejudice the districts' claim on state distributive funds by continuing [segregation.]"[63]

But many southern Illinois school districts persisted in their retention of segregated schools. In 1951, the Illinois state legislature, again at the behest of Representative Jenkins, amended its fund-withholding legislation by requiring local school superintendents to file sworn statements guaranteeing the operation of a nondiscriminatory school system and by establishing a special legislative committee to investigate compliance. The Jenkins Amendment increased pressure on recalcitrant school districts. Thirteen superintendents from the state's southern counties were subpoenaed to testify before the special legislative committee to explain – under oath – their level of compliance with the state's antisegregation mandate. Some school superintendents, who could now be held personally liable for state funds disbursed to schools that preserved segregation, refused to release state funds to certain schools under their jurisdiction.[64]

But a few southern Illinois school districts refused to yield to the legislative pressure. The primary holdouts were in Alexander and Pulaski counties in the southern tip of the state. The special legislative

from Thurgood Marshall to David Owens, Feb. 28, 1949, NAACP Papers, Box II-B-137.

[63] For East St. Louis, see NAACP Press Release, "E. St. Louis Ends Segregated Schools," Dec. 22, 1949, NAACP Papers, Box II-B-137; Ming, "The Elimination of Segregation in the Public Schools," p. 270; Associated Negro Press, "Illinois Town to End Jim Crow Schools Jan. 30," Dec. 28, 1949; Associated Negro Press, "Illinois Towns Score One For, One Against, Segregated Schools," Jan. 30, 1950, Barnett Papers, Box 350-5; "East St. Louis Will End School Race Segregation," *New York Times*, Dec. 22, 1949, p. 8. For the Edwardsville quote, see "Education Board Votes End to Act of Racial Bias," Apr. 15, 1951, Barnett Papers, Box 350-5.

[64] For 1951 legislation and its effects, see Valien, "Racial Desegregation of the Public Schools," p. 303; Ashmore, *The Negro and the Schools*, p. 73; Williams and Ryan, *Schools in Transition*, p. 93; Justin Fishbein, "School Segregation Is Still an Issue in Southern Illinois," *Chicago Sun Times*, June 20, 1954, p. 6; Ming, "The Elimination of Segregation in the Public Schools," p. 271.

committee investigating compliance with the fund-withholding law found that in these counties "[n]either the County Superintendent of Schools nor the District Superintendents, nor the School Trustee Boards are doing anything about obeying the law."[65]

One of the most notorious holdouts was the Alexander County town of Cairo, Illinois's southernmost community, with a long history of racial discrimination. In 1861, a newspaper in Cairo had quoted a fugitive slave who had surrendered to authorities as saying that four days free in Cairo were worse than four years in bondage. Blues composer W. C. Handy remembered hearing black workers in the Deep South in the late nineteenth century sing: "Hey-ooo-oo-o! Heyooooo. I wouldn't live in Cairo!" Cairo's racial history was influenced not just by the large number of white southerners who lived there, but also by its large black community. According to the 1950 census, 36 percent of Cairo's population was black, although many white residents believed that the census underreported the town's black population and that blacks comprised one-half to three-fourths of the town's population. Cairo was also one of the poorest towns in the state, with a median family income less than half the state average and a population in steady decline. A high proportion of the town's residents received public assistance. Cairo's large black population coupled with the town's shrinking economic base contributed to white insistence on racial separation and subordination.[66]

Cairo's schools, like the hospitals, churches, restaurants, public housing, and parks in this struggling town, were rigidly segregated – five for blacks and six for whites – with the black schools grossly inferior to their white counterparts. The Cairo school superintendent, whom the state legislative committee labeled "the main obstacle to the elimination of segregation," certified that his schools were in full compliance with the state's antisegregation law because, he claimed, no black child had ever sought admission to a white school. Cairo refused to assign children to school on the basis of geographic attendance zones, which would have resulted in substantial racial mixing. As one Cairo school official commented in early 1952: "[W]e'll never do that."[67]

---

[65] For holdouts, see Valien, "Racial Desegregation of the Public Schools," p. 305; for the quote, see ibid.

[66] For Cairo, see Voegeli, *Free But Not Equal*, p. 9; Williams and Ryan, *Schools in Transition*, pp. 82–3, 86–9; U.S. Bureau of Census, 1950. For the quote, see Langston Hughes, "A Sentimental Journey to Cairo, Illinois," *Chicago Defender*, May 15, 1954, in De Santis, *Langston Hughes*, p. 36.

[67] For the first quote, see Williams and Ryan, *Schools in Transition*, pp. 93–5; for the second quote, see ibid., p. 97. For segregation in Cairo, see Shagaloff and Bailey, "Cairo," p. 209.

In January 1952, the NAACP's national office dispatched two staff members to Cairo to build support for school desegregation among the city's black residents. At a mass meeting, the NAACP urged black parents to request transfers for their children to white schools at the onset of the second semester in late January and carefully explained the process for doing so. The black community in Cairo bitterly divided over the NAACP's integration efforts. Most Cairo blacks had long accepted segregation, in part because of their economic dependence on the city's white community and the town's history of racial oppression. Middle-class black families – particularly ministers, teachers, school principals, and policemen – uniformly refused to seek transfers, fearing retaliation. Indeed, several black teachers and principals, afraid of losing their jobs, urged Cairo's black parents to reject the NAACP's integrationist agenda. One black minister aggressively lobbied his parishioners not to seek transfers to white schools, reminding them of their economic dependency on the white community and disparaging the NAACP as an outside group. Fears of job loss were legitimate, as many black teachers in southern Illinois did lose their jobs in the wake of school integration in the early 1950s. At the same time, some local officials threatened – and eventually delivered on their threats – to terminate the relief checks of those blacks who insisted on integrated schools.[68]

But on January 28, 1952, the first day of the second semester, about 100 black students, accompanied by their parents, sought admission to a white school in Cairo. All of these children were turned away (though most gained admission a few days later). In the meantime, the city exploded in violence. A black doctor's home was bombed, crosses were burned near the homes of black families whose children had sought to attend white schools, a shotgun blast exploded through a black dentist's home, and unexploded dynamite was found at the business of a local NAACP official. David Lansden, a liberal white attorney who assisted the NAACP desegregation efforts, lost most of his white friends, experienced regular vandalism of his car and home, and eventually had a rifle shot fired through his front door. As a guide to the disgruntled, a neighbor placed a large, flashing red neon arrow in his yard pointing out Lansden's home. Lansden's brother and law

---

[68] For Cairo desegregation, see Williams and Ryan, *Schools in Transition*, pp. 81, 85–6, 98–9; Associated Negro Press, "Illinois NAACP Appeals to U.S. Attorney General to Intervene in Cairo School Fight," Mar. 10, 1952; Associated Negro Press, "White Salesman Arrested in Cairo, Ill. Bombing," Feb. 4, 1952, Barnett Papers, Box 350-5; "School Segregation Is Still an Issue in Southern Illinois," *Chicago Sun Times*, June 20, 1954, p. 6; Letter from Faith Rich to Gloster Current, Sept. 12, 1954, NAACP Papers, Box II-A-226; Shagaloff and Bailey, "Cairo," pp. 211–13.

partner fled Cairo to avoid the harassment. When the United States
Supreme Court issued it landmark decision in *Brown v. Board of Ed-
ucation* more than two years later in 1954, the neon arrow marking
Lansden's home still flashed and rocks still flew through his windows.
Life magazine described Lansden's plight in a 1954 story entitled "Dy-
namite Arrow."[69]

In early February 1952, one week after the Cairo black students
had sought admission to white schools, Cairo police arrested seven of
the black parents who had sought transfers and their attorney on the
outrageous charge of conspiring "unlawfully, fraudulently, maliciously,
wrongfully [and] wickedly" to endanger "the life and health of certain
children" by "forcing them" to enter Cairo's white schools. Eventually,
a grand jury refused to indict this little band of integrationists. But
the grand jury also refused to indict the white men who had been arrested for the bombing of the doctor's home and the cross burnings,
blaming instead the NAACP for these misfortunes: "[W]e feel [the
NAACP] . . . showed arrogance, abusiveness and utter lack of cooper-
ation, which could have very easily led to violence and upheaval, that
every effort was made to usurp our schools."[70]

Outraged at the refusal of the grand jury to indict the bombers, the
NAACP sought the intervention of the United States attorney general,
the Illinois attorney general, and Illinois governor and presidential
candidate Adlai Stevenson, labeling the grand jury's actions a "will-
ful, shameful and gross neglect of duty" and "an alarming breakdown
in the law enforcement machinery of Alexander county." Seeking
political advantage among black voters, the Illinois attorney general
intervened, with an assistant attorney general personally presenting evidence of the bombings to a second grand jury. Indictments and convic-
tions of five bombers followed. At the same time, both state police and

---

[69] Associated Negro Press, "White Salesman Arrested in Cairo, Ill. Bombing," Feb. 4,
1952, Barnett Papers, Box 350-5; Associated Negro Press, "Pupils Enroll in Cairo
Schools without Incident," Sept. 10, 1952; Associated Negro Press, "Eight Negroes,
One White Arrested in Cairo, Ill. School Integration Fight," Feb. 13, 1952; Associated
Negro Press, "Five White Men Indicted in Cairo, Ill. School Bombing Case," May
21, 1952; Associated Negro Press, "White Friends of Negroes Usually Suffer Insults,
Ostracism," Jan. 6, 1954, Barnett Papers, Box 350-6; Valien, "Racial Desegregation
of the Public Schools," p. 305; Williams and Ryan, *Schools in Transition*, pp. 99–100;
"Cairo Gripped by a Reign of Terror Against Anti-Bias Supporters," *The Crusader*,
Nov. 14, 1953, p. 2, NAACP Papers, Box II-A-229; Langston Hughes, "A Sentimental
Journey to Cairo, Illinois," *Chicago Defender*, May 15, 1954, in De Santis, *Langston
Hughes*, p. 36; "'Dynamite Arrow,'" *Life*, Feb. 1, 1954, p. 25.

[70] For the quotes, see Shagaloff and Bailey, "Cairo," pp. 263–4. See also Associated
Negro Press, "Eight Negroes, One White Arrested in Cairo, Ill. School Integration
Fight," Feb. 13, 1952, and Associated Negro Press, "Grand Jury Indicts Nobody in
Cairo Bombings," Feb. 25, 1952, Barnett Papers, Box 350-6.

FBI agents came to Cairo to prevent further threats and violence. Despite the violent environment, a few black children persevered: by the end of the 1951–2 school year, 17 of the approximately 100 black students who had originally sought transfers remained in mixed schools. In September 1952, Cairo schools opened with considerably more black students attending white schools, this time without violence, although some black students were still denied entry to white schools on the grounds that these schools were at capacity.[71]

The state fund-withholding legislation played an important role in the desegregation of the Cairo schools. In March 1952, the NAACP filed litigation demanding that the state superintendent of public instruction withhold all state education monies from Alexander County. In response to this litigation, on June 1, 1952, the state superintendent withheld funds from every Alexander County school district, including Cairo, which received in excess of $200,000 in state funds. Over the course of the next several months, *every* school district in Alexander County chose to comply with the state's antisegregation statute in order to restore their state funding. Two towns in Alexander County, Tamms and Ullin, had excluded all black students from local high schools, forcing them to travel twenty-five miles to a black high school in Cairo or Mound City. Faced with a cutoff of state funds, both Tamms and Ullin desegregated their schools. This desegregation, however, was not without incident; shortly thereafter, dynamite ripped through the Ullin city hall.[72]

Further north, in Alton, school authorities who had so vociferously resisted school desegregation during the first decade of the twentieth century quietly integrated their elementary schools in 1952, having

---

[71] For quotes, see Associated Negro Press, "Illinois NAACP Appeals to U.S. Attorney General to Intervene in Cairo School Fight," Mar. 10, 1952, and Associated Negro Press, "Eight Negroes, One White Arrested in Cairo, Ill. School Integration Fight," Feb. 13, 1952, Barnett Papers, Box 350-6. For the discussion of violence, see Associated Negro Press, "Five White Men Indicted in Cairo, Ill. School Bombing Case," May 21, 1952, Barnett Papers, Box 350-6; Williams and Ryan, *Schools in Transition*, pp. 101–3; Ming, "The Elimination of Segregation in the Public Schools," pp. 270–1; Ashmore, *The Negro and the Schools*, p. 73; "'Dynamite Arrow,'" *Life*, Feb. 1, 1954, p. 25.

[72] For fund withholding in Alexander County, see "Cairo School Situation," *The Crisis* 59 (Mar. 1952), pp. 143–4; Associated Negro Press, "Pupils Enroll in Cairo Schools without Incidents," Sept. 10, 1952, Barnett Papers, Box 350-6; Memorandum from June Shagaloff to Henry Moon, Sept. 18, 1953; Press Release, "More Than 100 Negro Students Attending Formerly All-White Public Schools without Incident in Cairo, Illinois," Sept. 10, 1953, NAACP Papers, Box II-A-229; for Tamms and Ullin, see Associated Negro Press, "Trend Is Toward Integration in Illinois Public Schools," Oct. 1, 1952; Associated Negro Press, "Jim Crow in Ullin, Illinois High School Smashed," Sept. 15, 1952, Barnett Papers, Box 350-5.

already desegregated their high schools a few years earlier. Again, the fund-withholding legislation prompted Alton's change of heart. Threatened with personal liability under the 1951 state legislation if he improperly disbursed state educational funds to a school district with segregated schools, the Madison County school superintendent withheld funds from the Alton schools; shortly thereafter, the Alton school authorities dropped their resistance to desegregation.[73]

In the fall of 1954, four months after the *Brown* decision, two of the last southern Illinois towns to retain segregated schools – Brookport and Mounds – finally opened their white schools to black schoolchildren. But at least one southern Illinois community in Madison County retained explicitly segregated schools until the mid-1960s, maintaining, in the words of the county school superintendent, "one [school] for the colored and one for the white." Finally, in the mid-1960s, the local school board desegregated these two schools.[74]

The successful desegregation of the schools in southern Illinois was due in large measure to the altered political climate in Illinois in the late 1940s and early 1950s that led to the fund-withholding legislation and to the efforts of the national office of the NAACP to build local support for integrated schools. The speed with which these southern Illinois school districts finally desegregated during the early 1950s was a function of the willingness of state legislators and education officials to withhold education funds from defiant school districts, as well as the NAACP's successful efforts to persuade local blacks to insist on integrated schools by requesting transfers to white schools and filing lawsuits when those requests were denied.[75]

But in other parts of the North, the NAACP confronted opposition to its desegregation agenda in both the black and white communities and was unable to secure fund-withholding legislation from the state legislature. In these areas, desegregation efforts during the 1940s and early 1950s proceeded more slowly. These efforts in Ohio proved particularly difficult. In 1939, a group of black parents secured the assistance of Cincinnati lawyer Theodore Berry to file a lawsuit challenging the Wilmington school board's decision to send all of the town's black elementary schoolchildren to a separate black school instead of to schools nearest their homes. The civil suit arose when a black parent

---

[73] Associated Negro Press, "Five White Men Indicted in Cairo, Ill. School Bombing Case," May 21, 1952, Barnett Papers, Box 350–6; Ming, "The Elimination of Segregation in the Public Schools," p. 271.

[74] For Brookport and Mounds, see Loth and Fleming, *Integration North and South*, p. 7; for the Madison County quote, see Letter from Wilbur Trimpe to Harvey Zeidenstein, Sept. 23, 1964, Armstrong Papers.

[75] Ming, "The Elimination of Segregation in the Public Schools," p. 270; Memorandum from June Shagaloff to Henry Moon, Sept. 18, 1953, NAACP Papers, Box II-A-229.

was jailed for withholding his two children from the black school after a nearby white school had refused to admit them. Berry solicited the involvement of Thurgood Marshall and the NAACP's national office. Marshall, who at the time was unfamiliar with the legal status of school segregation in Ohio, took special interest in the case and filed an amicus brief on behalf of the black litigants. The litigation, however, caused sharp division in the Wilmington black community, as many African Americans feared that it would antagonize whites and prompt retaliation against black teachers. As a result, Berry had great difficulty securing testimony from Wilmington blacks necessary to prove the extent of the school segregation; without that testimony, the case was lost.[76]

Division in the black community would remain a major obstacle to desegregation efforts in Ohio throughout the 1940s. When Thurgood Marshall arrived in Dayton in 1945 to build support for desegregation, black preferences for racially separate schools remained strong. Marshall complained that "[t]he biggest problem in Dayton is not a legal problem but is a problem of educating the Negro community to be in a frame of mind to fight segregated schools. The majority of the Negroes in Dayton are in favor of segregated schools and if this were not so, it would have been impossible to establish them." Marshall tried to find a local black lawyer in Dayton to file a desegregation lawsuit, but with no success. The inability of the NAACP to challenge school segregation in Dayton weakened the local branch and led to a sharp decline in NAACP membership in the mid-1940s in that city at a time when NAACP membership was increasing throughout the North.[77]

Part of the problem in Dayton was the outspoken support for segregation of Frederic McFarlane, the influential black principal of Dayton's all-black Dunbar High School. McFarlane was an enthusiastic proponent of Dunbar's racial character; he frequently addressed white downtown luncheon clubs, urging racial segregation. Black demands that the Dayton school board remove McFarlane from his

---

[76] For the Wilmington litigation, see "Parents Fight Jim-Crow School," *Cleveland Gazette*, Dec. 9, 1939, p. C2; Press Release, "Jailed for Opposing School Segregation; Parents File Mandamus Suit," Oct. 10, 1939, Barnett Papers, Box 362-5; Letter from Thurgood Marshall to Theodore M. Berry, Nov. 21, 1939; Letter from Theodore M. Berry to Thurgood Marshall, Nov. 9, 1939; Memorandum to Members of the National Legal Committee from Thurgood Marshall, July 17, 1940; Letter from Thurgood Marshall to Theodore M. Berry, July 16, 1940, NAACP Papers, Box I-D-99; *State ex rel. Lewis v. Board of Education of Wilmington School District*, 137 Ohio St. 145 (1940).

[77] For the Marshall quote, see Memorandum from Thurgood Marshall to Walter White, Nov. 6, 1945, NAACP Papers, Box II-B-146. For the discussion of Dayton, see Memorandum from Thurgood Marshall to Walter White, Nov. 6, 1945; Memorandum from Thurgood Marshall to Walter White, Oct. 29, 1945, NAACP Papers, Box II-B-146.

principalship failed. By 1954, 75 percent of the black children in Dayton attended what the school board termed "colored" schools. Segregation would continue in Dayton until after the 1954 *Brown* decision.[78]

African Americans resisted the school desegregation efforts of the NAACP in several other Ohio communities as well. In Chagrin Falls, just east of Cleveland, black parents had petitioned the school board to establish a separate black school during the 1930s. The school board complied, establishing an overcrowded, understaffed, "ram shackled" school, compared to the nearby white school housed in a modern building with superior equipment and adequate staffing. When the national office of the NAACP sent a field secretary to investigate school segregation in Chagrin Falls during the mid-1940s, the school's black teachers, fearing for their jobs, sharply opposed this "interference." School segregation would continue in Chagrin Falls until the 1950s. Similarly, when a local civil rights organization, the Future Outlook League, successfully sued the Mansfield, Ohio, school board in 1945 for establishing separate classes for black children in a mixed school, several of the school's black teachers announced that "their rights were disregarded" in the lawsuit and that they would "not teach white children."[79]

Dismayed at the resistance to school desegregation in the Ohio black community, Thurgood Marshall traveled to Ohio in 1946 to arouse interest in a comprehensive legal campaign against school segregation. Marshall convened a meeting in Columbus to assess the Ohio situation at which he secured the agreement of various branches of the NAACP to seek support in the black community for a litigation campaign against segregated schools. The national office of the NAACP prepared a short manual for local branches outlining methods of challenging school segregation in Ohio and dispatched attorney Robert Carter from the national office to build support among Ohio blacks for the desegregation campaign. Carter arrived with an ambitious agenda; he

[78] For McFarlane, see Associated Negro Press, "Dayton Luncheon Club Demands Negro Principal's Scalp," Nov. 1944, Claude Barnett Papers, Box 362–5; for all-black schools in Dayton, see *Brinkman v. Gilligan*, 583 F.2d 243, 247 and n.11 (6th Cir. 1978); Appendix to Brief in Opposition to Petition for Writ for Certiorari, p. 9a; Brief in Opposition to Petition for Writ for Certiorari, p.8 n.2, *Dayton Board of Education v. Brinkman*, 443 U.S. 449 (1979).

[79] For Chagrin Falls, see Memorandum from Noma Jensen, "Summary of Activities in Chagrin Falls, Mansfield, Warren, Columbus and Cleveland, Ohio and Detroit, Michigan," NAACP Papers, Box II-B-137; Press Release, "War on School Jim Crow Mapped by Ohio NAACP," Jan. 17, 1946, NAACP Papers, Box II-B-146. For Mansfield, see Memorandum from Noma Jensen, "Summary of Activities in Chagrin Falls, Mansfield, Warren, Columbus and Cleveland, Ohio and Detroit, Michigan," NAACP Papers, Box II-B-137.

proposed filing "as many cases simultaneously within the state attacking segregation in the school system as possible" to "show that we are determined to fight segregation throughout the State." Much of the Ohio black legal community, however, did not share Carter's enthusiasm for a sweeping litigation campaign. Carter expressed frustration with the support among so many African Americans for school segregation and the "fear on the part of the [Ohio] lawyers" that inhibited their willingness to file desegregation lawsuits.[80]

As a result, officially sanctioned school segregation persisted in a number of Ohio school districts until the early 1950s and in some instances until after the *Brown* decision. Indeed, by the early 1950s, some form of officially sanctioned segregation continued in Chagrin Falls, Cincinnati, Columbus, Dayton, Hamilton, Hillsboro, Middletown, Oxford, and Portsmouth. In 1952, for example, the Springmeyer School District in Cincinnati refused to admit three black children to their nearby white school and even rejected the local NAACP's appeal for monies to provide transportation for them to another school outside the district. As a result, these black children missed a year of school. The Ohio State Board of Education continued to ask local school boards to report the number of black children attending "separate schools for colored children" until 1955.[81]

The lack of support for integrated schools in the black community in parts of Ohio, the ongoing resistance in the white community, and the inability of NAACP leaders to secure fund-withholding legislation, as they had in New Jersey and Illinois, made desegregation efforts difficult in Ohio. Not surprisingly, in many communities, serious desegregation efforts did not take place in Ohio until after the *Brown* decision; indeed, more school desegregation litigation was filed in Ohio during the post-*Brown* era than in almost any other northern state. Finally, in

---

[80] For Marshall's trip to Ohio, see Al Dunmore, "Objectively Yours," *Pittsburgh Courier*, Jan. 5, 1946, NAACP Papers, Box II-B-146; Letter from Miley O. Williamson to Thurgood Marshall, June 7, 1945; Press Release, "War on School Jim Crow Mapped by Ohio NAACP," Jan. 17, 1946; Letter from Marian Williams to Roy Wilkins, Jan. 18, 1946, NAACP Papers, Box II-B-146. For the national office manual, see "Branch Action to Eliminate Segregated Schools," NAACP Papers, Box II-B-137. For Carter quotes, see Letter from Robert Carter to J. Maynard Dickerson, May 14, 1946; Memorandum from Robert Carter, undated; Letter from Robert Carter to George Johnson, Sept. 14, 1946, NAACP Papers, Box II-B-146.

[81] For continuation of segregation in Ohio, see Press Release, "War on School Jim Crow Mapped by Ohio NAACP," Jan. 17, 1946; Letter from Marian Williams to Roy Wilkins, Jan. 18, 1946, NAACP Papers, Box II-B-146; *Penick v. Columbus Board of Education*, 663 F.2d 24, 28 (6th Cir. 1981); *Brinkman v. Gilligan*, 583 F.2d 243, 249 (6th Cir. 1978). For segregation in Springmeyer, see Mjagkij, "Behind the Scenes: The Cincinnati Urban League," p. 282; Trotter, *River Jordan*, p. 157; for Ohio State Board practices, see *Penick v. Columbus Board of Education*, 663 F.2d 24, 28 (6th Cir. 1981).

1956, Ohio enacted legislation that gave authority to the State Board of Education to withhold state funds from those school districts that continued to operate segregated schools, legislation that helped accelerate the desegregation of the state's remaining recalcitrant school districts.[82]

Similar divisions in the black community in Pennsylvania harmed desegregation efforts in that state. By the 1940s, racially explicit pupil assignments remained pervasive in many parts of Pennsylvania. As it had in other northern states, the national office of the NAACP initiated a major effort in Pennsylvania during the late 1940s to challenge school segregation. In 1948, Marian Perry of the national legal staff of the NAACP convened a group of black attorneys and representatives of NAACP branches in Pennsylvania to discuss ways of attacking segregated schools. Perry, however, soon learned that the Pennsylvania black community was not united in its desire to file litigation challenging school segregation. The state NAACP president informed Perry that most black attorneys in Pennsylvania were "weak or afraid to try these cases."[83]

Confronted with a lack of support for school desegregation among much of the state's African-American population, the NAACP conducted an extensive survey of school segregation in Pennsylvania in the spring of 1948 similar to the one conducted the prior year in New Jersey. The NAACP found that more than a quarter of the surveyed school districts maintained some form of formal separation between black and white students – either racially separate schools or segregated classrooms within schools. The survey also found widespread teacher segregation, with only about a third of the school districts employing black teachers and only one – Pittsburgh – permitting black teachers to teach white children. In Philadelphia, school authorities retained teacher segregation even though the Philadelphia Board of Education had resolved to assign teachers on a nondiscriminatory basis in 1937. Armed with this survey, NAACP leaders in Pennsylvania met with members of the state legislature in June 1948 and urged the enactment of new legislation to end school segregation. Given the reluctance of many Pennsylvania blacks to file desegregation litigation, state NAACP leaders proposed legislation that would impose criminal sanctions on local school officials who defied the state's antisegregation

---

[82] Press Release, "Segregated Ohio Schools May Lose Funds," July 18, 1956, Barnett Papers, Box 362-6.

[83] For Pennsylvania desegregation efforts, see NAACP Press Release, Sept. 18, 1947; NAACP Press Release, Oct. 6, 1948, NAACP Papers, Box II-B-146. For the NAACP quote, see Letter from Joshua Thompson to Marian Wynn Perry, Dec. 3, 1948, NAACP Papers, Box II-B-146.

law. The legislature, however, refused to take additional action against segregation.[84]

In the meantime, some Pennsylvania blacks took action challenging school segregation. In 1945, a group of blacks petitioned the Harrisburg school board to end student and teacher segregation. At that time, Harrisburg permitted no black teachers to teach white children and required almost all of the city's black children to attend segregated schools through the use of racially explicit assignment policies. When the school board rejected the desegregation petition in 1947, the local branch of the NAACP secured a commitment from the NAACP's national office to help file a lawsuit. No litigation was initiated, however, because of the difficulty of finding a willing and suitable plaintiff. In the nearby community of Steelton, a black parent did file litigation in 1947 to secure admission for his daughter to a white school, but he subsequently relocated to another city and the lawsuit was discontinued. In both Harrisburg and Steelton, the lack of support in the black community for mixed schools undermined the litigation efforts. The national office of the NAACP also offered assistance for legal challenges to school segregation in Bryn Mawr and York, but no litigation was filed in either town due to a lack of local support. In fact, in an analysis of its "dead branches" conducted during the 1940s, the

---

[84] For the NAACP survey, see NAACP, "Race Policies and Practices: A Survey of Public School Systems in Pennsylvania" (1948), NAACP Papers, Box II-B-146. The NAACP found that Carlisle, Chester, Morton, West Chester, and York operated all-black elementary schools, while Washington, Downington, Kennett Square, Avondale, and Aliquippa operated segregated classrooms within integrated schools with black teachers teaching only black children. In some of these segregated classrooms, black children of various ages and abilities were combined in one room, resulting in an educational experience not only separate from but inferior to that offered white students. Letter from William M. Gilmore to Gloster B. Current, Jan. 21, 1950, NAACP Papers, Box II-B-146. Other school districts, not investigated by the NAACP, maintained similar practices. Williamsport, for example, placed black first, second, and third graders in a separate classroom in an integrated school. Memorandum from Ruby Hurley to NAACP Legal Department, Nov. 22, 1948; Letter from Marian Wynn Perry to Madison A. Bowe, Dec. 17, 1948, NAACP Papers, Box II-B-146. For Philadelphia, see Press Release, "'Invisible' Dual School System Slowly Engulfing Philadelphia," May 11, 1949; Press Release, "Quaker City School Board Abolishes Jim-Crow Rule Against Teachers," Apr. 1, 1937, Barnett Papers, Box 362-6.

For efforts to procure new legislation, see Letter from Marian Wynn Perry to J. O. Thompson, June 7, 1948; NAACP Press Release, "Urge Investigation of Pennsylvania Schools," June 10, 1948; Memorandum from Marian Wynn Perry to Gloster Current, Nov. 4, 1948; Memorandum from Marian Wynn Perry to Gloster Current, Nov. 24, 1948; Letter from Joshua O. Thompson to Marian Wynn Perry, Dec. 3, 1948; Letter from Marian Wynn Perry to Joshua O. Thompson, Dec. 7, 1948; Memorandum to Files from Marian Wynn Perry, Jan. 21, 1949, NAACP Papers, Box II-B-146.

NAACP found more such branches in Pennsylvania than in any other state in the nation.[85]

In a few communities, a local branch of the NAACP did support desegregation and pressured local school boards to make changes. In Williamsport, the local NAACP branch in 1948 petitioned the school board to end student and faculty segregation. As a result, the school board agreed to stop pupil segregation at the end of the 1948–9 school year. Similarly, in 1950, pressure from the Downington branch of the NAACP caused the local school board to cease its long-standing practice of segregating black children into separate classrooms within integrated schools.[86]

But by the time of the *Brown* decision in May 1954, several Pennsylvania school districts still maintained officially sanctioned segregated schools. The York school board, for example, still excluded two black elementary schools from the city's geographic assignment plan and barred black teachers from teaching white children. Segregation would also continue in Chester until after the *Brown* decision. The *Brown* decision, however, contributed to the end of explicit school segregation in Pennsylvania, as a number of school districts in the fall of 1954 adopted new geographic assignment plans encompassing – for the first time – black schools.[87]

---

[85] For Harrisburg, see Petition to Clarence Zorger, Oct. 18, 1945; NAACP Press Release, Sept. 18, 1947; Memorandum from Franklin H. Williams to Thurgood Marshall, Oct. 4, 1947; Letter from F. D. Gholston to Thurgood Marshall, Feb. 3, 1947; Letter from Franklin H. Williams to Millicent Ulen, Apr. 22, 1947; Letter from Franklin H. Williams to Superintendent, Harrisburg School District, Sept. 17, 1947; NAACP Press Release, Sept. 18, 1947; Letter from Franklin H. Williams to Justin Carter, Jr., Oct. 7, 1947, NAACP Papers, Box II-B-146. For Steelton, see Letter from George A. Jones to Franklin H. Williams, July 1, 1947; Memorandum from Franklin H. Williams to Thurgood Marshall, Oct. 4, 1947; Letter from George Kunkel to Franklin H. Williams, Oct. 13, 1948, NAACP Papers, Box II-B-146. For Bryn Mawr and York, see Letter from Edward R. Dudley to S. B. Randolph, Aug. 14, 1944; Letter from Thurgood Marshall to Warren F. Chew, Sept. 21, 1945, NAACP Papers, Box II-B-146. For dead branches, see "Dead Branches" (undated), NAACP Papers, Box II-L-14. The national office of the NAACP did continue, however, to urge litigation. For example, in August 1948, the national office, having learned of efforts in Lower Oxford to challenge school segregation, offered its assistance. Letter from Franklin H. Williams to Horace Mann Bond, Aug. 12, 1948, NAACP Papers, Box II-B-146.

[86] For Williamsport, see Memorandum from Marian Perry to Gloster Current, Nov. 4, 1948; Letter from Madison A. Bowe to Ruby Hurley, Nov. 10, 1948, NAACP Papers, Box II-B-146. For Dowington, see An Open Letter to the Board of Education and the Citizens of Downington, Feb. 17, 1950; Letter from William M. Gilmore to Constance Baker Motley, Feb. 22, 1950; Letter from William M. Gilmore to Gloster B. Current, Jan. 1, 1950, NAACP Papers, Box II-B-146.

[87] For York, see "High Court Rule Puts Focus on York Issue," *York Gazette and Daily*, June 29, 1954, NAACP Papers, Box II-A-228; Loth and Fleming, *Integration North and South*, pp. 9–10. For Chester, see Letter from A. H. Showalter to Chester School

The difference between the desegregation campaigns in Pennsylvania and neighboring New Jersey is striking. Even though southern New Jersey had a history of more extensive school segregation as well as fewer desegregation lawsuits than Pennsylvania, explicit school segregation ended sooner in southern New Jersey than in Pennsylvania. The difference between the two states was due to the fact that African Americans in New Jersey were more united in their opposition to segregation and were able to exercise greater political influence, leading to crucial support from the state government for desegregation.

School desegregation efforts in Indiana during the 1940s also suggest the importance of securing broader political and cultural support for desegregation. Indiana had been the only northern state to retain its nineteenth-century state legislation *permitting* local school districts to engage in school segregation. As in other northern states, the number of racially separate schools in Indiana increased during the first four decades of the twentieth century. For example, during the 1948–9 school year, almost 95 percent of the 11,300 black students in Indianapolis attended a racially separate school.[88]

Agitation for an end to school segregation increased in parts of Indiana during the 1940s. Although most of this agitation came from the black community, significant elements in the white community also supported an end to dual schools in Indiana. In 1946, the Gary school board passed a resolution to end discrimination against black students in the city's schools "in the spirit of fair play and democracy." The board noted that "experience in the principles of democratic living through education is an essential part of the heritage of American youth." A combination of forces converged to support an end to explicit school segregation in Gary. First, white elites sought to quell the potential for community unrest and to end the city's embrace of explicit and antidemocratic school segregation. In 1944, for example, a local newspaper editor had urged an end to racial segregation in Gary to prevent the possibility of widespread violence in his city: "I would look for an explosion if we were to expect the problems holding the races apart would be solved by neglecting them." Second, the new pupil assignment policy had limited impact on patterns of racial mixing, sending only 116 additional black students to white schools.

Board, Sept. 13, 1954; Memorandum from John W. Flamer to Gloster B. Current, June 3, 1954, NAACP Papers, Box II-A-228. For effect of *Brown*, see "Segregation Is Ruled Out by Steelton School Board," *Harrisburg Evening News*, Aug. 4, 1954, p. 27; "Segregation in Steelton Schools Ends," *Harrisburg Patriot*, Aug. 4, 1954, NAACP Papers, Box II-A-228; Press Release, "Parents Sue to End Bias at White School," Oct. 6, 1954, p. 27, Barnett Papers, Box 362-6.

[88] *United States v. Board of Commissioners*, 332 F. Supp. 655, 665 (S.D. Ind. 1971).

FIGURE 15   Shoe repair class at the segregated Crispus Attucks High School, Indianapolis, 1948. Reprinted with permission of the Indiana Historical Society, Indianapolis Recorder Collection, P0303, Box 9, Folder 3.

Residential segregation guaranteed that most children remained in racially separate schools. Moreover, those whites most affected by the policy change were from working-class immigrant families with limited political power. Although these families protested the city's desegregation policy and their children conducted a school strike in protest, their efforts failed. Union leaders, business leaders, several clergy, and the local newspaper opposed the student strike. The largest Congress of Industrial Organizations (CIO) local union in Gary adopted a resolution "warning CIO members who keep their children out of school that they are violating a national principle of the CIO opposing racial prejudice and discrimination." After two weeks, the strike ended in failure. Several weeks later, a pro-desegregation candidate won the mayoral election. The Gary desegregation experience reflected a combination of factors: the commitment in the postwar urban North to end obvious and explicit forms of racial discrimination and the limited actual effect of the city's desegregation policy, particularly outside of working-class immigrant neighborhoods.[89]

[89] For the Gary resolution, see Resolution, Gary School Board, Aug. 17, 1946, NAACP Papers, Legal Department Files, Box III-5. For the quote from the newspaper editor, see Tipton, *Community in Crisis*, p. 27. For the response to desegregation, see ibid., pp. 115, 118, 127, 134, 140–7; Reynolds, "The Challenge of Racial Equality," p. 178;

Desegregation efforts in Indianapolis, the city with the largest number of separate black schools in the state, proceeded with greater difficulty. As more black families moved into white neighborhoods during the 1940s, many black children were required to travel long distances to attend a racially separate school rather than their neighborhood school, which was reserved for whites. Finally, in 1947, a black attorney, Henry Richardson, requested that his children be allowed to attend their neighborhood school, Number 43, rather than travel sixteen blocks to a black school. When the Indianapolis school officials denied his request, the Indianapolis branch of the NAACP, along with other groups, urged the Indiana General Assembly to enact legislation banning school segregation throughout the state. Although these legislative efforts failed, two years later, in 1949 the Indiana General Assembly did enact a statute prohibiting school segregation throughout the state. The *Indianapolis Recorder* credited a "solid united front of all Negro groups" and "liberal white organizations" with the legislative success. The NAACP, for example, helped coordinate a mass lobbying campaign, warning state legislators "that more than 200,000 Negro citizens in the state 'have eyes on your vote on House Bill 242.'"[90] The Indiana antisegregation legislation, however, contained certain limitations that constrained its effectiveness. First, the legislation permitted a gradual phase-in period by grade, with full compliance delayed until 1954. Furthermore, it did not impose penalties on school districts

Letter from Henry J. Richardson to Thurgood Marshall, Jan. 30, 1947, NAACP Papers, Box II-B-138. One year later, in 1948, school authorities in Elkhart, Indiana, at the urging of the local NAACP branch and the local CIO union, also ended school segregation by including black children in their city's geographic attendance plan. Despite one cross-burning in protest, the desegregation proceeded relatively smoothly. "Board Votes to Quit Policy of Color Line in City Schools," *The Elkhart Truth*, June 22, 1948, p. 1; Letter from Marian Wynn Perry to Earl Drye, President, Elkhart Branch, NAACP, Aug. 19, 1948; Letter from Rheta and Al Pinsky to Mrs. Yankauer, Sept. 18, 1948, NAACP Papers, Box II-B-138.

[90] For 1947 desegregation efforts, see Educational Committee Report of the Indianapolis Branch to the Branch Secretary of the National Office, Oct. 1947; Letter from Henry Richardson to Thurgood Marshall, Jan. 30, 1947; Letter from Henry Richardson to Thurgood Marshall, Oct. 6, 1947; Memorandum to the Legal Department from Gloster Current, Oct. 6, 1947; Memorandum to Oliver W. Harrington from Gloster Current, Oct. 1, 1947, NAACP Papers, Box II-B-138. For statute, see Murray, *States' Laws on Race and Color*, pp. 145–6; Memorandum from June Shagaloff to Gloster Current, Sept. 29, 1953, NAACP Papers, Box II-A-231; for the quote from the *Indianapolis Recorder* and the NAACP warning, see Press Release, "Indiana NAACP Victorious in School Segregation Battle," Mar. 17, 1949, NAACP Papers, Box II-B-138. But not all Indiana blacks were united in the struggle against school segregation. At a 1949 regional conference of branches, NAACP leaders chastised their local Indiana branches for their failure to insist on nondiscriminatory treatment. Thornbrough, "Breaking Racial Barriers," p. 321.

that failed to comply. As a result, many Indiana school districts retained dual schools for several years. A staff member in the national office of the NAACP reported in September 1953 that "[d]espite the usual statements that de-segregation is being effected in Indiana on a state-wide basis, it has been reported that segregated public schools in southern Indiana is [sic] extensive and that no change of policy is being effected by local school boards." Moreover, even those school districts that did comply did so grudgingly. For example, Indianapolis did not convert to a geographic assignment plan until 1952. Even then, school district lines were grossly gerrymandered to preserve racial separation, and racially mixed neighborhoods were excluded from the assignment plan. Students living in racially mixed areas could choose which school to attend, a practice that tended to favor racial separation. In time, additional classrooms were built at certain black and white schools to accommodate the changing population density and to minimize racial mixing. The failure of the Indiana General Assembly to take additional action to enforce its antisegregation legislation would hamper the efforts of those seeking to require certain local school districts to comply with the statutory mandate.[91]

The Persistence of Racial Separation

Successful efforts to end the final vestiges of explicit and obvious school segregation in the North during the late 1940s and early 1950s did not mean an end to racial separation in many school districts. Particularly in urban areas, residential segregation – exacerbated by a variety of public and private actions intended to preserve racial separation – conspired to keep black and white children in separate schools. As northern state legislators enacted various antisegregation measures during the late 1940s, they did so with the knowledge that racial separation would continue. For example, although fund-withholding legislation had a dramatic impact on school segregation in Illinois's southern counties, it had no impact on Chicago, where racially separate schools flourished because of residential segregation and racially gerrymandered attendance lines.

In fact, as the last vestiges of dual school assignments in northern school districts were eliminated during the 1940s and early 1950s, racial separation sharply increased in much of the North. In Pittsburgh, for example, between 1945 and 1965, the percentage of black students enrolled in predominantly black schools increased from 45 to

---

[91] For the quote, see Memorandum from June Shagaloff to Gloster B. Current, Sept. 29, 1953, NAACP Papers, Box II-A-231; for desegregation in Indianapolis, see *United States v. Board of Commissioners*, 332 F. Supp. 655, 666–8 (S.D. Ind. 1971).

67 percent at the elementary school level and from 23 to 58 percent at the secondary school level. By 1965, the percentage of black elementary school students attending majority black schools in Chicago, Detroit, and Philadelphia ranged from 87 to 97 percent, a sharp increase from the 1940s. As the second half of the twentieth century wore on, these numbers increased. Whereas in 1950 whites comprised a majority of students in all of the nation's largest school districts except Washington, D.C., by 1980 every big-city school district in America had a student population that was at least two-thirds minority and most were at least three-fourths minority. And the region beset with the highest degree of racial separation? The North. In 1980, the five states with the highest percentage of black students attending predominantly black schools were all northern states: Illinois, Michigan, New Jersey, New York, and Pennsylvania. At the beginning of the twenty-first century, Illinois, Michigan, New Jersey, and New York still led the nation in terms of racial isolation in public schools.[92]

The reasons for this increase in racial separation in public schools are several. First and foremost, northern residential segregation steadily worsened following the end of World War II, with disastrous consequences for racially integrated schools. As historian Thomas Sugrue has noted: "The most visible and intractable manifestation of racial inequality in the postwar city was residential segregation." What caused this residential segregation? The most important factor was a series of private actions and public policies that whites used to restrict urban blacks to certain neighborhoods. Douglas Massey and Nancy Denton, in their superb 1993 study of residential segregation, drew these conclusions: "No group in the history of the United States has ever experienced the sustained high level of residential segregation that has been imposed on blacks in large American cities for the past fifty years. This extreme racial isolation did not just happen; it was manufactured by whites through a series of . . . well-defined institutional practices, private behaviors, and public policies by which whites sought to contain growing urban black populations." Although most northern whites came to support an end to explicit school segregation by the middle of the twentieth century, that support did not translate into enthusiasm for racially mixed housing. A 1942 poll found that 84 percent of white Americans believed that "there should be separate sections in towns and cities for Negroes to live in"; a 1961 poll found that

---

[92] For school demographic changes, see Glasco, "Double Burden," p. 90; Waller, "Holding Back the Dawn," p. 237; Kantor and Brenzel, "Urban Education and the 'Truly Disadvantaged,' " p. 374; Orfield and Eaton, *Public School Desegregation in the United States*, pp. 8–10. For current racial isolation patterns, see Orfield and Eaton, *Dismantling Desegregation*, p. 60.

61 percent of white Americans still agreed that "white people have a right to keep blacks out of [their] neighborhoods."[93]

As noted in earlier chapters, violence and threats of violence played a vital role during the first half of the twentieth century in controlling black settlement patterns in northern cities. Those blacks who ventured into white neighborhoods were frequently assaulted or threatened by their new neighbors. Moreover, racially restrictive covenants had a devastating impact on black residential patterns in northern cities, as whites effectively used these covenants to restrict blacks to certain neighborhoods. As a result, by the 1940s, the "foundations of the modern [black] ghetto had been laid in virtually every northern city"; in Chicago, for example, approximately 80 percent of residential real estate was covered by a racially restrictive covenant. Although the United States Supreme Court declared the enforcement of such covenants unconstitutional in 1948 in *Shelley v. Kraemer*, their use persisted in many northern communities in defiance of the Court's decision. In 1952, for example, the Cincinnati City Council debated whether to provide sewer and water connections to a new subdivision that explicitly restricted ownership and occupancy to whites.[94]

Moreover, real estate agents continued to conduct their business in a manner that reinforced the racial homogeneity of northern neighborhoods. Many real estate associations sharply criticized the Court's decision in *Shelley v. Kraemer*; the Los Angeles Realty Board even called for an amendment to the United States Constitution to reverse its effect. In 1948, the National Association of Real Estate Boards counseled its members that "madams, bootleggers, gangsters, and Negroes" were "blights" that should be kept out of respectable neighborhoods. Until 1950, Article 34 of the National Real Estate Board's Code of Ethics provided that a "realtor should never be instrumental in introducing into a neighborhood...members of any race or nationality or any individual whose presence will be clearly detrimental to property values in that neighborhood." On occasion this mandate was enforced; in 1948, the Seattle Real Estate Board expelled one of its members because he sold a home to an interracial couple in a white neighborhood. This discrimination would continue. Rose Helper's surveys of real estate practices during the 1950s found extensive discrimination against blacks in northern cities by both realtors and mortgage

---

[93] For the first quote, see Sugrue, *The Origins of the Urban Crisis*, p. 8; for the second quote, see Massey and Denton, *American Apartheid*, pp. 2, 10; for polls, see ibid., p. 49.

[94] For the quote, see Massey and Denton, *American Apartheid*, p. 31; for Chicago, see Biondi, *To Stand and Fight*, p. 114; for the reaction to *Shelley v. Kraemer*, 334 U.S. 1 (1948), see Meyer, *As Long as They Don't Move Next Door*, p. 97; for the Cincinnati city council, see "Restriction Is Hit by Locher," *Cincinnati Enquirer*, Apr. 3, 1952, p. 5.

lenders; other studies suggest that this discrimination continued thereafter.[95]

At the same time, federal housing policies contributed to the preservation of racial separation. The Federal Housing Administration (FHA), established during the 1930s, helped transform the nation's housing industry by guaranteeing the value of collateral used to secure loans by private banks. The FHA, however, reinforced patterns of residential segregation by stating a preference in its Underwriting Manual for single-race neighborhoods: "[I]f a neighborhood is to retain stability, it is necessary that properties shall continue to be occupied by the same social and racial classes." The FHA explicitly encouraged the use of racially restrictive covenants – its Underwriting Manual helpfully contained a model restrictive covenant – until 1950, two years after the Supreme Court declared enforcement of such covenants unconstitutional. As a result of FHA policies, the vast majority of the homes it insured were located in white suburbs; inner-city, black, and mixed-race neighborhoods received limited FHA help. Clarence Mitchell of the NAACP sharply attacked federal housing policies in 1951: "[W]hat the Ku Klux Klan has not been able to accomplish by intimidation and violence, the present Federal Housing Policy is accomplishing through a monumental program of segregation in all aspects of Housing which receive Government aid."[96]

The end of World War II also witnessed tremendous migration to the suburbs, fueled by urban housing shortages, the development of suburban real estate (aided by FHA loan policies), and a massive road construction program. Between 1940 and 1960, the nation's suburban population increased by more than 30 million, twice the comparable increase in the nation's center city population. This suburban migration would have profound consequences for residential segregation. The overwhelming majority of these suburban migrants were white, leaving major northern cities populated increasingly by racial minorities who continued to migrate from the South. Between 1950 and 1970, the percentage of residents in large northern cities who were black more than doubled, increasing, for example, from 14 to 33 percent in Chicago and from 16 to 44 percent in Detroit. As David Delaney has

---

95 For discriminatory real estate practices, see Biondi, *To Stand and Fight*, p. 234; for the reaction to the *Shelley* decision, see Meyer, *As Long as They Don't Move Next Door*, pp. 94–5; for the quote from the Code of Ethics, see Taylor, *The Forging of a Black Community*, p. 180; for Seattle, see ibid. For Helper's surveys, see Helper, *Racial Policies and Practices*, pp. 317–52; Massey and Denton, *American Apartheid*, pp. 50–1.

96 Massey and Denton, *American Apartheid*, pp. 52–7 (first quote, p. 54); King, *Separate and Unequal*, pp. 192–8 (second quote, p. 198); Biondi, *To Stand and Fight*, p. 121; Kirby, *Black Americans in the Roosevelt Era*, p. 34; *United States v. Board of Commissioners*, 456 F. Supp. 183, 187 (S.D. Ind. 1978).

noted, the migration of whites from urban centers to suburbs generated a separation of the races – both residentially and educationally – "unimaginable to the architects of the municipal segregation ordinances of the early part of the century." Given that almost all northern suburbs operated their own school districts, suburbanization would have a profound effect on racial isolation in urban public schools.[97]

School desegregation proponents well understood the connection between the increase in residential segregation and school segregation. As the Harlem Tenants Council noted in 1954 after the *Brown* decision: "Segregation in education, now outlawed by the Supreme Court, cannot really be eliminated until segregation in housing, too, is outlawed." But most white northerners viewed the Court's *Brown* decision as having no impact on northern residential segregation. In Minnesota, for example, where racial separation in the St. Paul schools was pervasive in the early 1950s, one of the state's U.S. senators declared on the day the *Brown* decision was announced: "We who live in states like Minnesota, where all children have free access to the same schools, must not forget that the so-called 'race problem' is no problem at all for us."[98]

Northern school officials exacerbated the effect of residential segregation by the widespread use of racially gerrymandered school district lines and the siting of schools in single-race neighborhoods. School districts across the North continually redrew school attendance zones during the 1940s and 1950s to minimize racial integration. Moreover, many of these school districts utilized liberal transfer provisions that allowed white children living in black school districts to transfer to another school. Not surprisingly, these transfer provisions contributed to the racial homogeneity of many northern schools.[99]

For example, school authorities in Chicago used racially gerrymandered attendance zones for much of the twentieth century coupled with "neutral zones" where students in mixed-race areas were given latitude to attend a school with children of their own race. Moreover, the Chicago school board subjected black schools to severe overcrowding, using double sessions and "portable" classrooms, due to an unwillingness to redraw school attendance lines in a manner that would place

[97] For population shifts, see Massey and Denton, *American Apartheid*, pp. 45–9; Rury, "Race, Space," p. 120; Fairclough, *Better Day Coming*, p. 298. By 1980, 77 percent of the black population but only 28 percent of the white population in the major metropolitan areas of the Midwest and Northeast lived in inner cities. Kantor and Brenzel, "Urban Education and the 'Truly Disadvantaged,'" p. 371. For the quote, see Delaney, *Race, Place, and the Law*, p. 182.

[98] For the Harlem quote, see Biondi, *To Stand and Fight*, p. 240; for the Minnesota quote, see Green, "'Critical Mass Is Fifteen Colored's!'" p. 319.

[99] Waller, "Holding Back the Dawn," p. 293.

black children in white schools. School officials in New York City also used racially gerrymandered attendance zones to preserve racial separation during and after the 1940s. As black neighborhoods expanded and black children entered nearby white schools, school officials redrew attendance lines to preserve the racial character of the schools. In some neighborhoods, like Washington Heights in upper Manhattan, white children were bused to a distant school to avoid attendance at a nearby predominantly black school in Harlem.[100]

Other urban school districts also utilized racially gerrymandered school district lines and overcrowded black schools to preserve the racial homogeneity of their schools. For example, in Cleveland, several black schools in the late 1940s were severely overcrowded, and yet local school authorities refused to transfer black students to nearby white schools. In 1948, the Hayes School housed 1,395 students, despite an 800-student capacity, and the Kinsman School housed 1,635 students, despite a 750-student capacity. Some classes in these schools had as many as 60 students and were conducted in gyms, basements, and school libraries. The Cleveland school board's response, however, was to shift children from these overcrowded black schools to other predominantly black schools, despite the presence of nearby predominantly white schools that were under capacity. At the same time, white students who lived in areas with a preponderance of black students were allowed to transfer to predominantly white schools.[101]

Racial gerrymandering was prevalent in smaller communities as well. The United States Commission on Civil Rights found "purposeful segregation by administrative action," including racial gerrymandering, by school officials in numerous smaller northern cities during the 1950s, including Gary, Indiana; Hillsboro, Ohio; New Rochelle, New York; East Orange, New Jersey; and Portland, Oregon. In Hillsboro,

---

[100] For Chicago, see Congress of Racial Equality, "Report on the Elementary and High Schools of Chicago," Oct. 5, 1943; "District Boundary Lines," Aug. 1945, unpublished statement; Citizens Schools Committee Papers, Box 5; "Survey Shows That Sixteen South Side Schools Operate on Double-Shift Basis," *Chicago's Schools*, Nov.–Dec. 1943; Letter from Mrs. Reid Bennett, of Chicago Woman's Club, to Mayor Edward J. Kelly, Apr. 5, 1939; Chicago Woman's Club, "Even a Portable May Be Better Than Half-Day Divisions, Double Schools, and Staggered Shifts," Apr. 4, 1939; "Leaders Ask for Longer School Day for Double-Shift Schools for Negro Children," *Chicago's Schools*, Oct. 1939, Citizens Schools Committee, Box 5; Associated Negro Press, "Governor Signs Law Authored by Negro to Ban Segregation in Illinois Schools," July 22, 1963, Barnett Papers, Box 350-5; "The People of Chicago," Chicago Urban League Papers. For New York, see Biondi, "The Struggle for Black Equality," pp. 163, 196–200.

[101] Moore, "The Limits of Black Power," pp. 65–6; *Reed v. Rhodes*, 422 F. Supp. 708, 718–24, 733–40, 750–3, 764–5 (N.D. Ohio, 1976); Russell H. Davis, "Civil Rights in Cleveland 1912 Through 1961," p. 106, 1973, Davis Papers, Container 9.

for example, the school board used grossly gerrymandered and non-contiguous geographic zones after the 1954 *Brown* decision to keep seven black children in the town's one black school, a plan the local school superintendent referred to as "temporary segregation." Finally, in 1956, the United States Court of Appeals for the Sixth Circuit ordered the Hillsboro school authorities to admit all of the black students to a white school.[102]

Similarly, in Hamilton County, Ohio, the school board in 1950 divided a local school district into two districts in order to preserve racial segregation. One of the new districts, Woodlawn, encompassed 17 percent of the students (a majority of whom were white) and 54 percent of the property tax valuation, while the remaining students (all of whom were black) were placed in the Lincoln Heights school district. A contemporary study of the Hamilton County schools found that the districts had been created so as to minimize interracial contact: "The district before the division was largely colored; after separation the new Woodlawn area was little less than half colored (in school enrollments) while Lincoln Heights was entirely colored. There are indications here that the white minority pulled out, taking with them the bulk of the wealth, in order to become a majority in the new Woodlawn district. For school purposes, the result of this division has been that a populous but impoverished area has been cut loose from the county system and left isolated to meet alone almost insuperable obstacles to financing an adequate educational system."[103]

Challenges to racial gerrymandering, either by legislation or litigation, generally failed during the pre-*Brown* era. For example, during the mid-1940s, the New York General Assembly considered legislation that would have barred racially gerrymandered school district lines. This proposed legislation failed – as it did throughout the North. Litigation challenging racial gerrymandering, as in Chicago, also failed. Northern states had eliminated most of the remaining vestiges of explicit school segregation by the time of the *Brown* decision, but would not begin to tackle the larger problems posed by racially gerrymandered school districts or entrenched residential segregation until the 1960s and 1970s. This general acceptance of racially gerrymandered districts reveals the limits of postwar racial liberalism – explicit forms of racial segregation were disfavored, but racial separation caused by residential patterns or by creative line

---

[102] For the Commission quote, see U.S. Commission on Civil Rights, *Racial Isolation*, I, p. 43. For Hillsboro, see *Clemons v. Board of Education of Hillsboro*, 228 F.2d 853, 855 (6th Cir. 1956); Press Release, "Ohio School Segregation Case May Prove Historic," Mar. 7, 1956, Barnett Papers, Box 362-5.

[103] Leigh, "Segregation by Gerrymander," p. 133.

drawing did not offend the egalitarian sensibilities of most white northerners.[104]

To be sure, some education officials criticized the use of racially gerrymandered school district lines. In 1952, a publication of the California State Department of Education labeled racially gerrymandered school attendance lines "a disservice to democracy and an unpatriotic denial of the doctrine that all men are created equal." The publication suggested that "[i]f America is to continue to guarantee fundamental human rights, schools must provide the democratic living and the group interaction essential to acceptance of the principles and ideals of America's democratic culture." Moreover, a few northern school districts took action to limit racial gerrymandering after the *Brown* decision. School authorities in Chester, Pennsylvania, for example, threatened with litigation, redrew racially gerrymandered school district lines and reduced racially motivated student transfers in the fall of 1954. But despite these efforts, the Pennsylvania Human Relations Commission found in 1964 that the Chester school board still utilized racially gerrymandered attendance lines.[105]

Finally, as had been feared during the early twentieth century, racially separate schools frequently meant disparately funded schools. During the early 1950s, financial support for black schools in many northern communities lagged considerably behind support for white schools. In New York City, for example, a 1954 study found that white elementary schools received three times the per pupil allocation for buildings and mechanical equipment that black and Puerto Rican schools received, almost eight times the per pupil expenditures for furniture and instructional equipment, and more than three times the total capital outlay. These disparities were also present at the junior high school level. Per pupil expenditures for children in white junior high schools were 26 percent higher than those in junior high schools attended by black and Puerto Rican children. For many northern

---

[104] For the New York proposed legislation, see International Labor Defense, *New York State Laws Against Discrimination on Account of Race, Creed, or Color*, Jan. 1945, Barnett Papers, Box 362-1; Biondi, "The Struggle for Black Equality," p. 196; for Chicago litigation, see Congress of Racial Equality, "Report on the Elementary and High Schools of Chicago," Oct. 5, 1943, Citizens Schools Committee Papers, Box 5. For the discussion of gerrymandering, see Biondi, "The Struggle for Black Equality," p. 205.

[105] For the California quote, see Reams and Wilson, *Segregation and the Fourteenth Amendment*, pp. 44–5; for Chester, see "Board Votes 7–2 to End Segregation in Schools," *Chester Times*, Aug. 24, 1954, NAACP Papers, Box II-A-228; "Chester Board Agrees 7–2 to End Segregation," *Chester Evening Bulletin*, Aug. 24, 1954, NAACP Papers, Box II-A-228; Pennsylvania Human Relations Commission, "The Chester Case," *Integrated Education* 13 (1965), pp. 15, 17–18.

blacks during the post-*Brown* era, the solution was to improve black schools and provide them with proper resources, as opposed to racial mixing. But other northern blacks, particularly those associated with the NAACP, favored racially mixed schools as the only way to prevent these disparities. Milton Galamison, for example, a forceful proponent of racial integration in the New York City schools during the 1950s, argued that black children would receive the same educational opportunities that white children enjoyed only in racially mixed schools. Decades later, the problem of unequally funded schools, and unequally funded school districts, would emerge as perhaps the most important issue in American education.[106]

By the late 1940s and early 1950s, the long struggle to end explicit forms of school segregation in northern communities had succeeded. World War II and its aftermath produced a set of political and cultural conditions that contributed to the ascendancy in the white North of a new racial norm that made *explicit* forms of racial segregation no longer acceptable. The NAACP took advantage of these new conditions by insisting – through litigation, political pressure, and public education initiatives – on an end to the remaining vestiges of explicit school segregation in the North.

The significance of the NAACP's victory, however, was diminished by its inability to address the problem of racially separate urban schools caused by residential segregation and racially gerrymandered school attendance lines. In fact, as the nation's attention turned to the complexities of southern school desegregation after the Supreme Court's 1954 decision in *Brown v. Board of Education*, the North would be left with the extraordinarily difficult question of what to do about the steady growth of racial separation in the region's urban schools.

[106] Waller, "Holding Back the Dawn," pp. 207–8, 339.

7

Conclusion

The long campaign to end explicit, officially sanctioned school segregation in northern states eventually enjoyed success, although that success was mitigated by the rapidly increasing racial separation in urban schools. While the NAACP celebrated its victories in the remaining pockets of segregationist resistance in the North during the early 1950s, many black children in northern cities continued to attend racially separate schools due to decades of white efforts to preserve residential segregation and the widespread use of racially gerrymandered school district lines. Indeed, by 1954, more northern black children attended predominantly black schools than ever before. And those numbers would steadily *increase* over the course of the next several decades. What, then, does the century-long struggle for desegregated schools in the North teach us about the relationship between law and racial change and about the long-standing debate in the northern black community over the importance of racially mixed schools?

Legal prohibitions operate in a complex social and political context. Cultural patterns, particularly those associated with race, have been remarkably resistant to change in this country's history, as entrenched racial attitudes have often proven impervious to the demands of court decisions and statutory enactments. The nineteenth-century antisegregation legislation *did* reflect a commitment among *some* northern whites to racial fairness. But many northern whites did not share that commitment, and when southern blacks began migrating north in significant numbers, white support for racial justice sharply declined. As scholars such as Leon Litwack have noted, claims of widely shared white commitments to full racial equality in the nineteenth-century (and early twentieth-century) North cannot withstand close scrutiny. As a result, efforts to enforce northern antisegregation legislation failed for almost seventy-five years to eliminate officially sanctioned segregation in many northern school districts.[1]

---

[1] See, for example, Litwack, *North of Slavery.*

African Americans seeking to eradicate the remaining pockets of explicit school segregation in northen states succeeded during the 1940s and early 1950s in significant measure because of important shifts in white attitudes toward the continued acceptability of obvious forms of racial segregation. Prior to that time, an implicit norm of racial hierarchy had dominated American social and political consciousness, with occasional outbursts of egalitarian sentiment, as during Reconstruction. After World War II, however, a new racial norm gained dominance among white elites in the United States (at least outside of the South), one that opposed *explicit* forms of racial separation. As political scientist Tali Mendelberg has noted, by the end of the 1940s "the central political institutions of the United States began to converge on the notion that... segregation and the ideology of white supremacy were illegitimate." The NAACP exploited this new racial norm by successfully pushing for an end to explicit forms of school segregation throughout the North.[2]

But this new racial norm did not reflect a broad reordering of white attitudes toward the desirability of racial mixing. Northern whites would and did take action to end obvious forms of racial segregation during the 1940s and early 1950s but tolerated and even encouraged more subtle forms of racial separation. This tension is best captured in the ongoing commitment to residential segregation and the widespread use of racially gerrymandered school district lines. Although some northerners criticized these efforts to preserve racial separation, their criticisms did not succeed in changing patterns of racial separation. For those whose goal was not just the elimination of government-mandated school segregation but also the education of black and white children together, the long campaign against northern school segregation had claimed a victory of decidedly mixed meaning.

What does the campaign against northern school segregation teach us about the relationship between law and racial change? Establishing rights through legislation or litigation is often essential to racial reform, but those legal victories are not likely to translate into meaningful social change unless they are accompanied by broader cultural and political support. Legal scholar Mark Tushnet has appropriately cautioned us "against overestimating the significance of legal victories" that are not grounded in such support. The antisegregation legislation of the nineteenth century did not reflect a broad commitment among northern whites to full racial equality, and the changing racial demographics of the early twentieth century further eroded

[2] Mendelberg, *The Race Card*, p. 70 (quote).

white commitments to racial mixing in public schools. Hence, the nineteenth-century legislation and the litigation enforcing it failed to alter patterns of explicit racial separation in northern schools until changing cultural and political attitudes produced an antisegregation imperative during the 1940s. Similarly, as we saw in Chapter 3, much of the antidiscrimination legislation of the 1880s prohibiting racial discrimination in public accommodations reflected temporary political imperatives such as the need to capture black votes in closely divided elections, and hence did not transform northern patterns of racial discrimination in public life.[3]

In recent years, many scholars have evaluated the use of litigation as a means of accomplishing social change. An early critique by political scientist Stuart Scheingold argued that many lawyers, with a simplistic view of the connection between litigation and social change, adopted a "myth of rights" perspective that judicial decisions directly produce social change, rather than a "politics of rights" perspective that views judicial decisions as political assets to be used as part of larger reform efforts: "Instead of thinking of judicially asserted rights as accomplished social facts or moral imperatives, they must be thought of, on the one hand, as authoritatively articulated goals of public policy and, on the other, as political resources of unknown value in the hands of those who want to alter the course of public policy. . . . The direct linking of rights, remedies, and change that characterizes the *myth of rights* must, in sum, be exchanged for a more complex framework, the *politics of rights*, which takes into account the contingent character of rights in the American system." The history of the campaign to eliminate northern school segregation supports Scheingold's observations. Litigation alone was incapable of ending northern school segregation, but it did play an important role in conjunction with other strategies. Litigation on occasion contributed to broader political efforts to promote school desegregation, as in Michigan and New York during the 1860s and 1870s, in part by calling attention to the injustice of racial segregation. On other occasions, desegregation proponents used litigation to enforce antisegregation norms that had already gained statewide acceptance, as in southern Illinois and southern New Jersey during the late 1940s and early 1950s. Indeed, litigation operates at peak effectiveness when used to enforce agreed-upon social norms. Not surprisingly, litigation seeking to overcome the effects of white migration to northern suburbs failed, as the United States Supreme Court

---

[3] Tushnet, "The Critique of Rights," pp. 23, 25 ("[T]he critique of rights distinguishes between winning legal victories and winning political ones. . . . [T]he critique of rights serves as a simple caution against overestimating the significance of legal victories").

declined in 1974 to order a highly controversial desegregation plan encompassing both urban and suburban school districts throughout the Detroit metropolitan area.[4]

The long campaign against northern school segregation also revealed deep divisions in the black community over the importance of racially mixed schools. What is striking about this debate is the similarity of concerns first articulated during the antebellum era that continued to resonate during the late nineteenth century and the first half of the twentieth century. Proponents of racial mixing have for almost two centuries urged the view that racial equality will come only when blacks and whites enjoy extensive contact with one another, beginning in the public schools, and government-mandated separate institutions are eliminated. Opponents, for the most part, argued that racial mixing was too often procured at the cost of black well-being, noting that black children in racially mixed schools frequently suffered at the hands of their white classmates and teachers, and black teachers were typically dismissed when schools were integrated. These concerns were not trivial. Even W. E. B. Du Bois, one of the great champions of racial integration, eventually despaired of the cost to black children of continued insistence on racial mixing. These dissenters from the campaign to end school segregation provided a reminder that in the context of a society with widespread antiblack sentiment, school desegregation was a mixed blessing. Proponents of racial mixing conceded that cost, but they argued that the ultimate goal of equal status in American life depended upon refusing enforced separation.

During the 1940s and early 1950s, the integrationist perspective gained the upper hand in the northern black community, reflected in the extraordinary increases in membership enjoyed by the NAACP. Across the North, blacks and white elites embraced an antisegregation perspective during the 1940s with unprecedented energy and commitment. In 1954, the United States Supreme Court legitimized this perspective in its decision in *Brown v. Board of Education.* But the debate in the black community over the importance of racially mixed schools continued during the post-*Brown* era. For example, when the United States Supreme Court considered in the early 1970s the question of whether to require local school districts to engage in extensive school busing as a remedy for de jure school segregation, the Congress of Racial Equality filed a brief with the Court urging it to reject extensive busing in favor of "community"-based schools, a clear expression

---

[4] For the quote, see Scheingold, *The Politics of Rights*, pp. 6–7; for the court decision, see *Milliken v. Bradley*, 418 U.S. 717 (1974).

of its preference for black control over the education of black children as opposed to integrated schools.[5]

Significantly, by 1979, the twenty-fifth anniversary of the *Brown* decision, even a few NAACP attorneys questioned the insistence on racially mixed public schools, suggesting that equal educational opportunity could be achieved through greater financial support for minority schools. Robert Carter, one of the NAACP litigators in *Brown*, articulated this perspective: "While we fashioned *Brown* on the theory that equal education and integrated education were one and the same, the goal was not integration but equal educational opportunity.... If [equal educational opportunity] can be achieved without integration, *Brown* has been satisfied." Derrick Bell, a former NAACP attorney involved in much of the school desegregation litigation of the 1960s, also questioned his organization's emphasis on racial mixing, which Bell characterized in an influential 1980 article as "in some cases inferior to plans focusing on 'educational components,' including the creation and development of 'model' all-black schools." Looking back on years of desegregation frustration, Bell wrote in 1986: "rather than beat our heads against the wall seeking pupil-desegregation orders the courts were unwilling to enter or enforce, we could have organized parents and communities to ensure effective implementation for the equal-funding and equal-representation mandates."[6]

Many factors account for this shift in perspective. As racial mixing became increasingly difficult, if not impossible, in large urban school districts with few nonminority students and the Supreme Court declined to order multidistrict desegregation remedies, an increasing number of proponents of minority education began to urge nonintegrationist alternatives to equal educational opportunity such as improved funding for minority schools. In 1977, the Supreme Court held that governmental defendants could be required to fund remedial and compensatory education programs in inner-city, predominantly minority schools as an alternative to racial mixing. That decision opened the door to litigation and political strategies designed to capture greater resources for urban, heavily minority schools as opposed to greater racial mixing.[7]

---

[5] Congress of Racial Equality, "A True Alternative to Segregation: A Proposal for Community School Districts," Feb. 1970, in "Brief for CORE as Amicus Curiae," *Swann v. Charlotte-Mecklenburg Board of Education*, in Douglas, *The Development of School Busing*, p. 259.

[6] For the Carter quote, see Carter, "A Reassessment of *Brown v. Board*," p. 27; for the first Bell quote, see Bell, "*Brown v. Board of Education* and the Interest-Convergence Dilemma," p. 528; for the second Bell quote, see Bell, *And We Are Not Saved*, pp. 112–13.

[7] *Milliken v. Bradley*, 433 U.S. 267 (1977).

By the 1990s, many racial minorities openly rejected the integrationist paradigm that had dominated earlier discussions of how best to ensure equal educational opportunity for all children, favoring instead a return to neighborhood schools. Black mayors in several major cities, including Cleveland, Denver, and Minneapolis, endorsed the termination of school desegregation plans.[8] In 1993, legal scholar Alex Johnson wrote an article subtitled "Why Integrationism Fails African-Americans Again," in which he suggested that "*Brown v. Board of Education* and its explicit adoption of integrationism" was "a mistake." Giving voice to the frustrations of many African Americans about the failure of racial mixing to improve their status in American society, Johnson conceded that his perspective constituted a break with the past. "Twenty or thirty years ago this Article would not have been written," Johnson noted. "The views presented . . . would have been so far outside the mainstream that, frankly, they would have been unthinkable by an African-American scholar." To be sure, many proponents of minority education have continued to insist on the importance of racial mixing to achieve equal educational opportunity, but the decline in support for school integration in the minority community has been striking.[9]

As America continues to confront the question of how best to provide an equal educational opportunity to all children, the question of the importance of racial mixing will remain. The long debate in the northern black community over school integration should provide context and insight to those who struggle with this issue today.

---

[8] Douglas, "The End of Busing?," p. 1731, n. 67. Moreover, many black parents prefer a return to neighborhood schools even if they mean the end of racial mixed schools. Days, "*Brown* Blues: Rethinking the Integrative Ideal," p. 54.

[9] Johnson, "Bid Whist, Tonk, and *United States v. Fordice*: Why Integrationism Fails African-Americans Again," pp. 1402, 1409.

References

Manuscript Collections

Cambridge, Massachusetts
　Schlesinger Library, Harvard University
　　Pauli Murray Papers
　Harvard Law School Library
　　William Hastie Papers
Chicago, Illinois
　Chicago Historical Society
　　Charles Barnett Papers
　　Citizens School Committee Papers
　University of Illinois at Chicago
　　Charles Armstrong Papers
　　Chicago Urban League Papers
Cincinnati, Ohio
　Cincinnati Historical Society
　　Printed Works Collection
Cleveland, Ohio
　Western Reserve Historical Society
　　Edward Bushnell Papers
　　Harold T. Clark Papers
　　Cleveland NAACP Papers
　　Russell Howard Davis Papers
　　Future Outlook League Papers
　　Sol Kahn Papers
　　Frank Lyons Papers
　　Henry Lee Moon Papers
　　Samuel V. Perry Papers
　　Urban League of Cleveland Papers
Columbus, Ohio
　Ohio Historical Society
　　Daniel A. P. Murray Colllection
　　George Myers Papers
Nashville, Tennessee
　Fisk University Library Special Collections
　　Charles Spurgeon Johnson Papers

Newark, New Jersey
  Newark Public Library, New Jersey Reference Division
    William M. Ashby Papers
    Harold Lett Papers
    New Jersey Urban League Papers
New Haven, Connecticut
  Yale University, Beinecke Rare Book and Manuscript Library
    James Weldon Johnson Papers
    Walter Francis White Papers
New York, New York
  New York Public Library, Schomberg Center for Research in Black Culture
    W. E. B. Du Bois Papers
    William Loren Katz Collection
    Henry Lee Moon Papers
    A. Philip Randolph Papers
    Joel and Amy Spingarn Papers
    Walter White Papers
    Franklin Williams Papers
Washington, D.C.
  Howard University, Moorland-Spingarn Research Center
    Charles Hamilton Houston Papers
    Joel Spingarn Papers
    Library of Congress
    NAACP Papers
    National Urban League Papers
    Arthur Spingarn Papers
    Moorfield Storey Papers

Newspapers

Alton (Ill.) *Daily Telegraph*
Asbury Park Press
Baltimore Afro-American
Brooklyn Daily Times
Chester Evening Bulletin
Chester Times
Chicago Defender
Chicago Tribune
Cincinnati Commercial
Cincinnati Enquirer
Cincinnati *Union*
Cleveland Advocate
Cleveland Call and Post
Cleveland Gazette
Columbus Statesman
Elkhart Truth
The Forum (Springfield, IL)
Frederick Douglass' Paper

Harrisburg Evening News
Harrisburg Patriot
Houston Informer
Indianapolis Freeman
Indianapolis Journal
The Liberator
Monmouth Democrat
Muscatine (Iowa) *Courier*
Muscatine Weekly Journal
Newark Evening News
Newark Herald
New Jersey Herald News
New York Age
New York Amsterdam News
New York Times
Norfolk Journal and Guide
The North Star
Ohio State Journal
Ohio State Monitor
Philadelphia Inquirer
Philadelphia Tribune
Pittsburgh Courier
Raleigh Daily News and Observer
York Gazette and Daily

Interviews

Robert Carter, Aug. 7, 2003
John Lee, July 23, 2002

Books, Articles, and Dissertations

Adams, Ezola Borden. "The Role and Function of the Manual Training and Industrial School at Bordentown as an Alternative School. 1915–1955." Ed.D. dissertation, Rutgers University. 1977.

Adler, Mortimer J., ed. *The Negro in American History*. Chicago: Encyclopedia Britannica Educational Corporation, 1969.

Aldridge, Derrick P. "The Social, Economic, and Political Thought of W. E. B. Du Bois During the 1930s: Implications for Contemporary African-American Education." Ph.D. dissertation, Pennsylvania State University, 1997.

Allen, Henry L. "Segregation and Desegregation in Boston's Schools, 1961–1974." In *From Common School to Magnet School: Selected Essays in the History of Boston's Schools*. James W. Fraser, Henry L. Allen, and Nancy Barnes, eds. Boston: Trustees of the Public Library of the City of Boston, 1979.

Anderson, Carol. *Eyes Off the Prize: The United Nations and the African American Struggle for Human Rights, 1944–1955.* New York: Cambridge University Press, 2003.

Anderson, John Robert. "Negro Education in the Public Schools of Newark, New Jersey During the Nineteenth Century." Ed.D. dissertation, Rutgers University, 1972.

Andrews, Charles C. *The History of the New-York African Free-Schools, From Their Establishment in 1787, To the Present Time; Embracing a Period of More Than Forty Years.* New York: Mahlon Day, 1830; New York: Negro Universities Press, 1969.

Annual Report of the Superintendent of Public Schools of the State of New Jersey, For the Year 1863. Trenton: David Naar "True American" Office, 1864.

Anyon, Jean. *Ghetto Schooling: A Political Economy of Urban Educational Reform.* New York: Teachers College Press, 1997.

Ashmore, Harry S. *The Negro and the Schools.* Chapel Hill: University of North Carolina Press, 1954.

Bagnall, Robert W. "Why Separate Schools Should Be Opposed." *The Messenger* 4 (Sept. 1922): 485–7.

Baker, Lee D. *From Savage to Negro: Anthropology and the Construction of Race, 1896–1954.* Berkeley: University of California Press, 1998.

Banks, William M. *Black Intellectuals: Race and Responsibility in American Life.* New York: W. W. Norton & Co., 1996.

Barnett, Claude A. "The Role of the Press, Radio, and Motion Picture and Negro Morale." *Journal of Negro Education* 12 (Summer 1943): 474–89.

Bell, Derrick. *And We Are Not Saved: The Elusive Quest for Racial Justice.* New York: Basic Books, Inc. 1987.

  "*Brown v. Board of Education* and the Interest-Convergence Dilemma." *Harvard Law Review* 93 (Jan. 1980): 518–33.

  Race, Racism, and American Law. Boston: Little, Brown, & Co. 1992.

Bell, Howard Holman, ed. *Minutes of the Proceedings of the National Negro Conventions, 1830–1864.* New York: Arno Press, Inc., 1969.

Benson, Lee. *The Concept of Jacksonian Democracy: New York as a Test Case.* Princeton: Princeton University Press, 1961.

Berry, Gail Estelle. "Wendell Phillips Dabney: Leader of the Negro Protest." M.A. thesis, University of Cincinnati, 1965.

Bertaux, Nancy. "Structural Economic Change and Occupational Decline among Black Workers in Nineteenth-Century Cincinnati." In *Race and the City: Work, Community, and Protest in Cincinnati, 1820–1970.* Henry Louis Taylor, Jr., ed. Urbana: University of Illinois Press, 1993.

Berwanger, Eugene H. *The Frontier Against Slavery: Western Anti-Negro Prejudice and the Slavery Extension Controversy.* Urbana: University of Illinois Press, 1967.

Bethel, Elizabeth Rauh. *The Roots of African-American Identity: Memory and History in Free Antebellum Communities.* New York: St. Martin's Press, 1997.

Bethune, Mary McLeod. "Certain Unalienable Rights." In *What the Negro Wants,* Rayford W. Logan, ed. Chapel Hill: University of North Carolina Press, 1944.

Betten, Neil and Raymond A. Mohl. "The Evolution of Racism in an Industrial City, 1906–1940: A Case Study of Gary, Indiana." *Journal of Negro History* 59 (Jan. 1974): 51–64.

Bigham, Darrel E. *We Ask Only a Fair Trial: A History of the Black Community of Evansville, Indiana.* Bloomington: Indiana University Press. 1987.

Towns and Villages of the Lower Ohio. Lexington: The University Press of Kentucky, 1998.

Billington, Ray Allen. *The Protestant Crusade, 1800–1860: A Study of the Origins of American Nativism.* New York: Macmillan Company, 1938.

Biondi, Martha. "The Struggle for Black Equality in New York City, 1945–1955." Ph.D. dissertation, Columbia University, 1997.

To Stand and Fight: The Struggle for Civil Rights in Postwar New York City. Cambridge: Harvard University Press, 2003.

Blascoer, Frances. *Colored School Children in New York.* New York: Negro Universities Press, 1915, reprinted 1970.

Blassingame, John W., ed. *The Frederick Douglass Papers.* New Haven: Yale University Press, 1979.

Blaustein, Albert P. *Civil Rights U.S.A.: Public Schools, Cities in the North and West, 1963, Camden and Environs.* Washington, D.C.: United States Commission on Civil Rights, 1963.

Bond, Horace Mann. *The Education of the Negro in the American Social Order.* New York: Prentice Hall, Inc., 1934.

"What the Army 'Intelligence' Tests Measured." *Opportunity* 2 (July 1924): 197–202.

Bowles, Samuel and Herbert Gintis. *Schooling in Capitalist America: Educational Reform and the Contradictions of Economic Life.* New York: Basic Books, Inc., 1976.

Brigham, Carl C. *A Study of American Intelligence.* Princeton: Princeton University Press, 1923.

Brown, George W. "The History of the Negro in Cleveland from 1800 to 1900." Ph.D. dissertation, Western Reserve University, 1934.

Brown, Ira V. *The Negro in Pennsylvania History.* University Park, PA: Pennsylvania Historical Association, 1970.

Bruce, Roscoe C. "The Stimulus of Negro Teaching." *Colored American Magazine* 17 (July 1909): 12–15.

Buck, Pearl S. "Democracy and the Negro." *The Crisis* 48 (Dec. 1941): 376–7.

Bunche, Ralph. "A Critical Analysis of the Tactics and Programs of Minority Groups." *Journal of Negro Education* 4 (July 1935): 308–20.

Buni, Andrew. *Robert L. Vann of the Pittsburgh Courier: Politics and Black Journalism.* Pittsburgh: University of Pittsburgh Press, 1974.

Burk, Robert Fredrick. *The Eisenhower Administration and Black Civil Rights.* Knoxville: University of Tennessee Press, 1984.

Bustard, Joseph L. "The New Jersey Story: The Development of Racially Integrated Public Schools." *Journal of Negro Education* 21 (Summer 1952): 275–85.

Carlson, Shirley Jean Motley. "The Black Community in the Rural North: Pulaski County, Illinois, 1860–1900." Ph.D. dissertation, Washington University, 1982.

Carter, Robert. "A Reassessment of *Brown v. Board.*" In *Shades of Brown: New Perspectives on School Desegregation.* Derrick Bell, ed. New York: Teachers College Press, 1980.

Cha-Jua, Sundiata Keita. *America's First Black Town: Brooklyn, Illinois, 1830–1915.* Urbana: University of Illinois Press, 2000.

Cheek, William and Aimee Lee Cheek. "John Mercer Langston and the Cincinnati Riot of 1841." In *Race and the City: Work, Community, and Protest in Cincinnati. 1820–1970.* Henry Louis Taylor. Jr., ed. Urbana: University of Illinois Press, 1993.

Chicago Commission on Race Relations. *The Negro in Chicago: A Study of Race Relations and a Race Riot.* Chicago: University of Chicago Press, 1922.

Clark, Kenneth. "Morale of the Negro on the Home Front: World Wars I and II." *Journal of Negro Education* 12 (Summer 1943): 417–28.

Cobb, Deirdre Lynn. "Race and Higher Education at the University of Illinois, 1945 to 1955." Ph.D. dissertation, University of Illinois, 1998.

Cohen, Ronald D. *Children of the Mill: Schooling and Society in Gary, Indiana, 1906–1960.* Bloomington: Indiana University Press, 1990.

Conner, Malcolm. "A Comparative Study of Black and White Public Education in Nineteenth Century New Brunswick, New Jersey." Ed.D. dissertation, Rutgers University, 1976.

Cottrol, Robert J. "Law, Politics and Race in Urban America: Towards a New Synthesis." *Rutgers Law Journal* 17 (Spring–Summer 1986): 483–536.

Cover, Robert. "The Origins of Judicial Activism in the Protection of Minorities." *Yale Law Journal* 91 (1982): 1287–316.

Crew, Spencer R. *Black Life in Secondary Cities: A Comparative Analysis of the Black Communities of Camden and Elizabeth, N.J., 1860–1920.* New York: Garland Publishing, 1993.

Crocco, Margaret Smith, Petra Munro, and Kathleen Weiler. *Pedagogies of Resistance: Women Educator Activists, 1880–1960.* New York: Teachers College Press, 1999.

Crowley, Mary R. "Cincinnati's Experiment in Negro Education: A Comparative Study of the Segregated and Mixed School." *Journal of Negro Education* 1 (Apr. 1932): 25–33.

"Comparison of the Academic Achievements of Cincinnati Negroes in Segregated and Mixed Schools." Ed.D. dissertation, University of Cincinnati, 1934.

Crummell, Alexander. *Africa and America: Addresses and Discourses.* Springfield, MA: Wiley & Co., 1891.

Cubberley, Ellwood P. *State and County Educational Reorganization: The Revised Constitution and School Code of the State of Osceola.* New York: Macmillan Company, 1914.

Current, Gloster B. "Exit Jim-Crow Schools in New Jersey." *The Crisis* 56 (Jan. 1949): 10–13, 29.

"Segregated Schools – On Trial in East St. Louis." *The Crisis* 56 (Mar. 1949): 77–9, 92.

Dabney, Wendell P. *Cincinnati's Colored Citizens: Historical, Sociological and Biographical.* New York: Negro Universities Press, 1926, 1970.

Dain, Bruce Russell. "A Hideous Monster of the Mind: American Race Theory, 1787–1859." Ph.D. dissertation, Princeton University, 1996.

Dalfiume, Richard M. "The 'Forgotten Years' of the Negro Revolution." In *The Negro in Depression and War: Prelude to Revolution, 1930–1945*. Bernard Sternsher, ed. Chicago: Quadrangle Books, 1969.

Daniel, Philip. "A History of Discrimination against Black Students in Chicago Secondary Schools." *History of Education Quarterly* 20 (Summer 1980): 147–62.

Daniels, John. *In Freedom's Birthplace: A Study of the Boston Negroes*. Boston: Houghton Mifflin Company, 1914.

Daniels, Roland H. "A Case Study of Desegregation in the Public Schools of Trenton, New Jersey." Ed.D. dissertation, Rutgers University, 1959.

Daniels, W. A. "Schools." In *Negro Problems in Cities*. Thomas Woofter, ed. New York: Negro Universities Press, 1928.

Dann, Martin E., ed. *The Black Press, 1827–1890: The Quest for National Identity*. New York: G. P. Putnam's Sons, 1971.

David, George. *Social Effect of School Segregation in Xenia, Ohio*. Wilberforce, Ohio: Combined Normal and Industrial Dept., Wilberforce University, 1932.

Days, Drew S., III. "*Brown* Blues: Rethinking the Integrative Ideal." *William and Mary Law Review* 34 (Fall 1992): 53–74.

Delaney, David. *Race, Place, and the Law, 1836–1948*. Austin: University of Texas Press, 1998.

Delgado, Richard and Jean Stefancic. *Failed Revolutions: Social Reform and the Limits of Legal Imagination*. Boulder: Westview Press, 1994.

Delton, Jennifer Alice. "Forging of a Northern Strategy: Civil Rights in Liberal Democratic Politics, 1940–1948." Ph.D. dissertation, Princeton University, 1997.

Department of the Interior, Bureau of Education. *Negro Education: A Study of the Private and Higher Schools for Colored People in the United States*, Vol. 2. Washington, DC: Government Printing Office, 1917.

De Santis, Christopher C. *Langston Hughes and the* Chicago Defender: *Essays on Race, Politics, and Culture, 1942–62*. Urbana: University of Illinois Press, 1995.

De Tocqueville, Alexis. *Democracy in America*. J. P. Mayer, ed. Garden City, NY: Anchor Books, 1969.

Devore, Wynetta. "The Education of Blacks in New Jersey, 1900–1930: An Exploration in Oral History." Ed.D. dissertation, Rutgers University, 1980.

Dickerson, G. Edward and William Lloyd James. "'The Cheyney Training School.'" *The Crisis* 25 (May 1923): 18–21.

Diner, Steven J. *A Very Different Age: Americans of the Progressive Era*. New York: Hill and Wang, 1998.

Dolson, Lee Stephen, Jr. "The Administration of the San Francisco Public Schools, 1847 to 1947." Ph.D. dissertation, University of California, Berkeley, 1964.

Douglas, Davison M., ed. *The Development of School Busing as a Desegregation Remedy*. New York: Garland Publishing, Inc., 1994.

"The End of Busing?" *Michigan Law Review* 95 (May 1997): 1715–35.

Douglass, Frederick. *Life and Times of Frederick Douglass Written by Himself*. New York: Macmillan Publishing Company, 1892, 1962.

Du Bois, W. E. B. "Does the Negro Need Separate Schools?" *Journal of Negro Education* 4 (1935): 328–35.

"Editorial – Close Ranks." *The Crisis* 16 (July 1918): 111.

"Editorial – Education." *The Crisis* 24 (Oct. 1922): 252.

"Editorial – Reconstruction." *The Crisis* 18 (July 1919): 130–1.

"Editorial – Resolutions of the Washington Conference." *The Crisis* 14 (June 1917): 59.

"Editorial – Segregation." *The Crisis* 1 (Nov. 1910): 10–11.

"The Immediate Program of the American Negro." *The Crisis* 9 (Apr. 1915): 310–12.

"Literacy Tests in the Army." *The Crisis* 18 (June 1918): 86.

"The Negro and the Northern Public Schools [Part I]." *The Crisis* 25 (Mar. 1923): 205–8.

"The Negro and the Northern Public Schools [Part II]." *The Crisis* 25 (Apr. 1923): 262–5.

The Philadelphia Negro: A Social Study. Philadelphia: University of Pennsylvania Press, 1899.

"Postscript." *The Crisis* 41 (Jan. 1934): 20.

"Postscript." *The Crisis* 41 (Feb. 1934): 52–3.

"Postscript." *The Crisis* 41 (Mar. 1934): 85–6.

"Postscript." *The Crisis* 41 (Apr. 1934): 115–17.

"Postscript." *The Crisis* 41 (May 1934): 147–9.

"Postscript – Pechstein and Pecksniff." *The Crisis* 36 (Sept. 1929): 313–14.

"The Tragedy of 'Jim Crow.'" *The Crisis* 26 (Aug. 1923): 169–72.

"William Monroe Trotter." *The Crisis* 41 (May 1934): 134.

Dudziak, Mary L. *Cold War Civil Rights: Race and the Image of American Democracy*. Princeton: Princeton University Press, 2000.

Duncan, Hannibal G. "The Changing Race Relationship in the Border and Northern States." Ph.D. dissertation, University of Pennsylvania, 1922.

Dunne, Matthew William. "Next Steps: Charles S. Johnson and Southern Liberalism." *Journal of Negro History* 83 (Winter 1998): 1–34.

Dykstra, Robert R. "Iowa: 'Bright Radical Star.'" In *Radical Republicans in the North: State Politics During Reconstruction*. James C. Mohr, ed. Baltimore: Johns Hopkins University Press, 1976.

Earhart, Amy E. "Boston's 'Un-Common' Common: Race, Reform, and Education, 1800–1865." Ph.D. dissertation, Texas A&M University, 1999.

Epstein, Richard A. *Forbidden Grounds: The Case against Employment Discrimination Laws*. Cambridge: Harvard University Press, 1992.

Erickson, Leonard. "The Color Line in Ohio Public Schools, 1829–1890." Ph.D. dissertation, Ohio State University, 1959.

"Toledo Desegregates, 1871." *Northwest Ohio Quarterly* 41 (Winter 1968–9): 5–12.

Erskine, Hazel Gaudet. "The Polls: Race Relations." *Public Opinion Quarterly* 26 (Spring 1962): 137–48.

Evans, Frank B. *Pennsylvania Politics, 1827–1877: A Study of Political Leadership.* Harrisburg: Pennsylvania Historical and Museum Commission, 1966.

Fairclough, Adam. *Better Day Coming: Blacks and Equality 1890–2000.* New York: Viking, 2001.

　Teaching Equality: Black Schools in the Age of Jim Crow. Athens: University of Georgia Press, 2001.

Farrar, Hayward. *The Baltimore Afro-American, 1892–1950.* Westport, CT: Greenwood Press, 1998.

Feinberg, Walter. *Reason and Rhetoric: The Intellectual Foundations of Twentieth Century Liberal Educational Policy.* New York: John Wiley & Sons, Inc., 1975.

Ferrell, Robert, ed. *Dear Bess: The Letters from Harry to Bess Truman, 1910–1959.* New York: W. W. Norton, 1983.

Finkelman, Paul. "Prelude to the Fourteenth Amendment: Black Legal Rights in the Antebellum North." *Rutgers Law Journal* 17 (1986): 415–82.

Finkle, Lee. *Forum for Protest: The Black Press During World War II.* Rutherford, NJ: Fairleigh Dickinson University Press, 1975.

Fishel, Leslie H., Jr. "The Negro in the New Deal Era." In *The Negro in Depression and War: Prelude to Revolution, 1930–1945.* Bernard Sternsher, ed. Chicago: Quadrangle Books,1969.

　"The North and the Negro, 1865–1900: A Study in Race Discrimination." Ph.D. dissertation, Harvard University, 1953.

Foner, Eric. *Free Soil, Free Labor, Free Men: The Ideology of the Republican Party Before the Civil War.* New York: Oxford University Press, 1970.

Foster, Paul Nathan. " 'Which September?' Segregation. Busing and Resegregation in the Columbus Public Schools." B.A. thesis, Harvard University, 1997.

Frank, John P. "Can the Courts Erase the Color Line?" *Journal of Negro Education* 21 (Summer 1952): 304–16.

Franklin, John Hope. *From Slavery to Freedom: A History of Negro Americans*, 3d ed. New York: Alfred A. Knopf, 1967.

Franklin, Vincent P. *The Education of Black Philadelphia: The Social and Educational History of a Minority Community, 1900–1950.* Philadelphia: University of Pennsylvania Press, 1979.

　"The Persistence of School Segregation in the Urban North: An Historic Perspective." *Journal of Ethnic Studies* 1 (Winter 1974): 51–68.

Frazier, E. Franklin. "The American Negro's New Leaders." *Current History* 28 (Apr. 1928): 56–9.

　The Negro in the United States. New York: Macmillan Company, 1949.

Fredrickson, George M. *The Black Image in the White Mind: The Debate on Afro-American Character and Destiny, 1817–1914.* New York: Harper & Row, 1971.

Fultz, Guy Michael. " 'Agitate Then, Brother': Education in the Black Monthly Periodical Press, 1900–1930." Ph.D. dissertation, Harvard University, 1987.

Gaines, Abner J. "New Jersey and the Fourteenth Amendment." *Proceedings of the New Jersey Historical Society* 70 (1952): 37–55.

Gaines, Kevin K. *Uplifting the Race: Black Leadership, Politics, and Culture in the Twentieth Century*. Chapel Hill: University of North Carolina Press, 1996.

Gerber, David A. *Black Ohio and the Color Line, 1860–1915*. Urbana: University of Illinois Press, 1976.

"Education, Expediency, and Ideology: Race and Politics in the Desegregation of Ohio Public Schools in the Late 19th Century." *Journal of Ethnic Studies* 1 (Fall 1973): 1–31.

"A Politics of Limited Options: Northern Black Politics and the Problem of Change and Continuity in Race Relations Historiography." *Journal of Social History* 14 (1980): 235–55.

Glasco, Laurence. "Double Burden: The Black Experience in Pittsburgh." In *City at the Point: Essays on the Social History of Pittsburgh*. Samuel P. Hays, ed. Pittsburgh: University of Pittsburgh Press, 1989.

Glaude, Eddie S., Jr. *Exodus!: Religion, Race, and Nation in Early Nineteenth-Century Black America*. Chicago: University of Chicago Press, 2000.

Glenn, Charles Leslie, Jr. *The Myth of the Common School*. Amherst: University of Massachusetts Press, 1988.

Goliber, Thomas J. "Cuyahoga Blacks: A Social and Demographic Study, 1850–1880." M.A. thesis, Kent State University, 1972.

Goodman, Paul. *Of One Blood: Abolitionism and the Origins of Racial Equality*. Berkeley: University of California Press, 1998.

Granger, Lester B. "Race Relations and the School System: A Study of Negro High School Attendance in New Jersey." *Opportunity* 3 (Nov. 1925): 327–9.

Green, William D. " 'Critical Mass Is Fifteen Colored's!' De Facto and De Jure Policies of Racial Isolation in St. Paul's Schools and Housing Patterns During the 19th Century, and Beyond." *Journal of Public Law and Policy* 17 (1996): 299–321.

"Race and Segregation in St. Paul's Public Schools, 1846–60." *Minnesota History* 51 (Winter 1996–7): 139–49.

Greenberg, Jack. *Crusaders in the Courts: How a Dedicated Band of Lawyers Fought for the Civil Rights Revolution*. New York: Basic Books, 1994.

Greenwood, Philip. "How History Was Made in the State of New Jersey." *The Crisis* 57 (May 1950): 277–81, 334–5.

Grimke, Francis J. "Segregation." *The Crisis* 41 (June 1934): 173–4.

Grimsted, David. *American Mobbing, 1828–1861: Toward Civil War*. New York: Oxford University Press, 1998.

Grossman, James R. "Blowing the Trumpet: The *Chicago Defender* and Black Migration During World War I." *Illinois Historical Journal* 78 (1985): 82–96.

Land of Hope: Chicago. Black Southerners and the Great Migration. Chicago: University of Chicago Press, 1989.

Grossman, Lawrence. *The Democratic Party and the Negro: Northern and National Politics. 1868–92*. Urbana: University of Illinois Press, 1976.

Hamblin, Thomas Dean. "Drive the Last Nail: John M. Palmer and the Blacks in Illinois and Kentucky." M.A. thesis, Southern Illinois University, 1976.

Hardy, Charles Ashley, III. "Race and Opportunity: Black Philadelphia During the Era of the Great Migration, 1916–1930." Ph.D. dissertation, Temple University, 1989.

Harney, Julia C. "The Evolution of Public Education in Jersey City." Ph.D. dissertation, New York University, 1931.

Harshman, Ralph Garling. "Race Contact in Columbus, Ohio." M.A. thesis, Ohio State University, 1921.

Hatfield, Eugene A. "The Impact of the New Deal on Black Politics in Pennsylvania 1928–1936." Ph.D. dissertation, University of North Carolina at Chapel Hill, 1979.

Heller, Herbert Lynn. "Negro Education in Indiana from 1816 to 1869." Ed.D. dissertation, Indiana University, 1951.

Helper, Rose. *Racial Policies and Practices of Real Estate Brokers*. Minneapolis: University of Minnesota Press, 1969.

Hendrick, Irving G. *The Education of Non-Whites in California, 1849–1970*. San Francisco: R & E Research Associates, Inc., 1977.

Henri, Florette. *Black Migration: Movement North, 1900–1920*. Garden City, NY: Anchor Press/Doubleday, 1975.

Hill, Leslie Pinckney. "The Cheyney Training School for Teachers." *The Crisis* 25 (Apr. 1923): 252–4.

Hine, Darlene Clark. "Black Migration to the Urban Midwest: The Gender Dimension. 1915–1945." In *The New African American Urban History*. Kenneth W. Goings and Raymond A. Mohl, eds. Thousand Oaks, CA: Sage Publications, 1996.

Hoffman, Frederick L. *Race Traits and Tendencies of the American Negro*. New York: Macmillan Company, 1896.

Homel, Michael W. *Down from Equality: Black Chicagoans and the Public Schools, 1920–41*. Urbana: University of Illinois Press, 1984.

"The Politics of Public Education in Black Chicago, 1910–1941." *Journal of Negro Education* 45 (Spring 1976): 179–91.

"Two Worlds of Race? Urban Blacks and the Public Schools, North and South, 1865–1940." In *Southern Cities, Southern Schools: Public Education in the Urban South*. David N. Plank and Rick Ginsberg, eds. New York: Greenwood Press, 1990.

Hopkins. Leroy T. "Door to Opportunity: Public Education for African Americans in Lancaster City, 1800–1895." *Journal of the Lancaster County Historical Society* 103 (Fall 2001): 126–52.

Horton, James and Lois Horton. *In Hope of Liberty: Culture, Community and Protest Among Northern Free Blacks, 1700–1860*. New York: Oxford University Press, 1997.

Hubbard, Maceo W. and Raymond Pace Alexander. "Types of Potentially Favorable Court Cases Relative to the Separate School." *Journal of Negro Education* 14 (July 1935): 375–405.

Hurt, R. Douglas. *The Ohio Frontier: Crucible of the Old Northwest, 1720–1830*. Bloomington: Indiana University Press, 1996.

Hyman, Herbert H. and Paul B. Sheatsley. "Attitudes Toward Desegregation." *Scientific American* 195 (Dec. 1956): 35–9.

Jackson, Reid. "The Development and Character of Permissive and Partly Segregated Schools." *Journal of Negro Education* 16 (1947): 301–10.

Jackson, Walter. *Gunnar Myrdal and America's Conscience*. Chapel Hill: University of North Carolina Press, 1990.

Jacobson, Matthew Frye. *Whiteness of a Different Color: European Immigrants and the Alchemy of Race*. Cambridge: Harvard University Press, 1999.

Janken, Kenneth Robert. *Rayford W. Logan and the Dilemma of the African-American Intellectual*. Amherst: University of Massachusetts Press, 1993.

Jensen, Noma. "Current Trends and Events of National Importance: A Survey of Segregation Practices in the New Jersey School System." *Journal of Negro Education* 17 (Winter 1948): 84–8.

Johnson, Alex. "Bid Whist, Tonk, and *United States v. Fordice*: Why Integrationism Fails African-Americans Again." *California Law Review* 81 (1993): 1401–70.

Johnson, Charles S. *Background to Patterns of Negro Segregation*. New York: Harper & Brothers, 1943.

    "Mental Measurements of Negro Groups." *Opportunity* 1 (Feb. 1923): 21–5.

    The Negro in American Civilization: A Study of Negro Life and Race Relations in the Light of Social Research. New York: Henry Holt and Company, 1930.

Johnson, Franklin. *The Development of State Legislation Concerning the Free Negro*. Westport, CT: Greenwood Press, 1919, 1979.

Johnson, James Weldon. *Negro Americans, What Now?* New York: Viking Press, 1934.

Johnson, Michael P. "Out of Egypt: The Migration of Former Slaves to the Midwest During the 1860s in Comparative Perspective." In *Crossing Boundaries: Comparative History of Black People in Diaspora*. Darlene Clark Hine and Jacqueline McLeod, eds. Bloomington: Indiana University Press, 1999.

Jorgenson, Lloyd P. *The Founding of Public Education in Wisconsin*. Madison: State Historical Society of Wisconsin, 1956.

Kaestle, Carl F. *Pillars of the Republic: Common Schools and American Society, 1780–1860*. New York: Hill and Wang, 1983.

Kantor, Harvey and Barbara Brenzel. "Urban Education and the 'Truly Disadvantaged': The Historical Roots of Contemporary Crisis." In *The "Underclass" Debate: Views from History*. Michael B. Katz, ed. Princeton: Princeton University Press, 1993.

Katzman, David M. *Before the Ghetto: Black Detroit in the Nineteenth Century*. Urbana: University of Illinois Press, 1973.

Katznelson, Ira and Margaret Weir. *Schooling for All: Class, Race, and the Decline of the Democratic Ideal*. New York: Basic Books, 1985.

Kellogg, Charles Flint. *NAACP: A History of the National Association for the Advancement of Colored People, Volume I, 1909–1920*. Baltimore: Johns Hopkins University Press, 1967.

Kendrick, Stephen and Paul Kendrick. *Sarah's Long Walk: The Free Blacks of Boston and How Their Struggle for Equality Changed America*. Boston: Beacon Press, 2004.

Kennedy, Louise Venable. *The Negro Peasant Turns Cityward: Effects of Recent Migrations to Northern Centers*. New York: Columbia University Press, 1930.

Kessen, Thomas Paul. "Segregation in Cincinnati Public Education: The Nineteenth Century Black Experience." Ed.D dissertation, University of Cincinnati, 1973.

King, Desmond. *Separate and Unequal: Black Americans and the U.S. Federal Government*. New York: Oxford University Press, 1995.

Kirby, John B. *Black Americans in the Roosevelt Era: Liberalism and Race*. Knoxville: University of Tennessee Press, 1980.

Kirp, David L. *Just Schools: The Idea of Racial Equality in American Education*. Berkeley: University of California Press, 1982.

Klarman, Michael J. "*Brown*, Racial Change, and the Civil Rights Movement." *Virginia Law Review* 80 (Feb. 1994): 7–150.

    From Jim Crow to Civil Rights: The Supreme Court and the Struggle for Racial Equality. New York: Oxford University Press, 2004.

Kliebard, Herbert M. *Schooled to Work: Vocationalism and the American Curriculum, 1876–1946*. New York: Teachers College Press, 1999.

Klineberg, Otto. *Race Differences*. New York: Harper & Brothers Publishers, 1935.

    "The Question of Negro Intelligence." *Opportunity* 9 (Dec. 1931): 361–7.

Klinkner, Philip A. and Rogers M. Smith. *The Unsteady March: The Rise and Decline of Racial Equality in America*. Chicago: University of Chicago Press, 1999.

Kluger, Richard. *Simple Justice: The History of* Brown v. Board of Education *and Black America's Struggle for Equality*. New York: Alfred A. Knopf, 1976.

Konvitz, Milton R. *The Constitution and Civil Rights*. New York: Octagon Books, 1946, 1977.

Kornbluh, Andrea Tuttle. "James Hathaway Robinson and the Origins of Professional Social Work in the Black Community." In *Race and the City: Work, Community, and Protest in Cincinnati, 1820–1970*. Henry Louis Taylor, Jr., ed. Urbana: University of Illinois Press, 1993.

Kousser, J. Morgan. "Before *Plessy*, Before *Brown*: The Development of the Law of Racial Integration in Louisiana and Kansas." *In Toward a Usable Past: Liberty Under State Constitutions*. Paul Finkelman and Stephen E. Gotllieb, eds. Athens: University of Georgia Press, 1991.

    Dead End: The Development of Nineteenth-Century Litigation on Racial Discrimination in the Schools. Oxford: Clarendon Press, 1986.

    "'The Onward March of Right Principles': State Legislative Actions on Racial Discrimination in Schools in Nineteenth-Century America." *Historical Methods* 35 (Fall 2002): 177–204.

Kryder, Daniel. *Divided Arsenal: Race and the American State During World War II*. New York: Cambridge University Press, 2000.

Kull, Andrew. *The Color-Blind Constitution*. Cambridge: Harvard University Press, 1992.

    "A Nineteenth-Century Precursor of *Brown v. Board of Education*: The Trial Court Opinion in the Kansas School Segregation Case of 1881." *Chicago-Kent Law Review* 69 (1993): 1199–1206.

Kusmer, Kenneth L. *A Ghetto Takes Shape: Black Cleveland, 1870–1930*. Urbana: University of Illinois Press, 1976.

"The Black Urban Experience in American History." In *The State of Afro-American History: Past, Present, and Future.* Darlene Clark Hine, ed. Baton Rouge: Louisiana State University Press, 1986.

Lane, Roger. *Roots of Violence in Black Philadelphia 1860–1900.* Cambridge: Harvard University Press, 1986.

William Dorsey's Philadelphia and Ours: On the Past and Future of the Black City in America. New York: Oxford University Press, 1991.

Lang, William Louis. "Black Bootstraps: The Abolitionist Educators' Ideology and the Education of the Northern Free Negro, 1828–1860." Ph.D. dissertation, University of Delaware, 1974.

La Plante, Bernard Raymond. "The Negro at Jefferson High School: A Historical Study of Racial Change." Ph.D. dissertation, University of Oregon, 1970.

Lawson, Steven F. *Running for Freedom: Civil Rights and Black Politics in America Since 1941.* Philadelphia: Temple University Press, 1991.

Origins of the Urban School: Public Education in Massachusetts, 1870–1915. Cambridge: Harvard University Press, 1971.

Leavell, R. H. "What Does the Negro Want? The Answer of the Douglass Public School." *Outlook* 29 (Aug. 20, 1919): 604–6.

Leigh, Patricia Randolph. "Segregation by Gerrymander: The Creation of the Lincoln Heights (Ohio) School District." *Journal of Negro Education* 66 (1997): 121–36.

Leskes, Theodore. "State Law Against Discrimination." In *A Century of Civil Rights.* Milton R. Konvitz, ed. New York: Columbia University Press, 1961.

Lewis, David Levering. "The Origins and Causes of the Civil Rights Movement." In *The Civil Rights Movement in America.* Charles W. Eagles, ed. Jackson: University Press of Mississippi, 1986.

W. E. B. Du Bois: The Fight for Equality and the American Century, 1919–1963. New York: Henry Holt, 2000.

Licht, Walter. *Getting Work: Philadelphia, 1840–1950.* Cambridge: Harvard University Press, 1992.

Lieberson, Stanley. *A Piece of the Pie: Blacks and White Immigrants Since 1880.* Berkeley: University of California Press, 1980.

Lipsitz, George. *The Possessive Investment in Whiteness: How White People Profit from Identity Politics.* Philadelphia: Temple University Press, 1998.

Litwack, Leon F. *North of Slavery: The Negro in the Free States, 1790–1860.* Chicago: University of Chicago Press, 1961.

Lockard, Duane. *Toward Equal Opportunity: A Study of State and Local Antidiscrimination Laws.* New York: Macmillan Company, 1968.

Lofgren, Charles A. *The Plessy Case: A Legal-Historical Interpretation.* New York: Oxford University Press, 1987.

Logan, Rayford W., ed. *What the Negro Wants.* Chapel Hill: University of North Carolina Press, 1944.

Long, Howard H. "Race and Mental Tests." *Opportunity* 1 (Mar. 1923): 22–8.

Loth, David Goldsmith and Harold C. Fleming. *Integration North and South: Progress Memorandum.* New York: Fund for the Republic, 1956.

Mabee, Carleton. *Black Education in New York State: From Colonial to Modern Times.* Syracuse, NY: Syracuse University Press, 1979.

Malcolm X. *The Autobiography of Malcolm X*. New York: Grove Press, 1965.

Mangum, Charles S., Jr. *The Legal Status of the Negro*. Chapel Hill: University of North Carolina Press, 1940.

Marks, Carole. *Farewell – We're Good and Gone: The Great Black Migration*. Bloomington: Indiana University Press, 1989.

Mason, Mame Charlotte. "The Policy of Segregation of the Negro in the Public Schools of Ohio, Indiana, and Illinois." M.A. thesis, University of Chicago, 1917.

Massey, Douglas S. and Nancy A. Denton. *American Apartheid: Segregation and the Making of the Underclass*. Cambridge: Harvard University Press, 1993.

Mayo, Amory. "Education in the Northwest During the First Half Century of the Republic, 1790–1840." In *Report of the Commissioner of Education*. Washington, DC: U.S. Government Printing Office, 1896.

McAdam, Doug. *Political Process and the Development of Black Insurgency, 1930–1970*, 2d ed. Chicago: University of Chicago Press, 1999.

McAfee, Ward M. *Religion, Race, and Reconstruction: The Public School in the Politics of the 1870s*. Albany: State University of New York Press, 1998.

McCaul, Robert L. *The Black Struggle for Public Schooling in Nineteenth-Century Illinois*. Carbondale: Southern Illinois University Press, 1987.

McElderry, Stuart John. "The Problem of the Color Line: Civil Rights and Racial Ideology in Portland, Oregon, 1944–1965." Ph.D. dissertation, University of Oregon, 1998.

McGinnis, Frederick Alphonso. *The Education of Negroes in Ohio*. Blancester, OH: Curless Printing Company, 1962.

McLagan, Elizabeth. *A Peculiar Paradise: A History of Blacks in Oregon, 1788–1940*. Portland, OR: Georgian Press Company, 1980.

McPherson, James M. "Abolitionists and the Civil Rights Act of 1875." *Journal of American History* 52 (Dec. 1965): 493–510.

Meier, August. "The Emergence of Negro Nationalism (A Study in Ideologies). Part I." *The Midwest Journal* 4 (Winter 1951–2): 96–104.

"The Emergence of Negro Nationalism (A Study in Ideologies). Part II." *The Midwest Journal* 4 (Summer 1952): 95–111.

Meier, August and Elliott Rudwick. *Along the Color Line: Explorations in the Black Experience* Urbana: University of Illinois Press, 1976.

"Early Boycotts of Segregated Schools: The Alton, Illinois, Case, 1897–1908." *Journal of Negro Education* 36 (1967): 394–402.

"Early Boycotts of Segregated Schools: The Case of Springfield, Ohio, 1922–23." *American Quarterly* 20 (Winter 1968): 744–58.

"Early Boycotts of Segregated Schools: The East Orange, New Jersey, Experience, 1899–1906." *History of Education Quarterly* 7 (Spring 1967): 22–35.

From Plantation to Ghetto, 2d ed. New York: Hill and Wang, 1966.

"Negro Boycotts of Jim Crow Schools in the North, 1897–1925." *Integrated Education* 5 (Aug.–Sept. 1967): 57–64.

"Negro Protest at the Chicago World's Fair, 1933–1934." In *The Negro in Depression and War: Prelude to Revolution, 1930–1945*. Bernard Sternsher, ed. Chicago: Quadrangle Books, 1969.

Meister, Richard Julius. "A History of Gary, Indiana: 1930–1940." Ph.D. dissertation, University of Notre Dame, 1967.

Mendelberg, Tali: *The Race Card: Campaign Strategy, Implicit Messages, and the Norm of Equality.* Princeton: Princeton University Press, 2001.

Ment, David Martin. "Racial Segregation in the Public Schools of New England and New York, 1840–1940." Ph.D. dissertation, Columbia University, 1975.

Meyer, Stephen Grant. *As Long as They Don't Move Next Door: Segregation and Racial Conflict in American Neighborhoods.* Lanham, MD: Rowman & Littlefield Publishers, Inc., 2000.

Middleton, Stephen, ed. *The Black Laws in the Old Northwest: A Documentary History.* Westport, CT: Greenwood Press, 1993.

Mims, Edwin. *The Advancing South: Stories of Progress and Reaction.* Garden City, NY: Doubleday, Page & Co., 1926.

Millender, Dharathula H. *Yesterday in Gary: A Brief History of the Negro in Gary.* Gary, IN: D. Millender, 1967.

Miller, Fredric. "The Black Migration to Philadelphia: A 1924 Profile." *Pennsylvania Magazine of History and Biography* 108 (1984): 315–50.

Miller, Kelly. "Is the Color Line Crumbling?" *Opportunity* 7 (Sept. 1929): 284.

Ming, William R., Jr. "The Elimination of Segregation in the Public Schools of the North and West." *Journal of Negro Education* 21 (Summer 1952): 265–75.

Minor, Richard Clyde. "The Negro in Columbus, Ohio." Ph.D. dissertation, Ohio State University, 1936.

Mirel, Jeffrey. *The Rise and Fall of an Urban School System: Detroit, 1907–81.* Ann Arbor: University of Michigan Press, 1999.

Mjagkij, Nina. "Behind the Scenes: The Cincinnati Urban League." In *Race and the City: Work, Community and Protest in Cincinnati, 1820–1970.* Henry Louis Taylor, ed. Urbana: University of Illinois Press, 1993.

Mohl, Raymond A. and Neil Betten. *Steel City: Urban and Ethnic Patterns in Gary, Indiana, 1906–1950.* New York: Holmes & Meier, 1986.

Mohr, James C. "New York: The De-Politicization of Reform." In *Radical Republicans in the North: State Politics During Reconstruction.* James C. Mohr, ed. Baltimore: Johns Hopkins University Press, 1976.

Mohraz, Judy Jolley. *The Separate Problem: Case Studies of Black Education in the North, 1900–1930.* Westport, CT: Greenwood Press, 1979.

Moon, Henry Lee. *Balance of Power: The Negro Vote.* Garden City, NY: Doubleday & Company, Inc., 1949.

"What Chance for Civil Rights?" *The Crisis* 56 (Feb. 1949): 42–4.

Moore, Clifford R. "Full Citizenship in New Jersey." *The Crisis* 56 (Oct. 1949): 272–3, 284.

Moore, Jacqueline M. *Leading the Race: The Transformation of the Black Elite in the Nation's Capital, 1880–1920.* Charlottesville: University Press of Virginia, 1999.

Moore, Leonard Nathaniel. "The Limits of Black Power: Carl B. Stokes and Cleveland's African-American Community." Ph.D. dissertation, Ohio State University, 1998.

Morris, Thomas D. *Free Men All: The Personal Liberty Laws of the North 1780–1861.* Union, NJ: The Lawbook Exchange, Ltd., 2001.

Morrow, E. Frederic. *Way Down South Up North*. Philadelphia: United Church Press, 1973.

Morse, George Chester. "New Jersey, New Laboratory in Race Relations." *Negro History Bulletin* 13 (1949–50): 156–63.

Mosey, Gerard Joseph. "Testing, Tracking, and Curriculum: The Isolation of Black Students in the Buffalo Public Schools from 1917 to 1956." Ed.D. dissertation, University of New York at Buffalo, 1998.

Moton, Robert R. *What the Negro Thinks*. Garden City, NY: Doubleday, Doran and Company, Inc., 1929.

Mumford, Kevin. "Double V in New Jersey: African American Civic Culture and Rising Consciousness against Jim Crow, 1938–1966." *New Jersey History* 119 (Fall–Winter 2001): 22–56.

Murray, Pauli. *Song in a Weary Throat: An American Pilgrimage*. New York: Harper & Row, 1987.

— ed. *States' Laws on Race and Color*, 2d ed. Athens: University of Georgia Press, 1997.

Myrdal, Gunnar, with Richard Sterner and Arnold Rose. *An American Dilemma: The Negro Problem and Modern Democracy*. New York: Harper & Row, Publishers, 1962.

Neier, Aryeh. *Only Judgment: The Limits of Litigation in Social Change*. Middletown, CT: Wesleyan University Press, 1982.

New Jersey Conference of Social Work, Interracial Committee. *The Negro in New Jersey*. New York: Negro Universities Press, 1932, 1969.

Niebuhr, Reinhold. "Race Prejudice in the North." *The Christian Century* 44 (May 12, 1927): 583–4.

Oak, Eleanor Hill. "The Development of Separate Education in the State of New Jersey." M.A. thesis, Howard University, 1936.

Oak, Eleanor H. and Vishnu V. Oak. "The Development of Separate Education in New Jersey." *Education* 59 (Oct. 1938): 109–12.

— "The Illegal Status of Separate Education in New Jersey." *School and Society* 47 (May 21, 1938): 671.

Orfield, Gary. *Public School Desegregation in the United States, 1968–1980*. Washington, DC: Joint Center for Political Studies, 1983.

— *The Reconstruction of Southern Education: The Schools and the 1964 Civil Rights Act*. New York: Wiley Interscience, 1969.

Orfield, Gary and Susan E. Eaton, *Dismantling Desegregation: The Quiet Reversal of Brown v. Board of Education*. New York: New Press, 1996.

Osofsky, Gilbert. *Harlem: The Making of a Ghetto: Negro New York, 1890–1930*. New York: Harper & Row, 1968.

Owen, Chandler. "Mistakes of Kelly Miller: Reply to Kelly Miller on Segregation in Education." *The Messenger* 4 (June 1922): 422–4.

— "Mistakes of Kelly Miller: Reply to Kelly Miller on Segregation in Education." *The Messenger* 4 (July 1922): 443–5.

Parillo, John J. "Images of Blacks, Native Americans, and Women in Textbooks Authored by Yankee Educators of Southern New England During the Age of Reform: 1830–1860." Ph.D. dissertation, University of Connecticut, 1996.

Parks, Gordon. *Voices in the Mirror: An Autobiography*. New York: Doubleday, 1990.

Partridge, G. E. *Genetic Philosophy of Education: An Epitome of the Published Educational Writings of President G. Stanley Hall*. New York: Sturgis & Walton Co., 1912.

Payne, E. George. "Negroes in the Public Elementary Schools of the North." *Annals of the American Academy of Political and Social Science* 140 (Nov. 1928): 224–33.

Pease, Jane H. and William H. Pease. *They Who Would Be Free: Blacks' Search for Freedom, 1830–1861*. New York: Atheneum, 1974.

Pechstein, L. A. "The Problem of Negro Education in Northern and Border Cities." *Elementary School Journal* 30 (Nov. 1929): 192–9.

Pennsylvania Department of Public Welfare. "Negro Survey of Pennsylvania." 1927.

Pennsylvania Human Relations Commission. "The Chester Case." *Integrated Education* 13 (1965): 15, 17–18.

Perkins, Samuel. *The World as It Is: Containing a View of the Present Condition of Its Principal Nations*. New Haven: T. Belknap, 1836.

Perkinson, Henry J. *The Imperfect Panacea: American Faith in Education*. New York: McGraw-Hill, Inc., 1991.

Perlmann, Joel. *Ethnic Differences: Schooling and Social Structure Among the Irish, Italians, Jews, and Blacks in an American City, 1880–1935*. Cambridge: Cambridge University Press, 1988.

Perry, Earnest L., Jr. "A Common Purpose: The Negro Newspaper Publishers Association's Fight for Equality During World War II." *American Journalism* 19 (Spring 2002): 31–43.

Pesin, Meyer. "Summary, Analysis and Comment on 'Anti-Discrimination' or 'Fair Employment Practices' Legislation of New Jersey." *New Jersey Law Journal* 68 (June 28, 1945): 1–5.

Pettigrew, Thomas F. *Negro American Intelligence*. New York: Anti-Defamation League of B'nai B'rith, 1964.

Phillips, Kimberley L. *AlabamaNorth: African-American Migrants, Community, and Working-Class Activism in Cleveland, 1915–45*. Urbana: University of Illinois Press, 1999.

Pierce, Bessie Louise. *Civic Attitudes in American School Textbooks*. Chicago: University of Chicago Press, 1930.

Porter, Jennie D. "The Problem of Negro Education in Northern and Border Cities." Ed.D. dissertation, University of Cincinnati, 1928.

Portwood, Shirley J. "The Alton School Case and African American Community Consciousness, 1897–1908." *Illinois Historical Journal* 91 (Spring 1998): 2–20.

Powell, Adam Clayton. *Marching Blacks*. New York: Dial Press, 1973.

Price, Clement Alexander, ed. *Freedom Not Far Distant: A Documentary History of Afro-Americans in New Jersey*. Newark: The New Jersey Historical Society, 1980.

"The Strange Career of Race Relations in New Jersey History." In *The Black Experience in Southern New Jersey*. David C. Munn, ed. Camden, NJ: Camden Historical Society, 1985.

"We Knew Our Place, We Knew Our Way: Lessons from the Black Past of Southern New Jersey." In *Blacks in New Jersey 1986 Report: A Review of Blacks in South Jersey*. Bruce Ransom, ed. New Jersey: New Jersey Public Policy Research Institute, 1986.

Price, J. St. Clair. "Current Literature on Negro Education." *Journal of Negro Education* 3 (Apr. 1934): 269–73.

Priest, Diana H. "A Historical Study of the Royal Elementary School." Ph.D. dissertation, University of Akron, 1993.

Proctor, Ralph. "Racial Discrimination against Black Teachers and Black Professionals in the Pittsburgh Public School System 1834–1973." Ph.D. dissertation, University of Pittsburgh, 1979.

Prosser, Inez B. "Non-Academic Development of Negro Children in Mixed and Segregated Schools." Ed.D. dissertation, University of Cincinnati, 1933.

Quillin, Frank U. *The Color Line in Ohio: A History of Race Prejudice in a Typical Northern State*. Ann Arbor, MI: George Wahr, 1913.

Rael, Patrick Joseph. "The Lion's Painting: African-American Thought in the Antebellum North." Ph.D. dissertation, University of California at Berkeley, 1995.

Ratner, Lorman. *Powder Keg: Northern Opposition to the Antislavery Movement 1831–1840*. New York: Basic Books, 1968.

Reams, Bernard D., Jr., and Paul E. Wilson, eds. *Segregation and the Fourteenth Amendment in the States: A Survey of State Segregation Laws 1865–1953: Prepared for United States Supreme Court in re* Brown v. Board of Education of Topeka. Buffalo, NY: William S. Hein & Co., Inc., 1975.

Reddick, Lawrence D. "The Education of Negroes in States Where Separate Schools Are Not Legal." *Journal of Negro Education* 16 (Summer 1947): 290–300.

Reed, Adolph L., Jr. *W. E. B. Du Bois and American Political Thought: Fabianism and the Color Line*. New York: Oxford University Press, 1997.

Reid, Ira De A. *Social Conditions of the Negro in the Hill District of Pittsburgh*. Pittsburgh: General Committee on the Hill Survey, 1930.

Reid, John B. "Race, Class, Gender and the Teaching Profession: African-American School Teachers of the Urban Midwest, 1865–1950." Ph.D. dissertation, Michigan State University, 1996.

Report of the New Jersey State Temporary Commission on the Condition of the Urban Colored Population to the Legislature of the State of New Jersey. Trenton: Temporary Commission on the Condition of the Urban Colored Population, 1939.

Reuter, Edward Byron. *The American Race Problem: A Study of the Negro*. New York: Thomas Y. Crowell Co., 1927.

Reynolds, Maureen Anne. "Politics and Indiana's Public Schools During the Civil War Era, 1850–1875." Ph.D. dissertation, Indiana University, 1997.

Reynolds, Maureen A. "The Challenge of Racial Equality." In *Hoosier Schools: Past and Present*. William J. Reese, ed. Bloomington: Indiana University Press, 1998.

Ripley, C. Peter, ed. *The Black Abolitionist Papers: The British Isles, 1830–1865*. Vol. I. Chapel Hill: University of North Carolina Press, 1985.

Robeson, Paul. *Here I Stand*. London: Dennis Dobson, 1958.

Robisch, Ann L. "Educational Segregation and Desegregation in Ohio, Especially Cincinnati." M.A. thesis, University of Cincinnati, 1960.

Rosenberg, Gerald N. *The Hollow Hope: Can Courts Bring about Social Change?* Chicago: University of Chicago Press, 1991.

Ross, B. Joyce. *J. E. Spingarn and the Rise of the NAACP, 1911–1939.* New York: Atheneum, 1972.

Rossell, Christine H. "The Convergence of Black and White Attitudes on School Desegregation Issues During the Four Decade Evolution of the Plans." *William and Mary Law Review* 36 (Jan. 1995): 613–63.

Rousmaniere, Kate. *City Teachers: Teaching and School Reform in Historical Perspective.* New York: Teachers College Press, 1997.

Rung, Margaret. *Servants of the State: Managing Diversity in the Federal Workplace, 1933–1953.* Athens: University of Georgia Press, 2002.

Rury, John L. "Race, Space, and the Politics of Chicago's Public Schools: Benjamin Willis and the Tragedy of Urban Education." *History of Education Quarterly* 39 (Summer 1999): 117–42.

Sacks, Marcy S. "'We Rise or Fall Together': Separatism and the Demand for Equality by Albany's Black Citizens, 1827–1860." *Afro-Americans in New York Life and History* 20 (July 1996): 7–33.

Samford, Thomas D. "Anti-Discrimination Policy in New Jersey: A Study in Administration and Application of Anti-Discrimination Policy by the New Jersey Division against Discrimination." Senior thesis, Princeton University, 1955.

Satterthwait, Linton. "The Color-Line in New Jersey." *The Arena* 35 (1906): 394–400.

Savage, Barbara Dianne. *Broadcasting Freedom: Radio, War, and the Politics of Race, 1938–1948.* Chapel Hill: University of North Carolina Press, 1999.

Scates, Douglas. "Cincinnati Colored Teachers Set a Standard." *Journal of Negro Education* 7 (Apr. 1938): 144–6.

Scheingold, Stuart. "Constitutional Rights and Social Change: Civil Rights in Perspective." In *Judging the Constitution: Critical Essays on Judicial Lawmaking.* Michael W. McCann and Gerald L. Houseman, eds. Glenview, IL: Scott, Foresman, 1989.

   The Politics of Rights: Lawyers, Public Policy, and Political Change. New Haven: Yale University Press, 1974.

Schultz, Stanley K. *The Culture Factory: Boston Public Schools, 1789–1860.* New York: Oxford University Press, 1973.

Schuyler, George S. "Do We Really Want Equality?" *The Crisis* 44 (Apr. 1937): 102–3.

Scott, Daryl Michael. *Contempt and Pity: Social Policy and the Image of the Damaged Black Psyche, 1880–1996.* Chapel Hill: University of North Carolina Press, 1997.

Shagaloff, June and Lester P. Bailey, "Cairo – Illinois' Southern Exposure." *The Crisis* 59 (Apr. 1952): 208–13, 262–5.

Silcox, Harry Charles. "A Comparative Study in School Desegregation: The Boston and Philadelphia Experience, 1800–1881." Ed.D. dissertation, Temple University, 1971.

Sitkoff, Harvard. "African American Militancy in the World War II South: Another Perspective." In *Remaking Dixie: The Impact of World War II on the American South*. Neil R. McMillen, ed. Jackson: University Press of Mississippi, 1997.

The Struggle for Black Equality, 1954–1980. New York: Hill and Wang, 1981.

Slevin, Kathleen F. and C. Ray Wingrove. *From Stumbling Blocks to Stepping Stones: The Life Experiences of Fifty Professional African American Women*. New York: New York University Press, 1998.

Smith, Rogers. *Civic Ideals: Conflicting Visions of Citizenship in U.S. History*. New Haven: Yale University Press, 1997.

Smith, Timothy L. "Native Blacks and Foreign Whites: Varying Responses to Educational Opportunity in America, 1880–1950." *Perspectives in American History* 6 (1972): 309–35.

Southern Education Reporting Service. *A Statistical Summary State by State of School Segregation-Desegregation in the Southern and Border Area from 1954 to the Present, 1965–66*. Nashville, TN: Southern Education Reporting Service, 1965.

Spann, Girardeau A. *Race Against the Court: The Supreme Court and Minorities in Contemporary America*. New York: New York University Press, 1993.

Spear, Allan H. *Black Chicago: The Making of a Negro Ghetto, 1890–1920*. Chicago: University of Chicago Press, 1967.

Squibb, John Roy. "Roads to *Plessy*: Blacks and the Law in the Old Northwest: 1860–1896." Ph.D. dissertation, University of Wisconsin, 1992.

Starr, Frederick. "The Degeneracy of the American Negro." *The Dial* 22 (Jan. 1. 1897): 17–18.

Stein, Judith. *The World of Marcus Garvey: Race and Class in Modern Society*. Baton Rouge: Louisiana State University Press, 1986.

Steinberg, Stephen. *Turning Back: The Retreat from Racial Justice in American Thought and Policy*. Boston: Beacon Press, 1995.

Stephenson, Gilbert Thomas. *Race Distinctions in American Law*. New York: AMS Press, 1910, 1969.

Stern, Edith M. "Jim Crow Goes to School in New York." *The Crisis* 44 (July 1937): 101–2.

Strane, Susan. *A Whole-Souled Woman: Prudence Crandall and the Education of Black Women*. New York: W. W. Norton & Co., 1990.

Sugrue, Thomas J. *The Origins of the Urban Crisis: Race and Inequality in Postwar Detroit*. Princeton: Princeton University Press, 1996.

Taylor, Quintard. *In Search of the Racial Frontier: African Americans in the American West 1528–1990*. New York: W. W. Norton & Co., 1998.

The Forging of a Black Community: Seattle's Central District from 1870 through the Civil Rights Era. Seattle: University of Washington Press, 1994.

Terman, Lewis M. *The Measurement of Intelligence: An Explanation of and a Complete Guide for the Use of the Stanford Revision and Extension of the Binet-Simon Intelligence Scale*. Boston: Houghton Mifflin Company, 1916.

Terman, Lewis M., Virgil E. Dickson, A. H. Sutherland, Raymond H. Franzen, C. R. Tupper, and Grace Fernald. *Intelligence Tests and School Reorganization*. Yonkers-on-Hudson, NY: World Book Company, 1923.

Thomas, Richard W. *Life for Us Is What We Make It: Building Black Community in Detroit, 1915–1945*. Bloomington: Indiana University Press, 1992.

Thomas, William B. "Black Intellectuals, Intelligence Testing in the 1930s, and the Sociology of Knowledge." *Teachers College Record* 85 (Spring 1984): 477–501.

"Urban Schooling for Black Migrant Youth: A Historical Perspective, 1915–1925." *Urban Education* 14 (Oct. 1979): 267–84.

Thompson, Charles H. "Court Action the Only Reasonable Alternative to Remedy Immediate Abuses of the Negro Separate School." *Journal of Negro Education* 4 (July 1935): 419–34.

"The Negro Separate School." *The Crisis* 42 (Aug. 1935): 230–1, 242, 247, 252.

"Editorial Comment: The Negro Teacher and Desegregation of the Public Schools." *Journal of Negro Education* 22 (Spring 1953): 95–101.

Thornbrough, Emma Lou. "Breaking Racial Barriers to Public Accommodations in Indiana, 1935 to 1963." *Indiana Magazine of History* 83 (Dec. 1987): 301–43.

The Negro in Indiana: A Study of a Minority. Indianapolis: Indiana Historical Bureau, 1957.

"Segregation in Indiana During the Klan Era of the 1920's." *Mississippi Valley Historical Review* 47 (1961): 594–618.

Thurston, Eve. "Ethiopia Unshackled: A Brief History of the Education of Negro Children in New York City." *Bulletin of the New York Public Library* 69 (Apr. 1965): 211–31.

Tifft, Henry N., Jr. "A Report of the Activities of the Division against Discrimination in New Jersey, 1945–1951." Senior thesis, Princeton University, 1951.

Tipton, James H. *Community in Crisis: The Elimination of Segregation from a Public School System*. New York: Bureau of Publications, Teachers College, Columbia University, 1953.

Trotter, Joe William, Jr. *Black Milwaukee: The Making of an Industrial Proletariat, 1915–45*. Urbana: University of Illinois Press, 1985.

River Jordan: African American Urban Life in the Ohio Valley. Lexington: University Press of Kentucky, 1998.

Turner, Edward Raymond. *The Negro in Pennsylvania: Slavery–Servitude–Freedom, 1639–1861*. Washington, DC: American Historical Association, 1911.

Turner, T. W. "What the Colored Teachers of Baltimore Are Doing for Their Race." *The Colored American Magazine* 13 (July 1907): 33–41.

Tushnet, Mark. "The Critique of Rights." *SMU Law Review* 47 (1993): 23–34.

Making Civil Rights Law: Thurgood Marshall and the Supreme Court. 1936–1961. New York: Oxford University Press, 1994.

The NAACP's Legal Strategy against Segregated Education, 1925–1950. Chapel Hill: University of North Carolina Press, 1987.

Tyack, David B. *The One Best System: A History of American Urban Education*. Cambridge: Harvard University Press, 1974.

and Larry Cuban. *Tinkering Toward Utopia: A Century of Public School Reform*. Cambridge: Harvard University Press, 1995.

and Elisabeth Hansot. *Managers of Virtue: Public School Leadership in America, 1820–1980*. New York: Basic Books, 1982.

Tyack, David, Thomas James, and Aaron Benavot. *Law and the Shaping of Public Education, 1785–1954*. Madison: University of Wisconsin Press, 1986.

United States Department of State. *Compendium of the Enumeration of the Inhabitants and Statistics of the United States*. [1840] Washington, DC: Thomas Allen, 1841.

United States Census. *Statistical View of the United States: Compendium of the Seventh Census*. [1850] Washington, DC: A.O.P. Nicholson, Public Printer, 1854.

United States Bureau of the Census. *Population of the United States in 1860*. Washington, DC: Government Printing Office, 1864.

United States Bureau of the Census. *The Statistics of the Population of the United States*. [1870] Washington, DC: Government Printing Office, 1872.

United States Bureau of the Census. *Statistics of the Population of the United States at the Tenth Census*. [1880] Washington, DC: Government Printing Office, 1883.

United States Bureau of the Census. *Report on Population of the United States at the Eleventh Census: 1890*. Washington, DC: Government Printing Office, 1895.

United States Bureau of the Census. *Twelfth Census of the United States, Taken in the Year 1900*. Washington, DC: United States Census Office, 1901.

United States Bureau of the Census. *Thirteenth Census of the United States: 1910*. Washington, DC: Government Printing Office, 1913.

United States Bureau of the Census. *Fourteenth Census of the United States, Taken in the Year 1920*. Washington, DC: Government Printing Office, 1922.

United States Bureau of the Census. *Fifteenth Census of the United States: 1930*. Washington, DC: Government Printing Office, 1933.

United States Bureau of the Census. *Sixteenth Census of the United States: 1940*. Washington, DC: Government Printing Office, 1943.

United States Bureau of the Census. *Census of Population: 1950*. Washington, DC: United States Government Printing Office, 1953.

United States Bureau of Education. *History of Schools for the Colored Population*. New York: Arno Press, 1969, 1871.

United States Immigration Commission. *Reports of the Immigration Commission: The Children of Immigrants in Schools* (5 volumes). Washington, DC: U.S. Government Printing Office, 1911.

Valien, Bonita. "Racial Desegregation of the Public Schools in Southern Illinois." *Journal of Negro Education* 23 (Summer 1954): 303–9.

van den Berghe, Pierre L. *Race and Racism: A Comparative Perspective*. New York: John Wiley & Sons, 1967.

Van Meeter, Sondra. "Black Resistance to Segregation in the Wichita Schools, 1870–1912." *The Midwest Quarterly* 20 (Autumn 1978): 64–77.

Voegeli, V. Jacque. *Free But Not Equal: The Midwest and the Negro During the Civil War*. Chicago: University of Chicago Press, 1967.

Wade, Richard C. "The Negro in Cincinnati." *Journal of Negro History* 39 (Jan. 1954): 43–57.

Waite, Cally Lyn. "Permission to Remain among Us: Education for Blacks in Oberlin, Ohio, 1880–1914." Ed.D. dissertation, Harvard University, 1997.

Walker, Francis A. "Restriction of Immigration." *Atlantic Monthly* 77 (June 1896): 822–9.

Waller, Lisa Yvette. "Holding Back the Dawn: Milton A. Galamison and the Fight for School Integration in New York City, A Northern Civil Rights Struggle, 1948–1968." Ph.D. dissertation, Duke University, 1998.

Walling, William E. "The Race War in the North." *Independent* 65 (1908): 529–34.

Wallis, Don, ed. *All We Had Was Each Other: An Oral History of the Black Community of Madison, Indiana*. Bloomington: Indiana University Press, 1998.

Warner, Robert Austin. *New Haven Negroes: A Social History*. New Haven: Yale University Press, 1940.

Washington, Michael Harlan. "The Black Struggle for Desegregated Quality Education: Cincinnati. Ohio 1954–1974." Ed.D. dissertation, University of Cincinnati, 1984.

Watras, Joseph. *Politics, Race, and Schools: Racial Integration, 1954–1994*. New York: Garland Publishing, Inc., 1997.

Weaver, Valeria W. "The Failure of Civil Rights 1875–1883 and Its Repercussions." *Journal of Negro History* 54 (Oct. 1969): 368–82.

Weinberg, Meyer. *A Chance to Learn: The History of Race and Education in the United States*. Cambridge: Cambridge University Press, 1977.

Weiss, Nancy J. *Farewell to the Party of Lincoln: Black Politics in the Age of FDR*. Princeton: Princeton University Press, 1983.

Wheeler, Joanne. "Together in Egypt: A Pattern of Race Relations in Cairo, Illinois, 1865–1915." In *Toward a New South? Studies in Post–Civil War Southern Communities*. Orville Vernon Burton and Robert C. McMath, Jr., eds. Westport, CT: Greenwood Press, 1982.

White, Arthur O. "The Black Movement against Jim Crow Education in Buffalo, New York, 1800–1900." *Phylon* 30 (1969): 375–93.

Wilkinson, J. Harvie, III. *From Brown to Bakke: The Supreme Court and School Integration, 1954–1978*. New York: Oxford University Press, 1979.

Williams, Lillian S. *Strangers in the Land of Paradise: The Creation of an African American Community. Buffalo, New York, 1900–1940*. Bloomington: Indiana University Press, 1999.

Williams, Patricia. *The Alchemy of Race and Rights*. Cambridge: Harvard University Press, 1991.

Williams, Robin M., Jr. and Margaret W. Ryan, eds. *Schools in Transition: Community Experiences in Desegregation*. Chapel Hill: University of North Carolina Press, 1954.

Wilson, Henry. "New Departure of the Republican Party." *The Atlantic Monthly* 27 (Jan. 1871): 104–20.

Wilson, Sondra Kathryn, ed. *In Search of Democracy: The NAACP Writings of James Weldon Johnson, Walter White, and Roy Wilkins (1920–1977)*. New York: Oxford University Press, 1999.

Wolters, Raymond. *Negroes and the Great Depression: The Problem of Economic Recovery*. Westport, CT: Greenwood Publishing Corporation, 1970.

Woodson, Carter G. *The Education of the Negro Prior to 1861: A History of the Education of the Colored People of the United States from the Beginning of Slavery to the Civil War*. New York: G. P. Putnam's Sons, 1915.

A *Century of Negro Migration*. Washington, D.C.: The Association for the Study of Negro Life and History, 1918.

ed., *The Mind of the Negro as Reflected in Letters Written During the Crisis, 1800– 1860*. Washington, DC: The Association for the Study of Negro Life and History, Inc., 1926.

"The Negroes of Cincinnati Prior to the Civil War." *Journal of Negro History* 1 (Jan. 1916): 1–22.

Woodward C. Vann. *Origins of the New South, 1877–1913*. Baton Rouge: Louisiana State University Press, 1951.

The Strange Career of Jim Crow. New York: Oxford University Press, 1955.

Woofter, Thomas Jackson, Jr., ed. *Negro Problems in Cities: A Study*. Garden City, NY: Doubleday, Doran & Co., 1928.

Wright, Giles R. *Afro-Americans in New Jersey: A Short History*. Trenton: New Jersey Historical Commission, Department of State, 1988.

Wright, Marion Thompson. *The Education of Negroes in New Jersey*. New York: Teachers College, Columbia University, 1941.

"Extending Civil Rights in New Jersey through the Division against Discrimination." *Journal of Negro History* 38 (Jan. 1953): 91–107.

"New Jersey Laws and the Negro." *Journal of Negro History* 28 (1943): 156–9.

"Racial Integration in the Public Schools of New Jersey." *Journal of Negro Education* 23 (1954): 282–9.

Yeazell, Stephen C. *From Medieval Group Litigation to the Modern Class Action*. New Haven: Yale University Press, 1987.

Index

abolitionists
  and black education 18–19
  and support for integration 53–4,
    68
Africa 42, 234
African Americans
  and age of children attending
    school 154
  and benefits of black schools
    182–3
  and challenges to school
    segregation 50–9, 68–82
  and crime rates 126
  decline in political influence 95
  and divisions over school
    integration 6–7, 45–50, 167,
    184–5, 193–5, 209–10, 256, 277
  and emigration from U.S. 27
  and employment opportunities
    22–3
  eschewing mass protest 224
  exclusion from public schools 149
  and fear of mistreatment in
    racially mixed schools 107–8
  and ignorance of antisegregation
    laws 239
  and importance of education 1,
    17–20, 60, 185
  increase in militancy 170
  as lawyers 107
  and opposition to school
    integration 7, 48–9, 107–12,
    172–86, 239
  response to increase in antiblack
    sentiment 168–9
  school attendance and graduation
    rates 179–80, 185–6
  and separatist views 170–2
  and support for school integration
    46–8, 167, 186–95, 219
  support for separate black
    institutions 167, 168–9
  insistence on school integration
    168
  see also antiblack sentiment
African Free Schools 18–19, 50
Akron (Ohio) 127, 175
Albany (N.Y.)
  and school boycott 50
  and school integration 40, 81,
    100
Alexander County (Ill.)
  and fund withholding 254
  and school segregation 104, 250
Alfred the Great 18
Alton (Ill.)
  and black teachers 118
  and desegregation efforts 117–22,
    254–5
  and litigation efforts 209, 246
  and persistence of segregation
    246
  and resistance to desegregation
    orders 121
American Civil Liberties Union
  223
American Colonization Society 26
American Creed 2
American Dilemma, An 5, 185, 235
American Federation of Labor
  166
American Jewish Congress 231
American Race Problem, The 162
Amityville (N.Y.) 102

antiblack sentiment
  in antebellum North 20–31
  after Civil War 63–5
  compared to response to white
    immigrants 32
  decrease during 1940s 236
  and denial of voting rights 12,
    30–1, 88
  and exclusion from communities
    129
  and exclusion from militias 29
  and fears of amalgamation 102
  and hostility to black education
    13, 32–3
  and increase of during early 20th
    century 124–31
  and job competition 22–3
  in Midwest 20, 21, 22, 25
  in New England 20, 41–4
  and race theory 21
  among school administrators
    156–7
  and state laws banning
    immigration of blacks 27–9
  among white students 48–9
  see also racial violence
Anti-Nebraska Party 37
antisegregation legislation (see
    legislation, antisegregation)
antislavery sentiment 31
Appeal in Favor of Americans Called
    Africans, An 22
Arizona 140, 145, 235
Arizona state legislature 140
Army (see U.S. Army)
Asbury Park (N.J.) 145
Asia 234
Asian Americans, and school
    segregation 67–8
Associated Negro Press 193
Atlantic City (N.J.) 149, 156, 191, 195

Bagnall, Robert 180, 189, 190, 215
Bailey, Thomas 124
Baltimore 179, 181
Baltimore Afro-American 171
barbershops, discrimination in 92

Bateman, Newton 37, 61, 66–7, 80
Bell Aircraft Corporation 165
Bell, Derrick 278
Belville (Ill.) 127
benevolent societies, and black
    education 19
Berlin (Germany) 233
Berry, Theodore 255–6
Berwyn (Penn.) 206, 210
Bethune, Mary McLeod 225
Bibb, Minnie 121
Bibb, Scott 118–21
Bible 58
Black Laws 25–6
  enforcement of 25
  in Illinois 25
  in Indiana 25
  in Michigan Territory 25
  in Ohio 20, 24, 25
  repeal of 25, 62
Blair, Austin 81
Boaz, Franz 162
Bond, Horace Mann 160, 161, 183,
    191
Bordentown Manual Training
    School 183, 240
Bordentown (N.J.) 175
Boston 22, 32
  and black teachers 176, 189
  and discrimination in hotels 134
  and preference of blacks for
    separate schools 48–9, 109
  and preservation of racially mixed
    schools 150
  and quality of black schools 44
  and school attendance rates 179,
    186
  and school boycott 54
  and school segregation 4, 40, 49,
    52–7, 60, 99
  and Women's Army Corps (WACs)
    224
Boston Guardian 217
Boston School Committee 40, 52,
    54, 56, 58
Boston Tea Party 225
Brazil (Ind.) 74

Brenholdt, John 119
Brigham, Carl 161–2
Brooklyn (Ill.) 139
Brooklyn (N.Y.)
    and black children in mixed
        schools 48, 108
    and black support for separate
        schools 107
    and black teachers 111
    and litigation over antisegregation
        law 102–3
    and mistreatment of black
        children 108, 177
    and school segregation 40, 102
    and vocational education 165
Brown, Homer 229
Brown, Jere 94
Brown v. Board of Education (1954) 4,
        9, 147, 162, 214, 220, 253
    and antisegregation view 277
    arguments in 3
    critique of 279
    degree of northern school
        segregation at time of 10
    and integrationist vision of 7
    and NAACP 5
    perceived effect on North 269
    and persistence of segregation
        after 4, 10, 11, 13, 265–73
    and racial change 8
Brueggemann, Henry 118
Bryn Mawr (Penn.) 260
Buck, Pearl 232
Buffalo Board of Education 165
Buffalo (N.Y.)
    and black teachers 176
    and exclusion of blacks from
        technical schools 165
    and influx of black migrants 132
    and quality of black schools 44
    and racial views on school
        segregation 155, 184
    and school attendance rates 186
    and school desegregation 51, 100
    and school segregation 40, 46
    and use of intelligence tests 163–4
Buffalo Technical High School 165

Buffalo Urban League 165
Bulkley, William L. 186
Bunche, Ralph 187, 218
Bureau of Intelligence (*see* U.S.
    Bureau of Intelligence)
Burns, Anthony 57

Cairo (Ill.)
    economic condition of 251
    and fears of retaliation 252
    and grand jury indictments 253
    and loss of black teachers 252
    and police retaliation 253
    and population of 251
    and racial violence 252–3
    and Republican control of 95
    and school desegregation in 251
    and school segregation 245, 251,
        254
California
    and ban on discrimination in
        public accommodations 91
    and black political influence
        230
    and black population 227–8
    and compliance with
        antisegregation law 105
    and desegregation litigation 72,
        207
    and exclusion of blacks 28–9, 65
    and fund-withholding law 68
    and repeal of Black Laws 62
    and residential segregation 137
    and school segregation 67, 97
California State Department of
    Education 272
California Supreme Court 105
Cambridge (Mass.) 216, 217
Camden (N.J.) 107, 149, 243, 245
Canaan (N.H.) 43–4
Canada 24, 27
Canterbury (Conn.) 42
Cape May (N.J.) 141
Carnegie Foundation 236
Carter, Carey 72–3
Carter, Robert 249, 257–8, 278
Carver, George Washington 177

Catholic schools 58
Cayton, Horace 221
CBS Radio 232
Central High School (Cleveland)
    144, 164
Chagrin Falls (Ohio) 257, 258
Champion Elementary School
    (Columbus, Ohio) 146, 175
Chase, Salmon 23
Chester High School 142
Chester (Pa.) 123, 142, 145, 261
    and black teachers teaching white
        children 174
    and racially gerrymandered
        school district lines 272
    and retaliation for challenging
        segregation 211
    and school segregation 149
Chew, Benjamin 94
Cheyney Training School for
    Teachers 198–9
Chicago
    and black population 125, 268
    and black schools 192
    and discrimination in hotels 134
    and discrimination by realtors
        136
    and election of 1948 230
    and employment discrimination
        138
    establishment of segregated
        schools in 195
    and increase in residential
        segregation 129, 137
    and influx of black migrants 132,
        133
    and litigation challenging school
        segregation 207
    and mistreatment of blacks by
        white principals 177
    and NAACP branch and school
        segregation 246
    and persistence of segregation
        during 1950s 265, 266
    and racial conflict 130
    and racially gerrymandered school
        district lines 147–8, 269–70, 271
    and racist textbooks 217

and restrictive covenants 267
and school attendance rates 66,
    186
and student achievement in 161
and support for school
    segregation 109, 139, 184
Chicago Commission on Race
    Relations 154
Chicago Defender 180, 204
    and southern migration 132, 133
    and support for school integration
        185, 186, 193
Chicago Tribune 138
Chicago World's Fair (1933) 248
Child, Lydia Maria 22
Chillicothe (Ohio) 104
Christian Recorder 109
Cincinnati 18, 22, 25, 93
    and black children in mixed
        schools 108, 180
    and black leadership 182
    and black schools 19, 36, 96
    and black support for separate
        schools 107, 184
    and black teachers 174, 176,
        189
    and discrimination by realtors
        136
    division in black community over
        school integration 193–5
    and influx of black migrants 132
    and mulattoes 35
    and NAACP branch 187
    and racial violence 24
    and removal of blacks 25
    and response to antisegregation
        law 104
    and school segregation 144, 149,
        258
    and support of white students for
        school segregation 157
    and undistricted attendance zones
        148–9
Cincinnati Chamber of Commerce
    138
Cincinnati City Council 267
Cincinnati Daily Gazette 25
Cincinnati Enquirer 23, 65

Cincinnati School Board 35, 149,
194–5
Cincinnati *Union* 186, 193
Civil Rights Act of 1875 82, 90
Civil Rights Act of 1964 9, 11
Civil Rights Cases (1883) 89, 90,
93
Civil Rights Protective League
(Springfield, Ohio) 215
Civil War and racial idealism 61,
62–3
Clark, Kenneth 222, 223
Clark, Peter 88
Clark v. Board of Directors (1868)
76–8
Cleveland
and antiblack sentiment 184
and black population 125, 228
and blacks favoring racial
separation 168–9
and black teachers 109, 111,
175–6, 189
and discrimination in public
accommodations 128, 134
and influx of black migrants 132,
134
and increase in employment
discrimination 129
and increase in residential
segregation 128, 137
and NAACP 172
and overcrowded black schools
270
and racially separate classrooms
144
and school attendance rates 181,
186
and school integration 60
and school segregation 96, 144
and support for neighborhood
schools 279
and tracking of blacks and whites
164
and vocational education 165
and voter registration 228
Cleveland Association for Colored
Men 168
Cleveland *Call and Post* 144

Cleveland Gazette 110–11, 168, 184
criticism of pro-segregation views
201, 215
support for school integration
186, 215
Cleveland *Journal* 168
Cleveland Leader 96
Cleveland Plain Dealer 131
Cleveland School Board 175
Clifford, Nathan 71
Cold War 10, 220, 227, 234
colonization of slaves 26–7
Colorado 90
Colorado constitution of 1876 68
Colorado Territory 68
*Colored Patriots of the American
Revolution* 53
Columbus Board of Education
(Ohio) 146–7, 175
Columbus (N.J.) 159
Columbus (Ohio)
and influx of black migrants 132
and racially gerrymandered
school district lines 146–7
and racially separate classrooms
144
and school desegregation 69, 96,
257
and school segregation 195, 258
and support for school
segregation 155, 157
and use of black teachers 111, 175
Commentaries on the Constitution 114
common school movement
in antebellum North 13–16
and assimilation 15
growth in number of schools 14
and inclusion of blacks 31–41
in the Midwest 16
in New England 16
reasons for 14–16, 31–2
and reduction of crime 15–16
and stability of government 14–15
in the Western Reserve 16
communism 234
compulsory education laws 58–9,
87–8
Congress (*see* U.S. Congress)

Congress of Industrial Organizations (CIO) 263
Congress of Racial Equality (CORE) 7, 277
Connecticut 21
  and antisegregation law 84–5
  and ban on discrimination in public accommodations 90, 91
  and black education 40
  and black population 97
  and black voting rights 30, 63, 88
  and school segregation 4, 41, 99
Connecticut state legislature 42
Connecticut Supreme Court of Errors 42
Cook, E. F. 46
Cook County Circuit Court 207–8
Cook County (Ill.) 248
Cooley, Thomas 114
Corwin, Thomas 1
Cory v. Carter (1874) 73, 74
Cottrol, Robert 8, 30
Couch, William T. 226
Crandall, Prudence 42
Crawford (Penn.) 79–80
The Crisis 181, 188
  and black support for World War II 223
  and Cheyney School controversy 198
  and costs of segregation 197
  and Du Bois 195, 204
  and financial problems 204
  and inaugural issue of 195
  and 1934 debate over school integration 200
  supporting integration 199
critical race theory 8
Crowley, Mary Roberts 181
Crummel, Alexander 18, 49
Cubberly, Ellwood 153
Current, Gloster 247, 249
curriculum, in black schools 45
Curtis-Wright Corporation 165

Dabney, Virginius 226
Dabney, Wendell 193–4, 199
Darby (Penn.) 157
Davis, Frank Marshall 193
Davis, Samuel H. 12
Dayton (Ohio)
  black opposition to separate schools 212
  black support for separate schools 107, 110, 184, 212
  and black teachers 174, 211, 213
  and desegregation efforts in 256
  lack of compliance with desegregation order 213–14
  and litigation challenging school segregation 211–13
  mistreatment of blacks by white teachers 177
  and NAACP 212, 256
  and persistence of school segregation 258
  racially separate classrooms 144, 214
  and retaliation for challenging school segregation 211
  and school segregation 4, 149
Dayton School Board 144, 211, 213
Decatur County (Ind.) 35
Delany, David 268
Delany, Martin 27
Delaware 190
democracy
  and relationship to antisegregation efforts 220, 222–3, 234–5
  and war for 222
Democratic Party
  and antiblack sentiment 23
  and black vote 88–9
  and judges on state supreme courts 105
  in Ohio 90–1
Denton, Nancy 266
Denver (Colo.) 279
Des Moines 175
De Tocqueville, Alexis 22, 62

Detroit Board of Education 85,
  113–15
Detroit Bureau of Government
  Research 154
Detroit (Mich.)
  and antiblack animus 113
  and black population 125, 228,
    268
  and desegregation efforts in 1970s
    277
  and discrimination in hotels 134
  and establishment of schools 114
  increase in school segregation
    during 1950s 266
  and influx of black migrants 132
  and litigation to enforce
    antisegregation laws 112, 113–15
  and mistreatment of blacks by
    white teachers 177
  and poor support for black
    schools 114
  racial conflict during World War II
    231
  and removal of blacks 25
  and riot of 1943 225, 232
  and school segregation 46, 85
  and use of black teachers 176,
    189
Dickerson, G. Edward 198
Die Wehrmacht 236–7
Dorchester (Mass.) 158
Douglass, Frederick
  and arguments for integration 47
  and employment barriers 22–3
  and integration strategy 60
  and school desegregation in
    Rochester (N. Y.) 51
  and sons of 68
Dowington (Penn.) 261
Downing, George 47, 88
Dred Scott v. Sanford (1857) 73
Driscoll, Alfred 241–2, 245
Du Bois, W. E. B. 167, 171
  call for moratorium on racial
    protest 197
  and changing views on school
    segregation issue 195, 200

and controversy of 1934 200–3
and debate over Cheyney School
  198–9
and debate over school
  integration 195–205
and hotel discrimination 134
and increase in black population
  125
and increase in segregation 188
and litigation challenging school
  segregation 210
and mistreatment of blacks in
  racially mixed schools 177
and Philadelphia schools 101
and problems of racially mixed
  schools 197–8
resigns from The Crisis 204
and rift with Walter White 204
and support for school integration
  195–6, 197, 277
support for school segregation
  201–5
and support for separate training
  for black officers 196
and World War I 169, 226
Dubuque (Iowa) 4, 77–8
Dunbar High School (Washington,
  D.C.) 199
Dunbar Junior and Senior High
  School (Dayton, Ohio) 214, 256
Dwight, Timothy 32

Earhart, Amy 58
East Orange (N.J.) 139, 159, 270
East Pulaski School (Gary, Ind.)
  143
East St. Louis (Ill.) 245, 249–50
East St. Louis School Board 249–50
Eaton, Horace 1
Eaton, John 87
education,
  decentralized nature of 99
  and equality 1–2
  and exclusion of blacks 2–3, 13, 31
  and graded classes 45
  importance of 1
  and poverty 1

education (*cont.*)
  prohibition on teaching free
    blacks 2
  prohibition on teaching slaves 2
  and republican government 82
  and social stability 87
  and unequal black schools 2
Educational Equality League 183,
  217
Edwardsville (Ill.) 250
Elizabeth (N.J.) 68
Elkhart (Ind.) 191, 234
Ellwood (Ind.) 129
Emancipation Proclamation 63,
  67
employment discrimination
  domestic work for blacks 130
  by employers 138, 221
  increase in early 20th century 129
  by labor unions 138, 165, 221
  among teenagers 186
  by white workers 138
Englewood (N.J.) 69
Equal Protection Clause (*see* U.S.
  Constitution)
equality 1
eugenics 126
Evanston (Ill.) 175
Evansville (Ind.) 28, 64, 127–8

Fair Employment Practice
  Committee 225, 236
Fair Haven (N.J.) 101
federal housing policies 268
Federal Bureau of Investigation
  (FBI) 254
Federal Home Owners Loan
  Corporation 137
Federal Housing Administration
  (FHA) 137, 268
Felicity (Ohio) 113
fifteenth amendment (*see* U.S.
  Constitution)
Fisk University Jubilee Singers 92
Flint (Mich.) 175
Flushing (N.Y.)
  and school segregation 102

and support for school
  segregation 157
Foner, Eric 25
Foraker, Joseph 89, 93–4
Fort Scott (Kan.) 178
fourteenth amendment (*see* U.S.
  Constitution)
Frank, John 136
Franklin, John Hope 138
Frazier, E. Franklin 160, 162, 170,
  187
Frederick Douglass High School
  (Chester, Penn.) 142
Frederick Douglass School
  (Cincinnati) 182
Freedmen's Bureau 64
Freedmen's Schools 130
Freedom's Journal 17
Free Soil Party 36, 57, 93
Fugitive Slave Act of 1850 20, 27, 57
fugitive slaves 20
Fulton School (Springfield, Ohio)
  215–16
Fultz, Michael 185
Future Outlook League 257

Gaines, Kevin 1
Galamison, Milton 273
Galesburg (Ill.) 69
Gallipolis (Ohio) 157
Garfield School (Dayton, Ohio) 144,
  211–14
Garrison, William Lloyd 27, 43
  and Boston integration 53
  and Crandall's school 42
Garvey, Marcus 170–2
Gary (Ind.) 199, 219
  and black support for school
    segregation 182–3
  and conflict between NAACP and
    UNIA 172
  and desegregation efforts during
    1940s 262–3
  and employment discrimination
    129
  and racially gerrymandered
    school district lines 270

and school boycotts in support of
    segregation 157, 233–4
and school segregation in 143, 148
and support for racial equality 235
and use of black teachers 176
and white support for school
    segregation 155–6, 157
Gary Evening Post 129
Geneva (N.Y.) 86, 100
Georgia 127, 184
Germany 221, 222, 231, 234
gerrymandered school district lines
    (by race) 3, 113, 146–8, 191,
    269–72
    in East Orange (N.J.) 270
    effect on school segregation
        269–72, 273, 275
    in Gary (Ind.) 270
    in Hillsboro (Ohio) 270–1
    in Indianapolis 265
    legal challenges to 271
    in New Rochelle (N.Y.) 146, 270
    in Portland (Ore.) 270
Gilmore High School (Cincinnati)
    19
Girls High School (Brooklyn, N.Y.)
    165
Glassboro Teachers College (N.J.)
    241
Goebbels, Joseph 237
Goshen (N.Y.) 103
Grant, Ulysses S. 87
Gray, William 113
Greathouse, Archie 210
Great Migration 131–3, 219
    and decline in foreign
        immigration 132
    and economic concerns 132–3
    and educational opportunity 133
    and employment opportunity 132
    and impact on northern white
        hostility toward blacks 134–8
    and increase in segregation 203
    and labor agents 132
    and numbers of migrants 227
    and racial oppression 133
    and southern agriculture 132

support of migrants for school
    segregation 183–5
Greensburg (Ind.) 127
Grimke, Francis 201
Grossman, James 133
Grossman, Lawrence 88

Hackensack (N.J.) 159
Haiti 27
Hall, G. Stanley 126–7
Halliwell, Henry J. 100
Hall v. DeCuir (1878) 71
Hamilton County (Ohio) 271
Hamilton (Ohio) 258
Hamtramck (Mich.) 217
Hancock County (Ind.) 34
Handy, W. C. 251
Harper's Weekly 82
Harrisburg (Ill.) 246
Harrisburg (Penn.) 260
Harlem
    and black attitudes in 221
    and intelligence tests 162
    and riot of 1943 225
    and school quality in 192
    and school segregation 152
    and voter registration 228
Harlem Tenants Council 269
Harriet Beecher Stowe School
    (Cincinnati) 194
Hartford (Conn.)
    and NAACP branch 187
    and school segregation 4, 40, 41,
        84
Hartranft, John 94
Hastie, William 187
Hayes School (Cleveland) 270
Helper, Rose 267
Here I Stand 101
Hillburn (N.Y.) 103, 229
Hill District (Pittsburgh) 174, 191
Hill, Leslie Pinckney 198
Hillsboro (Ohio) 258, 270–1
Hilton, John 47
Hitler, Adolph 221–2, 231
Hitlerism 234
Hoadly, George 89, 92–3, 110

Hoffman, Frederick 126
Holmes, Dwight 190
Hopkins, W. R. 134
hotels, discrimination in 92
housing, and federal loan programs
    137
Houston, Charles H. 187
Howard Law School 187
Howard University 187
Hunter, Jane Edna 168
Hyde Park Improvement Protective
    Club 129, 139

Illinois
    and antiblack sentiment 24, 118
    and antisegregation legislation
        85–6, 98
    and ban on court testimony by
        blacks 29
    and ban on discrimination in
        public accommodations 90, 91,
        229, 248
    and ban on employment
        discrimination 229
    and black education 37, 67
    and black population 88, 104,
        125
    and common schools 16
    and desegregation efforts during
        1940s and 1950s 240, 245–55,
        276
    and election of 1948 230
    and enforcement of
        desegregation orders 115–21
    and exclusion of blacks from
        public schools 33, 34, 65, 66–7,
        89, 149
    and exclusion of blacks from state
        27, 28
    and fund-withholding law 248,
        250, 265
    and increase in black political
        power 248
    and increase in black population
        227, 248
    and increase in school segregation
        140

and inferiority of separate black
    schools 191
and influx of blacks to 64, 131
and litigation challenging school
    segregation 80
and litigation to enforce
    antisegregation laws 106, 207,
    209
and NAACP support for school
    integration 185
and petitions challenging school
    segregation 69
and presidential vote 95
and racially segregated school
    swimming pools 145
and racial views 20
and repeal of Black Laws 62
and response to antisegregation
    law 104–5
and retaliation for desegregation
    efforts 112
and school segregation 5, 33, 104,
    245–6, 266
Illinois Attorney General 253
Illinois Colored Historical Society
    121
Illinois Commission on Human
    Relations 248
Illinois constitutional convention of
    1847 33
Illinois constitutional convention of
    1869 67
Illinois General Assembly (see Illinois
    state legislature)
Illinois Journal 119
Illinois State Conference of NAACP
    Branches 247
Illinois state legislature 37, 67, 248,
    250
Illinois State School Directory
    246
Illinois State Superintendent
    of Public Instruction 246,
    248
Illinois Supreme Court 80, 86,
    115–16, 117, 120, 211, 246
Imes, William Lloyd 198

immigration
  and assimilation 162–3
  and employment of white
    immigrants 130
  from Germany 24
  and hostility toward Irish 55
  increase in 125, 127–8
  from Ireland 24, 32
  and school attendance rates 185–6
Independence (Kan.) 79
Indiana
  and antiblack sentiment 20, 24,
    32–3, 65, 95
  and antisegregation legislation 83,
    219, 238, 264–5
  and ban on discrimination in
    public accommodations 90, 91
  and black population 28, 65, 88
  and black schools 19
  and black voting rights 30, 88
  and campaign for black education
    rights 65–6
  and colonization of blacks 26
  and common schools 16
  and desegregation efforts during
    1940s 262–5
  and elections 95
  and exclusion of blacks from
    public schools 33, 65, 74, 89
  and exclusion of blacks from state
    27–8
  inferiority of separate black
    schools 191
  and Ku Klux Klan 158
  and law permitting limited school
    integration 74
  and law permitting school
    segregation 5
  and litigation challenging
    exclusion from schools 72–5
  and litigation challenging school
    segregation 207
  and litigation mandating school
    segregation 75
  and lynchings 127
  and migration of ex-slaves 64
  and mulatto education 34
  and opposition to desegregation
    265
  and racially segregated school
    swimming pools 145
  and repeal of Black Laws 62
  and Republican Party 95
  and school segregation 5, 33, 140,
    152–3, 262
  and support of black teachers for
    segregation 110
  and testimony of blacks in court
    29
Indiana constitutional convention of
  1816 30
Indiana constitutional convention of
  1850 27–8, 32
Indiana Constitution of 1851 73
Indiana General Assembly 29
  and antisegregation law 264
  authorization of segregation 72,
    152
  and challenges to school
    segregation 207
  and common schools 16
  and opposition to antisegregation
    law 95
  and opposition of black teachers
    to desegregation 110
  and provision of black education
    66, 74
Indianapolis
  and black population 228
  and black teachers 174, 176
  and branch of NAACP 264
  and challenges to school
    segregation in 210
  and common schools 16
  discrimination in hotels 134–5
  and discrimination by realtors
    136
  and mistreatment of black
    children 108
  and residential segregation
    136
  and school desegregation during
    1940s 264–5
  and school segregation 152–3

Indianapolis Chamber of Commerce
    152
Indianapolis *Freeman* 134
Indianapolis Journal 73, 74
Indianapolis Recorder 152, 264
Indiana Superintendent of Public
    Instruction 66
Indiana Supreme Court 34, 75
    and antiblack decisions 28, 73–4,
    75
intelligence tests
    black opposition to use of 160–1
    and explanation of racial
        differences 161–2
    and school segregation 160–1
international concerns and effect on
    desegregation efforts 220
interracial committees 237
Iowa
    and ban on court testimony by
        blacks 29
    and ban on discrimination in
        public accommodations 90
    and black population 75, 78, 88,
        97
    and black voting rights 30, 63, 78
    and desegregation litigation 75–8,
        85
    and exclusion of blacks from
        schools 33
    and exclusion of blacks from state
        27, 28
    and repeal of Black Laws 62
    and school segregation 4
Iowa Constitution of 1846 75
Iowa Constitution of 1857 75
Iowa state legislature
    abolishes state board of education
        76
    requires school segregation 75
Iowa state superintendent of
    education 76
Iowa Supreme Court
    declaring discrimination in
        steamboat travel unlawful 77
    declaring school segregation
        unlawful 75, 76–8

Irish Catholics 57–8, 88
    conflict with blacks 113
Italy 222, 234

Jacksonian democracy 23
Jackson (Mich.) 81
Jamaica (N.Y.) 102, 103
Japan 221, 231, 234
Jaymes, Sully 215
Jenkins Amendment 250
Jenkins, Charles 248, 250
Jersey City (N.J.) 68
Johnson, Alex 279
Johnson, Charles S.
    on black goals 226
    on effect of World War II on race
        in America 233
    on mistreatment of blacks in
        racially mixed schools 178
    and *Opportunity* 160
    on overage schoolchildren 154
    on racial conflict 236
Johnson, James Weldon and Du Bois
    controversy 202–3
Johnson, Lyndon 2
Johnstown (Penn.) 137
Journal of Negro Education 187
Julian, George 25
Jury service and exclusion of blacks
    from 12, 29

Kaestle, Carl 21
Kansas 28
    and antisegregation legislation 87,
        98
    and exclusion of blacks from
        schools 65, 67, 79
    and increase in school segregation
        140
    and inferiority of separate black
        schools 191
    and litigation to enforce
        antisegregation legislation
        207
    and migration of ex-slaves to 64
    and racially segregated school
        swimming pools 145

and racially separate classrooms
    208
Kansas City (Kan.) 140
Kansas-Nebraska Act of 1854 57
Kansas state legislature
    and antisegregation legislation 87
    permits school segregation 79,
        139–40
Kansas Superintendent of Public
    Schools 140
Kansas Supreme Court strikes down
    school segregation 78–9, 140
Kansas Territory 57
Kentucky 20, 26, 64
Kentucky constitutional convention
    of 1850 26
Keokuk (Iowa) 4, 78
King, Charles F. 216
Kinsman School (Cleveland) 270
Klarman, Michael 95
Klineberg, Otto 162
Know Nothing Party 57–8
Konvitz, Milton 210
Kousser, Morgan 71
Ku Klux Klan 215, 268
    and resurgence in 1920s 158–9

labor unions
    support for desegregation 263
    see also employment
        discrimination
Lancaster (Penn.) 36, 39, 101
Lansden, David 252–3
Lawrenceburg (Ind.) exclusion of
    blacks 129
Lawrence Township (Ind.) 72
law, and role in racial change 7,
    8–10, 274–7
legislation, antisegregation
    campaign for 82–99
    congressional efforts to enact
        82–3
    defiance of 6
    effect on patterns of school
        segregation on 98, 99–105
    enactment of 3, 6, 9, 62
    enforcement of 10, 62

failure to eliminate school
    segregation 7–8, 62
ignorance of 153
impact of inefficiency of dual
    schools on 95–7
reasons for 84–99
sanctions for violations of 98–9
legislation, fund-withholding 10, 240
legislation, prohibiting
    discrimination in public
    accommodations 90–1, 92, 99,
    135, 276
    penalties for violation of 91–2
legislation, prohibiting employment
    discrimination 230–1
legislation, providing for black
    education 62
Liberator, The 42, 53, 57
Liberia 27, 42
Life magazine 221, 232, 253
Lincoln, Abraham 20, 128
Lincoln Heights School District
    (Cincinnati) 271
Lincoln School (New Rochelle, N.Y.)
    146
Lincoln School (Quincy, Ill.) 115–16
Lincoln University 191
literacy rates 14, 66
literary societies and black
    education 19
litigation, challenging school
    segregation 7, 50, 54–6, 69,
    75–80, 82, 89, 208
    contributes to legislative action
        80–2
litigation, to enforce antisegregation
    legislation 3, 105–9, 122, 207–8,
    239
    and class actions 112
    and cost of 107
    and dearth of 209
    and defiance of court orders
        113–21, 211
    difficulties finding plaintiffs for
        209
    and failure of 8, 106–22, 167
    impediments to 112, 209–16

litigation (*cont.*)
  and importance of state supreme
    courts 105
  and limits on relief granted 211
  and retaliation for 211
  role of state Attorneys General in
    107
  role of white lawyers in 107
Litwack, Leon 45, 274
lobbying, legislative and school
  desegregation 7
Locke, Alain 151, 160, 187
Lockport (N.Y.) 69
Logan (Ohio) 12–13
Logan, Rayford 187
Long Branch (N.J.) 243
Long, Howard H. 160
Long Island 20
Los Angeles (Cal.)
  and increase in black population
    228
  and intelligence tests 162
  and riot during World War II 225
Los Angeles Realty Board 267
Louisiana 232
Lovejoy, Elijah 117, 128
Lowell (Mass.) 52
Lower Oxford (Penn.) 142
Low, Seth 124
lynchings 127
  and Great Migration 133
  following World War I 170
  during World War II 221
Lynn, Winfred 223

Madison County (Ill.) 255
Madison (Ind.) 157
Maine 30
  and black education 40
  and black population 97
  and school integration 61
Malcolm X 7, 178
Manhattan Trade School for Boys
  166
Mann, Horace 16
Mansfield (Ohio) 257
Marion County (Ind.) 72

Marshall, Thurgood
  and desegregation in Dayton 256
  and desegregation in East St.
    Louis 249
  and desegregation in Ohio 257
  and desegregation in Wilmington,
    Ohio 256
  fighting school segregation in the
    North 238
  refusal to support war resisters 223
  and segregation in Illinois 246,
    247
Marshall, William 85
Maryland 190
Maslow, Will 231
Mason (Mich.) 178
Massac County (Ill.) 104
Massachusetts
  and antisegregation legislation 20,
    56–7, 59, 61, 99
  and ban on discrimination in
    public accommodations 62, 90,
    91
  and ban on railroad segregation
    52
  and black education 40
  and black population 97, 99
  and compulsory education 87
  and discrimination at hospital 224
  and importance of education
  and miscegenation ban 52
  and school segregation 4
Massachusetts Antislavery Society 56
Massachusetts state constitution 56
Massachusetts state legislature
  and legislation banning school
    segregation 56–7
  and legislation providing equal
    rights 54
Massachusetts Supreme Judicial
  Court 56, 70
Massey, Douglas 266
Maxville (Ore.) 149
Mayor's Commission on Conditions
  in Harlem 151, 165–6
McCord, George 159
McFarlane, Frederic 256

McLean County (Ill.) 80
Measure of Intelligence, The 159
Meeting Street School (Providence, R.I.) 99
Mendelberg, Tali 275
Messenger, The 186–7, 190, 192–3
Michigan
  and antisegregation legislation 81, 85
  and ban on discrimination in public accommodations 90, 91
  and black education 37–8
  and black population 88, 97
  and black voting rights 30
  and increase in black population 227
  and influx of black migrants 132
  and litigation challenging school segregation 81, 276
  and litigation to enforce antisegregation legislation 207
  and patterns of school segregation 100
  and persistence of racial separation in 266
  and Republican legislature 85
  and School Integration Act 85
Michigan state legislature 115
Michigan Supreme Court 81, 114
Middleton (Ohio) 258
Midwest
  and migration of ex-slaves to 64
  and school integration 61, 97
migration
  of emancipated slaves 78, 97
  of southern blacks 3, 10, 98, 124–5, 220, 227
  to suburbs after World War II 268–9
Miller, Kelly 140, 180
Milwaukee 170
Ming, Robert 249
Minneapolis
  and lack of black teachers 175
  and refusal to hire blacks 138
  and support for neighborhood schools 279

Minnesota
  and antisegregation legislation 85, 98
  and ban on discrimination in public accommodations 90
  and black education 37, 38
  and black population 88, 97
  and black voting rights 30, 63, 85
  and patterns of school segregation 100
  and perceived effect of *Brown* decision 269
  and racially restrictive covenants 137
  and Republican legislature 85
Minnesota constitution of 1857 14
miscegenation
  and Massachusetts ban 52
  and proposed federal ban 128
Mississippi 137
Mississippi River 117
Missouri and black teachers 20, 64, 111
Missouri Compromise 57
Mitchell, Clarence 268
Mohraz, Judy 125
Montana 97
Montclair (N.J.) 145, 224
Moore, Harry 242
Morris Township (N.J.) 38
Morrow, Jeremiah 14–15
Morton, Oliver 66
Morton (Penn.) 191
Moton, Robert 124
Mound City (Ill.) 254
mulattoes 12–13
  exclusion from white schools 13, 34–6
  harassment of 48–9
  prejudice against 13
  and school segregation 100
Muscatine (Iowa) 76
Mussolini, Benito 222
Myers, Nannie Jackson 217
Myrdal, Gunnar 2, 5, 185, 235
  importance of black press 240

Nantucket (Mass.)
and school boycott 52, 69
and school integration 52, 59
Nation, The 95
National Association for the
Advancement of Colored
People (NAACP) 6, 10, 107, 168
and antidiscrimination efforts
during World War II 225–6,
233
and black support for school
segregation 7
and black teachers in New York
City 176
and campaign against northern
school segregation 2, 10, 188–9,
237–65, 273, 275
and campaign against southern
school segregation 5, 6
and challenges to racially
gerrymandered school district
lines 191
and Cheyney school controversy
198
and Cincinnati branch 194–5
and desegregation efforts in Cairo
(Ill.) 252, 253, 254
and desegregation efforts in
Chagrin Falls (Ohio) 257
and desegregation efforts in
Dayton (Ohio) 212
and desegregation efforts in East
St. Louis (Ill.) 249
and desegregation efforts in
Harrisburg (Penn.) 260
and desegregation efforts in
Indianapolis 207
and desegregation efforts in New
Jersey 245
and desegregation efforts during
the 1940s 273, 275
and desegregation efforts in Ohio
257
and desegregation efforts in
Pennsylvania 259–60
and desegregation efforts in
Springfield (Ohio) 215
and desegregation efforts in
Wilmington (Ohio) 256
and desegregation efforts in York
and Bryn Mawr (Penn.) 260
and Du Bois controversy 200–5
and financial problems 204
and importance of school
integration 167, 171–2
and lack of interest of local
branches in desegregation 209
and litigation challenging school
segregation 207, 209–10, 217
and membership increases 220,
225
and mistreatment of blacks by
white teachers 178
and preservation of black teacher
jobs 239
and prominence during World
War II
and refusal to support war
resisters 223–4
and resisting school segregation
167, 170
and school segregation in New
York City 151
and support for hiring black
teachers 189
and support for school integration
185, 187–9
and support for World War II
222–3
and surveys of school segregation
183, 243–4, 259
National Association of Real Estate
Boards 267
National Convention of Colored
Citizens (1843) 12
National Housing Act of 1934 137
National Negro Business League 168
National Opinion Research Center
236
National Real Estate Board Code of
Ethics 267
National Urban League 221, 225
Native Americans and school
segregation 68

natural law 77
Navy (*see* U.S. Navy)
Nazism 224, 233
Nebraska 28
  and ban on discrimination in
    public accommodations 90
Nebraska Territory 57
Negro Americans, What Now? 202–3
Negro Convention Movement 17, 41,
    45, 50
  and Dayton (1848) 27
  and Indianapolis (1847) 17
  and Philadelphia (1830) 24
  and Philadelphia (1832) 17
  and Rochester (1848) 18
neighborhood associations 136
Nell, William 53, 54, 59
Nevada
  and exclusion of blacks from
    schools 65, 68
  and litigation challenging school
    segregation 72
Nevada Supreme Court 68
New Albany (Ind.) 26, 28
Newark (N.J.)
  dearth of black teachers 175
  petition challenging school
    segregation 68
  poor quality of black schools
    191–2
New Bedford (Mass.) 22, 52, 59
New Brunswick (N.J.) 107
Newburgh (N.Y.) 39, 100
New Deal 228
New England
  and antiblack sentiment 41–4
  and black education 31, 40, 41–4
  and black population 99
  and black voting rights 30
  and Great Migration 150
  and increase in school segregation
    150
  and school integration 61, 99
New Hampshire
  and black education 40, 43–4
  and black population 97
  and school integration 61

New Haven (Conn.)
  efforts to establish black school
    41–2, 43
  and increase in school segregation
    150
  quality of black schools 44, 45
  quality of black teachers 45
  and school segregation 40, 41, 84,
    99
New Haven School Visitors 44
New Jersey
  and antiblack sentiment 156
  and antidiscrimination state
    agency 241
  and antisegregation legislation 4,
    96, 101
  and ban on discrimination in
    public accommodations 90, 135
  and black education 38
  and black lawyers 107
  and black political power 88, 241
  and black population 89, 98, 125,
    227
  and black press criticizing
    segregation 224
  and black school attendance rates
    179
  and black support for school
    segregation 172, 183
  and black teachers 175
  and black voting rights 30, 64
  and dearth of desegregation
    litigation 209
  and desegregation efforts during
    the 1940s 240–5, 262, 276
  and fund-witholding law 241
  and ignorance of antisegregation
    laws 239
  and increase in number of black
    teachers 242
  and inferiority of separate black
    schools 191
  and law prohibiting racial
    discrimination against teachers
    242
  and law permitting school
    segregation 4

New Jersey (*cont.*)
    and litigation to enforce
        antisegregation laws 106, 207
    and petitions challenging school
        segregation 68
    and racially segregated classrooms
        143
    and racially segregated school
        playgrounds 145
    and racially segregated school
        swimming pools 145
    and school segregation 4, 5, 96,
        141–2, 153, 266
    and support of white school
        administrators for segregation
        155
    and survey of school segregation
        183
    and thirteenth and fourteenth
        amendments 64
New Jersey constitution of 1844 38
New Jersey constitutional
    convention of 1947 241
New Jersey Division against
    Discrimination 241–2, 244–5
New Jersey Herald News, support for
    school integration 186
New Jersey state legislature 38–9
New Jersey State Temporary
    Commission on the Condition
    of the Urban Colored
    Population 229, 241
New Jersey Supreme Court 4–5
New Mexico
    and laws permitting school
        segregation 4
    and litigation challenging school
        segregation 207
    permits school segregation 140
New Orleans 19
Newport (R.I.) and school
    segregation 41
New Richmond (Ohio) 113
New Rochelle (N.Y.) 146, 191, 270
newspapers, black 186–7
    and importance of education
        17
    and opposition to racial
        discrimination 224
    and support for school
        desegregation 239
    and support for World War II 223
newspapers, white, and Black Laws
    23, 26
New York 60, 216
    and antisegregation law 229
    and assimilation of immigrants
        163
    and attitudes toward blacks 20
    and ban on employment
        discrimination 229, 230–1
    and black education 38, 39–40
    and black population 102, 125,
        227
    and black teachers 50
    and black voting rights 30, 64
    and common schools 14
    controversy in NAACP branch
        over war resisters 223
    and effect of antisegregation law
        100, 102–3
    and importance of black vote 88
    and influx of black migrants 132
    and interpretation of
        antisegregation law 102–3
    and litigation challenging school
        segregation 72, 81, 276
    and persistence of racial
        separation in 266
    and quality of black schools 44
    and racially segregated school
        swimming pools 145
    and school integration 61
    and school segregation 5, 39–40
New York Age 92
New York City
    and black education 18–19
    and black population 125, 228
    and black school attendance rates
        179
    and black support for separate
        schools 107
    and black teachers 111, 176–7,
        189

and debate over school
integration 197
and discrimination in public
accommodations 92, 134
and disparate funding of black
and white schools 272
and immigrants 186
and influx of black migrants 132
and intelligence tests 162
and mistreatment of black
children 108
and poor quality of black schools
192
and protest against segregation
235
and Puerto Rican schools 192
and racially gerrymandered
school district lines 270
and racial violence 127
and school segregation 40, 140,
150–2
and vocational training 165–6
New York City Board of Education
and black schools 46
New York Commercial 124
New York Commercial Advertiser 15,
18–19
New York Court of Appeals 86, 103,
105
New York General Assembly 86, 103,
271
New York Herald 59
New York *Journal of Commerce* 41
New York Manumission Society 18
New York Public School Society 50
New York State Commission against
Discrimination (SCAD) 231
New York State Employment Service
231
New York State Temporary
Commission on the Condition
of the Urban Colored
Population 151, 166
New York Times 74, 119, 124
New York Tribune 23
Niagara Movement 168
Niebuhr, Reinhold 134

North Providence (R.I.) 98
North Star 17
Nott, Eliphalet 21–2
Noyes Academy 43

Oakland (Cal.) 97, 228
Oberlin College 130–1
Oberlin (Ohio) 130, 216
Ohio 22
and antiblack sentiment 20, 24
and antisegregation law 83, 89,
92–4, 96, 182
and ban on discrimination in
public accommodations 90–1,
229
and ban on employment
discrimination 229
and black education 36–7
and black opposition to
antisegregation law 104
and black political power 88, 94
and black population 88, 89, 94,
98, 125, 227
and black support for school
segregation 109–10, 172
and black voting rights 30
and common schools 14, 16
and defiance of court orders 113
and Democratic Party 89, 92, 93
and desegregation efforts during
1940s 255–8
and desegregation litigation after
1954 258
and difficulty of desegregation
efforts 258
and discrimination in public
accommodations 128
and effect of antisegregation law
103–4
and efforts to repeal
antisegregation law 104
and election of 1883 89
and election of 1885 93
and exclusion of blacks from
public schools 12, 33, 34
and exclusion of blacks from state
27, 63

Ohio (*cont.*)
  and fears of black teacher loss
    111
  and fears of racial mixing 93
  and fourteenth and fifteenth
    amendments 64
  and fund-withholding law 259
  and inferiority of separate black
    schools 191
  and influx of black migrants 131
  and intelligence tests 161
  and justification for school
    segregation 181
  and Ku Klux Klan 159
  and litigation challenging school
    segregation 72, 82, 208
  and litigation to enforce
    antisegregation laws 106, 207
  and migration of ex-slaves 64
  and mulatto education 35
  and petitions challenging school
    segregation 69
  and quality of black schools 44
  and racially segregated classrooms
    144
  and racially segregated school
    swimming pools 145
  and Republican Party 89, 92
  and retaliation for desegregation
    litigation 112–13
  and school segregation 5, 96–7,
    140, 258
  and support for integration 47–8
  and support of local NAACP
    branches for desegregation
    257
  and testimony of blacks in court
    29
Ohio Commissioner of Common
    Schools 44
Ohio Commissioner of Education
    37
Ohio constitution 14
Ohio Director of Education 147
Ohio River 24, 26, 64
Ohio State Board of Education 4,
    258

Ohio state legislature
  and antisegregation law 92, 94
  and black education 36–7
  and common schools 15–16
  considers legislation permitting
    segregation 140
  and law requiring segregation 96
Ohio Supreme Court
  and black education 36
  and Dayton litigation 4, 213
  and mulattoes 11, 13, 34–5
  and racial classifications 12–13
  and testimony of blacks in court
    29
Opportunity 160, 221
Oregon 28
  and exclusion of blacks from
    public schools 149
  and exclusion of blacks from state
    29
  and Ku Klux Klan activity 159
  and litigation challenging school
    segregation 72
  repeal of Black Laws 62
  and school integration 97
Oregon City (Ore.) 159
Ottawa (Kan.) 78–9
Owen, Chandler 186, 190–1, 192
Oxford (Ohio) 112, 258
Oxford (Penn.) 139

Palmer, John 67, 115, 118
Panic of 1873 96
Park, Robert 162
Parks, Gordon 178
Partridge, G.E. 126–7
Paterson (N.J.) 68
Pearl Harbor 224, 233
Pechstein, Louis A. 156, 180–1, 199
Pennsylvania
  and antisegregation law 86–7, 94
  and ban on discrimination in
    public accommodations 229
  and ban on employment
    discrimination 229
  and ban on segregation in public
    transit 62

and black education 38, 39
and black lawyers 107
and black political power 88, 94
and black population 125, 227
and black support for school
    segregation 172
and black teachers 174
and black voting rights 30
and Cheyney School controversy
    198
and common schools 14
and Democratic support for
    antisegregation law 94
and desegregation efforts in 1940s
    259–61
and exclusion of blacks from state
    22
and failure to enforce
    antisegregation law 106
and financial support for schools
    190
and hearings on teacher
    discrimination 229
and increase in school segregation
    140, 142–3
and influx of black migrants 131
and legislation authorizing or
    requiring school segregation
    80, 96
and litigation challenging school
    segregation 72, 79–80
and litigation challenging racially
    separate classrooms 208
and litigation to enforce
    antisegregation legislation 207
persistence of school segregation
    after 1954 261, 266
and racially separate classrooms
    143
and Republican support for
    antisegregation law 94
and school segregation 5
Pennsylvania Association of Teachers
    of Colored Children (PATCC)
    183
Pennsylvania Human Relations
    Commission 272

Pennsylvania state constitutional
    convention of 1837 22
Pennsylvania State Equal Rights
    League 49, 50
Pennsylvania state legislature 39
    enacts antisegregation legislation
    80
Pennsylvania Superintendent of
    Common Schools 39
Pennsylvania Supreme Court 80
Peoria (Ill.) 69
Perlmann, Joel 164
Perry, Marian 259
personal liberty laws 31
petitions challenging school
    segregation 50, 68–9, 239
    in Boston 52
    in Ohio 89
    in Rochester 51
petitions supporting school
    segregation 107, 172
Philadelphia 43, 189
    and black education 19, 39, 48–9
    and black population 125, 228
    black support for school
        segregation 107, 183
    and black teachers 101, 111, 259
    and black voters 94, 228
    and campaign against racist
        textbooks 217
    and Cheyney School 198
    and Court of Common Pleas 94
    and employment of blacks as
        domestics 130
    and inferiority of separate black
        schools 191
    and influx of black migrants 132
    and publication of textbook 216
    and quality of black schools 44
    and racial violence 127
    refusal to hire black teachers 49
    relative inactivity of NAACP
        branch 210
    and school attendance rates 179,
        186
    and school segregation 94, 100–1,
        142–3, 149, 195, 266

Philadelphia (*cont.*)
  and support for segregation to
    secure black teachers 109
  and support of school
    superintendent for segregation
    155
Philadelphia Board of Education
  100, 259
Philadelphia *Record* 94
Philadelphia Tribune 183
  and campaign to remove racist
    textbooks 217
  support for black teachers in
    racially mixed schools 189
  support for school integration 186
Philanthropist, The 24
Phillips, Wendell 82
Phyllis Wheatley Association 168–9
Picturesque Geographical Reader, The
  216
Pittsburgh
  and black education 39
  and black exodus to Canada 27
  and black population 125
  and black teachers 111, 174, 176,
    189, 259
  and discrimination by realtors
    136
  and increase in school segregation
    during 1950s 265–6
  and inferior black schools 191
  and influx of black migrants
    132
  and school attendance rates 186
Pittsburgh Board of Education 96,
  229
Pittsburgh Commercial 73
Pittsburgh Courier 173
  on black disillusionment 222
  and Double V campaign 223
  support for hiring black teachers
    189
  support for school integration
    186
Plessy v. Ferguson (1896) 56, 71, 127
PM 236–7
political power of blacks

  increase in during World War II
    10, 220, 227–30, 240
  and swing votes of blacks 230
population, northern black 10, 88,
  97–8, 131
  growth in urban areas 125, 228
  increase during World War II
    227–8
Porter, Jennie 180
  and benefits of black schools 182
  petitions for separate black school
    193–5
Portland (Maine) 40
Portland (Ore.)
  and Cold War concerns 234
  and Klan activity 159
  mistreatment of blacks by white
    teachers 177, 178
  and opposition to school
    segregation 233
  and racially gerrymandered
    school district lines 270
  and school segregation 145
Portsmouth (Ohio) 258
Portwood, Shirley 117
Poughkeepsie (N.Y.) 40, 100
Powell, Adam Clayton, Jr. 219, 224,
  225
presidential election of 1944 230
presidential election of 1948 230
Price, Joseph St. Clair 160
Princeton (N.J.) 101, 141
Princeton University 233
private schools for black children 19
Prosser, Inez 181
protest movement, black 13–14
Providence Journal 47
Providence (R.I.)
  and mistreatment of black
    children 108
  and preservation of racially mixed
    schools 150
  and race riots 42
  and retaliation toward
    prodesegregation blacks 112
  and school segregation 40, 41, 99
  and vocational education 164

public accommodations
  discrimination in 128
  increase in discrimination after
    Great Migration 134–5
Puerto Rican schools 272
Pulaski County (Ill.) 104, 250

Quakers 34, 42
  and black education 19, 33
  and emancipated slaves 26
  and racial views 20
Queens (N.Y.) 81
  and desegregation litigation 103
  and litigation to enforce
    antisegregation laws 112
Quincy (Ill.) and desegregation
    efforts 115–16

Race Differences 162
Race Orthodoxy in the South 124
race riots (*see* racial violence)
racial liberalism, emergence during
    1940s 235–6
racial unrest
  efforts to quell 227
  increase during 1940s 236
racial violence 137–8, 267
  in antebellum North 23–4
  in Cairo (Ill.) 252–3
  in Chicago 137–8, 236
  in Detroit 113, 136, 236
  in early 20th century 127–8
  in East St. Louis (Ill.) 137–8
  in Evansville (Ind.) 127–8
  and Great Migration 136–7
  in Harlem 236
  in Los Angeles 236
  in New Hampshire 43–4
  in Oakland 236
  in Philadelphia 137, 236
  post–Civil War 64
  against private black schools 33
  in Providence (RI) 42
  in response to school
    desegregation 112–13
  in San Diego 236
  in Springfield (Ill.) 121

  in Syracuse (N.Y.) 137
  following World War I 170
  during World War II 220, 225, 236
Radical Republicans (*see* Republican
    Party)
railroad segregation 52
Randolph, A. Philip 183, 186, 236
real estate practices, racially
    discriminatory 136, 267–8
Reconstruction 62, 275
  and racial idealism 10
Red Cross 221
Reid, Ira de A. 160
Republican Party 93
  and animus toward Irish-Catholics
    88
  and antiblack sentiment in Illinois
    118
  and antisegregation laws 84–7, 122
  ascendancy during late 19th
    century North 95
  and blacks 20, 88
  and embrace of public education
    87–8
  judges on state supreme courts
    105
restaurants, racial discrimination by
    224
restrictive covenants, racially 136,
    137, 226, 267
Reuter, Edward 162
Rhode Island
  and antisegregation law 84, 99
  and ban on discrimination in
    public accommodations 90, 91
  and black education 40
  and black population 97, 150
  and black voting rights 30
  and desegregation efforts 59
  and school segregation 41
Rice, V. M. 46
Richardson, Henry 264
Richmond (Ind.) 26, 75
Roberts, Benjamin 54
Roberts v. City of Boston (1850) 55–6,
    70–1, 77, 82
Robeson, Paul 101

Robinson, James Hathaway 182
Rochester (N.Y.)
　black preference for separate
　　schools 49
　and division over integration 51
　and school boycott 51, 69
　and school integration 40, 51–2,
　　60
　and school segregation 40
Rochester School Board 51
roller skating rinks, discrimination
　in 92
Roosevelt, Eleanor 231
Roosevelt, Franklin 228, 231
Roosevelt School (Gary, Ind.) 183
Roosevelt, Theodore 103
Rosyln (N.Y.)
　and desegregation litigation 206
　and school segregation 102, 103
　and student protest 206
Rush, Benjamin 15
Russia (see Soviet Union)

Sacramento (Cal.) 105
St. Louis 117–18, 179
St. Paul (Minn.) 85, 119, 269
St. Paul School Board (Minn.)
　38
Salem (Ind.) 129
Salem (Mass.)
　and school boycott 69
　and school integration 52
　and school segregation 40
San Francisco
　and black population 228
　and residential segregation 137
　and school segregation 97
Savannah (Georgia) 148
Scheingold, Stuart 276
Schenectady (N.Y.) 100
school attendance rates 14, 16, 60
school boycotts
　in Alton (Ill.) 119, 205
　in Berwyn (Penn.) 206
　in Boston 53, 54
　in Buffalo (N.Y.) 50–1, 69
　in California 206

　in Chicago 139, 205
　in Cincinnati 157
　in East Orange (N.J.) 205
　in East St. Louis (Ill.) 249
　in Englewood (N.J.) 69
　in Gallipolis (Ohio) 157
　in Gary (Ind.) 157, 233, 263
　in Hillburn (N.Y.) 224
　in Illinois 206
　in Long Branch (N.J.) 243
　in Massachusetts 205
　in Nantucket 52
　in New Jersey 206
　in New York 50, 205
　in Ohio 206
　in Oxford (Penn.) 205
　in Pennsylvania 206
　and school desegregation 7, 50,
　　69, 205–6, 224, 239
　in Springfield (Ohio) 215
　in Wichita (Kan.) 205
school closures 113
school curriculum
　and tracking of white and black
　　children 163–4
　and variations between white and
　　black schools 163–6
school riots
　in Chicago 139
schools, black
　age of 191–2
　inferiority of 44–5
schools, overcrowded 270
　disparities between black and
　　white schools 272–3
schools, technical, exclusion of
　blacks from 164–6
school transfer policies 3
Schuyler, George 134
Scott, Emmett 169
Seattle Real Estate Board 267
segregation, residential 123
　effect on school segregation 3, 10,
　　220, 265, 269, 273
　government support for 137
　increase in early 20th century
　　128–9, 188

increase after Great migration
136–7
increase after World War II 266,
275
white attitudes toward 266
segregation, school
and black opposition to 221–7,
237
and change in white attitudes
toward 220
within classrooms 144–5
and continuation of during 1950s
265, 274
de jure 3
end to explicit forms of 219
and exclusion of blacks from high
schools 149
at graduation ceremonies 145
and increase during early 20th
century 3, 153–4, 163
and increase after Great Migration
138, 153–4, 188
leads to inferior schools for blacks
190–1
linked with fascism 233–4
among other ethnic groups 6
in recreational activities 145
in school activities 145
on school playgrounds 3, 145
and separate buildings and
classrooms 3, 8, 143–4
and separate American flags 3
and stigma 82
and support for from white
education scholars 156, 159–60
support for from white parents
157
and support for from white school
administrators 155
and support for among white
students 157–8
and support for from white
teachers 155–6
and undistricted school zones
148–9
and white insistence on 123,
124–31, 170, 219

Shaw, Lemuel 56
Sheffield (Mass.) 139
Shelley v. Kraemer (1948) 267
Shils, Edward 185
Shoop School (Chicago) 207
Sitkoff, Harvard 134, 226
slaves, emancipated 26
and migration northward 64
Smith, Harry C. 110, 168, 184
opposition to segregation in
Dayton 212
Smith, James McCune 49
Smith School (Boston) 52–4, 59
Smith, Thomas 54
Social Darwinism 126
social scientists
and racial discrimination 235
and racial outcomes 162
soldiers, black (*see also* U.S. Army)
and mistreatment during World
War II 225–6
and protest against discrimination
224
Soldiers and Sailors Club
(Milwaukee) 170
South Topeka (Kan.) 79
Southern Society of Chicago 183
Soviet Union 234
Spencer, John 51
Springfield (Ill.) 121, 127–8
Springfield (Ohio)
and black petition for separate
school 215
and desegregation litigation 82
and disregard of desegregation
order 214, 216
and fears of black teacher loss 111
and litigation challenging school
segregation 211
and racial violence 127
and retaliation for challenging
school segregation 211
and school segregation 89
and support for school
segregation 159
Springmeyer School District
(Cincinnati) 258

Stapleton (N.Y.) 102
Starr, Frederick 126
State and County Educational Reorganization 153
Steele, O.G. 50
Steelton (Penn.) 260
Stetson, Paul 212
Story, Joseph 16
Straubmuller Textile High School (New York City) 165
Strauder v. West Virginia (1880) 71
strikebreaking and black employment 130
Study of American Intelligence, A 161
suburban migration (*see* migration)
Sugrue, Thomas 266
Sumner, Charles
    argument in *Roberts* case 55–6
    support for antisegregation legislation 82
Sunday schools and black education 19
Sweet, Ossian 136
swimming pools, racially segregated in schools 145
Syracuse (N.Y.) 40
Syracuse (Ohio) 129

Tallahassee (Fl.) 233
Tamms (Ill.) 254
Taney, Roger 73
teachers
    black educator support for school integration 187
    black teacher opposition to school desegregation 109–10, 183
    criticism of black teachers for support for segregation 110
    fears of black teacher loss with desegregation 111–12
    hiring of black teachers 174–86
    impact of black teachers on black retention rates 179
    importance of black teachers 109–12
    job loss following antisegregation legislation 181–2

leadership role of black teachers 181–2
    and mistreatment of black children by white 177–8
    nurturing quality of black 49, 173–86
    percentage of black college graduates who are 181
    quality in black schools 44–5
    refusal to hire black teachers 49–50
    refusal to use black teachers in racially mixed schools 174, 175–6, 186, 219
    white teachers and black students 48
Technical High School (Providence, R.I.) 164
Terman, Lewis 159, 160
Terrell, Mary Church 131
testimony, court, denial to blacks 12, 29
textbooks
    efforts to remove those with racist views 216–17
    and unflattering portrayals of blacks 216
Thompson, Charles 181, 187
Tillman, Ben 128
Toledo (Ohio) 69, 187
Toms River (N.J.) 156
Trenton (N.J.)
    ban on black teachers teaching white children 175
    black support for separate schools 107
    and black teachers 176
    and desegregation efforts during the 1940s 241
    increase in school segregation 141, 149
    support of school superintendent for school segregation 155
Trotter, William Monroe 217
Troy (N.Y.) 100
Troy (Ohio) 33
Truman Administration 230

Truman, Bess 230
Truman, Harry S. 225, 230
Trumbull, Lyman 63
Turner, Nat 42
Tushnet, Mark 275

Ullin (Ill.) 254
Underground Railroad 130
Union College 21
United Negro Improvement
    Association (UNIA) 170–2
U.S. Army, segregation in 221
U.S. Bureau of Education 153
U.S. Bureau of Intelligence 221, 226,
    231
U.S. Commission on Civil Rights 270
U.S. Congress 62, 64, 74
    and antimiscegenation bill 128
    and antisegregation legislation 61
    and civil rights legislation 62
    and House committee on public
        lands 15
    and public accommodations
        legislation 82–3
    and Republican support for
        antisegregation legislation 86–7
U.S. Constitution 63, 69
    and equal protection clause 70,
        114
    and fifteenth amendment 62, 64,
        88
    and fourteenth Amendment 62,
        64, 71, 77, 78–9
    and privileges or immunities
        clause 70
    and proposed amendment
        guaranteeing education 87
    and thirteenth amendment 62, 80
    and using fourteenth amendment
        to challenge school segregation
        70, 71, 73, 80
U.S. Court of Appeals for Sixth
    Circuit 271
U.S. Immigration Commission
    176
U.S. Navy, discrimination in 221
U.S. Steel 129

U.S. Supreme Court 56, 71, 73, 74,
    89, 127, 136, 226, 235
    and *Brown* decision 3, 277
    and compensatory remedies
        278
    and restrictive covenants 267
    and school busing 277, 278
    and suburban migration 276
University of Cincinnati School of
    Education 180–1, 199
University of Illinois 248
University of North Carolina Press
    226
Upper Alton (Ill.), and
    desegregation efforts 116–17,
    120
Ursuline convent (Boston) 32

Valentine, Daniel 79
Valentine, William 183, 240
Van Camp, Enos 12–13
Vann, Robert 173, 189
Vardaman, James K. 128
Venice (Ill.) 119
Vermont 40, 61, 97
Vicksburg (Miss.) 148
Virginia 42
Visalia (Cal.) 105
voting and race 63–4
    black voter registration numbers
        228
    denial of right to blacks 12
    legal challenges to exclusion of
        blacks 226

WACs (*see* Women's Army Corps)
Walling, William English 128
War Camp Community Service 170
Washington, Booker T. 169, 171
Washington, D.C. 191, 199, 235,
    266
    and black attendance rates school
        179
    and black teachers 111
Wayne County (Ind.) 34
Webster School (New Rochelle,
    N.Y.) 146

Western Reserve (Ohio) 20, 26, 33, 128
Westhampton Township (N.J.) 156
West Pulaski School (Gary, Ind.) 143
What the Negro Wants 226
Whig Party 36, 57
Willard School (Dayton, Ohio) 212–14
White, Walter
  on black despair with racism 221
  and black support for World War II 222
  and campaign against racist textbooks 217
  and Du Bois controversy 203, 204
  on increase in black militancy 221
  and NAACP litigation policy 209
  and prominence during World War II 225
  and school segregation 188, 194, 210, 246
White Plains (N.Y.) 177
Wichita (Kan.) 140, 145
  and racially segregated school playgrounds 145
  and school segregation 140
Wilkie, Wendell 232
Wilkins, Roy 233, 247, 249
Williams, Franklin 247
Williams, Patricia 7
Williamsport (Penn.) 261
Wills, J. Walter 168
Wilmington (Ohio)
  and desegregation efforts 255–6
  and division in black community 256
Wilson, Henry 87
Wisconsin
  and ban on discrimination in public accommodations 229
  and black education 37, 38
  and black population 88, 97
  and black voting rights 30, 63
  and patterns of school segregation 100
  and school integration 61
Wisconsin constitutional convention of 1847 38
Wogaman School (Dayton) 214
Women's Army Corps (WACs) 224
Woodlawn School District (Cincinnati) 271
Worcester (Mass.) 59
Workman, Joseph 114
World War I 131
  blacks in military service 169
  impact on black consciousness 169, 172
  and racial segregation in military 169–70
World War II 218, 219
  black loyalty during 227
  and black refusal to enlist 221
  effect of on white attitudes toward racial equality 227–34
  effect of racial discrimination on war effort 231–3
  impact on antisegregation efforts 220, 221–4, 275
  increase in black militancy 221
  increase in black political power 227
  and racial protest during 224
Wright, Joseph 63

Xenia (Ohio) 104, 113

Yale University 41
YMCA 169, 172
York (Penn.) 260, 261
Young, Kimball 160
Youngstown (Ohio) 111
Ypsilanti (Mich.) 100
YWCA (Cleveland) 169

Zanesville (Ohio) 33
zoning regulations 136